# HOW DO YOU DO IT?

*The Selected Works of Gerald Russello*

# *How Do You Do It?*

## THE SELECTED WORKS OF GERALD RUSSELLO

*Edited and Introduced by*
David G. Bonagura, Jr.

CLUNY
*Providence, Rhode Island*

CLUNY EDITION, 2024

*All previously published works by Gerald J. Russello have been reprinted with permission.*

For more information regarding this title
or any other Cluny Media publication,
please write to info@clunymedia.com, or to
Cluny Media, P.O. Box 1664, Providence, RI 02901

ONLINE AT WWW.CLUNYMEDIA.COM

❧



ISBN: 978-1685953652

Cover design by Clarke & Clarke
Cover image: Ernest Lawson, *Brooklyn Bridge*,
between 1917 and 1920, oil on canvas
Courtesy of Wikimedia Commons

# TABLE OF CONTENTS

# *Introduction*

## DAVID G. BONAGURA, JR.

"How do you do it?" This question was asked often by friends and admirers of Gerald Russello, who amazed them with all he accomplished in a day. He was a husband, father of three, hardworking lawyer in major New York City firms, editor of *The University Bookman*, adjunct professor of law, avid reader, regular writer and reviewer for multiple publications, advisor and board member to multiple institutions, friend of many. To this question, which had variations—"Where do you find the time?" or "Do you ever sleep?"—Gerald never gave a straight answer. His eyes would twinkle, sometimes in embarrassment and sometimes with a hint of mischief, and he would flash his mirthful, magnetic smile, and then say something to deflect attention from himself, if he would say anything at all. One response stands out over the years: "I have elves."

Gerald accomplished all these things not because—or at least not solely because—he was a talented, bright, and highly motivated individual. He did them all because he loved people, he loved what he was doing, and he loved to bring people together in the causes he held most dear. His love generated an incomparable generosity from which he gave his time, his expertise, his friendship. Conscious that God had blessed him with many talents, Gerald felt an obligation to serve others with them, which he did until his life was cut short on November 7, 2021, at age fifty, after a yearlong battle with cancer.

Gerald's true passion was writing, a skill he wielded to express his love for the causes that motivated him. The combination of family, neighborhood, faith, and an inspiring liberal arts education shaped Gerald into the man whom many knew, and whom so many more knew indirectly through his copious published works. He was a lover of family, of local communities, and of his country. He was a devoted Catholic who loved his faith and his Church while ever conscious of his own failings to live up to the creed he professed. He was an imaginative conservative in the mold of Russell Kirk who, after years of study, became the subject of Gerald's only full-length book, *The Postmodern Imagination of Russell Kirk*. Gerald was a passionate humanist who knew the gifts the liberal arts could bestow on individuals and societies. He was a skilled lawyer who not only wrote occasionally about the law itself, but also employed his legal knowledge to combat challenges facing Catholicism, conservatism, and localism.

These causes shine brightly in this volume of Gerald's most representative essays and reviews. It does not contain all of his writings; quite a few pieces remain scattered across the Internet and in dusty journals. *How Do You Do It? The Selected Works of Gerald Russello* pays tribute to a scholar who wrote in service of the causes he loved while highlighting some key lines of his thought. But above all, it presents to posterity what Gerald Russello loved and why his loves were worth defending and sharing.

Gerald Joseph Russello was born on July 27, 1971, the oldest child of Charles and Anne Russello. Native New Yorkers of Italian descent, the Russellos made their home in Old Mill Basin, Brooklyn, an Italian, Irish, and Jewish enclave on the recesses of the world's most cosmopolitan city. "We lived in a tiny apartment near the butcher shop," Gerald would later recall in writing about the day when, at age three, he was almost abducted by a stranger a few blocks from home. "The living room looked out into a backyard, bare apart from a couple of clotheslines, and the view was dominated by a building covered in graffiti." Together with his sister, born two years later, Jerry, as he was called then by all who knew him, grew up close to his family and friends in a tightly knit ethnic neighborhood that featured all the stereotypes: working class life centered around the parish church, Saturday night dinners with the grandparents and cousins, personal relationships with the proprietors of every store in the area. His was not an extravagant life. "We were poor too. We sometimes got free milk and big blocks of government-issued cheese from my grandmother, who had worked out some complicated plan to get more than her share at the food bank." Yet he loved this life and this neighborhood, where the people and the places forged "connections that made me who I am." From these experiences grew his commitment to localism, the bedrock of the conservative principles that would define his adult life.

Young Jerry walked around the block to Mary Queen of Heaven Church for school and for Mass. The church, in keeping with the neighborhood motif, was functional rather than beautiful. It blended Irish and Italian pieties, particularly devotions to the saints, that became a lasting part of Jerry's Catholicism. A precocious student, he earned a scholarship to the prestigious Regis High School in Manhattan, to which he commuted over an hour one way by bus and subway. The Jesuit school's strong program in the humanities opened Jerry to the life of the mind and planted the seeds of his vocation as a scholar and writer. Unlike many of his classmates, he became enthralled with Latin. He was inspired by his history teacher Mr. John Connelly, whom school legend revered as the smartest man in the world, to dig more deeply into the treasures of Western Civilization that he would later defend with his pen. Mr. Connelly also introduced him to Christopher Dawson, the British Catholic historian of culture who argued that "religion is the key to history." Dawson would become one of two leading intellectual influences on Jerry's life.

Jerry remained intensely loyal to Regis long after graduation, and he kept in regular contact with Mr. Connelly, whom he called "The Magister," and with whom he and a small group of friends would dine once or twice a year. After graduating from Regis in 1989, Jerry enrolled in Georgetown University, where his conservative dispositions, his love of faith, family, and neighborhood, and his liberal arts education coalesced into a full intellectual symphony. Determined to pursue eternal truths, he majored in classics. In addition, he studied with Dr. George Carey and Father James Schall, S.J., leading conservative thinkers in Georgetown's Department of Government. He joined and became highly involved in the Knights of

Columbus, a national Catholic fraternal organization. With a group of friends, he marshalled his nascent understandings of intellectual conservatism to begin his first foray into writing: in 1991 he co-founded *The Georgetown Academy*, a conservative campus newspaper. To prepare for this endeavor, as he later recalled, Jerry and his friends devised a reading list, and "[s]omeone suggested [Russell Kirk's] *The Conservative Mind.* I spent the summer reading and rereading that book, and quickly got my hands on as many other Kirk books as I could find. They were a revelation."

That summer Jerry's future was launched. In addition to devouring Kirk's books, he attended a few Kirk lectures in Washington, DC, and even wrote letters to him, who responded in turn. After Kirk died in 1994, his wife Annette founded the Russell Kirk Center for Cultural Renewal at his home in Mecosta, Michigan. Jerry would visit and remain actively involved with the Kirk Center for the rest of his life. Kirk was his intellectual lodestar, serving as both the subject and the inspiration of his research and writing. Jerry's conservatism was Kirkean in every sense, as the writings in this volume make plain.

At Georgetown, Jerry entertained attending graduate school to study the classics, but his practical side forged in Old Mill Basin overcame his intellectual idealism: he chose to return home to study law at New York University. Upon arriving he effected a minor self-transformation: he now preferred to be called Gerald, as he would be known professionally and personally thereafter. Yet he never disavowed his roots, nor did he dismiss his passion for the intellectual life: upon graduating law school in 1996, he pursued not a celebrated position at a major law firm, but a judicial clerkship under Justice Daniel J. O'Hearn of the New Jersey Supreme Court. Law clerks are essentially legal academics: they research the legal background relevant to given cases and then help the judge write opinions. Not surprisingly, Gerald loved this job. After his one-year tenure under Justice O'Hearn concluded, Gerald worked as an associate at Donovan Leisure Newton & Irvine before advancing to a second, more prestigious clerkship on the United States Court of Appeals for the Third Circuit under Judge Leonard I. Garth. After this tenure, he returned to the New York City law scene, where, with the exception of working for the U.S. Securities and Exchange Commission from 2002–2006, he would spend the rest of his career.

The law also opened another door for Gerald: as a summer law intern in Washington, DC, Gerald met fellow intern Alexandra Hines. The two New Yorkers began courting, and they married in New York City in May 1998. They made their home in Brooklyn Heights, which like his beloved Old Mill Basin, "appeal[led] to all sorts of conservative instincts for small-scale neighborhoods traversable without a car, [was] home to few if any big-box or chain stores (and those easily ignored), and [had] a focus on local producers. We bought produce directly from farmers, loved finding the newest purveyor of organic ice cream, did not need to drive a car for weeks at a stretch, and lived within five miles of where my father and ancestors are buried." But over the next thirteen years, hipsters swooped into the area and snatched up its old-world charm. In an essay in this volume, Gerald tells how he and his family of five fled Brooklyn for the suburbs, where they rediscovered the feel of a neighborhood—albeit one enabled by the regular use of a car.

For Gerald, the law paid the bills. His heart was in the academy. While still in law school, he forged an arrangement that, though often dissatisfying due to the incongruence of his desires with the demands of the legal profession ("Law is a harsh mistress," he would often say when forced to abandon lunches, dinners, and intellectual pursuits for work obligations), became a regular feature of his life: lawyer by (long) day, scholar by night and weekend. At age twenty-five he had already begun publishing essays, yet simultaneously he undertook a grander project: editing a volume of essays of Christopher Dawson. In 1998, The Catholic University of America Press published Gerald's edition *Christianity and European Culture: Selections from the Work of Christopher Dawson*.

At that time, Dawson was remembered only by very few specialists. Gerald's edition, which includes a superb twenty-two-page introduction to Dawson's thought and significance, catalyzed a twenty-first-century revival in Dawson studies, which included The Catholic University of America

Press obtaining the rights to reprint twelve of Dawson's books. In the introduction, Gerald writes that the essays he selected "are of more than antiquarian interest. They represent an innovative attempt to revive the idea of Christian culture in an age when religious approaches are less respected than they used to be." In this, Dawson was ahead of his time—as was Gerald, who perhaps felt in his bones Dawson's conviction that "severing a society from its defining faith will have tragic moral, social, and political consequences" as he watched Old Mill Basin rapidly transform from a religiously-based ethnic community into a hazardous place to live.

Aside from his work on Dawson, in the years before and after his thirtieth birthday, Gerald preferred writing longer essays, often of the footnoted, scholarly variety, as opposed to the shorter essays and reviews that comprise the bulk of his work after 2010. "Early Gerald" wrote scholarly pieces on the Catholic novel and on Catholic social teaching that are included in this volume. He also began reviewing books on Latin, Roman antiquity, and the American founding. In 2000, he was appointed fellow at the Chesterton Institute of Seton Hall University, an affiliation he would maintain for the rest of his life; he regularly contributed reviews, three of which are included here, to the Institute's *Chesterton Review*. In 2003, he began applying his legal expertise to Catholic and religious liberty issues through an occasional column in the *National Catholic Register*; three of these columns are reprinted below. And whereas practicing the law was sometimes trying for Gerald, teaching it was not. For three years he taught a seminar in securities litigation and enforcement at Cardoza Law School in Manhattan, a labor of love that was, in certain ways, an extension of his writing vocation, only with a live audience.

But the most significant subject of Gerald's early work, one that would remain central throughout his career, was the person and work of Russell Kirk. Gerald's early research yielded "Russell Kirk and Territorial Democracy," which appeared in the scholarly journal *Publius* in 2004. It traced Kirk's understanding of federalism and his grounding of rights within United States history as opposed to ethereal universalism. He later incorporated these ideas into his *magnum opus*, a critical study of Kirk's thought entitled *The Postmodern Imagination of Russell Kirk*, which was published in 2007 by The University of Missouri Press.

It was a striking choice for a title. Imagination was central to Kirk's thought, for through it, men and women, in Gerald's summary, are "able to bridge the otherwise impassable gap between individual minds," for it "has great potential to unify sentiments, loyalties, and ideas that are usually considered opposed." The imagination was Kirk's answer to the dreary rationalism that modern liberalism championed. By contrast, Kirk, though he used the term "postmodern," did not consider himself a postmodernist. Yet Gerald saw Kirk as a postmodern thinker in the sense that his championing of imagination not only helped conservatism contend against rationalism, but also because he believed Kirk's understanding of imagination could appeal beyond typical conservative circles to those who prefer sentiment over rationality. Through imagination and sentiment, Gerald hoped, Kirk could pitch to postmoderns, who generally oppose strong truth claims, the conservative case for order and tradition as the bulwarks of a healthy society.

The book was a critical success, focusing on Kirk's general cultural and conservative thought, understanding of history and historiography, political philosophy and statesmanship, jurisprudence and rights. It established Gerald as a leading authority on Kirk and as a gatekeeper in reviewing books about him. He received his greatest compliment from the renowned British philosopher Sir Roger Scruton, who wrote in *Conservatism: An Invitation to the Great Tradition* that Gerald's "writings about Kirk are far clearer in this matter [of explaining conservative principles] than Kirk himself."

In 2010, Gerald was made partner at Bingham McCutchen LLP. The demands of his new role seemed to have prevented him from larger book projects, though he did manage to contribute as a coauthor to the legal textbook *Securities Litigation and Enforcement in a Nutshell*, published in 2016 by West Academic Publishing. Yet "late Gerald" was every bit as prolific as his pre-partner self. He reviewed and wrote short essays at a tremendous rate given the demands on his time. Reviews, in particular, thrilled him as a bibliophile, for in them he combined his two favorite things: reading and writing. As books came into his home, he had a personal rule: unread books would remain on a chair until they were read; only then could they find a place on his library shelf. Gerald reviewed books on Kirk, conservatism, Latin, American history and culture, Catholicism, and law. His reviews, true to his personality, were never caustic nor demeaning. Most begin with a panorama of the subject before diving into the particulars of the book itself; in these opening paragraphs, Gerald's personal thoughts on the topic can often be gleaned. He typically left his most salient point to his final sentence. Gerald generally praised the books he reviewed, though he would include one perceived shortcoming in his critique. Only rarely did he review a book that he thought fell short of the mark.

In addition, Gerald served as the editor of *The University Bookman*, a quarterly review of books founded by Russell Kirk himself. Appointed in 2005, Gerald oversaw the transformation of the *Bookman*, as it is affectionately known, from a quarterly print edition to an online-only publication that, with weekly postings, required more regular attention. In doing so he broadened the *Bookman's* focus to include humanistic books, both fiction and non-fiction, that appealed to a wide readership. Gerald also opened the *Bookman's* Twitter account in 2011. To the surprise of many, he loved the medium, posting missives, requests, celebrations, retweets, and, near the end of his life, prayer requests. Gerald took a regular ribbing from his friends over whether he met his billable hours quota because he spent too much time tweeting. Twitter is often marked by cruel and crude vitriol, but never on Gerald's handle: his tweets were an extension of his personality: joyful, gregarious, engaging, affirming.

Writing placed Gerald in the public eye, but he preferred to pass unnoticed in the background. As a law partner, he went out of his way to serve as an unofficial mentor to many young lawyers. As *Bookman* editor, he spent time cultivating young writers, teaching them the art of reviewing books. As a lawyer who cared about religious and cultural institutes, he served as a board member of several organizations. As an enthusiastic friend, he lent his encouragement to start up enterprises in the Catholic world and in the conservative movement. He never sought credit nor recognition; he desired only that the good might flourish.

Amid all this, Gerald most loved sneaking out of the office for lunch or dinner with friends from Regis, Georgetown, the legal profession, and the conservative movement. True to form, he preferred to talk about anything that did not center around him. He may have been a bookworm, but he was an outgoing people person at heart. Ideas were important for Gerald, but only because they were at the service of people.

In November 2020, while working from home during the Covid-19 pandemic, Gerald had a health scare: while on a Zoom call, he suddenly could not speak. He and his wife Lexi rushed to the doctor. He underwent tests and received a devasting diagnosis: he had glioblastoma, an aggressive brain cancer for which there is no cure. He flew to Duke University Medical Center, which specializes in glioblastoma treatment, for surgery; chemotherapy and radiation followed. Gerald continued his legal work and his editing for *The University Bookman* during this period, though at a reduced rate. He even managed to write when he felt up to it. His final piece, "Milites Christi," which appeared posthumously in *The Lamp*, is included here, and its subject matter is fitting for a man grappling with terminal illness: the importance of handing on the faith to the next generation. Gerald had been teaching catechism to eighth graders in his parish, and he believed his mostly unchurched students needed a new approach: he threw away the lesson plans because, he realized, "their faith needed to be introduced to them as an adventure, not another class in school. They needed to see it as a living guide to understanding the world."

As he wrote those words, Gerald's own adventure in this world was coming to an end, and his faith was helping him through. After checking into hospice care, he passed away on the evening of November 7, 2021. A beautiful sunset coincided with his passing. In the prime of his life, Gerald had been called home to God, who, we pray and reasonably hope, has rewarded him for his love, generosity, and faithful service.

*How Do You Do It? The Selected Works of Gerald Russello* presents Gerald's preeminent essays and reviews sorted by theme. The first, and appropriately given his humility, briefest, section provides glimpses of Gerald himself, a neighborhood man of community and of faith. These first-person essays—a rare style for him—are invitations to see through his eyes the world that molded him. He wanted his readers not merely to know about Brooklyn and his faith, but to know the impact these milieux had on him. From this perspective, Gerald's defense of regionalism and localism in the tradition of Russell Kirk and Bill Kauffman, which he articulates in multiple pieces in this volume, gains heft. To be wedded to a place is part of the human longing for community and love, and Gerald shows that localism can thrive in the big city as much as in the country.

Gerald's work on Russell Kirk and conservatism is his most enduring intellectual legacy. The sections devoted to each complement each other, as Gerald's conservatism was that of Kirk. Conservatism, as Kirk and Gerald often noted, is not an abstract philosophical theory, nor is it merely the posture of those opposed to liberalism. Rather, it begins from a disposition of the soul to preserve life's permanent things—truth, beauty, goodness, family, religion, community, order—and develops certain principles based on human nature and lived experiences. Conservatism learns from the past and preserves its best features in order to flourish in the present.

When Gerald jumped into the conservative movement in 1990, the Soviet Union had just collapsed. With it, the fusion of three types of conservatives that coalesced after World War II—cold warriors, social conservatives, and laissez-faire capitalists—began to unravel. As the conservative movement warily embarked on new terrain, Gerald followed Kirk in advocating for social conservatism rooted in local and regional traditions while opposing both military adventures abroad and unbridled capitalism. For this reason, Gerald believed, again following Kirk, that culture precedes and shapes political priorities, which "are at root only reflections of philosophical and religious conviction." In this vein, Gerald's caution from 2007 is every bit as relevant today: "Power must be contained.... What Kirk reminds us is that conservatives should seek power only as a means to accomplish something particular and should never mistake it as an end in itself."

Like Kirk, Gerald was an imaginative conservative who realized that "mystery—not reason—lies at the heart of each individual and the societies the human race creates." Community life and political order, therefore, will differ by locale according to human ingenuity and circumstance. Gerald's conservative principles are best articulated in the essays that bookend Part III of this volume. The 2016 presidential election threw the conservative movement into disarray. In response, Gerald offered "Beauty is the Heart of True Conservatism" as "an opportunity for a reconsideration of conservatism beyond the northeast Acela corridor." With this sentence Gerald was exercising his customary restraint, as the essay is really a *cri de coeur* for conservatism "to recall the centrality of beauty, and the power of images to work with man's reason to fashion again stories and a culture that is beautiful.... As [T. S.] Eliot did with modernist poetry, conservatism must use our current fashions to rejoin a salutary populism with its higher transcendent ends, our *mythos* with *logos* once again."

Deeply learned in the conservative intellectual tradition, Gerald considers other thinkers and issues in Part III. Three reviews consider the thought and legacy of the grandfather of modern conservatism, Edmund Burke, while another three weigh books of Sir Roger Scruton, the leading light of the conservative movement in Great Britain. One review considers the entirety of the conservative tradition from Burke to the present. There is also his review of Rod Dreher's 2006 book *Crunchy Cons*, which presents a kind of conservatism "lived outside the mainstream of the Republican Party." The book resonated with Gerald, and he referred to it often in his other writings, likely to draw attention to conservative principles overlooked by mainstream culture. Another repeated theme is the "unwritten constitution," an idea Kirk found in the writings of Orestes Brownson, and which comprises, in Gerald's summary, "all the mores, customs, and ways of life that together form American political culture and support the written Constitution." Gerald also believed that "conservatism cannot be separated from Christianity, because of its doctrine that original sin clouds our reason and our passions." From the doctrine of original sin comes conservatism's caution towards power.

With so many thoughtful and encompassing pieces, it is not an exaggeration to call Gerald's writings contained in Parts II and III a thematic history of the conservative movement, with special concentration on the period from 1990–2020.

Subsequent sections of this volume group Gerald's other intellectual interests. Part IV introduces leading humanists whose ideas impacted their times—and Gerald personally. Appropriately, the lead four pieces consider Christopher Dawson's work and impact. Writing in 1996 at age twenty-five, Gerald argued that "the contemporary value of Dawson's work lies in this recognition and explication of the continuing mission of the Church to use the present world situation of increased communication and ease of travel to bring about a new evangelization and to fill the great spiritual need that exists alongside of great wealth and technological advances." Other essays highlight key contributions from other nineteenth- and twentieth-century luminaries: G. K. Chesterton, Orestes Brownson, Jacques Barzun, David Jones, Dietrich von Hildebrand, and T. S. Eliot. Like a good teacher, Gerald's essays on these humanist heroes include brief biographies to connect these thinkers to an audience likely unfamiliar with them, and like a good scholar, he makes ready references to other commentators' work.

"The Catholic Thing" is a phrase that refers to the specific ways Catholics bring the universal teachings of Jesus Christ into the particulars of daily life. It is also the name of a website to which Gerald contributed a few essays, one of which concludes this volume. The selections of Part V showcase Catholicism's big tent, with essays and reviews on Catholic social teaching, economics, and fighting discrimination against Catholics and the Church herself. One of Gerald's abiding interests was the art of the Catholic novel; three pieces here, including a long scholarly essay, explore particulars of what Gerald called the purpose of the Catholic novel: to explore "a distinctive Catholic way of seeing reality and interpreting experience, which blends 'natural feeling, sentiment, and insight with what is believed in faith.'"

If ever Gerald found the practice of law dull, he successfully applied his knowledge to advance conservative and Catholic causes. The essays in Part VI consider habeas corpus and the rights of incarcerated terrorists; the law of status and specialized courts; reviews of books on judges and judicial opinions; the unwritten constitution versus the living constitution; the role of religion in law; and religious freedom cases. As in other areas, Gerald's philosophy of law stems from Kirk: "Kirk believed legal and political problems were at first philosophical, then theological problems. A community that was confused about its founding principles would be confused as to its laws. Understanding the customs and traditions of a nation must inform our understanding of the written Constitution."

Gerald never penned original essays on the ancient classics or the American founding, yet Parts VII and VIII cover books he reviewed on these topics, drawing on his liberal arts background, his Georgetown education, and the history he learned studying conservatism. On the latter theme, Gerald's thoughts were shaped by Kirk and by historian David Allan Shain, who, Gerald wrote, "argued that the generations leading up to and including the founding were not lovers of an abstract liberty or an untrammeled individualism. The sentiments and mores of the colonists were based not in Locke or some post-Renaissance 'republicanism,' but in small-town Calvinist Protestantism and a strong sense of the heritage of English liberty." The founding and individual founders are considered here in this light.

As a conservative, Gerald constantly measured the health of American culture. He was fond of a frequent saying, borrowed from St. Paul, of Kirk: the task of conservatives is to "redeem the time," that is, in Kirk's words, "to conserve the Permanent Things, to raise up the human condition to a level less unworthy of what Pico della Mirandola called 'the dignity of man.'" This can be done, Kirk continued, "by brightening the corner where you are; by improving one human unit, yourself, and helping your neighbor." The final section of this volume covers several key cultural issues dear to Gerald: the transformation of American holidays brought about by secularization, and what that means for the nation; the dangers of addiction to technology; reviving the virtue of thrift; and considering ways to renew the culture. Not surprisingly, in these assessments Gerald repeated a theme of his conservatism: he cautioned not to "mistake art for politics. Beauty will save the world, not govern it." As a good conservative, he did not seek grand solutions in the form of a central plan, imposed from the top down, that would remake America. This, Gerald knew, again following Kirk, would cause far more harm than good. Authentic renewal, rather, begins like conservatism itself: with a disposition from within the individual soul before reaching out to society at large.

As a life-long Latin student, Gerald would have known Horace's famous ode in which he sings praise to himself and predicts immortality for his poetry: "I have created a monument more lasting than bronze, and higher than the royal foundation of the pyramids." Gerald had no such pretension for his work; he did not even keep a curriculum vitae listing it all. Gerald did not write for immortality nor for fame; he wrote for love. In this, we are right to remember and esteem him, for he has communicated life's greatest mystery to us through his pen.

# PART ONE

## *Glimpses of the Man*

# *Almost Abducted*

**The red balloon** was a new detail. In my mind's eye, there was never a balloon.

When I was about three, I was almost abducted. I was outside a butcher shop on Bath Avenue in Brooklyn. The whole experience couldn't have lasted long—maybe a few minutes until I was recovered. So far as I know, nothing was done to the man who tried to take me.

This was in the early 1970s, when New York City was tipping into disaster but had not quite gotten to the bottom. Brooklyn was an Italian enclave, just one of many ethnic neighborhoods keeping the city at bay as it started its million-person population drop. The Bronx had not yet burned, and the Son of Sam had not yet become the symbol of urban terror. The subways were filthy, the parks not for visiting, and crime was on the rise. For some, the city's ethnic enclaves still held out a hope of safety and stability.

In those days, Bath Avenue was the center of Brooklyn's Italian population. We lived in a tiny apartment near the butcher shop: my mother, my father, my sister (then about one), and me. The apartment had two bedrooms; my sister slept in my parents' room. The living room looked out into a backyard, bare apart from a couple of clotheslines, and the view was dominated by a building covered in graffiti. My mother was also Italian, but from the factories of Niagara Falls rather than the proto-*Goodfellas*, pre-*Saturday Night Fever* of my father's Bensonhurst. She had escaped one ethnic neighborhood at eighteen, taking the bus to New York, but had ended up in another.

Originally published in *Harvard Review Online*, December 3, 2020.

In addition to the violent crime that was taking hold of the city—murders passed the 2,000 mark in 1972—people were also starting to panic over child abductions. The bulk of child abductions were, and are still, committed by people known to the child, usually a parent. According to some estimates, 250,000 of these occur every year, but the smaller number of stranger abductions only seemed to magnify the trauma of each one. The 1970s were filled with fears about pedophiles and what we now would call human traffickers, as well as Lindbergh baby-type kidnappings with demands for ransom. Enough cases were in the news in the 1970s to create to a movement to put pictures of the missing children on milk cartons, a predecessor of sorts to AMBER Alerts.

On the day I was almost abducted, my mother and father were both at work. My sister and I were with my grandmother and her sister, who lived together in a big pile of a house a few blocks away. My grandfather had a barbershop, where he ran books in the back. He was busy gambling away what little money he had, something we did not find out about until later. For a long time, I thought my great-aunt had never been married, that she just was always in that house. But many years later, I saw some wedding pictures and learned there had been a husband. He, it was whispered, had been an abusive husband. Her brother, it was also whispered, had driven him out of the house. My great-aunt never mentioned that she'd been married, but her brother's wayward children were always welcome in her house.

Of the butcher shop that day, I do not recall much. I have an image of myself holding hands with a stranger on a corner, but this cannot be a true memory. The image is *of* me holding someone's hand, from some distance away, not the view I would have had at the time. Psychologists refer to a period around the age of three as the time when a person's memories start to form and remain in one's recollection. Before that, we all experience something so common that it has a name: *infant amnesia*. No one really knows why it is that most of us cannot remember events that occurred before we were about two or three years old, or why we cannot remember our own births. Some think of this as a problem of ability: our minds have not developed to the point where we can form memories at all. Others think the problem is one of retrieval: the early memories are there, but our minds have overgrown them with later experiences and we don't know how to retrieve them. This memory of me holding someone's hand is retrievable and must have come later. I don't remember being told what happened; I only remember what it was I was told.

In my current job, I spend much of my time exploring people's memories. I listen to people tell me about events that happened weeks, months, or even years before. In most of the stories I hear, something bad happened and most people don't want to take the blame. So they construct memories of what happened—out of embarrassment, to protect themselves or others, or to avoid getting involved. Or maybe infant amnesia never really goes away. We all perform hundreds of individual tasks, hundreds of actions every day; how could one remember them all? Even events in the relatively recent past can be forgotten, and memories one does not think especially important disappear. My job is to go over the memories of many different people to try to find a reasonable facsimile of what really occurred. Sometimes one detail sticks out that makes the rest of the story make sense and helps you separate what likely happened from what likely didn't. But sometimes you never really know.

As I recall, my mother told me the story of what happened only once. My grandmother and great-aunt were arguing with the butcher. They were poor despite their house, which was bought by their parents with loans from friends and was in a steady state of collapse. We were poor too. We sometimes got free milk and big blocks of government-issued cheese from my grandmother, who had worked out some complicated plan to get more than her share at the food bank. Anyway, one sister, followed shortly by the other, went into the butcher's shop. I was left outside, a hand on the stroller holding my sister.

When my parents came home, the story came out. My grandmother had come out of the store and had an altercation with a man holding my hand who said he was taking me somewhere safe, perhaps a friend's house. That is the detail that confirms this was an abduction and not someone who saw a child on the street and tried to help. My mother remembers me being yelled at and blamed for walking away from my baby sister with some stranger. The sisters tried to deflect the blame, and suggested I had in fact wandered off. That would not have been like me: I was an introverted child even then, not one to act contrary to instructions. But walking away with someone who extended a hand, who may have appeared friendly, yes, I could see myself doing that.

In part because of my father's concern about his family's ability to watch me, we left soon after, moving to the other end of the borough, and my mother stopped working. A couple of years later a young boy around my age was abducted from a Soho street. His was perhaps the most famous of the high-profile cases of children who were taken seemingly at random. A police officer who was assigned to the case lived on our block. It was not solved until decades later, almost by accident.

When I mentioned it to her as an adult, my mother was surprised that I even knew about the incident. She had forgotten that she had told me about it, but her recall was quick, even after four decades. "The red balloon," she said. "That was how your grandmother found you. You weren't with your sister where you were supposed to be. She saw it bobbing down the street and she went after it."

# *Leaving Brooklyn*

❧

**My family had been in Brooklyn** (or, as I will ever call it, God's country) for over a century, refugees from the Lower East Side and a Jacob Riis-style life in early-twentieth-century New York. My father didn't speak much about his youth in Bensonhurst, but what he did say was enough to fill that neighborhood—which we visited every Saturday for dinner at my grandparents' house, with several dozen cousins and hangers-on—with myth.

Now a transient place full of hipsters, bond traders, and actors, as well as actors and hipsters who are the children of bond traders, all searching for an "authentic" place to replace the Midwestern suburbs and rural towns they came to Brooklyn to escape, Brooklyn for me will always be Flatbush Avenue and Rudy Giuliani, Bernie (Goetz, not Madoff), and Ed Koch, block parties, radios murmuring Yankees games on back porches (all of us too poor to afford air conditioning, which kept us outside in that great urbanist semi-public space), the blackout of 1977 and the blizzard of 1995, Mickey Rivers and Bucky Dent, not to mention the wild cast of characters appearing in the *Daily News*, a paper that practically taught me to read. (Although my mother, a Niagara Falls native, reminds me that *she* taught me how to speak; no "dese and dose" with her, but the flatter vowels of upstate New York.)

My neighborhood, Old Mill Basin, was one of the city's white ethnic redoubts. On the far edge of Brooklyn, abutting Jamaica Bay, it was "unequivocally remote," as the *New York Times* once called it, culturally as well

Originally published in *First Things*, April 2013.

as geographically, from Manhattan. Irish, Italian, and Jewish to its core, it was a neighborhood Norman Rockwell might have recognized, had his father been from Calabria and his mother from Derry. My Little League season opened with Mass, midsummer's highlights were the church bazaar and projects organized with the parish youth group, and each fall the shofar could be heard for blocks.

The title of a classic sociological study, *Canarsie: The Jews and Italians of Brooklyn Against Liberalism*, sums up my cultural and social surroundings. We sort of knew Norman Lear was making fun of Archie Bunker, but so much of what Archie said made sense that we didn't fully get the joke.

I had left Brooklyn for college but after a brief stint of Manhattan living came back for what I thought was for good—which in this case meant twelve years. But instead of living in Old Mill Basin or Bay Ridge, Marine Park or Bensonhurst, those neighborhoods I knew like I knew myself, my family landed in Brooklyn Heights.

Some may recall the paeans this neighborhood, and the adjoining Carroll Gardens and Boerum Hill, received in Rod Dreher's book *Crunchy Cons*. And he was not wrong. The neighborhoods are friendly and appeal to all sorts of conservative instincts for small-scale neighborhoods traversable without a car, home to few if any big-box or chain stores (and those easily ignored), and with a focus on local producers. We bought produce directly from farmers, loved finding the newest purveyor of organic ice cream, did not need to drive a car for weeks at a stretch, and lived within five miles of where my father and ancestors are buried.

During the dozen years we were in the Heights, we made good friends, who through their example continue to teach us how to live a rich and rewarding life. Since Rod's book was published in 2006, Brooklyn's growth into a center of individual handicrafts, small-scale producers, and eco-friendly business has exploded, along with the real-estate prices.

And yet, and yet. The celebrated small shopkeepers, holdovers in large part from the time when the neighborhoods were more coherent, usually lived elsewhere. The owners of my favorite deli, for example, where we went every Sunday after Mass, had moved out long before to raise their children in Pennsylvania and drove back every day to the store. Their hipster replacements are doing cool things, to be sure, but whether they can create a stable culture like the one that has all but disappeared is unclear.

The cultural rhythms of our life in Brooklyn had also become jarring. Institutions matter, and how people recognize community and the values that motivate them is important. Centuries after Christian missionaries co-opted the pagan festivals and converted them to Christ, Brooklyn, like many communities of the affluent elite, is undergoing a sort of re-paganization.

The holidays of the traditional Christian calendar are being either replaced by fake ones (Earth Day) or simply hollowed out. Valentine's Day, for example, has assumed a ridiculously large presence and is, so far as I can tell, the only time the word "saint" can be safely mentioned in a secular school. Halloween, too, is now reserved for candy distribution and completely removed from the feast of All Saints.

This is all old news, of course, to anyone even peripherally familiar with the culture wars, but to see it played out daily was more of a shock than I had expected. One anecdote: Our older daughter's "winter sing" contained respectful songs celebrating Hanukkah, Kwanzaa, and the Chinese New Year; Christians got "Jingle Bell Rock." The end of the year featured a "Maypole" dance, severed from its cultural realities and imbued with a neutral, multicultural vibe.

One can take only so much. These events spoke to the need of every community to have rituals, and a deep thoughtfulness went into creating traditions that would be open to all, or almost all. But to me, all this seemed to be the beginnings of a new culture ultimately incompatible with what I believed.

Our parish church, where all of our children were baptized and which I imagined being the church of my daughters' weddings (and my funeral), was wonderful, if half-filled and always in danger of being consolidated with other churches. But because, I think, of the combined effect of affluence and the busyness of life in the city, it was no longer a center of the lives of the Catholics who attended Mass there.

Moreover, there was little overlap between the families we knew in our parish and the families we saw the rest of the week in school or at other activities. Although I appreciate the need to be a leaven in a secular culture, the contrast was affecting our ability to convey a Christian worldview to our children; I needed help.

I'd like to say that all these changes were the reasons we moved north from Brooklyn to suburban Westchester, shaking the dust of the secular city from my feet. Alas, I am not so strong-willed. Out of nostalgia and inertia I likely would have stayed, but the cold logic of the dismal science was the final straw.

Paying three private-school tuitions was crushing, especially as I grew less enchanted with the education, and the public-school options were byzantine and unsure. As for the Catholic schools, there were none—none—nearby that served Brooklyn Heights, a commentary that speaks volumes about the state of the Church in affluent neighborhoods that, a few decades ago, might have supported not only traditional parochial schools but perhaps a Catholic high school charging competitive private-school tuition. My wife, who is far more reasonable and who could more patiently put up with what so exasperated me, and I decided that leaving was the best option for us.

The suburbs have their own tradition of anomie and cultural dissolution, of course, and my crunchy-con friends will surely blanch at our easy acceptance of the demon automobile. But the church here is bursting, the religious-education program is an order of magnitude larger, and there's even a very active Knights of Columbus chapter, a group I had not been involved with since college.

The entire town speaks a cultural and religious language I had not heard in years, and one I had not realized I missed very much. In the end, I decided I would rather drive almost everywhere and forgo artisanal pickles than lose those connections that made me who I am.

# *Milites Christi*

Last May, Pope Francis formally recognized the lay ministry of catechists, after a request from the Synod of Bishops. "Being a catechist is a vocation," Francis wrote, "and is a true and genuine ministry in the Church." This decision could not have come at a better time in the United States. As many diocesan school systems dissolve, the duty to instruct children in the faith—more so than at any other time in recent memory—has fallen to lay volunteers.

And more laymen, at least while lockdowns were instituted, had found the time to take on this duty. In my own parish, a number of us who were working from home began volunteering for the weekday religious education program, where there never were enough catechists. I had taught similar classes earlier in my life on Sundays, first in college and then again when I had small children. In the first round, I instructed mostly younger children, for whom the weekly lessons were often about being nice to others and accepting God's love, along with some Jesus stories. The second time, when I was volunteering at my parish, I joined forces with a friend who had a graduate degree in theology. He did the main work of the teaching, and he was not afraid to explain the sacraments and the life of Christ, including Good Friday and why the authorities pursued the Lord and John the Baptist. More of an assistant catechist, I just tried to keep the kids focused.

This time around, instead of teaching second graders about the sacraments, the Church calendar, and the people in the Gospels, I was handling

---

Originally published in *The Lamp*, Christmas 2021.

the oldest students in eighth grade, the year most children are confirmed. I loved it, but I soon realized that the class needed to be something different than what I had expected. Typically, in the lower grades at a grammar school, one teacher handles all the basic courses. Only a few classes, such as music, art, or foreign languages, are taught by separate teachers. But by the time a student reaches seventh or eighth grade, he often has a different teacher who specializes in his respective subject.

Unlike the usual courses taught in school, mature religious education should combine multiple disciplines in each class: history, philosophy, theology, Church doctrine, art, prayer, and literary criticism. Many of these subjects appear for the very first time in religion class. Theology, for example, is completely new to many students. And because it is not included in their secular education, they may not know why it is important. History, which they do learn, often does not cover the events that they need to know, let alone why they should remember them. The Battle of Lepanto, the Crusades, Saint Francis, how Christianity changed the cultures it entered—these were just a few milestones I needed to present. Even to begin religious education, we catechists were required to introduce, to explain, and to justify the existence of multiple disciplines before the students were ready to understand our lessons.

My fellow catechists were marvelous and to be thanked greatly for volunteering, but they struggled with the same challenges that I did. Some of the material we presented to our students resembled the facts and formulas that they memorized in school, except it was all a bit less obviously important to their lives. And we could only present our specifically religious themes, which the students weren't likely to encounter again in school, once a week. It is hard to expect anyone to remember things that they encounter so infrequently.

Most of us were not professional teachers or academics, so we were rather handicapped. After all, a lot of Catholic families only show up for religious education when it is a so-called "sacramental" year. While I am happy for their presence, this often means they have some basic gaps in their knowledge. Other catechists report that, along with these gaps, the adults in these families are unable to give their children answers. Then the catechist's role is doubled: he finds himself trying to lead along both the parent and the child in the latter's religious education.

A religious education program can easily become an incomprehensible mess. It is difficult enough just to find catechists and to make good use of diocesan resources, which oftentimes have been depleted because of sexual abuse settlements during the past few decades. And anyway, volunteer catechists made more sense in a culture in which everyday life was saturated with the Church. Now teachers often find themselves starting from the very beginning, with basic lessons about Mary, the apostles, and all the saints. In the old Catholic neighborhoods, this wasn't necessary: their names were on the street signs, their prayer cards in local stores.

In the very first class I noted one statue of Our Lady, after whom our parish is named, and another of Saint Jude in the classroom. I asked the students what I thought was an easy question: who were these two people in our classroom with us? No one knew. And so we had a good discussion about how to read identifiers in a church statute: colors, tools, clothing, or instruments of their martyrdom. We had a similar discussion about the readings from Mass that week, just in case some of the students did not understand them on Sunday. I tried—but I am no theologian—to explain the Scriptures. Both discussions were focused on the same theme: the Church is not random. Each detail in the statues has a deliberate meaning; they tell us something specific about the saints and Our Lady, on which we can reflect. Neither were readings chosen by accident; they speak to one another and show us how the Gospel is the culmination of God's plan.

Eventually, I largely ditched the book and the lesson plan. I tried something new, beginning with an explanation of why we were here. The Church was asking the students to become *milites Christi*, soldiers of Christ. What did that mean? I explained that they needed weapons (prayers), tools (rosaries), and officers (the saints). They were not simply students; they were preparing to be warriors and adventurers in a world that often knows nothing of the faith, or, just as likely, may know it and be hostile to it. This seemed to perk them up. They were all good kids, but they were in need of a new approach: their faith needed to be introduced to them as an adventure, not another class in school. They needed to see it as a living guide to understanding the world, even as they may forget their eighth-grade biology.

# PART TWO

## *The Wisdom of Russell Kirk*

# *Captain Kirk: An Interview*

**Clinton Rossiter** once quipped that Russell Kirk "has the sound of a man born one hundred and fifty years too late and in the wrong country." *National Review Online* contributor Gerald J. Russello nevertheless wants to update Kirk for twenty-first-century Americans—the University of Missouri Press has just published his book, *The Postmodern Imagination of Russell Kirk*.

Russello is also editor of *The University Bookman*, a fellow of the Chesterton Institute at Seton Hall University, and the editor of *Christianity and European Culture: Selections from the Work of Christopher Dawson*. He recently spoke to *NRO*'s John J. Miller about postmodernism, crunchy cons, and whether Kirk would have watched ESPN's SportsCenter.

**John J. Miller**: To a modern-day conservative, what's the importance of Russell Kirk?

**Gerald Russello**: Kirk provides a way for conservatives to talk and live as conservatives. From early on, he was convinced that liberalism had exhausted itself because of what he called its lack of imagination. He was looking beyond liberalism into what would come after, in a time that had discarded both liberal rationality and the pre-modern tradition represented, for example, by Burke. This new age, which Kirk identified with postmodernism in an early essay, was still too inchoate to define. In 1980,

Originally published in *National Review*, June 28, 2007.

he wrote that "We seem to be entering upon the Post-Modern Age... and new thoughts and new sentiments and new modes of statecraft—or *re*newed thoughts, sentiments, modes—may take on flesh soon. The Post-Modern Age surely will be an epoch of big battalions and Napoleonic figures; possibly it may be also a time of renewed poetic imagination, and of the reflection of poetry in politics." The way he did this—through narrative and imagination, primarily—provides I think a sharp contrast to most conservative controversialists, who are too focused on political controversies and electoral victory to take the long view that Kirk did.

**Miller**: So is this a time of "renewed poetic imagination" or "poetry in politics"?

**Russello**: It may be, although I am a little less optimistic than perhaps Kirk was in 1980. A lot of younger conservatives are breaking with the established right wing and focusing more on individual cultural issues—Rod Dreher has called this a "crunchy con" phenomenon, but I think it is broader than that. That new flowering of younger conservative thinkers may yet bear fruit in politics, probably not in 2008 but at some point.

**Miller**: Was Kirk the original "crunchy con"?

**Russello**: Yes, and no. Certainly Kirk was concerned with what he called the Permanent Things, such as truth and beauty, and found in much of modern life obstacles to realizing them, so in that sense he was a little crunchy. Being something of a bohemian himself, I think he would have appreciated some crunchy efforts to go off the grid, which was easier in his less-regulated time. But I think the terms of that debate are not his; Kirk spoke fondly of certain cities, for example—including old Detroit, and defended family farms and small neighborhoods on the basis of their historical continuity and naturalness, which only roughly corresponds with some of the crunchy arguments I have seen.

**Miller**: When I hear the word "postmodern," I think of graduate students who wear black turtlenecks, hang out in coffee bars, and wish they were French. How is Kirk's imagination "postmodern," as the title of your book has it?

**Russello**: That is what I thought as well, but I discovered two things while researching this book. First, historically, a conservative was one of the very first people even to use the word "postmodern." The Episcopal cleric Bernard Iddings Bell, whom Kirk admired and whose book *Crowd Culture* is a must-read, was one of the first to use the term "postmodernism," in a book published in 1926. Bell's postmodernism is explicitly religious, the solution to a crisis of faith in an unbounded reason. In its place, Bell proposed a postmodernism comfortable with both modern science and miracles, and which placed the good of existence—sacralized through the Incarnation—at the center of its understanding of the world. Though I don't know if Kirk ever read this book, parts of it are consistent with his outlook.

Secondly, I found that a number of other conservative scholars are exploring the new opportunities postmodernism opens for conservatives who reject core principles of modernity. Vigen Guroian and Peter Augustine Lawler have both written very insightfully on the postmodern condition and what it may mean, but they are only the most recent in a longer series of anti-modern writings that touch on themes we would now call postmodern.

Kirk's conservatism is "postmodern" in the sense that it was never modern, and therefore is not burdened as liberalism is with the weaknesses of the Enlightenment worldview. Kirk's emphasis on imagination, his concern for the imagery a society creates of what it admires or condemns, his treatment of tradition and history as not objective but one in which we participate and can change, and his devotion to what Burke called the "little platoons" of society all have parallels in postmodern thought. Moreover, Kirk himself saw this. In 1982, he wrote in *National Review* that "the Post-Modern imagination stands ready to be captured. And the seemingly novel ideas and sentiments and modes may turn out, after all, to be received truths and institutions, well known to surviving conservatives." With liberalism moribund, it "may be the conservative imagination which is to guide the Post-Modern Age."

**Miller:** Kirk always maintained that conservatism was not an ideology. What did he mean by that?

**Russello:** Kirk contended that ideology is a type of religious dogmatism in a political context, and one completely inconsistent with a conservative outlook. It eliminates the nuances and shades of gray that exist in actual political or social life. "For the ideologue, humankind may be defined into two classes: the comrades of Progress, and the foes attached to reactionary interests," who are not only incorrect but who must be destroyed. The proponent of ideology "resorts to the anesthetic of social utopianism, escaping the tragedy and grandeur of true human existence by giving his adherence to a perfect dream-world of the future. Reality [the ideologue] stretches or chops away to conform to [a] dream-pattern of human nature and society." Because ideology is a replacement religion, when injected into the public sphere it makes politics, at least as Kirk defines it, impossible.

It should be stressed that Kirk opposed even conservative efforts at ideology creation, thinking that it enshrined an objectionable and false abstractness to historically contingent beliefs. Conservatism, because it is based on a realistic assessment of human nature and a rejection of utopia, could never be ideological. He wrote that while "some Americans, conservatively inclined ones among them, might embrace an ideology of Democratic Capitalism or New World Order," such an embrace was fraught with difficulty. Even if done with innocent motives, the imposition of such a construct would, Kirk thought, have disastrous results.

**Miller:** Does that mean he was a paleocon?

**Russello:** Not really, though he certainly had an affinity with some of what are called paleocon positions. He wrote for *Chronicles*, for example, and supported Pat Buchanan. However, Kirk parted company with the positions of some paleocons, which I touch on in the book. He went his own way, as Adam Wolfson noted in an article in the *Public Interest*.

**Miller**: It's amazing to think that Kirk had any influence at all, living in tiny Mecosta, Mich., rather than in Manhattan or Washington. This was before the Internet, after all. How did he pull it off?

**Russello**: I'm not sure, but would like to know! In large part, of course, it was that what he had to say people found appealing and persuasive. But at a more practical level, Kirk's influence was a result of his work ethic: Kirk wrote consistently throughout his career, and in a remarkable variety of venues, even places like *Cosmopolitan*. The sustained, substantive output caught a lot of people's attention.

**Miller**: That doesn't seem to impress Alan Wolfe. In Wolfe's recent attack on Kirk in *The New Republic*, he called Kirk "prolific without being profound" and described Kirk's brand of conservatism as "provincial, resentful, bigoted."

**Russello**: The funny thing is that *The New Republic*, which published Wolfe's nasty and uninformed piece, published some very favorable pieces on Kirk after his death in 1994. Wolfe just recycles old canards about Kirk and conservatives that were dated even in the 1960s, and merely uses scare words to motivate his liberal readers, without analyzing the substance much. As a man who traveled all over the world, and who took into his home refugees from any nation on Earth, to call Kirk provincial or bigoted is simply ridiculous. As with his writings on American religion, Wolfe entirely misses the point of Kirk's work.

**Miller**: How did you first learn about Russell Kirk? Did you ever meet him?

**Russello**: I first heard of Russell Kirk in the summer of 1990, when some friends and I were selecting a reading list for the summer in preparation for launching a conservative newspaper at our college. Someone suggested *The Conservative Mind.* I spent the summer reading and rereading that book, and quickly got my hands on as many other Kirk books as I could find. They were a revelation. I met him briefly a couple of times in Washington, D.C., when he was giving lectures, and he signed my edition of his book *John Randolph of Roanoke.* He was also kind enough to answer some of my letters.

**Miller**: Why hasn't anybody written a definitive biography of Kirk—a book that tells his life story, as opposed to a book that mainly grapples with his ideas?

**Russello**: I am not sure, though books by Jim Person and Wes McDonald are great places to start. Perhaps because until recently Kirk's letters and other papers at his home in Mecosta had not been catalogued, and they would be the natural first step for any scholar. Any foundation willing to support that work, feel free to call me!

**Miller**: If you could have interviewed Kirk during your research, what's the one question you would have asked him?

**Russello**: I would have asked him why he never wrote more specifically about traditions as he knew them. There are glimpses of what he would have said in some of his work, especially his early essays on Scotland, but for the most part he seemed content to defend tradition without delving into details about specific American customs or folkways. I would have loved to hear him on sports, for example, which conservatives like George Will have written about.

**Miller**: Sorry, but I just can't picture Russell Kirk watching *SportsCenter.*

**Russello:** Me either! But he had a great sense of play, and I think would have had interesting things to say on the role sport and games play in human society.

**Miller:** Have you read Kirk's ghost stories?

**Russello:** Yes, most of them. They are fun to read, of course, and also an important way in which Kirk expressed his conservatism. They also give a flavor for the variety of his character. Kirk was not a stuffy antiquarian character. In 1987, for example, Kirk published both *The Wise Men Know What Wicked Things Are Written on the Sky*, a collection of lectures given at the Heritage Foundation, and he also appeared in *The Color of Evil*, a collection of horror stories that also featured Stephen King, H. P. Lovecraft, and Shirley Jackson.

**Miller:** Do you have a problem with stuffy antiquarians? Now I'm worried that they're going to flood *NRO* with e-mailed complaints. Except that they probably don't use e-mail.

**Russello:** Not really, as I am something of one myself. Indeed, part of the argument I make in the book is that Kirk's pose as a figure of "antique grandeur," a phrase he used, was in part to sharpen the contrast between the fullness of conservatism and what he found to be desiccated modernity.

**Miller:** You're the editor of *The University Bookman*, a publication that Kirk founded years ago. What is it?

**Russello:** *The University Bookman* is a quarterly review of books that Kirk founded in 1960. I took over as editor a couple of years ago and it is essentially a forum for the discussion of serious books that may have escaped the attention of the mainstream press, and even of some conservatives. In recent issues, for example, we have covered books of interest to conservatives that were published in Italy, France, and elsewhere, as well as review essays on science fiction, the "pulps," and a host of other topics. We also republish classic Kirk essays in each issue.

**Miller**: If somebody who has never read anything by Kirk asks for advice on where to start, what do you suggest?

**Russello**: That's a tough one. I think his book *Eliot and His Age* is one of his best, but for someone who just wants to browse and find out what Kirk is about, ISI has just published a collection called *The Essential Russell Kirk*, which certainly covers the major themes of his thought.

# *An American Tory*

A FEW YEARS AGO, C-SPAN's "American Writers" series featured a segment on Russell Kirk (1918–1994). The episode toured Kirk's Italianate home in the small Michigan town of Mecosta, decorated with furniture Kirk collected from his wide travels, or saved from church sales or old hotels about to be demolished, and exhibited his library, a converted toy factory lined with heavy bookshelves. Kirk himself cast a quiet, dignified figure, almost always pictured (even as a young man) with waistcoat and watch fob, but with a twinkling eye and a taste for good Scotch and a tall tale well told. In an historical irony, Kirk was paired in the segment with William F. Buckley, Jr. In sharp contrast to the urbane Buckley, who excelled and reveled in the verbal sparring that characterized "Firing Line," the television interview/debate series he hosted, Kirk despised television, belittling "Demon TV" in his published work, and was himself a less-than-brilliant public speaker. Yet the two will be forever joined as the co-founders of modern American conservatism. What Kirk called his "prolonged essay in the history of ideas," published in 1953 as *The Conservative Mind*, was one of a small cluster of books—including Whittaker Chambers's *Witness* (1952) and Robert Nisbet's *The Quest for Community* (1953)—that enabled American conservatives in the 1940s and 1950s to collect what had been a disorganized collection of eccentrics, anti-Communists, and traditionalists into something resembling a coherent social force.

Indeed, the conclusion that without Kirk, modern American conservatism would not have existed, alone merits the recent publication of *The*

Originally published in *The New Criterion*, January 2007.

*Essential Russell Kirk*, a collection of his writings. The young Buckley thought as much, and he traveled from New York to the wilds of Michigan to see whether Kirk would be interested in lending his name to a conservative newsmagazine that would eventually become *National Review*. Kirk agreed; he went on to contribute a column to the magazine for the next twenty-five years. His major books—*The Conservative Mind*, *Eliot and His Age*, *The Roots of American Order*, *America's British Culture*—created the intellectual latticework from which he and other conservatives could feel comfortable in challenging liberalism. They were not, as mainstream liberal culture thought, outcasts; instead, they were representatives of a living tradition.

This path to becoming the twentieth century's most successful conservative cultural critic was not obvious: it began, of all places, at Utah's Dugway Proving Ground, where Kirk was stationed during World War II. In its vast expanse, with few duties to occupy him, Kirk came to realize his life's calling. As he recounted in his memoir (in the third person), Kirk had concluded that "[h]is was no Enlightenment mind, Kirk now became aware: it was a Gothic mind, medieval in its temper and structure. He did not love cold harmony and perfect regularity of organization; what he sought was a complex of variety, mystery, tradition, the venerable, the awful." As a result of this conclusion, tradition and mystery, and not abstract rationality, became cornerstones of his conservatism.

Kirk came of old Protestant stock, the son of a railroad engineer in the small Michigan town of Plymouth. His grandfather, a bank president, was a serious man devoted to good books and conversation, whose grandson adored him. Other relations supplied an equally important but quite different influence: clustered around "Piety Hill," the home in which he was to live as an adult, these relatives were devoted spiritualists of the pre-New Age Swedenborgian variety. They imbued in Kirk a love of mystery and a lifelong belief in the reality of ghosts and the supernatural. Kirk expressed his devotion to both these inheritances by composing both big books of intellectual history, and award-winning Gothic tales of the supernatural.

After his discharge from the Army, Kirk received a graduate degree from Duke and made his way to Scotland's University of St Andrews, where he received a doctorate, and whose academic robes, in typical fashion, he later took to using as a Halloween costume. Always shy and laconic, Kirk found the courtly and reserved manners of St Andrews and rural Scotland to his liking. The many "ghostly tales" and stories of hauntings surrounding the Scottish great houses continued Kirk's fascination with the occult and the gothic. And although Kirk bore many of the marks of his low-church Puritan ancestors, the aristocratic and medieval trappings of Scotland's peers appealed to him. This close connection with Scotland shaped Kirk's lasting persona in the United States. So strong was the Scottish stamp that when he returned to the United States and began writing for American periodicals some conservatives suspected him of harboring a preference for aristocracy or an established church. Kirk did little to alter this perception, even after he had more permanently settled in the United States. Instead, Kirk appropriated the persona and crafted an image of himself as a "figure of antique grandeur." Pictures of him from this time—still a relatively young man—show him dressed severely in old-fashioned costume. He combined this façade as lower-case Scottish laird with the stoicism of the Roman philosopher-emperor Marcus Aurelius, whose *Meditations* he had read while at Dugway. This Scottish resolve never left him, even after, late in life, he converted from a generic religiosity to Catholicism and incorporated the work of Christopher Dawson, among other Catholic thinkers, into his critique of modern life.

After a short stint in academia, Kirk set himself up in his Michigan home (always referred to as "ancestral"), and surrounded himself with the cast-offs, both human and otherwise, of modernity's whirl. For the following four decades he issued several dozen elegantly written books and hundreds of essays and reviews on everything from urban planning to children's literature, sallying forth on occasion to debate the leading lights of the Left. He railed against politicized education, and brutalized culture, wore antique waistcoats, did not drive, disdained Communism without being a Cold Warrior, and preferred storytelling to economics or party politics.

For some, this was too much. No one seemed to know what to make of this antiwar, deliberately old-fashioned storyteller who hated cars and "Behemoth University," who embraced old buildings and planted trees, a thinker with many admirers but no disciples. Critics from the right, such as Frank Meyer, thought Kirk's emphasis on community obligations and an ordered society was a form of crypto-collectivism. Others critics, mostly from the left, took from Richard Hofstadter the notion that conservatism was the expression of a mental defect, a regrettable "paranoid style" that needed to be contained and dismissed. One reviewer wrote that the purpose of *The Conservative Mind* was merely to soothe the "pent-up injury, forlornness and frustration" for those conservatives left behind by contemporary life. More recently, some, such as Rod Dreher, have tried to baptize Kirk as a "crunchy con" *avant la lettre*, his conservative principles watered down into a modern "authenticity." Others have tried to discredit him as a poor historian seeking an ordered hierarchical world that never existed. This remains the most significant criticism: the conservatism Kirk argued for was all in his mind, and did not reflect the actual America around him. And despite his influence, his reputation has in recent years languished, due to his opposition to the First Gulf War and from his contention that conservatism was not ideological.

But Kirk becomes a more complex figure from the vantage point of a decade and more after his death. The typical caricature of Kirk as an ersatz eighteenth-century gentleman turns out to be wrong, made by a too-hasty assessment based on appearances. It is belied by Kirk's own expressed distaste for that period, which he once described as "an age of gilded selfishness and frivolous intellectuality—an age almost without a heart." To the contrary, Kirk was keenly aware of his time, and his use of Burke and others was part of a deliberate design. Kirk's exaggerated persona of the "Bohemian Tory," and the sometimes out-of-the-way subjects he wrote about—"Will the Habsburg Return?" was a typical column subject—were attempts to jar his readers out of complacency. But instead of the theatrics of the Beats and their hippie descendants, which were tired agitprop even then, Kirk was trying to spur deeper reflection on the tradition he uncovered in his books, running from Burke to T. S. Eliot, and from the revelations of Jerusalem to Philadelphia's ordered liberty. For this reason, Kirk was even cautiously optimistic about postmodernism. While he recognized the nonsense that that term often denotes, nevertheless, in sounding the final death knell of rationalistic liberalism, he suggested that postmodernism could provide an opportunity for a resurgence of the conservative imagination.

*The Essential Russell Kirk*, edited by the distinguished literary critic George Panichas, is a significant contribution to understanding his place in American intellectual history. The volume is arranged thematically, and includes generous selections on subjects ranging from architecture to constitutionalism, literature to politics, from the beginning of Kirk's career to his posthumous memoir, *The Sword of Imagination*. Of particular interest are the pieces on education; Kirk was for many years perhaps best known for his trenchant critiques of indoctrination masquerading as education. He complained that higher education "has been rearing up not a class of liberally educated young people of human outlook, but a series of degree-dignified elites, an alleged meritocracy of confined views and dubious intellectual and moral credentials," a tyranny of the "quarterschooled" such as those inflicted on developing countries in Africa and Asia.

Representative essays such as "Reflections of a Gothic Mind," "Eigg, in the Hebrides," and considerations of Orestes Brownson, Paul Elmer More, George Santayana, and Max Picard remind us that Kirk, who after all made his living by writing for a popular audience, perfected a style that was reserved without being rigid. It was a deliberate attempt to express the compression of time that was an important feature of his conservatism: the past is here with us, now, as the future melts into the present. Kirk's writing was almost defiantly imaginative, frustrating even his admirers for not being sufficiently "analytic." He concentrated on the formation of images and the cultivation of imagination, for "[w]hether to throw away yesterday's nonsense to embrace tomorrow's nonsense, or whether we find our way out of superficiality into real meaning, must depend in part upon the images which we discover or shape." Often his work begins with an autobiographical reflection; visiting Burke's home, or having tea with Eliot in a

London club. Such scenes provide the concrete links between present and past that he thought critical for any civilization.

Kirk is most often, and with obvious justification, thought of as the great antagonist of liberalism. *The Conservative Mind*, after all, was intended as an explicit contrast with the liberal mind, then so dominant that critics such as Lionel Trilling could think of no alternative to it. What his admirers sometimes miss, however, is that even in his earliest writings Kirk was looking beyond the end of liberalism. Although as a political movement liberalism began with the great conflagration of the French Revolution and was tied, to varying degrees, to Enlightenment rationalism, utilitarianism, individualism, anti-Christianity, and socialism, those were for Kirk insufficient bases for a full and humane social philosophy, and liberalism eventually succumbed to its internal contradictions. Liberalism soon "ceased to signify anything, even among its most sincere partisans, [other] than a vague good will." In a 1955 piece collected here, "The Dissolution of Liberalism," Kirk was already writing its obituary.

> The liberal system attained popularity because it promised progress without the onerous duties exacted by tradition and religion. It is now in the process of dissolution because, founded upon an imperfect and distorted myth, it has been unable to fulfill its promise, and because it no longer appeals in any degree to the higher imagination. It has been undone by social disillusion.

Aside from some totalitarian revolution—unlikely in the United States—Kirk suggested that a "Macchiavellian scheme founded upon self-interest and creature comforts" would take hold in American culture. The countercultural excesses of the 1960s and 1970s and the adult baby boomers' materialist narcissism (masquerading as social concern) were the expected results of liberalism's disintegration.

Yet just because liberalism could no longer guarantee the allegiance of the rising generation did not mean conservative principles would naturally triumph. From the ruins of liberalism, Kirk saw what he called the Age of Sentiments, whose central feature was television and the false images it projects, intended to act upon its viewers' emotions. "The immense majority of human beings will feel with the projected images they behold upon the television screen; and in those viewers that screen will rouse sentiments rather than reflections. Waves of emotion will sweep back and forth, so long as the Age of Sentiments endures." But because "conservatism is sustained by a body of sentiments," albeit of a different kind, it has a better hope of success than liberalism in surviving even among a television-saturated nation. Without right feeling, the intellect is useless, perhaps even dangerous, a lesson that the proponents of rationalism had forgotten.

The abiding feature of Kirk's work was hope, which makes his work especially attractive in a time of electoral defeat and conservative disarray. Given his Christian convictions about sin and redemption, he did not despair even when the causes for which he fought seemed no closer to victory than when he started. This cautiously optimistic view avoids the disillusionment of liberal utopians when reality does not match their plans for heaven on earth, and it also avoids the postmodern despair of meaning, which cannot distinguish between decadence or progress. That narrow path remains a fruitful one for conservatism.

# *Russell Kirk and Postmodern Conservatism*

THIS WEEK marks the ninetieth anniversary of the birth of Russell Kirk. Kirk, who died in 1994, is best remembered for his role in helping to create the postwar conservative movement in America. His groundbreaking work, *The Conservative Mind*, received national attention when it was published in 1953, upsetting the settled elite consensus (as articulated most famously by Lionel Trilling) that liberalism was the only intellectual tradition in America.

The son of an engineer, Russell Amos Kirk grew up during the Depression in the Michigan railroad town of Plymouth. As a child, Kirk also spent time in the tiny town of Mecosta, Michigan, where his family—fallen-away Protestants and spiritualists—had a rambling place called Piety Hill, so named because of the séances and occult services held there. (Kirk later inherited the property and made it his own home.) He converted to Christianity as an adult but was still much influenced by this side of his family; among his many accomplishments, he became a collector, teller, and award-winning writer of what he called "ghostly tales." His early exposure to the possibility of the supernatural convinced him that rationalist materialism could not explain the whole of life.

After service in the Army in World War II (an experience that soured him on big government), Kirk began graduate work at Duke, writing his master's thesis on John Randolph of Roanoke. He did his graduate work at St. Andrews University in Scotland, and his doctoral thesis became *The Conservative Mind.* The book was an intellectual sensation—full reviews

---

Originally published in *First Things*, October 24, 2008.

were published in *Time* and the *New York Times Book Review*—and it launched Kirk's career. He followed it with some two dozen other books on subjects ranging from Robert Taft to multiculturalism, hundreds of essays and reviews, and a long-running column on educational subjects for *National Review*.

The problem Kirk faced, along with most conservatives, was that the Enlightenment, with its universalizing equality, secularism, and blinkered rationality, was already destroying traditional Western culture. How can a tradition be preserved if it is already dissolving into what theorist Zygmunt Bauman called "liquid modernity?"

Kirk's answer was twofold. First, he uncovered (some would say, "created") a counter-tradition, one that rested not on the rationalism of the Enlightenment, the ideological fervor of the French Revolution, or the modern vogue for limitless "rights." Rather, it began with Edmund Burke's defense of the lived experience of Britain as a bulwark of liberty and the protection of rights. Moreover, Kirk claimed that this tradition connected Britain and America, and included such varied figures as Samuel Taylor Coleridge and John Henry Newman, Orestes Brownson and Benjamin Disraeli, Irving Babbitt and Paul Elmer More, John Adams and W. H. Mallock.

The second strategy was more daring. Kirk was criticized, then and later, for writing in an anachronistic style, one not suited to confronting the seemingly rationalist arguments of liberalism. In order to defend what they thought to be worth conserving, some conservatives believed that they had to engage liberalism on its own terms, in a "dialectic" mode that is foreign to the conservative language of custom and tradition. Kirk rejected this approach.

As early as the 1950s, he had become convinced that liberalism would exhaust itself because it could not inspire and sustain what he called the "moral imagination." For conservatives to buy into its premises would seal their defeat. Something else would replace liberalism eventually, and Kirk offered a richly imaginative vision of conservatism that could survive liberal modernity's collapse. One element of that vision was a revived respect for religious faith.

As early as 1982, in an essay for *National Review*, Kirk suggested that "the Post-Modern imagination stands ready to be captured. And the seemingly novel ideas and sentiments and modes [of postmodernism] may turn out, after all, to be received truths and institutions, well known to surviving conservatives." He went so far as to state that he thought that it "may be the conservative imagination which is to guide the Post-Modern Age." (One of the earliest uses of the word *postmodern* was by the conservative Episcopalian cleric Bernard Iddings Bell, in a book of that title published in 1926; not surprisingly, Bell was an early influence on Kirk.)

Kirk had little patience for the trendy radicalism and sometimes simply nonsensical expressions of postmodern hacks. Nonetheless, he saw in postmodernism a chance to escape the strictures of liberalism and reconnect with the older, pre-Enlightenment tradition of the West. This approach has its weaknesses—Kirk, for example, too often simply assumed the existence of historical continuity, and perhaps did not sufficiently confront the corrosive effects of liberalism on the kinds of social forces he believed could sustain tradition. Nevertheless, his work stands as a stark alternative to a much bleaker postmodern future.

Kirk's intellectual legacy remains widespread, if too often unacknowledged by the movement he helped create. Two of the journals he founded, *The University Bookman* and *Modern* Age, continue to appear, and his books remain in print. The localist writer Bill Kauffman has outlined a defense of regionalism that is very much in Kirk's spirit. Kauffman wants to reclaim the particularities of the American experience from the domination of big government and the monotone culture emanating from Hollywood, Washington, and New York. His lyrical prose elevates half-forgotten episodes and figures in American history and weaves them into a compelling counter-cultural story.

Scholars such as Robert Kraynak and Peter Augustine Lawler have followed Kirk in studying postmodernism through a traditionalist lens, and popular writers such as Rod Dreher, author of the provocative *Crunchy Cons*, draw from Kirk's writings to support a localist, organic lifestyle. Despite Kirk's suspicion of the cult of technology, a number of influential bloggers also look to him for inspiration in shaping their own conservative visions, rejecting purely utilitarian views of rationality and promoting the ideal of the "postmodern conservative" who transcends traditional political labels of left and right.

In addition, scholars like Barry Alan Shain, in their writings on early America, have confirmed Kirk's contention that that the colonies were not Lockean utopias expressing the values of modern political theory, but closely knit, highly religious Protestant villages for whom "Christian liberty" had real meaning. The world of the Founders was not, in other words, an earlier version of our own secular society.

Fourteen years after his death, Kirk would not be surprised at our cultural problems. But neither would he be surprised at the progress made by those who confront these problems in political and intellectual battle. Believing Christian that he was, Russell Kirk never despaired of the future; cheerfulness, he liked to say, will always break in.

# *Whispers from Kirk*

**Stan Evans** has described bodies of thought as having "lifecycles"; they emerge, thrive for a while, and, unless continually nourished, eventually hollow out and pass away. Having reached the end of its lifecycle, liberalism, as a coherent body of thought, is dead. There are still liberals, of course. But the tradition derived variously from John Locke, John Stuart Mill, and Montesquieu, which was transmuted in the 1950's by the Cold War and transmogrified beyond recognition by the social revolutions of the 60's and 70's and the influence of Michel Foucault and company, has not been able to sustain itself. The ethos of revolution, which was tied, in varying degrees, to Enlightenment rationalism, utilitarianism, individualism, anti-Christianity, and socialism, has proved itself to be an insufficient basis for a full and humane social order. Liberalism's culture of individual rights has become increasingly unworkable and has made politics impossible. Moreover, liberalism has metastasized into a corrosive popular culture that even many liberals oppose. Finally, as a direct rebuke to liberal visions of a gradually secularizing world, nonliberal and traditional religious movements are now stronger than they have been in perhaps a century.

What does this mean for conservatives? For one thing, it means that what Adrian Woolridge has called the "Coulterization" of conservatism is a dead end. "Movement" conservatism's shrill condemnation of the "liberal" bogeyman is falling on deaf ears, as it is becoming increasingly

---

Originally published in *Chronicles*, September 2007.

detached from social and political reality. On issues ranging from foreign policy to the environment, the political landscape is shifting, but mainstream conservatives are not paying attention. The growing opposition to the Iraq war is the most recent, and the most significant, case in point: Many mainstream conservatives seemed to favor any Republican so long as he supported the war, while long-time conservatives were blacklisted, or worse, for opposing it. This tunnel vision justifies critics who say that conservatism has no real substance to it and is, at most, a reaction to the dominant liberalism.

Russell Kirk is often thought of as the great antagonist of liberalism. His *Conservative Mind* (1953), after all, provided an explicit contrast with the liberal one, which was, at the time, so dominant that critics such as Lionel Trilling could think of no alternative to it. Some may think Kirk would have little to offer regarding the challenges conservatism faces in this century. After all, he died in 1994, which, in our post-September 11 world, seems like a long time ago. Before his death, many had already written him off, for, among other things, his opposition to the Gulf War. Even Kirk's admirers sometimes forget that, even in the 1950's, Kirk was looking beyond the end of liberalism. Because of its inherent faults, liberalism soon was emptied of content and "ceased to signify anything, even among its most sincere partisans, [other] than a vague good will." In "The Dissolution of Liberalism" (1955), Kirk was already writing its obituary:

> The liberal system attained popularity because it promised progress without the onerous duties exacted by tradition and religion. It is now in the process of dissolution because, founded upon an imperfect and distorted myth, it has been unable to fulfill its promise, and because it no longer appeals in any degree to the higher imagination. It has been undone by social disillusion.

What would come next? Would there be a totalitarian takeover of some sort? After all, the communists were, at the time, working to infiltrate American society. No, said Kirk, it is far more likely that a "Machiavellian scheme founded upon self-interest and creature comforts" would take hold on American culture. The excesses of the counterculture of the following two decades, and the baby boomers' materialist narcissism masquerading as social concern that characterized the 80's and 90's, were, for Kirk, expected results of liberalism's disintegration.

The challenge for conservatives is to create a substantive program within their own tradition without having to feed off the carcass of liberalism. Part of that challenge involves re-imagining that tradition, as Kirk did in his day and as writers such as Bill Kauffman have done more recently, by calling on lesser-known figures and movements in American history that give the lie to the ossified divisions of contemporary politics.

In 1954, Russell Kirk published *A Program for Conservatives*, which was reissued in 1989 as *Prospects for Conservatives*. It is the closest Kirk ever came in writing to discussing actual policies that suited his romantic, imaginative conservatism, though, in the book, he explicitly disclaims any sort of political program. Rather, he sets forth a framework for conservatives for analyzing political issues.

In *Prospects*, Kirk devotes an entire chapter to the question of power; it is worth rereading, because conservatives seem to have forgotten its central lesson: Power must be contained. These days, conservatives often seem to want to acquire and hold onto power without knowing why. This is an unfortunate consequence of the successes of the Reagan years and the Gingrich Revolution of 1994. What Kirk reminds us is that conservatives should seek power only as a means to accomplish something particular and should never mistake it as an end in itself.

Kirk also addressed two facets of the challenge of power. On the national level, he found the constitutional scheme of ordered liberty and federalism to be the "chief attainment of American political philosophy." On the international level, he was a staunch opponent of exporting ideology in the name of democracy. Kirk was no anarchist, of course. He believed that there is a place for the proper exercise of government power, exercised primarily through states and localities and constrained by tradition and custom. Thus, he parted ways with the libertarians, whose obsessive focus on freedom detached from tradition is the flip side of liberalism. Invoking the example of Lincoln, for whom he maintained a decent respect throughout his career, he chose the "middle path" between absolute sovereignty and absolute liberty.

Kirk thought the decay of federalism and the institutions of self-government in America would increase the temptation to use government power for seemingly good causes. In *Prospects*, he uses the example of a federal school-lunch program. Who could be against providing lunches for schoolchildren? Kirk's whimsical example reminds us that we can always come up with a reason to use power. The temptation to look to the central government for the solution to our problems—even national problems—must be resisted. Conservatives "must stand firm against centralization, legislation that offers to substitute a passing 'security' for prescriptive liberty, and the conversion of republican government into plebiscitary democracy."

On the use of American power abroad, Kirk was just as clear: "A 'preventive' war, whether or not it might be successful in the field...would be morally ruinous to us." Although written as part of a critical reflection on the decision to destroy Hiroshima and Nagasaki, Kirk's arguments ring true, perhaps even more so, today. In the 1989 edition of his book, Kirk takes his critique of U.S. foreign policy a step further. He criticizes the "pragmatists" who see conservatism as a means of "placating or serving certain powerful interests—and so warding off radical interests." Such an approach can only be self-defeating and self-destructive, as the Iraq debacle demonstrates.

In the 1989 edition of *Prospects*, Kirk could confidently declare that American policies had not been much improved after almost a decade of Republican rule. Yet he refused to give up hope that the various conservative factions might join together for political purposes. More generally, given his Christian convictions about sin and redemption, he did not despair, even though the causes for which he fought seemed no closer to victory than when he started. This cautiously optimistic view avoids the disillusionment of liberal and conservative utopians, which inevitably sets in when reality does not line up with their plans.

# Reagan and Kirk

**Ronald Wilson Reagan** and Russell Amos Kirk would seem to have little in common. Reagan was known as the Great Communicator. Kirk was once described as "communicative as a turtle." Reagan lived in the glare and cameras of Hollywood. Kirk preferred a converted toy factory in rural Michigan. Reagan of course became governor, then president. Kirk sought no political office, and served in none, except for justice of the peace.

Yet despite their differences, each had a profound respect for the other. And it is safe to say that conservatism as we know it would not have existed without the both of them. The conservative intellectual movement Kirk inspired through books such as *The Conservative Mind* bore political fruit in the 1980 election of Reagan. Reagan, in turn, was able to communicate the conservative message—increased liberty, smaller government, hope in America, and traditional values—to an electorate exhausted with the scandals of Watergate and the Carter malaise.

In a collection of essays, Kirk chose Reagan's election in 1980 as one of the ten conservative events worth remembering. It was a turning point for America, and the world. Kirk spent many years looking for an American statesman that could carry on the mantle of Edmund Burke, the first modern conservative. Nixon, Eisenhower, Hoover, and even Taft ultimately fell short of the abilities Kirk thought were needed to present the conservative case.

Reagan was of a different mold entirely. He came closest among contemporary American politicians to Kirk's idea of a creative and imaginative

---

Originally published in *National Review*, June 10, 2004.

political leader. In his autobiography, *The Sword of Imagination*, Kirk credits Reagan with winning the presidential nomination with his "humor, candor," and "the vigor of his speeches." The ability to conjure images and evoke feelings through words is a skill long honored in the West under the name of rhetoric. Reagan had it, in spades. There was no elitism in his speeches. He simply called on all Americans to succeed. The elites disparaged this combination of strong rhetorical skill with equally strong belief. They preferred the cult-like language of policy, open only to chosen initiates.

In his reliance upon settled American truths, Reagan evoked the language of Lincoln, a political hero he shared with Kirk. Kirk wrote that Lincoln was the first defender of order in America from the common clay—that is, not the aristocracy. He represented the best of what America could offer. In his first inaugural, Reagan too invoked Lincoln, saying that "[w]hoever would understand in his heart the meaning of America will find it in the life of Abraham Lincoln."

The Southern conservative Richard Weaver, in his book, *The Ethics of Rhetoric*, stated that traditional rhetoric has a "spaciousness" because it relies on settled truths to communicate with an audience. Reagan intuitively connected to these truths, and conveyed them in a language that was immediately comprehensible. Kirk said of him:

> Had a few more Republicans apprehended the drift of public opinion in the United States, and understood how the popular rhetoric of Mr. Reagan spoke to American minds, Mr. Reagan might have been elected years earlier...
>
> Ronald Reagan will be remembered as the President who gave hope to the American people—even great expectations. Old sureties that the ritualistic liberal had mocked were unshaken in Ronald Reagan's mind; and President Reagan's reaffirmation of those ancient convictions began to arouse the nation from the discouragement of twenty years or more.

Further, Reagan "really was the Western hero of romance...audacious, dauntless, cheerful honest—and skilled at shooting from the hip." Indeed, it was these abilities that made Reagan so effective. In speaking of Reagan, Kirk reminds us of William Butler Yeats, who "tells us that everyone ought to make a mask for himself, and wear it, and become what the mask represents. Ronald Reagan put on the mask of the Western hero...and truly lived the part, and became the Western hero." This was no criticism by Kirk, and turned on its head the criticism that Reagan was "just an actor." T. S. Eliot, in his essay "Tradition and the Individual Talent," reminds us that we have to participate in tradition to maintain it, and we do that by taking on the role that history and choice assign to us. Assuming that role takes imagination, and an understanding of the larger story in which you are involved. In speeches such as his D-Day praise of "the boys of Point du Hoc," Reagan placed us within the broad sweep of Western history and American liberty.

Kirk was occasionally offered posts within the administrations. He consistently refused them, preferring the life of an independent writer. But in 1989, Reagan awarded Kirk the Presidential Citizens Medal for his achievements.

Kirk died ten years and one month ago. With the loss of Reagan the conservative movement has lost the other half of the intellectual and political partnership that propelled American conservatism into the twenty-first century.

# The Conservative Mind *at* 60

**In his great work,** *The American Republic*, written in 1866, the American Catholic political writer Orestes Brownson—who ranks with Calhoun and John Adams as among the finest political minds America has produced, and who still remains somewhat neglected—wrote this about the nation's political order.

The constitution of the United States is twofold, written and unwritten, the constitution of the people and the constitution of the government.

The written constitution is simply a law ordained by the nation or people instituting and organizing the government; the unwritten constitution is the real or actual constitution of the people as a state or sovereign community, and constituting them such or such a state. It is Providential, not made by the nation, but born with it. The written constitution is made and ordained by the sovereign power, and presupposes that power as already existing and constituted.

This dual structure also informs the work of Brownson's greatest intellectual descendant, the conservative writer Russell Kirk (1918–1994), whose major book *The Conservative Mind* celebrates its sixtieth anniversary this year. Kirk drew explicitly upon Brownson in that book, arguing that constitutions must first be drawn from historical experience, and are the product of slow growth. Indeed, Kirk says that whatever the form of government that has grown up in a nation, that "must" therefore be the best form of government for that nation. For constitutional government, the same rule holds, with Kirk writing that "no matter how admirable a

Originally published in *Law & Liberty*, July 1, 2013.

constitution may look upon paper, it will be ineffectual unless the unwritten constitution, the web of custom and convention, affirms an enduring moral order of obligation and personal responsibility." In the subsequent forty years of writing, until his death in 1994, Kirk rarely strayed from that conviction, but he did explain in further detail what his early work set out only in outline.

Although Kirk is not primarily known as a legal thinker, over the course of his career, and especially in the last fifteen years of his life, Kirk devoted several important essays and articles to legal themes. A collection of his writings on the law are found in a posthumous work, *Rights and Duties*, which combines previously unpublished pieces with an earlier book-length work, *The Conservative Constitution*. His writings on the law, justice, and the Constitution present a conservative perspective that is opposed not only to a liberal theory based on abstract rights but also to what are considered more classically conservative approaches. Kirk may be classed among the originalists, in that he believes the Constitution does reflect a consistent meaning that relates back to the meaning it had during the founding period, and that judges should exercise restraint in interpreting the Constitution. However, his concern is really with the cultural underpinnings that make a written constitution workable in the first place. Paraphrasing the Harvard critic Irving Babbitt, Kirk believed legal and political problems were at first philosophical, then theological problems. A community that was confused about its founding principles would be confused as to its laws. Understanding the customs and traditions of a nation must inform our understanding of the written Constitution.

In his works, which primarily concern intellectual history and biography, Kirk delineated a comprehensive critique of liberalism. He focused on finding (some would say creating) a tradition of conservative thought, descended from the Whig statesman Edmund Burke, to counter what he saw as the desiccated rationality of the Enlightenment and the coming post-liberal age that Kirk termed the Age of Sentiment. His individual studies of writers such as Burke and T.S. Eliot, and his more thematic works such as *The Conservative Mind* or *America's British Culture*, were intended to identify enduring cultural norms upon which, Kirk believed, civilizations must rely. His writing was for this reason narrative and evocative rather than purely analytical, deliberately creating a conservative style of thought that was—rhetorically and substantively—a counterpoint to what he saw as liberalism's excessive devotion to scientism and abstract rationalism.

His mode of writing about the law is in this vein. Kirk is not interested, really, in professional arcana like statutory interpretation or parsing precedent. In constitutional law, as in other areas, Kirk displays his central themes: a suspicion of centralized power and rule by "experts," a devotion to tradition, and a commitment to the nation's federal structure. He repeatedly states that the purpose of the law is a simple one—it is to keep the peace. Because it is intended to keep the peace, the law must evolve gradually out of actual disputes and compromises of a living community. The law must not be imposed top-down, as such an enforced peace is not peace at all. Moreover, such a legal system reduces certainty and fairness, and turns the legal system into a struggle for power.

But at the same time, Kirk believes in an overarching moral order that also—as much as local custom or convention—informs both the law and the Constitution. However, Kirk developed his own perspective on whether, and to what extent, that law has to do with positive law. He emphatically rejected a view that the Constitution required "substituting [the] personal and shifting value judgments of nine judges—who can form no consensus among themselves—for enduring moral standards derived from religion, philosophy, and a people's custom and convention." That perspective, unfortunately for those seeking a Kirkian "system," does not reduce itself to a series of propositions or statements of "right" answers. Rather, Kirk was a forceful voice for multiplicity and diversity in constitutional arrangements, but those arrangements must be adjusted and modified at local levels and across a myriad of courtrooms and other fora. The conservative obsession, at least since the 1980s, with fixing the "original meaning" of the Constitution had little resonance for him given his larger cultural concerns.

The historian Clinton Rossiter once quipped that Kirk was born in the wrong country a hundred and fifty years too late, and Kirk was criticized by fellow conservatives (such as the libertarian Frank Meyer) for promoting a static social order of squire and servant rather than a free republic. But amidst the sweeping history of *The Conservative Mind* is a chapter titled, "Legal and Historical Conservatism: A Time of Foreboding," which treats the work of Henry Sumner Maine, Leslie Stephen, and W.E.L. Lecky. This chapter has not received significant attention, but in it Kirk undercuts the vision of him as a faux-aristocrat. First, he approves Maine's assessment that the transition to the modern world is from status to contract. Contract accords each of us the right of freely entering into agreements. In his discussion of Maine, Kirk notes that "the source of social wisdom is the knowledge of past ages, but that dreary imitation of what once lived will stifle the most gifted peoples." Kirk was no reactionary.

Kirk is often challenged for his statement in *The Conservative Mind* that civilized society "requires orders and classes, as against the notion of a 'classless society'," and that some such hierarchy was necessary for a stable social order. Kirk's argument is typically misunderstood as an approval of a *particular* social order, specifically that of late eighteenth-century Britain, and that such a social order must mean people stay in place. Neither of these mischaracterizations are true. Kirk in fact had no patience for the eighteenth century, which he called "an age of gilded selfishness and frivolous intellectuality—an age almost without a heart." His preference for Burke over other thinkers of the same era, for example, Bolingbroke was because, for Kirk, Burke was "essentially a modern man, and his concern was with our modern complexities." Rather his point is that every society has such hierarchies and orders, and to pretend otherwise—either by inventing a Marxist "classless society" or an equally imaginative egalitarian utopia, actually undermined both order and liberty.

The "science of jurisprudence" likewise cannot be weighed down by the dead hand of the past but must change with "the passage of the generations." The law is not, Kirk says, "immutable." But the fact that the law changes was less important to Kirk than how it changes. In the

Anglo-American tradition, Kirk identified several prerequisites, foundational principles upon which the rule of law rested. The most important of these are first, that the law is not an arbitrary system to be used by those in power against those who are not; second, the notion that no one is "above" the law; and third, that the sources of law are custom, tradition, and precedent. These features, for Kirk, it must be stressed, not themselves part of the rule of law or the formal "legal system," but rather arise from the historical experience of the West. Taken together, they represent a strong preference for gradual, piecemeal development of the law, with few if any abstract, universal principles imposed from outside.

This approach can be frustrating, and Kirk—in part because he came to legal discussions rather late in his life—never fully developed, for example, how he would reconcile both his belief in an enduring moral order with his approach to specific legal questions. Some essays, however, give an example. In 1986, he wrote a long essay on the Supreme Court's pornography jurisprudence. Kirk's thesis was simply that local communities needed to decide how to treat such materials, or even to permit them at all. The moral absolute of free speech—if such there was—applied only to political speech. To find otherwise, and to let judges, especially the Supreme Court, apply their own pet theories as to whether something was obscene, was a recipe for social disaster. One thing the precedent demonstrates was the "imprudence of transferring to an arbitrary central authority decisions that have traditionally been made by local communities or state legislatures." In short, such arrangements might differ across the country. It is liberalism, not conservatism, that was imposing a moral straitjacket on the country. In this he sounds something like Willmoore Kendall, in his 1964 article on the school prayer cases, who made the same point. "We the people" must live together in our various communities, and the law should reflect our considered sense of justice.

Kirk wrote several important essays on the "natural law," which he sharply distinguished from the doctrine of "natural right," an ideology he traced to the French revolution. Some have criticized Kirk's reliance on the natural law, which they say was both too commanding and yet too vague to be of real use. Drew Maciag, for example, in his recent book on Edmund Burke and his reception in America, finds Kirk's invocation of the natural law underwhelming and indeed "slippery." For Maciag, Kirk's proposition "that humans could not determine where natural law began or ended, and should neither define it too precisely or too vaguely, but should be guided by it" made little sense, and was more a romantic, antirational invocation of romantic sensibility than a persuasive account of the natural law, much less the details of its operation.

But this overstates Kirk's use of the natural law. First, in the everyday world of disputes, the natural law will be little invoked. Indeed, he wrote that the "Christian doctrine of natural law cannot be made to do duty for 'the law of the land'; were this tried, positive justice would be delayed to the end of time. Nevertheless, if the Christian doctrine of natural law is cast aside utterly by magistrates, flouted and mocked, then positive law becomes patternless and arbitrary." Natural law is "more than a guide for statesmen and jurists. It is meant primarily for the governance of persons—for you and me, that we may restrain will and appetite in our ordinary walks of life." Careful attention to historical development and actual community norms would be a better guide to the natural law than philosophic theorizing, to which judges are unsuited.

Kirk himself warned against this use of natural law as trump in his recounting of the controversy between Senator William Seward and Orestes Brownson. In a speech on the Senate floor in 1850, Seward stated there was a "higher law than the Constitution" regarding laws about slavery. This speech caused Brownson to write in reply one of his more famous essays, the 1851 "The Higher Law," which argued that while the law of God may indeed be above that of the Constitution, the Constitution is not intended to channel private judgment about what that law is.

Nevertheless, both progressives and conservatives have called upon the natural law to serve their purposes, often deriving various principles out of elaborate theories. Yet for Kirk the natural law had a public purpose only in the most narrow of circumstances—tyrannicide is the only clear historical example Kirk uses, when arguing that those conspiring to kill Hitler were justified in doing so. Kirk sees the natural law as a bulwark against a conception of law that does not acknowledge any boundary to the lawgiver's power. Kirk termed this as positivist law, which rests all authority only in the state.

This brings us now to the Constitution. Kirk objected strongly to the view that the Constitution reflected a Lockean state of nature. Indeed, he wrote a famous essay titled "The Constitution Was not Written by John Locke." The "social contract" was a dangerous fiction, and if there were any such agreement it was one between generations and bound by sentiments such as love of neighbor and a sense of duty. The Founders were not Lockeans, and the majority of Americans at the time, the ones who actually ratified the Constitution, were small-town communalist protestants more influenced by moralist Thomas Browne (and Burke) than Locke.

Instead, the Constitution was the final flower of the "great tree" of Anglo-American jurisprudence, and not something born simply of the minds of the fifty-five men gathered in Philadelphia. He did acknowledge the novelty in some respects of the American governmental system, as defended for example in the *Federalist*. Kirk saw that the tripartite federal system, with its division of powers, extended over such a large republic, was new in political science, and was without clear British or classical models. Nevertheless, at the state and local levels, much remained of British practice, not least the strong tradition of common law and the use of British precedent and legal treatises. Kirk saw political parties, the presidential cabinet, and the primary system as important supports for our written constitutional orders.

That system rests in turn on the "postulates" of Christianity. In an important 1983 lecture, Kirk draws on Maine, again, and more recent legal writers such as Roscoe Pound to claim that the particular forms of Anglo-American law reflect, even if opaquely, certain Christian assumptions. Without those assumptions, the legal system will collapse, and be used merely as a tool for social engineering and "judicial metaphysics."

The law that judges mete out is the product of statute, custom, convention, precedent yet back of statute, custom, convention, and precedent may be discerned, if mistily, the forms of Christian doctrines, by which statute and custom and convention and precedent have been much influenced in the past. And the more that judges ignore Christian assumptions about human nature and justice, the more are they thrown back upon their private resources as abstract metaphysicians—and the more the laws of the land fall into confusion and inconsistency.

It should not be necessary to state what Kirk is not saying. He is not saying the United States is a "Christian commonwealth," or one whose legal code need match the Christian moral code (indeed, he stated in a lecture given at the Heritage Foundation that the "state is unconcerned with sins unless they lead to breaches of the peace, or menace the social order.") And certainly much of the practice of the modern administrative state is quite removed indeed from the postulates of human nature Kirk refers to here; rather Kirk is making an historical point that our legal system comes from a very specific, concrete, and long tradition that should not be ignored.

Kirk presents a challenging historical and legal vision of the Constitution for conservatives, accustomed now for almost three decades to fight over the legitimacy of the Supreme Court and the true meaning of the Constitution. Important as the battles over constitutional meaning are, the stability of the constitutional structure lay elsewhere.

# *The Unwritten Constitution*

**The battle** over the confirmation of Brett Kavanaugh to the Supreme Court is only the most recent—if perhaps one of the more disturbing—examples of how important control of the law has become in the ongoing, never-quite-dead culture wars. In a sense, the merits of this particular candidate did not matter much. Liberals and progressives were going to oppose any pick for the Court—remember the left-wing group that accidentally issued a prewritten opposition to Trump's pick with the name of the candidate blank? The opposition was so fierce because what was at stake was not only a Court seat, but a vision of the nation itself.

That vision is one in which judges, and in particular five justices of the Supreme Court, lead us all into a promised land. Russell Kirk called this vision "archonocracy," or rule by judges. Before the election, liberal elites openly defended the idea of the Supreme Court as an agent of social change. In 2016, for example, the liberal law professor Mark Tushnet famously argued that liberals should abandon a "defensive" liberalism and instead use the courts aggressively to advance their causes. Those who opposed such social engineering should realize, according to Tushnet, that conservatives lost the culture wars, and the victorious liberals should treat them as a defeated enemy. Even earlier, in a book called *Making Our Democracy Work* (2010), Justice Stephen Breyer characterized the acceptance of judicial supremacy as a "habit" that has developed in the American people. This habit not only accepts that the Supreme Court must pass on the Constitution's meaning, but also that its interpretation is superior to

Originally published in *The New Criterion*, January 2019.

those of Congress or the president. This supremacy must be recognized because only the courts can protect the "rights" they have discovered in the constitutional text; left to the other branches, freedom would dissipate under the threat of majoritarian tyranny.

This position echoes the 1992 decision *Planned Parenthood v. Casey*—not the famous "mystery of life" passage, but one that is just as troubling. The Court said that the belief in Americans as a people "is not readily separable from their understanding of the Court invested with the authority to decide their constitutional cases and speak before all others for their constitutional ideals." Archonocracy, indeed.

Of course, now that has all apparently changed. Liberals are calling for the expansion of the Supreme Court's membership, or some other way to dilute the Court's power. Funny what an election will do to principle. Now the cry is to hold democracy sacred—protected by the elites against the wrong kind of populism. But these calls for upending judicial structure are only a temporary diversion from the issue of what the law is and what it is supposed to do. Those who hold views such as Tushnet's have not discovered states' rights or originalism, and they have not abandoned the progressive effort to move the nation to the left partially through elections but mostly by capturing the judiciary. On this view, the arc of history bends towards justice, but that arc is bent by liberal justices and held there even if it is over the people's throats.

Kirk and Orestes Brownson can help us respond to this legal progressivism. For those who may not know him, Brownson was an American original. After spending three days visiting with Brownson, Great Britain's Lord Acton wrote to a colleague, "Intellectually, no American I have met comes near him." He was praised by Arthur Schlesinger Jr. (who wrote a short book about him) and Woodrow Wilson. Kirk placed him "in the first rank of American men of ideas" and wrote about him as early as 1954.

Brownson lived mostly as a writer and a preacher; his collected essays and articles, including those from *Brownson's Quarterly Review*, which he edited and almost completely wrote, total more than twenty volumes. His most famous book-length work is the political treatise *The American*

*Republic*, published in 1865. After Alexis de Tocqueville's *Democracy in America*, it has been called the best book on American democracy. Brownson employed two terms to understand American legal culture: territorial democracy and the unwritten constitution.

Territorial democracy is based on the conviction that political power must be centered on a geographic unity, a territory, within which the people participate in governance. Thus, when separating from the United Kingdom, "in the Declaration of Independence [the colonies] declared themselves independent states indeed, but not severally independent. The declaration was not made by the states severally but by the states jointly, as the United States. They unitedly declared their independence; they carried on the war for independence, won it, and were acknowledged by foreign powers and by the mother country as the *United* States." Democracy is "not territorial because the majority of the people are agriculturists or landholders, but because all political rights, powers, or franchises are territorial."

As Robert Moffitt of the Heritage Foundation notes in an article on Brownson and federalism, "Acting in convention, the sovereign people authorize a dual system of government, federalism, which assures national unity and yet secures their liberty and diversity: This division of the powers of government...rendered possible and practicable by the original constitution of the people themselves, as one people existing and acting through state organizations, is the American method.... The American method demands no...antagonism, no neutralizing of one social force by another, but avails itself of all the forces of society, organizes them dialectically, not antagonistically, and thus protects with equal efficiency both public authority and private rights." Brownson himself describes it this way:

> The general government governs supremely all of the people of the United States and territories belonging to the Union, in all their general relations and interests, or relations and interests common alike to them all; the particular or state government governs supremely the people of a particular state.... The powers of each are equally sovereign, and neither are derived from the other. The state

> governments are not subordinate to the general government, nor the general government to the state governments. They are coordinate governments, each standing on the same level, and deriving its powers from the same sovereign authority. In their respective spheres neither yields to the other. In relation to the matters within its jurisdiction, each government is independent and supreme in regard of the other, and subject only to the convention.

On this view, the general government is able to protect individual rights against state oppression, while at the same time state independence serves as a bulwark against an encroaching central government. And even within states, both Brownson and Kirk note the need for strong local government to protect against state power. Thus a territorial system of democracy can protect against what Brownson sometimes called "humanitarian democracy," which was the concentration of power in a centralized, national government pushing for a pure egalitarianism. This humanitarian democracy "scorns all geographical lines, effaces all individualities, and professes to plant itself on humanity alone, has acquired by the war new strength, and is not without menace to our future." It is a menace because it brooks no opposition to its organizing principle of equality and would destroy actual rights developed through the common understanding of a political society. Kirk, writing in the 1950s, said that the humanitarian would not stop at erasing geographic boundaries or local rights and privileges. Presently, he would also attack the family and assail private property as unequal.

Kirk explains that "Brownson distinguishes between the old American territorial democracy founded upon local rights and common interests of the several states and smaller organs of society, and the pure democracy of Rousseau, which later writers call 'totalitarian democracy.'" This pure democracy is characterized by centralized administration in the name of an abstract "People," with little authority or freedom at the local level. For Kirk, this meant the dissolution of true democracy. The conversation Kirk envisions among the democratic localities, indirectly democratic states, and a representative national government was the genius of the American system. "If the federal character of American government decays badly, then American democracy also must decline terribly, until nothing remains of it but a name; and the new 'democrats' may be economic and social levellers, indeed, but they will give popular government short shrift."

But a constitution cannot be sustained simply through its written form; indeed, for Brownson as for Kirk, that would not be possible. How the Constitution reconciles state with national interest, and individual rights with our obligations toward our community, relies on another feature of American society. That was the "unwritten constitution," which supplements and pre-exists the written Constitution. The unwritten constitution includes all the mores, customs, and ways of life that together form American political culture and support the written Constitution. As Kirk explained, "[N]o matter how admirable a constitution may look upon paper, it will be ineffectual unless the unwritten constitution, the web of custom and convention, affirms an enduring moral order of obligation and personal responsibility." Bruce Frohnen argues that "Brownson recognized that the unwritten constitution of a people is primary in that it constitutes the customs (e.g., a common culture and the common law) necessary to make a written constitution work, and because we must look to its customs and practices to understand the meanings and purposes of the written constitution's text." In other words, the unwritten constitution is not the progressives' "living Constitution," through which elites conform political practice to their norms by means of a kind of top-down command.

Kirk in his writings on the law understood that if the customs of a people change, then the law changes as well, even if written texts remain the same. So it was important for citizens to be mindful of and preserve those traditions that supported local government and established practices and understandings. And as Kirk noted, a thoroughly secular state was not a neutral one, and combined with its increasing powers would seek to act on its own vision of the common good. The unwritten constitution, in Kirk's usage, has both a spatial and temporal aspect. Geographically, state and nation overlap, but each territory has its own historical imagination and narrative of itself, which is necessary for self-government and a stable social order. Kirk only hints at what the other aspects of these customs might be, but they include such things as the tradition of voluntarism, private associations, a rough-and-ready American tolerance, and so on, refracted through the particular circumstances in communities across the nation. We can also point to such things as the traditional deference lawyers have for the procedures of the law and its officers, something increasingly less in evidence in some of our law schools.

Without those attachments, self-government suffers. And those attachments are only partially attributable to reasoning from abstract rights. We have become too Lockean. We understand ourselves as rights-bearing, autonomous individuals entering the public square to which we give our contingent consent. It is unclear whether our constitutional structure can survive on such a thin basis, especially when our notion of the rights that an individual bears expands endlessly. When that happens, especially when not accompanied by a shared sense of responsibilities, the only solution to prevent disorder is to let government be the continued and repeated arbiter of disputes. The law therefore becomes an instrument in a power struggle as groups compete for recognition of their rights against others, a situation that is itself a form of disorder.

Brownson and Kirk rejected this Lockean formulation. As Peter Lawler writes, Brownson agreed with Locke that there were natural rights, but he based them on an anti-Lockean principle. The reason that "one man… can have in himself no right to govern another" is that a "man is never absolutely his own, but always and everywhere belongs to his Creator." That is, we can reasonably affirm that the natural law originates with a Creator, and that we are dependent on Him for all that is and all that we are. It is this affirmation—the virtual antithesis of the Lockean principle of self-ownership—that provides the proper foundation of human equality, or the doctrine that we have "equal rights as men." All governments that truly protect individual rights depend on the assumption that man is not God. A political society is not a contract but a kind of covenant.

Progressives have tried their own version of the unwritten constitution. Indeed, the prominent law professor Akhil Amar in 2012 published a book with that title. But that is a world away from what Brownson and Kirk meant. For Amar and those who agree with him, law is a source of rights divined by experts, then circulated through the population by judicial fiat. But as Ted McAllister puts it: "law is not the source of higher-order goods, but rather the means of pursuing those goods. Law is normative in the sense that it reflects and sometimes expresses (or crystallizes) social norms. Rooted, therefore, in concrete social experience, laws emerge out of existing social arrangements and practices." Particular and imperfect, these laws reflect "the integrations of historical expectations—rooted in circumstance and practice—with permanent principles stemming from the order of reality, or natural law; it is best understood as historically grounded normative reasoning." The law encompasses what Allen Mendenhall describes as "a mode of preserving and transmitting knowledge about the human condition that develops out of ascertainable facts rather than abstract speculation. It is bottom-up, reflecting the embedded norms and values of the community as against executive command or legislative fiat." In Kirk's phrase, the purpose of the law is relatively simple: to keep the peace.

For Amar, however, the unwritten constitution is a tool to undermine those customs and practices and to serve as a mode of disruption rather than an instrument of civil peace. It is used to change "the written constitution according to the values and desires of powerful contemporary elites in charge of propagating meanings and even civil religious doctrine." Indeed, Amar has a series of documents and events he calls the "symbolic" Constitution. Now, symbols are something conservatives are comfortable with, but his are all of a piece, promoting a progressive view of the Constitution. Those who disagree with these symbols are on the wrong side of history. In this Amar is in the line of liberal justices such as William Brennan, for whom the law was primarily a weapon available to the individual against the community.

Kirk, in contrast, saw the danger in allowing that weapon to be used only according to the dictates of judges; to do so would risk rendering the unwritten constitution meaningless and would reduce the court to an "infallible and omniscient body of moral authorities," an absurd result.

While there may be universal human rights, these cannot substitute for the actual political rights filtered through the historic practices of a particular community; Kirk warned that the assertion of those rights should be done "only as a last resort, ordinarily." Why? Because he wished to avoid the situation that we have now, where law is a weapon of my rights against all others, and private judgment as to what I "am entitled to" rules the day.

With his usual prescience, Brownson saw individualism as a threat to American self-government. Individualism sees government as the agent of particular individuals who comprise it, and not the collective sense of the community. If that is the case, government becomes merely a tool to express our rights—which necessarily leads to disorder as everyone determines how much they may choose to provide to the government. Thus, the rights of the individual can properly be understood and maintained only in community, particularly a community whose members share similar beliefs as to what constitutes a right. Indeed, Kirk essentially rejected the idea of "human rights" as improperly descended from the dangerous abstractions of the French Revolution. True rights grow from "old custom, usage, and political tradition, and from judges' common-law decisions." The Constitution, in part, protects individual rights by allowing a space for community standards of morality. Adam White wrote a piece elaborating on Justice Alito's Burkean constitutional vision, which is "attuned to the space that the Constitution preserves for local communities to defend the vulnerable and to protect traditional values." Abstraction of either the Left or the Right will ultimately disempower citizens and eliminate the space for free self-government.

As Lawler writes, "the freedom of the person that territorial democracy supports accounts for the richness of personhood as seen in man's spiritual, political, familial, and economic relations, which must be supported and protected by the authority of the state.... A good polity will connect and reconcile the free and relational person with self-government and law and thereby engender devotion to the common good." In other words, the law is more like a tool to assist in constructing a stable social order than a weapon. But to use a tool properly, you have to know what it is for, and what you are trying to build.

# "Little Money but Good Canoeing"

❧

**Deep in James E. Person, Jr.'s** captivating and illuminating collection of letters, entitled *Imaginative Conservatism: The Letters of Russell Kirk*, Russell Kirk (1918–1994) writes, during the annus horribilis of 1968, of the protests then sweeping through college campuses, that "the rootless are always violent, and the lonely and bored find riot a welcome diversion." In the half century since, the atmosphere on campuses has only intensified. The old conservative complaint was that colleges made students liberals and resentful of where they came from. Now, after a generation or more of left-wing dominance of academia, students arrive at elite liberal arts campuses having learned almost nothing of their civilization and expecting to be entertained and not have their opinions, which largely mimic the ambient liberal culture, challenged. (When such challenges occur, as with conservative speakers on campuses across the country, riot has again become a diversion for spoiled students ungrateful for the stupendous riches they have inherited.)

The quote also reveals something about its author. Kirk believed that stability was the first requirement of a tolerable society, and that the first obligation of political leaders was to preserve it. Fostering the connections among citizens, and between citizens and the common enterprise of the nation, was one way to preserve such stability. We must value our Burkean little platoons even as we recognize the larger, institutional supports such as the Constitution. We must endeavor individually to preserve what we can, even as we support larger movements to do so on a bigger scale. Being

Originally published in *National Review*, May 28, 2018.

rootless does not make us free; rather it makes us bored because we have nothing to which we have committed ourselves and so we are blown about by every ideological wind or frisson of political action.

Kirk was famously rooted in Michigan "stump country," and his devotion to his family's ancestral town of Mecosta is evident throughout this collection. This was more than a mere emotional attachment, or even a matter of intellectual conviction (though it was that); Kirk was showing by example how to lead a conservative life. In a 1972 letter, included here, to Irving Kristol (whom Kirk described in another letter three years later as "a force for good"; the two were on pleasant terms despite disagreements), Kirk explains that "in general, my approach is historical; yet I am concerned not with civilization in general, but rather with the institutions and beliefs which underlie the American personal and social order." He was describing the book that became *The Roots of American Order* (1974), intended as "an attempt to wake some of the rising generation to awareness of their own cultural and institutional roots." Politics was an important, but distinctly secondary, cause for Kirk—though he wrote at least one lengthy letter to the *Wall Street Journal*, in 1968, detailing his assessment of the Goldwater campaign. Kirk contended that Goldwater, like much of the conservative movement in the 1960s, had moved away from an unrealistic "individualism" to a more balanced conservatism. (In 1954, Kirk had written to conservative activist Victor Milione: "I never call myself an individualist; and I wish that you people hadn't clutched that dreary ideology to your bosom.")

The enemy was not simply collectivism, as strong as that was, but the characteristics of modern life that dissolve natural connections such as family and local bonds. People, wherever they are, are tradition-making beings, and so conservatism must shore up those natural instincts beyond a simple individualism. Kirk wrote to science-fiction writer Jerry Pournelle in 1963 that "there remains in this country a large body of support for an imaginative conservatism," and that conservatives should be bold in their defense of principles: "One does not compromise with the silly people, but rather overawes them or leads them into ways of wisdom."

This is the first collection of Kirk's considerable correspondence, and it is a great service to American intellectual history generally and to that of conservatism in particular. The letters cover Kirk's entire adult life, beginning in 1940, when he was a graduate student at Duke (where he would complete his first book, a study of John Randolph of Roanoke), through his journeys throughout Scotland as he completed the manuscript that became *The Conservative Mind* (1953), and visits afterward, up through a month before his death in 1994. Kirk's correspondents include T. S. Eliot, publisher Henry Regnery, automotive executive B. E. Hutchinson, Felix Morley, Herbert Hoover, historian Ross Hoffman, Ray Bradbury, Henry Kissinger, William F. Buckley Jr., and many others. Even a younger Arianna Huffington (née Stassinopoulos) makes an appearance; Kirk wrote to her in 1979 about a review of her book *After Reason*.

The voice in the early letters is that of a young man who was quite confident of himself. But several years sitting in the Utah desert while in the Army allowed him time to read and reflect on his future. That future was in the University of St Andrews, and we see in letters to friends back home the gestation of Kirk's landmark study. We also see his growing relationships with some of Scotland's landed families. The letters recount how such people as Hew Lorimer, a renowned Scottish sculptor, and Ralph and Margret Christie, of Durie House, took Kirk in and exposed him to what he would later call "the unbought grace of life," which in turn became a cornerstone of his conservative imagination. James Person, in his helpful notes, states that Kirk's intellectual and emotional evolution "was greatly aided...by the examples of wise, goodhearted men and women in Scotland and England who befriended him and sometimes took him in as a houseguest for extended periods." Scotland added to his conservatism a physicality that even Kirk's time in the American South had not. Scotland gave life to his sense of tradition as concrete, as much social as intellectual. Hospitality, good manners, and gratitude were as important to civilization as other milestones, and Kirk took these lessons back with him to Michigan, where Piety Hill, his home, became for decades a civilized refuge for people from around the world. Scotland also fortified Kirk's love of ghost stories. These letters properly include many discussing Kirk's novels and short stories, one of which ended up as an episode of *Night Gallery*, and which were as important to Kirk as his other works.

Person's excellent selections explain Kirk's work and his enduring themes, and provide context on important events of the moment; they explore as well Kirk's independence of mind. He bucked a lot of the Right by opposing the first Iraq War and wrote to the editor of the *Wall Street Journal* to agree with Arthur Schlesinger Jr. (and the late Robert Taft) that presidential power to make war is limited. Historians of conservatism will lament that many letters between Kirk and such figures on the right as Albert Jay Nock and Roy Campbell have not survived, as Kirk started regularly keeping copies of his letters only in the mid 1960s, but they will especially value the exchanges with Buckley. The two met in the 1950s, and Kirk began writing a regular column for *National Review* in 1955, continuing it for over two decades. The numerous letters here express admiration and friendliness, along with literary gossip and plans to meet, though Kirk was never one to decline to offer criticism of the magazine if he felt it was going off track. When Buckley resigned as editor in 1990, Kirk wrote to him that "no one else could have made a success of such an undertaking; before you commenced it, I had despaired of the creation of a conservative weekly or fortnightly.... *National Review* will be your most enduring monument." Person includes a long response to a series of questions Buckley posed about Kirk's religious faith.

In a 1990 letter to Wendell Berry, Kirk described Mecosta as having "little money but good canoeing" and promised "handsome lodging and abundant food." Among other intellectual delights, these letters provide a picture of a life well lived.

# PART THREE

## *The Conservative Imagination*

# *Beauty is at the Heart of True Conservatism*

**What is the point** of contemporary conservatism? Whatever one thinks of the victory of Donald Trump to the presidency, he is not a conservative of any expected kind. But he has thrown the various strands of conservatism into disarray and has caused a remarkable level of self-reflection and self-criticism. And his administration has opened up an opportunity for a reconsideration of conservatism beyond the northeast Acela corridor.

In *Vision of the Soul*, James Wilson's important book returns to a conservatism in the tradition of Burke, Eliot, and Russell Kirk. For it is obvious that in a certain, significant sense, political conservatism has lost: lost the culture war, lost in the popular imagination, and it is no longer the imaginative underpinning of what Russell Kirk called "our civil social order." There is no serious argument, for example, that the country is more conservative now than in, say 1990 or even 1980. The Republicans, insofar as they were the embodiment of a conservative political program, are imploding under a combination of scandals and an inability—after eight years of complaining about President Obama—of getting anything done that resonates with their constituents, including the populist wave that brought Trump to power.

Amidst the ruins, various groupings are trying to claim the mantle of the Right. These various iterations include the Never Trumpers, the recrudescence of neoconservatism, reformicons of the Ross Douthat stripe, and the provocative crowd around the new journal *American Affairs* promoting

Originally published in *Crisis*, November 21, 2017.

a Trumpism without Trump. But none of these movements has displaced the conservative establishment or its Republican epigones.

Moreover, liberalism is also facing a crisis, arguably a bigger one than conservatism. Liberalism has in recent years transformed into progressivism. Progressivism has lost the notion of a common reason to which people of differing faiths could consent, even of the possibility of an objective order that may govern individual or community moral lives. And it has also taken on some of the characteristics of an intolerant religion, such as its antipathy toward free speech and its elevation of ideas such as tolerance and diversity as god terms. Some have called this moment at the end of liberalism postmodernity. Postmodernity has had a lot of nonsense spoken about it but its core principle as formulated by the late Peter Lawler remains a workable definition for our present moment. Postmodernity is liberalism without the notion of human perfectibility. And without that (which of course was itself a utopian project), liberalism loses even the veneer of wishing for a common good. As witnessed on campuses across the nation a post-liberal left is at ease with totalitarian methods, while an increasingly post-religious right, as Douthat has noticed, threatens to descend into atavistic racial politics.

Conservatism in a postmodern moment must therefore be different than the conservatism that motivated Burke or Taft or Disraeli or Reagan. The school of conservatism that might be most fitted for this moment, is paradoxically, the one that is the one least inclined to modernity. This would be a form of conservatism known as traditionalist, espoused most prominently by Russell Kirk. James Matthew Wilson has grasped the Burkean insight that to love our country (or our culture) one must first make it lovely. And making things lovely is at the core of conservatism and must remain at the center of any true conservative revival. Wilson reminds us that "[t]he conservatism of Burke and Coleridge sought to remind modern man, in an age of revolutionary upheaval, that politics was an activity built on art, meaning, representation, and community." Because of this, there is, thankfully, little to nothing here about policy prescriptions or election prospects. If a culture is healthy, those things sort themselves; if it is not, those things do not ultimately matter.

Wilson is a poet, and literature is at the foundation of his conviction for a cultural revival. In years past, this has been the weakness of this school: other conservatives thought it fine to invoke the literary history of conservatism but preferred not to delve too much into what that might mean. At worst, these conservatives took the insights from the literary tradition and watered them down into a political program. Wilson addresses the central problem that many in the conservative "movement" see conservatism as "a static and received, putatively sacred, order before which life must kneel and growth must stultify." But that is not how the exemplars of modern conservatism have seen it. T.S. Eliot, for example, was quite firm that by entering into a tradition one also changes it; tradition is the dynamic relationship between what Wilson here calls *mythos* and *logos*. Wilson relies on Eliot in his marvelous opening salvo "the drama of cultural conservatism." Burke, for Wilson, presents the truly modern attack on the ahistorical revolutionaries. For Kirk, too, his project was very much attuned to our contemporary moment: he built an alternative history of conservatism to present a narrative of unity and tradition against the massage of liberalism and now postmodernity's fragmentation.

Liberalism, by contrast, was and remains primarily political. It was born in the thought of Locke and Hume, Hobbes and Rousseau. The French Revolution and all the schools afterward brought it forward. Its central characteristics have been an irrational rationality and an ahistorical utopianism. Even today, when liberalism has morphed into an extreme individualism, with "choice" at its center, politics is inescapable. For the new liberalism needs the state to protect the ever-expanding list of individual rights. Further, it always needs an enemy which it can condemn as reactionary and against which it must wage an eternal fight.

Wilson, thankfully, largely avoids another tired debate about the future of liberalism, or contemporary conservatism, though he does have harsh words to say about both. Instead, he wants us to focus on beauty and its place in Western culture. The book is a strong defense of that culture, but not an unthinking one. In a striking passage, he takes Plato's *Symposium* as a metaphor for the larger Western tradition. That tradition is in some ways a riotous mess, "obtrusive and violent like Alcibiades, passionately irrational like Phaedrus, solipsistic like Aristophanes, pretentious and vapid like Agathon, self-serving like Pausanians, and reductive and therapeutic like Eryximaches." The only thing that makes sense of this is "Beauty. If we do not hold fast to that word, we have not simply missed something important, we have missed everything."

And Wilson notes that that tradition has garnered a populist audience: "there is a salutary populism, a potentially wide practical political appeal, to conservative thought that belies what, for the better part of two centuries, was taken as its merely literary, merely intellectual, vaguely aristocratic pretensions." That populism rejects the nihilistic materialism of the Marxist and the rootless plastic individualism of the progressive, to search for a community whose ends transcend "either individual material comfort or the uprooting and restructuring of society" according to some bureaucratic ideal. To move conservatism forward, we need to recall the centrality of beauty, and of the power of images to work with man's reason to fashion again stories and a culture that is beautiful. Drawing on Jacques Maritain, whose work on aesthetics attempted to do this in the middle years of the last century, Wilson notes that Maritain in works like *Art and Scholasticism* took "as his starting point the fashions and prejudices of his age." We must do the same but that means expanding conservatism beyond a literary tradition. Most people do not look to texts as their primary force of culture. In a sort of reverse-medievalism, people once more use images to sort their reality, either movies, video games, or the endless internet stream. Conservatism must find and create beauty there, too, as well as in other non-textual space such as the liturgy. As Eliot did with modernist poetry, conservatism must use our current fashions to rejoin a salutary populism with its higher transcendent ends, our *mythos* with *logos* once again.

# *Conservatism's Contested Tradition*

❧

**Early in his magisterial history** *Conservatism: The Fight for a Tradition*, Edmund Fawcett identifies the twin projects of conservatism. "Conservatives fight to identify and protect traditions that liberal modernity undermines," he writes, "and they fight among themselves for ownership of their own conservative tradition." So discussions of conservatism typically do two things: defend particular ideas about what conservatism is, and explain how conservatives defend it from its opponents.

Fawcett, a longtime correspondent for *The Economist*, has also written a well-received volume on liberalism. At the beginning of this book, he gives the game away by positioning liberalism at the center of the Western political tradition and conservatism as useful only insofar as it serves liberalism. "To survive, let alone flourish, liberal democracy needs the right's support," he writes, "needs, that is, conservatives who accept liberal and democratic ground rules." Moreover, he argues, such acceptance has been good for conservatives, who have been better combatants than liberals on the ideological-political chessboard over the past two centuries. For Fawcett, three "advantages—the backing of wealth, institutional support, and electoral reach—helped the right prevail at the liberal democratic game." He continues: "Puzzling as it sounds, conservatism's ultimate reward for compromising with liberal democracy was domination of liberal democracy."

To explain why the advantages accrued to conservatism, Fawcett presents perhaps the most comprehensive view of "the conservative mind"

---

Originally published in *National Review*, January 21, 2021.

since Russell Kirk's classic book (1953) of that title, discussing thinkers from the United Kingdom, the United States, Germany, and France. His roster includes, among others, Enoch Powell, Roger Scruton, David Willetts, John Kekes, Yuval Levin, Peter Sloterdijk, and Arnold Gehlen. The opening chapter is devoted to modern conservatism's forerunners, including Edmund Burke, Joseph de Maistre, and other critics of revolution. Because of such antecedents, critics of conservatism often assume that it must always be reactionary, a wish to restore an *ancien régime*. It can't be restored, so how can conservatism make any sense?

The European forerunners of modern conservatism did defend hierarchical society, which was opposed to the cultural and social solvent of revolutionary thought. Maistre, writes Fawcett, stood for the "hard authority of punishment," which "proscribed reasoning in politics,...celebrating instead faith and obedience." Burke, on the other hand, was "more open," which is one reason that he has been a more attractive figure in the Anglo-American conservative tradition. Burke's authority was the soft one of custom, Fawcett notes; he "insisted on the need for shared customs and a common faith within a unified society, without which, argument risked slipping into intellectual warfare." But that is an understatement of Burke's concern. He thought that what Fawcett describes as "intellectual warfare" was in large part impossible without prerational commitments.

That is why a common culture is so important, even one (such as that of England or the United States) that can accommodate great diversity. Invocations of "norms" may be politically motivated, but for people to make any sense at all to one another, they must have some understanding of what any given norm is and of its importance relative to other norms. Further, they must recognize that, regardless of its political effect, the refusal to violate a norm should be respected. No amount of "explainers" will paper over differences in shared assumptions about what counts as normative and whose authority can be recognized.

To his credit, Fawcett does not take the route of conservatism's critics. Instead, he proposes two responses. First, the forerunners of conservatism handed on not so much their defense of a lost society—or a case for restoring it—as a stock of arguments, images, and rhetorical tools that conservatives could draw on to attack liberalism as it too evolved in the succeeding decades. We can see this in some of the powerful images Burke used in his defense of social order, and in the attacks that he, Maistre, Friedrich von Gentz, and others made on ideas about the power of human reason or on the notion that society is perfectible.

The second response is framed by James Madison, Fawcett's last forerunner. Madison balanced the revolutionary fervor of Jefferson with an inclination to preserve authority and social stability. The U.S. Constitution, which Madison had such a large part in shepherding, entails a "belief in the need for popular control of government," but he "thought peace and prosperity elusive without overall central power and uniform national laws." Interestingly, Fawcett does not discuss John Adams, whom Kirk, for example, thought a bedrock thinker of American conservatism because Adams believed a republic could survive only with a virtuous citizenry. Without it, conservatives have argued, the structures in which Madison trusted would not work as intended. That need for virtue would also apply even if you accepted Fawcett's presumption that conservatives should support liberal democracy; the proceduralism favored by so many liberals is not enough.

The constitutional structure was an attempt to set the principles of order and liberty in a fruitful tension, and in a way unknown in the Old World. The Constitution itself then became part of the "common culture" that conservatives in America would seek to preserve against various progressive or left-wing movements, as well as, at times, right-wing movements such as the John Birch Society or, more recently, the alt-right.

Fawcett divides his chronology into four sections, deftly crosscutting political and cultural developments in his four countries: resisting liberalism (1830–80), adaptation and compromise (1880–1945), political command and intellectual recovery (1945–1980), and the fourth, current phase, hyper-liberalism and the hard Right. Conservatism is both political practice and "aesthetic" or philosophical opposition to modernity. At the same time, writers as diverse as W. H. Mallock (1849–1923) in England

and, in America, the Southern Agrarians have all tried to formulate their own vision of conservatism against the forces of liberalism.

Relatively few pages are devoted to the role of Christianity in the development of conservative thought. In a sense this is not surprising; Christianity is a liberationist, revolutionary religion, and in any event it resists neat ideological categorization. Nevertheless, in the Western context, conservatism cannot be separated from Christianity, because of its doctrine that original sin clouds our reason and our passions. The teaching tracks closely the conservative suspicion of ideological plans and the assumption that their failure is almost inevitable. The most explicit discussion of Christianity deals with John Henry Newman, Orestes Brownson, and a handful of other nineteenth-century figures concerned with the decline of the public appeal of religious arguments. Fawcett omits Cardinal Edward Manning and other conservative English figures but does note that Brownson in America argued that religion and democracy were inseparable and that a rejection of religious faith would ultimately doom even a pluralist, constitutional democracy.

In Fawcett's view, conservatism made its crucial turn after 1945. In the post-war period, the defense of an overarching Christian-inflected culture came undone and was transformed into a more generic defense of "culture." This term became detached from long observance of human nature and from religious precedent and came to mean practices that were simply either "useful" or "nonideological," which made them vulnerable to attack on utilitarian grounds. Similarly, conservative defense of government and business working together to support a larger culture furthering a common good was replaced with a defense of "the market," independent of formerly widely shared assumptions about humanity and God.

Fawcett implies that conservatives have actually won the political battle with liberalism, thanks to conservatism's triple advantages (wealth, institutional support, electoral reach). Indeed, Fawcett says we "are living in an era of the right." But this misses the mark. Take, for instance, his contention that conservatives have the wealthy class as their support. While economic interests wish to hold their own, they do not further any identifiable conservative social goals, and indeed have been captured by "woke" forces to a very large degree. Wall Street and Silicon Valley are strongholds of social and cultural liberalism and have strongly supported liberal policies.

A lot of Fawcett's argument depends on the question of why modern liberal societies need an articulated conservative opposition. Is it because liberal premises about unbounded autonomy and the perfectibility of society are self-destructive? If so, why does Fawcett think conservatives should accept these premises? He does not really address this tension; he seems to suggest that conservatives simply need to slow liberalism down but ought to generally accept its view of the individual, the non-binding character of religious or family obligations, and related positions that liberals have taken at different times. Is it instead that capitalism is a danger to organic human affection and communities and that conservative defenses of human dignity provide some protection for the weak? If so, perhaps a conservative state with a liberal opposition is preferable to the reverse. In referring to "liberal principles," Fawcett may instead mean values—democracy, rejection of any social structure that impedes the individual will, and a supposed lack of religious orthodoxy (in favor of a kind of secularism)—that are more attractive to modern societies.

Fawcett does not believe that conservatism represents a tradition of thought that should try to replace liberalism as the West's cultural and political baseline. He is fair enough, however, to bring to light the ideas of thinkers from Maistre to Scruton about what such a baseline might look like and how it would differ from liberal assumptions. With its reach and breadth, *Conservatism* is a significant contribution to the scholarship on conservatism, especially in its cross-cultural analysis. It is one of the fairest accounts of the conservative intellectual tradition to be published in recent years.

# *Postmodern Burke*

**Edmund Burke** occupies a premier place in American conservative thought. Russell Kirk's foundational 1953 book, *The Conservative Mind*, bore the subtitle *From Burke to Santayana*, and from the mid-1950s Burke was a right-wing touchstone in the Cold War. Peter Stanlis's 1958 *Burke and the Natural Law* inserted the Whig statesman into the philosophical school of Thomas Aquinas. On this view, Burke had a developed epistemological system based on appeals to transcendent principles derived from what Stanlis described as "right reason."

Kirk and others in that first generation took Burke's career to be a model of nuanced conservative thought. In his opposition to the French Revolution, Burke was the great adversary of ideology; in his defense of Britain, the great spokesman for tradition and hierarchy; and in his support for Irish Catholics, American revolutionaries, and the oppressed peoples of India, a master of mixing politics with principle. But not all conservatives agreed with this view: some considered his invocations of tradition and custom only a cover for a baser utilitarianism. Most famously, Richard Weaver favored Lincoln's "argument from principle" against Burke's "argument from circumstance" as a model for conservative thought.

Burke's legacy now stands in disarray. The conservative movement has chosen other heroes, who more closely fit its current self-conception based in the creative destruction of global capitalism and endless foreign adventures. The Burke who thundered against the corruption bred by the East India Company finds little support in the age of Halliburton and

---

Originally published in *The American Conservative*, January 9, 2012.

Abu Ghraib. And of the natural law Burke, there is nary a sound—his arguments seem the fossilized remnants of a generation past. His claims for tradition are invoked more than practiced, and the importance he placed on the non-political conditions of political life finds little traction on the right except when fulminations in the "culture wars" prove useful for fundraising.

In his new book *Edmund Burke for Our Time: Moral Imagination, Meaning, and Politics*, William F. Byrne, a professor of government and politics at St. John's University, wants to rescue Burke from those who would claim him for either the natural law or utilitarian movements. In Byrne's view, Burke believed in universally applicable principles but did not, contra the natural law crowd, believe they could be expressed in eternal cultural forms. How Burke walked that line, Byrne believes, holds lessons for contemporary politics.

Burke lived in a time when an old order was collapsing; in that sense, he confronted problems similar to those of us living in the postmodern age. Liberal certainties about reason, culture, and politics—derived from the Enlightenment, which replaced the order in which Burke grew up—are themselves dissolving. The question that confronted Burke was the crucial one of how to preserve a relatively stable political order when the bases of that order were no longer taken for granted. The same difficulty confronts us: "under liberal pluralism there is little assertion of a common ethos, but without a common ethos, liberal society disintegrates," writes Byrne. His Burke is not the placid political thinker deriving abstract truths through the application of rational theorems, but a deeply engaged partisan trying to make sense of a changing political and social climate.

Byrne's interpretation centers on the concept of the "moral imagination," a phrase used first by Burke that, while much quoted since, has received "relatively little explication or philosophical development." The term appears in a key passage in *Reflections on the Revolution in France* that refers to the "wardrobe of the moral imagination, which the heart owns, and the understanding ratifies" being "rudely" torn off by the new ideas coming from France. This phrase embodied all the elements of the old order that Burke saw coming apart: education, habit, custom, the rule of law, and what he described as "the spirit of religion" and the "spirit of a gentleman" at the root of Western civilization.

Byrne investigates Burke's neglected *English History*, specifically his commendation of Pope Gregory's policy of allowing pagan customs to exist alongside Christian ones in order to speed England's conversion to Christianity. Byrne uses this example to challenge the usual understanding of Burkean conservatism as one that endorses gradual change simply for the sake of its gradualness. "Burke's focus is not on the objective problem of whether or not the innovation is 'good,' or even whether the change is suitable for the circumstances at hand. His focus is on the subjective experience of the people. This emphasis on subjectivity is one key to Burke's approach to fundamental problems of order, meaning, and the good." Seen from this perspective, Burke's support for Indians, Americans, and the Irish Catholics, and his opposition to the French revolutionaries, takes on a unifying character. In each instance, the subjective experience was wrenching, as a new order was placed upon a people, destroying in the process the "experiential" view of the world that Burke considers crucial to a stable civil order.

Byrne relocates Burke's aesthetics as a central feature of his moral imagination. Burke knew that culture affects the quality of one's judgment, and he believed that our experience of beauty or the sublime was an important component of that culture. This is not romanticism or elevation of the individual will. Burke's aesthetics "did not point to the sort of expansive, undisciplined willfulness that is commonly associated with some forms of romanticism. Instead, Burke's perspective points in the opposite direction: toward humility, toward reverence, toward a sense of order and of moral values," rooted in the mystery of human experience.

Earlier thinkers, especially those who saw a natural law Burke, were uneasy with his aesthetics since it clearly invokes non-rational feelings like dread and reverence as a basis for moral judgments. But Byrne explains that these feelings, and the imaginative effort used to form judgments, are the link between Burke's aesthetics and his politics. Human experience is too varied and subtle, too mysterious, to be completely accounted for by political theory or metaphysics. To avoid the temptation to do so, Burke turned to tradition, for "paradoxically, the best way to set standards above the vagaries of human society is to anchor those standards firmly in that society."

Yet society must itself be informed by sensitivity to the effects of its cultural components and attuned to the ways politics can destroy those components. Right-wing ideology can be just as destructive as the left's, and Byrne does a good job in explaining that Burke is opposed to abstract assertions of "rights" from either side for the same reason: such demands allow too much expression of will and arbitrariness to enter political debate, when what is needed is humility and order.

The example of the East India Company is instructive. That imperial episode combined military force, arbitrary authority, and extractive capitalism, and Burke saw the whole project as not only inimical to India but dangerous for England on account of the culture that such an experience created when young colonial Englishmen, some newly enriched, returned home. The parallels to our foreign entanglements and their cultural risks could not be clearer.

*Edmund Burke for Our Time* advances an effort engaged in by some conservative writers to position the conservative tradition as a postmodern reaction to the end of Enlightenment modernity. Russell Kirk, perhaps the foremost exponent of this school, was adamant that the reductionist ideologies of both the left and right were giving way to a time more amenable to the imagination, and he shared with Burke a reverence for existence that should, he felt, inform political thinking. Byrne usefully separates Burke from the pure natural law school without diminishing Burke's convictions, and shows him to be still, as Kirk saw five decades ago, the beginning of a conservative reconstruction.

# *Un-American Conservative*

**In the 1950s,** American conservatives—then a scattered group of fugitives—sought an intellectual ancestor who embodied their principles and whose writings could be applied to the contemporary United States. Books like Peter Stanlis's *Edmund Burke and the Natural Law* and, most famously, Russell Kirk's *The Conservative Mind* repackaged the eighteenth-century Anglo-Irish statesman Edmund Burke into an all-purpose conservative champion. Where Burke stood against Jacobinism during the French Revolution, conservatives could resist communism during the Cold War. As Burke had stood for eternal verities in 1790, so too he could now stand for the natural law against an emerging liberal relativism.

Although in retrospect seemingly obvious, this choice was not one everyone would have made. In his own day Burke was not a reactionary or even a conservative in our sense but a reforming Whig. Moreover, while he is eminently quotable, his words are just as suitable to support liberal causes as conservative ones. In the nineteenth century writers such as the historian George Bancroft considered Burke an admirable, but outdated, opponent of tyrannical power not suited for emulation in democratic, egalitarian America; others labeled him a simple utilitarian.

Russell Kirk forcefully rejected this interpretation, both in *The Conservative Mind* and in his later biography of Burke. For Kirk, the defense of tradition Burke mounted conveyed not some utilitarian calculus but rather an argument that customs that had developed over centuries—while perhaps also representing the greatest good for the greatest number—were at root an expression of enduring principle. This was the farthest thing from what Kirk derisively termed "Benthamism," a utilitarianism that would

Originally published in *The American Conservative*, July 3, 2013.

change customs and tradition as soon as some abstract principle bid it to do so. Rather, Burke championed the principle of order, which Kirk described as "an anticipatory refutation of utilitarianism, positivism, and pragmatism, an affirmation of that reverential view of society which may be traced through Aristotle, Cicero, Seneca, the Roman jurisconsults, the Schoolmen, Richard Hooker, and lesser thinkers."

Burke, therefore, was for the ages. But not all conservatives agreed with the picture Kirk and others were painting. Libertarian-minded thinkers like *National Review* senior editor Frank Meyer rejected Kirk's conservatism as an aristocratic collectivism. Richard Weaver, author of the seminal conservative work *Ideas Have Consequences*, wrote a famous essay arguing that Burke's "argument from circumstance" was, from a conservative point of view, inferior to Lincoln's "argument from principle." Yet the view of Kirk and Stanlis has prevailed: Burke is now routinely considered a founder of American conservatism.

Drew Maciag considers why Burke's stock has risen so high on the American intellectual right in this study of the reception and use of Burke in the U.S. since the Founding. *Edmund Burke in America* is a concise treatment of the many ways Americans have thought of Burke, and Maciag presents an important historiographical treatment of the emergence of a Burkean conservatism—even as he concludes it is something of an artificial growth on these shores.

Burke inspired ambiguous reactions shortly after the Founding. He had, after all, been the agent of New York colony prior to the Revolution, and he supported the colonists' grievances through the 1760s and 1770s. In a telling detail Maciag recounts, the Continental Congress toasted to Burke's health in 1775 as a friend of liberty. But his interest in the colonies lasted only so long as they were a part of the Empire; once that was no longer the case, it disappeared.

Not until 1791 did Burke's *Reflections on the Revolution in France* reach America, and when it did his former admirers and friends, such as Thomas Paine, were disappointed by his fervent stance against the French Revolution. Burke's relation to the new nation changed. By that time, according to Maciag, the die had been cast: America was a revolutionary nation, even if that revolution was qualified by respect for certain British political traditions. Burke's devotion to a hereditary king and aristocracy, however, was bound to fall on deaf ears.

Burke became a controversial if not disfavored figure among the Founding generation. Maciag highlights this in a chapter comparing Burke to John Adams, who is sometimes considered a sort of American Burke. The Englishman himself understood his mission as being to "apply the brakes to the momentum of Enlightenment overreach." But Adams was an American and sought to implement "Enlightenment thought in some workable, responsible manner." The two were aligned in opposition to the French Revolution, but even there Maciag sees a difference. As the only Federalist president,

> Adams fit the bill for the forces of order and continuity, as well as Jefferson did for the forces of innovation and progress. If the Republican-Enlightenment ideal was to become the dominant national vision, and so give rise to an ideology of liberalism and progress, then certainly a counter-persuasion, loosely defined as conservative, was needed in order for the dynamic progress to function.

Maciag also devotes chapters to Jacksonian America; the antebellum Whigs, who attempted a partial restoration of Burke's reputation in reaction against the mob rule of "King Andrew" Jackson; the post-Civil War period and Gilded Age, when John Morley and E.L. Godkin identified Burke as a utilitarian; and Theodore Roosevelt, who alternately detested and admired a conservatism that owed less to Burke than "religious fundamentalism, monopoly capitalism, and 'tory' attitudes toward culture and society." Roosevelt leads to Woodrow Wilson, who wrote substantially, and positively, about Burke in the 1890s. Wilson's Burke was opposed to abstraction and favored responsible reform; he was getting closer to the postwar conservative's vision.

The second part of the book, "Postwar America," considers how and why Burke became the right's intellectual standard-bearer. Maciag rightly focuses on larger intellectual movements, such as the revival of "natural law thinking" on Catholic campuses in the late 1940s, as well as on more concrete factors, such as the 1948 publication of Burke's correspondence. The conservative reappropriation of Burke brings Maciag to his second theme: for Maciag, conservatism is a vital but junior partner in the American political culture. He writes that "American Burkeans quickly learned that they were unlikely to prevail. The exceptionalist environment proved too resistant to the innate traditionalism of the Burkean message. In reaction to this, the Burkean perspective became transformed into a perennial counterpoint that was played against the major themes of egalitarianism and competitive material progress." In other words, conservatism is destined to play "the loyal opposition—strong enough to influence the agenda, not strong enough to set it."

Maciag's treatment of Kirk, whom he calls "the greatest postwar Burkean," is sympathetic while focusing on a central problem. For Kirk, Burke represented the entire intellectual ancestry of the West sharpened to a point thrust at the heart of revolutionary France. Kirk clearly wants Burke to be the source of a tradition opposed to what he called "defecated rationality," yet one still connected to the primordial wisdom of the natural law, about which Burke said little explicitly. But because Kirk took a "holistic and inseparable view of civilization," he could not incorporate "the modern ideals of progress, equity, democracy, and the pursuit of happiness." In that sense, Kirk was more reactionary than Burke ever was: "while Burke was a progressive reformer who defended British traditions that were declining but not yet extinct, Kirk condemned liberal reformers and sought to impose ancient, foreign, and vague traditions that had never really existed in the United States." This is for Maciag ultimately a mistaken endeavor because Burke can never quite fit in America, and his resurgence in the 1950s was merely an opportune moment for a movement looking for a father.

Kirk never really explained—in the way, say, T.S. Eliot did for

England—what traditions defined the nation. He wrote little, for example, on American creations like jazz or even baseball, often a go-to source of pop wisdom for right-wingers. Yet Maciag does not fully address what Kirk was doing with his invocation of Burke. Kirk was waging a battle of imagination, not only with liberalism and other strains of conservatism—a nuance Maciag notes but whose significance he passes over—but with what he saw coming after liberalism, what Kirk called the Age of Sentiment. Kirk, like others such as Daniel Bell, Marshall McLuhan, and Philip Rieff, saw liberalism and the rational Enlightenment that brought it into being coming to an end. What would replace it had the potential to be shaped by a powerful imaginative vision of human society, a vision Kirk saw in Burke. This was not a rigid aristocratic vision but one that recognized society as an interlocked union of communities. It's a vision that caused one writer, Catholic University professor of politics Claes Ryn, to call Burke the first postmodern. In this, Kirk was Burke's true heir: Kirk once went so far as to say that it "may be the conservative imagination which is to guide the Post-Modern Age."

Conservatives are ever in the minority, for Maciag, because modernity has unleashed a power that can go in only one way: "you cannot turn back the clock." But as Chesterton responded to that aphorism, since a clock is manmade, as is culture, the clock can be turned anywhere we like. Maciag notes the (in some ways) changing nature of conservatism but without addressing the changing nature of liberalism. A century ago, many liberals were eugenicist elitists who would no more have supported gay marriage or a liberal welfare state than does Rush Limbaugh today. To argue that conservatism must always be a junior partner, merely correcting liberalism's excesses, implies that there is a definitive direction not only to liberalism but to history itself, a contention that, if it is not unfalsifiable, certainly has little to confirm it.

Seen in this way, the conservative reappropriation of Burke becomes more comprehensible. Burke's mysticism and reliance on some form of natural law were not meant to convey a legalistic structure of metaphysics, with "ought" confidently derived from "is." Nor is Burke's common resort to "circumstance" a rejection of natural principles. Rather, it is a recognition that mystery—not reason—lies at the heart of each individual and the societies the human race creates, thus conservatives are enjoined to eschew social engineering and respect the bewildering array of ways in which we can organize our life together. There are enduring principles, but they must be sifted from particular facts, not theorizing.

Although Maciag defines Kirk and his supporters as premodern "anti-rationalists," the reality is more complicated. Maciag is right that at times Kirk seems to be speaking from a world "that had already passed away." But that is what makes the imaginative vision of Burke, as seen through the work of Kirk, the most formidable alternative to liberalism among the conservatisms vying for attention today.

# *Burkean Aesthetics*

In 2006, Stanley Kurtz, writing at *National Review Online*, lamented that conservatives had given up on the culture. Rather than talking about the importance of social conditions to a stable society, conservatives had yielded that ground to the left. The devotion of the left to multiculturalism and various forms of "cultural studies" made such talk unnerving to conservatives, who preferred the supposedly separate spheres of politics and economics. Moreover, conservatives too often simply asserted absolute rights against what they saw as liberalism's cultural relativism. But, aside from being alien to conservatism, such language was not a long-term electoral winner. "Let's get back," Kurtz wrote, "to Burke and Tocqueville—not as a way of rejecting the notion of individual rights, but as a way of understanding the social and cultural foundations required to make a rights-based democracy work in the first place."

Kurtz was prescient, for an Edmund Burke revival of sorts has been underway. David Bromwich's book is one of a new clutch of studies about the great Whig statesman, including a biography by the British Conservative MP Jesse Norman. William Byrne has produced an interesting study titled *Burke for Our Time*, focusing on the importance of aesthetics and sensibility to his subject's political views. Drew Maciag has traced the contested history of Burke in America, where followers from utilitarians to traditionalists have tried to claim him. Most recently, Yuval Levin has received praise for his work *The Great Debate*, which sets Burke against his

Originally published in *The New Criterion*, February 2015.

friend and great antagonist Thomas Paine and locates the origins of the modern right and left in their arguments over liberty and the social order.

But Kurtz was right to pair Tocqueville (1805–1859) with Burke (1730–1797), for they have been consistent touchstones of American self-understanding. Tocqueville is the later of the two, coming to America in the 1830s. By then, Burke had been dead for over thirty years, and his work on America and the larger questions of social change and revolution a generation past. Tocqueville forced Americans to examine what it meant to be a nation in which the spirit of equality entered into every social and political interaction, from the national government to marriage and the family.

Burke too recognized that spirit. In his 1775 speech on conciliation with the American colonies, he wrote that "a love of freedom is the predominating feature which marks and distinguishes" America. But Burke, unlike Tocqueville, represented a concrete connection with America. He had, after all, served as the agent in Parliament for the New York colony, with his health toasted by the revolutionaries in 1775. The American question was one of his great causes, along with India and the French Revolution. If Tocqueville reminded Americans of what was new about the nation, Burke reminded them of what was owed to their tradition. Indeed, Burke attributed the characteristic American love of liberty to, among other things, the colonists' Protestant religion and British heritage. The conservative thinker, and perhaps the greatest American Burkean, Russell Kirk, wrote that Burke represented a tradition of thought extending back to Richard Hooker and the great Roman jurisprudents, and that he was as influential as Locke among the founding generation, if not more so.

Even in his own time, Burke was considered a great man, but he was not a particularly successful public man. Bromwich, a Sterling Professor of English at Yale, wants to identify "the originality and continuities" of Burke's thinking across aesthetics, politics, and morals and "not the rise and fall of his fortunes." *The Intellectual Life of Edmund Burke* covers, in seven chapters, the first three decades of Burke's public life, beginning with the 1756 anonymous publication of *The Vindication of Natural Society* and the more important *Enquiry into the Origin of the Sublime and the Beautiful* in 1757 through his famous speech at the Bristol Guildhall in 1780; another volume is expected to cover Burke's campaign against the depredations of Warren Hastings, and his confrontation with the French Revolution. There is little pure biographical detail here, nor much political context. This is an intellectual biography, exploring almost exclusively the development of Burke's thought.

Burke faced several monumental events during his career as a parliamentarian and member of the Rockingham Whigs: the loss of the American colonies, the fight over the East India Company's treatment of its possessions, and the events in France beginning in 1789. What Bromwich notes is the consistent "fit between his private and public views." And the theme that runs through both is a hatred of injustice and an opposition to arbitrary power:

> The purpose of enlightened government is to prevent such persons or groups from acquiring an excess of the "very corrupting thing" that power is. Though Burke lived and moved in proximity to the powerful, his lot was never cast in them. He meant to act as a reminder of the cost of power, and a curb against the perpetual danger of its abuse.

This is one reason why Burke, no democrat, remains critical reading for those in democratic societies. Not just kings or lords, but, as Bromwich writes, "a mass of men playing at being lords [or] a new class of moneyed men carving up the world for advantage" may all at times be rightfully resisted. One wonders what Burke would have thought of the Lois Lerners or Mark Zuckerbergs among us.

Early in the book, Bromwich dismisses claims that would identify Burke "as the father of modern conservatism," based on what he implies is current scholarly consensus, though he more asserts than supports this statement. It is true that some recent scholarship has cast Burke as a thinker less reliant on the "natural law" than some contended in the 1950s and 1960s. Writers such as the late Peter Stanlis had recruited Burke as the great exponent of the Western natural law tradition against an immoral communism. The problem with that position is that Burke did not use the term "natural law" very often. He spoke in different moral categories and his aesthetics and sensitivity to feeling have always been an awkward fit for those who saw him as championing an unbreakable set of universal laws.

But that has never been the whole of conservative reflection on Burke, and Bromwich does not really address those who do consider Burke to be a source of conservatism. Byrne, for example, emphasizes the importance of Burke's aesthetics in forming his moral judgments and roots his defense of tradition in Burke's sympathy for the experiences of others. Kirk, in his book *The Conservative Mind: From Burke to Eliot*, closely identifies his "principles of conservatism" with Burke. He connects, as Bromwich does, Burke's defense of the colonies' liberties, inherited from the British, with his rejection of the abstract rights of the French *philosophes*. Like Kirk, Bromwich compares Burke to Rousseau as opposed, but equally influential, figures. Even Maciag, who is no conservative, recognizes that Burke became, in postwar America, the thinker presented as a counterpoint to a reckless egalitarianism and a consumerist liberalism because of his defense of tradition and the British civil order.

This is a blind spot in what is otherwise a very fine study, which draws not only on Burke's public writings, but also on his extensive correspondence. Bromwich seems content rather to point to Burke's opposition to injustice, and his role as a mildly progressive (as understood in that period) Whig as proof that he would not be in accord with his later, conservative admirers. But Bromwich's careful scholarship and sensitivity to Burke's thought end up belying this position. Indeed, some points of Bromwich's analysis support the conservative understanding of Burke. Thus Bromwich focuses on Burke's use of the word "sympathy," which is "the faculty of imagining the feelings of others in the place of others." This is a core conservative insight. Byrne, for example, identifies Burke's feeling for the other as key to understanding his opposition to arbitrary power and his love of localized tradition. Sympathy, imaginative engagement, and respect for tradition work together to create the basis for a stable social order, and include an emphasis on the world of culture outside politics.

Burke did not, as some conservatives have asserted, completely disregard universal rights or the claims of humanity, though he parted company with those who would try to impose such abstractions on a living community. Bromwich reminds us that in his famous speech of the "little platoons," Burke explains that to "love the little platoon we belong to in society is the first principle (the germ as it were) of public affections. It is the first link in the series by which we proceed towards a love to our country and to mankind." Burke reaches out from those closest communities of family, locality, or interest, to which we owe our first loyalty, to those wider circles of people to whom we also owe a duty, though of lesser degree, based on our common humanity. Bromwich summarizes Burke's view here as moving "from sympathy with our neighbors or clan or tribe to a feeling about mankind at large," and seems to think this separates Burke from conservatism.

But this does not mean conservatives are wrong to claim Burke as a defender of those little platoons; they are, after all, the "germ" of all other attachments. It is liberalism that disdains those platoons and values, perversely, those farther away more than those closer. But because liberalism lacks Burke's basis in warm affection for those familiar to us, liberalism ends up being a distant, cold bureaucracy at best, and at worst a system more inclined to oppress in the name of freedom than to empower citizens to be free themselves. The history of the last century is littered with examples of despotic regimes who claimed to love "humanity," while persecuting those actual humans unfortunate enough to live under such regimes. It is precisely because Burke prioritizes the initial personal connection that he can then claim our allegiance to larger circles. In this, again, Rousseau is the opposing figure, preaching liberation, but abandoning his own children to the orphanage.

And when Bromwich writes that "[t]he people have no *interest* in disorder," with his italics, he expresses a sentiment that Kirk could, and did, express. Order is the first need of society, said Kirk, explicitly invoking

Burke. Bromwich agrees, though he places more emphasis on the sovereignty of the people than Kirk thought it would bear. But even there, Bromwich writes, when the people make an error and mistakenly (because they would not intentionally) choose disorder, then it is up to a statesman to interpret the disorder and to figure a way to right it. Few conservatives would challenge that statement.

In the end, *Edmund Burke* is not concerned with contemporary political affiliations. One need not agree with the inferences he draws to conclude that Bromwich has done a great service in so lucidly explaining Burke's thought.

# *The Rise of Bohemian Burkeans*

**After September 11, 2001,** Rod Dreher, then a writer for *National Review* and now an editor at the *Dallas Morning News*, wrote a series of articles exploring how some conservatives were rejecting the free market and individual liberty espoused by Republicanism and were returning to an older tradition of human-scale living and traditional ways of production and consumption. Based on his colleagues' comments that his enthusiasm for an organic market in Brooklyn was "too lefty," Mr. Dreher began to identify himself as a "crunchy con," that is, a conservative who lived outside the mainstream of the Republican Party.

At first, the term sounds like a meaningless hook. Defining and redefining the various right-wing groups has long been a conservative pastime, and so it would be tempting to ignore this book as a publishing exaggeration. That would be a mistake. *Crunchy Cons: How Birkenstocked Burkeans, gun-loving organic gardeners, evangelical free-range farmers, hip homeschooling mamas, right-wing nature lovers, and their diverse tribe of countercultural conservatives plan to save America (or at least the Republican Party)*, even with its weaknesses, may be a clarion call for conservatives who have come to realize that the most important things in life cannot be found either in politics or the marketplace, and that what passes for political discourse is largely empty of meaning.

This is no academic treatise but rather a look at what America has become since the revolutions of the 1960s and the Reagan era. The ethos of "do your own thing," promoted by 1960s radicals and latter-day libertines,

---

Originally published in the *New York Sun*, February 28, 2006.

has been combined with a capitalist system all too happy to separate people from traditional commitments and to remake them instead into atomistic consumers tossed amid the "creative destruction" of the marketplace. The results have been broken families, destroyed neighborhoods, environmental degradation, and neglect of the duties one generation owes to another.

Mr. Dreher recounts his own journey to crunchy conservatism and those of others who have opted out, in various ways, from the dominant culture. We see here organic farmers, home schoolers, natural farmers, devotees of traditional urban architecture, and others who "don't buy into the consumerist and individualistic mainstream of American life." Mr. Dreher organizes his chapters thematically, with subjects such as "Home," "Food," and "Education." Each chapter is centered around Mr. Dreher's own experiences, or those of others of a similar disposition. Thus, in the "Home" chapter, he describes how he and his wife selected a home in an urban Dallas neighborhood rather than a suburb, so they would not have to rely on a car and where the neighborhood architecture lent itself to living on a human scale.

The results are impressionistic, but no less impressive. Mr. Dreher has tapped into an undercurrent of conservative (mostly Republican) dissidents, who have more in common with those few remaining hippies than they do with the mainstream Republican juggernaut. And at times, Mr. Dreher sounds just as harsh as any liberal critic of the free-market utopia promised by the party's leaders: "Consumerism has become our religion, and it is difficult to identify anything within the contemporary Republican Party that stands against the dogma of the Market Supreme." His jeremiads against the cult of efficiency are likewise worthwhile: Unless we know to what ends our economy is directed, efficiency is an empty word.

The Democrats, too, have bought into the same false promises of progress and materialism as the Republicans, with the added liability of having positions on issues such as abortion and biotech issues that do not endear them to crunchy cons who may otherwise approve of their position on, say, the environment. The appeal of Mr. Dreher's book, however, is that it largely eschews politics. His crunchy cons, generally, are just trying to live their lives, sometimes in accord with what they perceive as a religious vocation, and sometimes not.

This crunchy conservatism is not new, of course; there is a long tradition of conservative critique of materialism and consumerism. Moreover, left-wing writers from Christopher Lasch to George McGovern to—gasp—a former president, Jimmy Carter, all echo, in varying degrees, Mr. Dreher's concerns. Mr. Dreher has done his homework, and he names Russell Kirk, the founder of traditionalist conservatism and a figure rarely praised by the official conservative "movement," as the godfather of crunchy cons. Kirk wrote his books from his family home in rural Michigan, and he had little patience for a conservatism that promoted an uncontrolled free market, or "liberty" unconstrained by morality or tradition. Mr. Dreher has traded in Kirk's trademark suit and watch fob for Birkenstocks and shopping at Whole Foods, but the effect is the same.

But how real is all this? While Mr. Dreher is obviously excited about the kindred spirits he has found, there are limits to crunchy conservatism, and it is too early to tell whether it is a stable trend. For one thing, the elements of crunchiness Mr. Dreher points to, such as gentrified architecture and organic foods, are largely made possible in this generation only by the larger materialist culture that has enabled smaller artisan producers to survive. In other words, without all those hedge fund managers, no Whole Foods. Other areas of life that most Americans would consider important—health care, for example—remain untouched by Mr. Dreher's analysis. We do not see, for example, people making their own clothes or flocking to open small farms.

This is not surprising, of course, as Mr. Dreher is not advocating a wholescale rejection of modern convenience. However, without a more nuanced defense of the crunchy con viewpoint, his assertions become little more than matters of taste. Everyone agrees that neighborhoods are important; if I choose to live in a prefab McMansion and spend weekends at the country club, what is it to you? Mr. Dreher wants to say that such choices are somehow less authentic or more harmful in the long run than others, and we may well agree; but assertion is not argument, and it is unlikely to persuade those who do not share Mr. Dreher's predilections.

The risk of Mr. Dreher's crunchy conservatism is its potential to become just another "lifestyle choice" that the market is perfectly happy to satisfy. Rock music can be used to sell cars, so why not country music to sell the crunchy con lifestyle? The rejection of (some types of) consumerism is itself inseparable from a free market that makes consumerism possible. Crunchy cons may end up little different from David Brooks's bourgeois bohemians, who go barely mentioned here. Crunchy cons would have their virtue and still live in enclaves of liberal cities that provide the crunchy amenities unavailable, say, in East Coast rust-belt towns.

*Crunchy Cons* has jump-started a serious conversation among young conservatives who are discovering, once again, that happiness lies not in Mammon or power but in brightening the corner where you are.

# *Cold War Conservatives Who Influenced Reagan*

**In one sense** Laurence R. Jurdem's new book is like a time capsule for those with a deep interest in American conservative political history. In the course of *Paving the Way for Reagan: The Influence of Conservative Media on U.S. Foreign Policy*, we see the emergence of *Human Events*, *National Review*, and *Commentary* as influential journals of opinion. They had their idiosyncrasies but were united on how they positioned the United States as a strong, global opponent of communism. We see controversies that once preoccupied the political classes—Vietnam, SALT II, Rhodesia, China's admission to the United Nations and its threatening of Taiwan. Figures such as Muammar Gaddafi and Robert Mugabe dominate the book. Hard to see many millennials knowing who or what any of these are, or why they mattered.

And yet. Mugabe is still around, if out of power in Zimbabwe. Gaddafi, killed after being overthrown as Libya's dictator, remains part of American consciousness. And China is still pushing to isolate Taiwan, most recently by forming stronger economic ties with other Pacific islands. More important for the purposes of this book, the conservative media are still around, though changed and still changing. So *Paving the Way for Reagan* comes at an opportune time to examine the legacy of the conservative media, at least in the area of foreign policy.

Jurdem's account helps explain, in a roundabout way, how figures like David Frum, Bill Kristol, Max Boot, and others thought they could convert America into a permanent war machine against "Islamofascism" after

Originally published in *Law & Liberty*, May 1, 2019.

the attacks of September 11, 2001. Conservative media have been arguing for military intervention and an aggressive foreign policy for decades. This book analyzes attempts by media conservatives to change crucial foreign policy decisions from the time of the Vietnam War up to Reagan's victory in the presidential election of 1980. It focuses on three journals, *Human Events*, *National Review*, and *Commentary* and their respective editors, Allan Ryskind, William F. Buckley, Jr., and Norman Podhoretz.

*Human Events* (which in 2013 became an online-only publication, and which was purchased recently by new owners intending to relaunch it under a pro-Trump banner) is the oldest, having been founded in 1944 by conservatives upset with Franklin Roosevelt and the big government programs of the New Deal. Of the three, it focused perhaps the most on publishing news stories as opposed to opinion.

*National Review*, founded in 1955, was and is a broader journal, owing to founder Buckley's more diverse interests, and his clearer desire (as Jurdem astutely notes) to remain within the corridors of power.

*Commentary*, founded in 1945 by the American Jewish Committee, came more fully to the anticommunist cause later in the 1960s, once Podhoretz and others became disillusioned with the New Left. *Commentary*'s editors' "move to the Right, particularly in the arena of foreign policy, sent a powerful signal to America's intellectual elites that the once-vital center of the Democratic Party, symbolized by its passionate commitment to anticommunism, no longer existed." From about 1968 on, anticommunism became increasingly the occupation of the Right.

In the late 1960s, these journals went on the attack against what they saw as a liberal "failure of nerve" to promote American interests abroad and aggressively to confront the global Soviet threat. "Writers for these publications claimed that the fortunes of the country were being subverted not only abroad but at home," writes Jurdem. In the face of Soviet and Cuban communism and especially during the withdrawal of U.S. forces from Vietnam, "conservatives believed that a once-active foreign policy that promoted democracy and freedom had been transformed by liberal elites into a policy of appeasement and self-doubt." Those arguments—until the advent of Donald Trump, at least—remained baseline conservative opinion on foreign policy, though at least since 9/11 there has been an increasing conservative revival of its own antiwar and anti-interventionist traditions.

Jurdem devotes chapters to several key events in U.S. foreign policy, including Vietnam, the SALT II treaty, relations with China, and the United Nations, and ends with the Iranian hostage crisis of 1979, which famously ended shortly after the election of Reagan. In the hindsight of the seemingly never-ending wars in the Middle East that some of these same publications advocated after 9/11, this account makes for at times sobering reading.

Conservatives were vociferous in their resistance to any fallback or withdrawal from Vietnam. When American forces left South Vietnam, conservatives argued for continued economic support for the nation to resist the North, and when South Vietnam finally fell and the United States engaged in peace talks, some conservatives looked for any misstep by North Vietnam to restart the conflict.

And the less said about the Right's strong support for racist Rhodesia, the better. It is impossible to read *National Review*'s support for Rhodesia outside of its then-antipathy toward the American civil rights movement. *National Review* supported Rhodesia's separation from Great Britain for complicated (some might say opaque) anticommunist reasons. Jurdem summarizes the view of people like senator and presidential candidate Barry Goldwater (R-Ariz.) as believing that "when the United States penalized a 'friendly nation,' it sent communist states the message that supporting its close ally Great Britain was more important than taking a strong position in the Cold War," because Britain had trading interests with communist countries. The magazine went so far as to call Rhodesia's Ian Smith that nation's "George Washington."

Similarly with SALT II and the Soviet Union. Here, as throughout, Jurdem has conducted thorough research among the relevant publications' archives, and has done lengthy interviews. The Strategic Arms Limitations Talks were meant as a way to de-escalate the arms race with the Soviet

Union. In May 1971, Nixon announced an agreement with the Russians regarding limits on the use of antiballistic missiles. But this was viewed by conservatives as a show of weakness.

Nixon's tense relations with the Right are a recurring theme. Jurdem highlights a rare unpublished column by Buckley, in which the *National Review* editor listed the ways in which Nixon had, he felt, betrayed conservative principles in his negotiations with the Russians. The thirty-seventh President, for his part, never quite forgave conservatives for not supporting him in the early 1960s, or for failing to understand that negotiations needed to run both ways. Nixon's National Security Advisor and later Secretary of State, Henry Kissinger, and Nixon aide Pat Buchanan were employed as go-betweens to keep channels of communication open with the Right. (This mostly meant with Buckley; Nixon had little time for *Human Events* or most other conservative commentators.) Conservatives, especially Buckley and senior *National Review* writer James Burnham, remained respectful of Kissinger but saw him (and President Nixon) as too pragmatic.

Their suspicions were only confirmed by Nixon's visit to China. Buckley, one of the editors and journalists who accompanied Nixon on that trip, according to Jurdem "charged that the great struggle against communism—a war that many believed as one of good against evil—had now evaporated." The decision of the Carter administration to open a formal relationship with Beijing was cause for further anguish on the Right.

So Jurdem is correct that conservative publications paved the way for Reagan, and he shows that Reagan was reading *Human Events* and *National Review* since his General Electric days. At times, Reagan cribbed directly from these publications to attack those seen as softer on communism. Likewise members of Congress (particularly Senators John Tower of Texas and Strom Thurmond of South Carolina) used conservative editorials to bolster their own arguments. Reagan's staunch anticommunist stance found support and confirmation in the editorials and articles he spent decades reading.

*Commentary*, although important in its own right, especially after it became more clearly associated with the neoconservative cause, receives the least attention of the three in this study, with one significant exception: the 1979 article by Georgetown political scientist Jeane J. Kirkpatrick, "Democracy and Double Standards," which was to have a big influence on the Reagan administration. Kirkpatrick, who was to become Reagan's ambassador to the United Nations, argued that America had misunderstood the ideological revolutions that were toppling states that had been allies, and that we should be friendly to non-democratic regimes (such as Iran under the shah) that were friendly to us. As Jurdem phrases it, Kirkpatrick argued that "whereas autocracies had the capacity for change, societies under the totalitarian system could not alter themselves, as it was not the rulers but the principles of communism that held control." Thus conservatives' support for all manner of regimes so long as they were not totalitarian, that is, communist.

The conservative media's scorecard is decidedly mixed. Conservatives opposed the peace talks with Vietnam, and lost. They opposed the opening to China, and lost. SALT II was a more complicated story. The ratification of the treaty was delayed by the Soviet invasion of Afghanistan in 1980, and voted down by the Senate Armed Services Committee headed by neoconservative hero Senator Henry "Scoop" Jackson (D-Wash.). But even in the mid-1980s, Reagan argued for abiding by the terms of arms-limitations treaties so long as the Soviets displayed the same restraint, which did not sit well with some conservatives. On whether or not the United States should relinquish control of the Panama Canal, the positions were switched: Buckley, who favored transferring the canal to Panama, famously debated this with his friend Reagan, who opposed it (as did *Human Events*).

All of these controversies need to be seen in light of the real threat emanating from Leonid Brezhnev's Soviet Union, and the mood of the country was, throughout this period, still heavily in support of efforts to resist communism. Yet it is also clear that conservative publications—themselves often staffed by those like Burnham and Frank Meyer, who were apostates from the Soviet cause—were apt to see every conflict through that lens, whether this was called for or not.

Jurdem writes that the three journals he has singled out "viewed the dominant foreign policy events of the 1960s and 1970s through a specific ideology that eventually came to define the activist agenda of the Reagan Administration in regard to the Cold War." True enough, but there were two strands to this ideology. Some conservatives, like Ambassador Kirkpatrick, were fine with authoritarian regimes so long as they were not communist. But another side of conservative foreign policy writing existed alongside this *realpolitik* position: that American power should be used specifically to promote democracy against any non-democratic regime.

This ambiguity is not brought out too clearly by Jurdem. President Reagan in fact used both kinds of rhetoric in his speeches. And once the Cold War ended, the democracy-promotion strand remained, and grew stronger. The mistake these journals made was to confuse this activist agenda with conservatism itself.

# *The Ability to See*

**Through books on subjects** ranging from wine to hunting, music to environmentalism, British philosopher Roger Scruton has constructed a multifaceted attack on liberalism. In his latest book, *The Soul of the World*, Scruton addresses the contention that religion is a byproduct of our culture or our genes, and therefore ultimately some kind of a fantasy projection. Liberals have convinced themselves that biology explains God, and that the philosophical traditions of the West, as well as the other great world cultures, have nothing to say about human nature. Scruton, drawing on figures as diverse as Hegel and Mozart, shows that religious concepts are perfectly consistent with scientific reasoning (properly understood), but they point beyond science to something that can be, and has been, understood as transcendence. The core problem with liberalism, he wrote in an essay some years ago, has been

> the relentless scoffing at ordinary prohibitions and decencies and the shrill advocacy of "alternatives" that ordinary people in their hearts are unable to recognize. Liberal sarcasm is the ideology of a ruling class.

Religion embodies those prohibitions and decencies enshrined in ritual, concepts of the sacred and profane, and a personal relationship with the divine. Conservatives need to convince society to return to a sort of piety, even if the postliberal world is not ready for a return to explicit theism.

---

Originally published in *Chronicles*, November 2014.

Having been in Paris in the disastrous year 1968, Scruton witnessed firsthand the radicalism that has come to define the last half-century. The experience awakened in him a conservatism of which he had previously been unaware. In his memoir, *Gentle Regrets*, he writes that, "[f]or the first time in my life, I felt a surge of political anger, finding myself on the other side of the barricades from all the people I knew." Thus began a long journey into a kind of conservatism that is similar to, but not the same as, the various types of American conservatism. He is no neoconservative publicist for war and "creative destruction," and his respect for the free market does not include devotion to an abstract "capitalism." Scruton's closest counterpart, in tone if not in style, in the United States is perhaps the late Russell Kirk. In their different ways (Scruton is a trained philosopher; Kirk was primarily an historian), both have offered a defense of tradition and habit as a natural part of the human condition, which cannot be discarded without severe damage to our understandings of persons and the societies in which they live.

Read broadly, Scruton's work defends religious belief against two sets of attacks. The first is the anthropological and sociological argument, which was greatly influential in the late nineteenth and twentieth centuries but is of lesser importance today. Thus, Sir James Frazer thought magic both a precursor to more intellectual "religion" and an early form of science, which was primitive man's way of understanding the forces of nature. Extrapolating from a few such examples, anthropologists tried to make all religious reflection analogous to some sort of cultural response to the mysteries of the prescientific world. The second, more recent set of attacks comes from the so-called New Atheists, such as Sam Harris and Richard Dawkins. Relying on supposed insights from evolutionary biology, they, too, have an explanation for religion. Religion is a "meme" that is somehow encoded in our genes, helping us to survive. The New Atheists discard an anthropological explanation of culture in favor of theories of reproductive survival and fecundity. Religion, especially with its emphasis on family relations, marriage, and children, is (they claim) simply a way to maintain tight control over reproductive faculties to further the interests of individual and group genes. Once its evolutionary origins are understood, these writers assert, then religion and its cultural influence will disappear.

The search (at times a desperate one) by secularists for a "natural" explanation for religious belief is, of course, nothing new. The British historian Christopher Dawson, for example, in his 1947 Gifford Lectures (later published as *Religion and Culture*) addressed what he called Natural Theology—that is, a discipline that is competent to study the nature of God and the relationship of man with Him. The book closes with a consideration of the effect of the unification of the world cultures under the dominance of "scientific knowledge and technique." Dawson notes that scientific advances, by themselves, have no political program or agenda. That makes them all the more dangerous when separated from their founding relationship with Western political and religious culture. "The new scientific culture is devoid of all positive spiritual content," Dawson argued—a statement as true today as it was when he wrote that scientific methods are "no culture of all in the traditional sense—that is to say it is not an order which integrates every side of human life in a living spiritual community."

Pope Benedict XVI developed a similar theme in his 2006 Regensburg lecture. He cautioned that the scientific method—which judges the validity of statements only insofar as they conform to mathematical or empirical tests—necessarily excludes religion. But doing so imprisons, rather than liberates, human reason. Then ethical, or moral, questions fall to the individual to decide,

> on the basis of his experiences, what he considers tenable in matters of religion, and the subjective "conscience" becomes the sole arbiter of what is ethical. In this way, though, ethics and religion lose their power to create a community and become a completely personal matter. This is a dangerous state of affairs for humanity, as we see from the disturbing pathologies of religion and reason which necessarily erupt when reason is so reduced that questions of religion and ethics no longer concern it. Attempts to

> construct an ethic from the rules of evolution or from psychology and sociology end up being simply inadequate.

Scruton develops a similar critique in his opening chapter, "Believing in God." Here he argues that evolutionary thinking simply has "no bearing on the content of our religious beliefs and emotions." Such thinking "overlook[s] the aspect of our mental states that is most important to us, and through which we understand and act upon each other's motives, namely, their intentionality or 'aboutness.'" That is, evolutionary biology does not explain how we experience what our genetic programming commands or forbids. Moreover, the materialist explanations of the New Atheists cannot "take note of the internal order of our states of mind." Like philosopher Mary Midgley and neuroscientist Raymond Tallis, Scruton grants, as he must, that evolutionary biology has taught us much. But he denies that biology can explain, or explain away, how we experience the world and, especially, one another.

Scruton addresses the evolutionary biologists' favorite trait, altruism. For them, altruism is simply selfishness in another guise. One helps others as a part of an evolutionary strategy to build allies and protectors and so to allow one's genes to survive into the next generation. But this leaves out, according to Scruton, what we think altruism is about:

> a considered response, based sometimes on agape or neighbor love, sometimes on complex interpersonal emotions like pride and shame, which are in turn founded on the recognition of the other as another like me. In all cases altruism in people involves the judgment that what is bad for the other is something that I have a motive to remedy.

That complex set of emotional and intellectual reactions cannot be reduced to an evolutionary survival game.

The same goes for religion. Without denying any biological imperatives, Scruton insists that

> [t]o explain religion in terms of its reproductive function is to leave unexplained and indeed unperceived the central core of the phenomenon, which is the religious thought—the aboutness of the urge to sacrifice, of the need to worship and obey, of the trepidation of the one who approaches holy and forbidden things and who prays for their permission.

Christians' experience of religion is with a real Person, "who can be addressed, implored, reasoned with, and loved." In a chapter titled "Looking for People," Scruton explores what that relational religious experience means. Atheistic materialism cannot explain the "I" speaking to another "I," but that "web of interpersonal relations" is what makes common life possible and provides the possibility of communication with that other Person who exists outside our experience of reality.

The materialism of the New Atheists creates a false duality: We are not mere biological machines, but biological machines that operate within a framework of emotional and mental states, interpersonal relationships, and experiences that cannot be explained by that machinery. The Western tradition is filled with examples, real and in art, literature, and music, of individuals facing tragedy and what Scruton calls annihilation "as free and self-conscious individuals," not collections of genes. This is the way of true humanism, which is also the escape from ruling-class liberal ideology.

# *Roger Scruton, on the Heart of Conservatism*

WHEN A HISTORY OF CONSERVATIVE THOUGHT (as opposed to the conservative "movement," which perhaps already has its authoritative treatment in George Nash's history, and many other studies) in the twentieth century is written, it is likely to describe three broad areas. The first will be that of William F. Buckley Jr., who brought modern American conservatism into being and connected it with larger themes and thinkers in America and beyond. The second is the narrative traditionalism of Russell Kirk, who developed a sophisticated response to the challenges of liberal rationalism. And the third is very likely to be the defense of conservative thinking proffered by British philosopher Roger Scruton.

His most recent effort, *How to Be a Conservative*, is only the latest of a series of books Scruton has been writing that extend and defend a conservative outlook, from the very personal (*England: An Elegy* and *Gentle Regrets*) to the more explicitly philosophical (including the recent *Soul of the World*). Scruton is, unlike Buckley or Kirk, a trained philosopher and he has been confronting the basic objections liberalism has been making to conservatism and has developed a sophisticated affirmative case for conservatism in areas from economics to the environment. Rather than Burke or Eliot, Scruton finds his conservative philosophy in other thinkers, Hegel perhaps above all. Hegel taught Scruton that the search for freedom is the core of human activity, but that this freedom is only most fully realized through our actions with others, and in "the recognition of mutual rights and duties." This mutuality, also recognized

Originally published in *National Review*, January 5, 2015.

by Kirk, is the core of a conservative temperament and the basis for a stable social order.

Scruton starts with the empirical defense of conservatism, addressed to audiences within what has been called the Anglosphere. Conservatism, Scruton writes, is a natural human impulse, perhaps the first impulse: to preserve the good things of one's society. Conservatism starts from the "sentiment that all mature people can readily share: the sentiment that good things are easily destroyed but not easily created." But that universal urge to preserve the good things of human society is refracted through particular circumstances and traditional of specific societies. "Good things" is not a free-floating category; to become preservable, they must be particularized, desired, and defended by specific people.

Scruton has written this book for those societies that are heirs to the British tradition of ordered liberty. Americans, like the British, have inherited a specific set of good things that are worth defending and that are under attack, such as "the ability to live our lives as we will; the security of impartial law, through which our grievances are answered and our hurts restored; the protection of our environment as a shared asset, which cannot be seized or destroyed at the whim of powerful interests; the open and enquiring culture that has shaped our schools and universities," as well as more specific products such as democratic elections and writs of habeas corpus.

These shared goods are not, as liberals like to think, universals that one can invent or modify at will. Indeed, the lack of willfulness is part of the point: No one power or authority developed them, and no one power or authority has, or should have, the ability to destroy them.

Scruton uses the organic growth of institutions as the starting point for his conservatism. Freedom and institutions go together, indeed they can hardly exist apart: "The process whereby human beings acquire their freedom also builds their attachments, and the institutions of law, education, and politics are part of this—not things that we freely choose from a position of detachment, but things through which we *acquire* our freedom, and without which we could not exist as fully self-conscious agents."

Liberal theory, therefore, which asserts autonomous individuals, is wrong both as a matter of theory and practice. The intrusion by government into every aspect of life hinders this process of acquiring freedom—even though (contrary to libertarian theorists) government is necessary—because while we are institution-builders, some of those institutions can be detrimental to the common good. Institutions can hinder that process of mutuality and common recognition of our being joined in a society. This is the positive insight of socialism, in a chapter Scruton titles "The Truth in Socialism," which recognizes that all of us live in a community; other chapters treat multiculturalism, nationalism, and environmentalism similarly. The main flaw in socialism, Scruton finds, is that socialism must by necessity pit one part of the community against another. It can live only by envy.

Associations can generate inequality; thus, the great liberal drive for equality, which had beneficial effects in the civil-rights movement, has more recently sought to impose a drab secular uniformity, with, for instance, the contraceptive mandate. Inequality results from our natural search for freedom, and the only real counter to this lies in opportunity, which has been brought to us in the modern age through capitalism. But here, too, liberal government missteps: In using the power of the state to interfere in our natural association-making, government reduces opportunity rather than expands it. Laws become means of acquiring power, rather than liberating citizens.

Like all of Scruton's books, *How to Be a Conservative* is elegantly written and scrupulously fair to opposing arguments—the fairness in itself is a lesson in how to be a conservative. But his deeper meaning is that being a conservative means being joined to earlier generations through institutions and the environment, in our founding documents and public buildings, and in our clubs and all those things that together compose, across space and time, what Scruton calls our "dwelling." Modern liberal society, in part because of the disappearance of religious faith, instead imposes a "contagious hardness of heart," Scruton writes. "There is neither love nor happiness—only fun." Modern liberalism rejects the traditional

Western response—rooted in its Christian heritage but which Scruton finds throughout great Western art that still speaks even to the nonbeliever—which is to "bear each loss *as* a loss" and thereby redeem that loss. That response helps us resist the void of despair that liberalism would force us to gaze into, forever, and to recover both respect for the past and a true hope for the future.

# Second Person Politics

❧

**For our intellectual and cultural elites,** conservative ideas can never win. When the Cold War ended, conservatives got little credit; they supposedly had nothing left to fight against and now had to "invent" enemies, such as terrorism, to avoid their fall into irrelevance. When Barack Obama was president, conservatives were on the losing side of history, as the "arc" bent toward justice. Now with Trump, liberals are crowing again, about how his election shows that conservatism is incoherent and in disarray.

Roger Scruton will have none of this. As the preeminent exponent and defender of Anglo-American conservatism, he has spent his career explaining why conservative ideas endure. Author of books on topics ranging from fox-hunting to wine, Spinoza to sex, Scruton has perhaps done more to create the vision of a conservative way of life than any writer in English other than Russell Kirk and William F. Buckley Jr. As with those authors, reading Scruton is an aesthetic as well as an intellectual revelation; conservatism becomes much more than political positions or arguments to own the liberals, as fun as those are. Drawing on the work of David Hume, Michael Oakeshott, Pierre Manent, and Kirk, as well as lesser-known writers such as the Hungarian economist Peter Bauer, Scruton, in his new book, *Conservatism: An Invitation to the Great Tradition*, explicates the major lines of what he calls "philosophical" and "cultural" conservatism. Scruton argues that conservatism is about home, how we figure out what home is and how to create and sustain one.

---

Originally published in *National Review*, June 7, 2018.

Although the book is designed as an introductory text, even those who have followed Scruton will find it full of insight and a handy overview of the conservative tradition. Of particular note is how Scruton defends the relational aspect of conservative thought. Conservatism is not the unbounded "I" of the progressives (and some libertarians), but neither is it the undifferentiated mass of the socialist state. Rather, Scruton posits that the essence of conservatism is the I–thou, the "second person" perspective "in which the 'we' of social membership is balanced at every point against the 'I' of individual ambition." This tension therefore allows for communication between people of differing views to whom we owe an obligation, which allows for society and political organizations. In contrast, to posit an endless array of fully autonomous individuals—as, for example, Rousseau did—is to render civil society impossible.

The problem with understanding conservatism is that it has two creation stories. Liberalism really has only one: The French Revolution combined a political ideology of overthrowing the old European order with the vision of a new man unencumbered by religion or tradition. Although this vision has antecedents in Western history, it was the French Revolution that cemented the "liberal person" for the next two centuries through today. Political conservatism, too, was born in the French Revolution's aftermath, as a reaction to its excesses; we can see this birth most prominently in the work of Edmund Burke (who receives much attention in this volume).

Scruton recognizes that "we will understand modern conservatism as a political movement only if we see that some elements of liberal individualism have been programmed into it from the outset." Political theorists, including Locke, and social and political movements have rendered "reaction" obsolete; but that does not render conservatism itself unintelligible. That is because conservatism did not have only a political birth. Conservatism is older than the 1789 revolution, and built into the human condition. "Modern conservatism is a product of the Enlightenment. But it calls upon aspects of the human condition that can be witnessed in every civilization and at every period of history." The most important is what can be called the physicality of conservative belief in the person. The person is not self-created and limitlessly changeable, subject only to the individual will. A conservative believes in contingency; individuals do have choice, but our identities are shaped by loyalties and communities not of our own choosing. Society must balance "the need for custom and community" with "the freedom of the individual." Scruton sees that "extreme individualism" is a myth; it ignores "the indispensable part played by social membership in the exercise of free choice."

This social membership is in part what we call tradition, which, echoing Oakeshott, Scruton defines as a kind of knowledge. Tradition helps us to know how to act in accord with our human needs and relational obligations. Political bonds among liberal individuals are weak, because there are no other bonds. For Scruton, this is a category mistake in understanding how political societies come into being and how they remain stable, even under great pressure. For the basic bond is pre-political. That is, legitimacy precedes consent, not the other way around. We recognize a political authority as ours, made by a particular people at a particular place for goals we share. This is why people continue to live peaceably in a society even when the vote might go against their wishes. The recent liberal mantra that Trump is "not my president" is therefore a breakdown of democratic order, not a sign of its health.

So when conservatives say they defend "freedom," it is not some abstraction: "What they mean is *this* kind of freedom, the freedom enshrined in our legal and political inheritance, and in the free associations through which our societies renew their legacy of trust. So understood, freedom is the outcome of multiple agreements over time, under an overarching rule of law." How this happens, how a society maintains the balance between freedom and order, is conditioned by history, religion, custom, and tradition. Without these things the only option is some kind of reactionary authoritarianism, or its left-wing counterpart, political correctness. That is to say, the alternatives to conservatism replicate the very weaknesses liberals say they find in conservative thought.

Now one can already hear the liberal reaction: This view of political life is exclusionary, in that it deliberately cuts out of political society some who are not "like us." Scruton disagrees. Where we live matters, and every modern society is in some sense a society of strangers. Therefore, we have to find common bonds upon which to build, and we must start with the ones right in front of us: our neighborhood and nation, and our rights as citizens of a particular polity to which we give our consent. This is not a racial or religious concept, as those are false bases on which to build a modern political society. Because conservatism incorporates a respect for the individual, it can accommodate both political freedom and societal coherence. "The language of politics is spoken in the first person plural." We the People rule and should decide our own destiny.

In a concluding chapter, Scruton describes the current state of conservatism, which he places as a bulwark against both the "culture of repudiation" on the left and the rise of Islam within Europe. As a transnational "pre-political loyalty that is defined without reference to territory," Islam threatens the European nation-state system in ways that echo international socialism. Western-style tolerance is no defense against such a challenge, because such tolerance assumes common goals. Conservatism has an initial organizational disadvantage because it is local, concerned with particular communities, and so sometimes cannot see a threat until it is almost too late. Here, Scruton argues that European Christian civilization gives us a resource to "find credible alternatives" to extremism, in the injunction to love one's neighbor. The nation "is the means to reconcile people of different faiths and lifestyles." For progressives or religious extremists, there is no such thing as a nation, no obligation to understand and defend your neighbors simply because they are your neighbors and not try to change them into socialist man or "woke" citizens. Neighborliness at its best means peace, and conservatism is a necessary strand of any political practice wishing to attain it.

# *Who Are These People?*

**Perhaps because** of their beleaguered status for much of the postwar period, conservatives have had a special penchant for the conversion narrative, tapping into an American tradition of the redeemed sinner finding God in an unfaithful world. By now, the conservative *Bildungsroman* is a well-established genre. After living under liberal illusions, a chance encounter—a book, a professor, some event—opens the protagonist's eyes to conservative truths. The question that traditionally has occupied the conservative audience for such books concerns the type of conservatism the narrator will adopt. Would the young recovering liberal hero reject von Mises? Embrace Willmoore Kendall? What are his (or, sometimes, her) views of the South? Of tradition? These conversion narratives, in other words, reflected the intellectual ferment within conservatism and among conservatives as much as they related the mere rejection of liberalism.

*Why I Turned Right: Leading Baby Boom Conservatives Chronicle Their Political Journeys* is a celebrity version of the old tale, with a generational twist. Edited by Mary Eberstadt, the collection features contributions from "leading Baby Boom conservatives" who "chronicle their political journeys." Contributors include humorist P. J. O'Rourke, *New York Times* editorial writer David Brooks, *National Review's* Rich Lowry, psychiatrist and AEI Fellow Sally Satel, Heather MacDonald, an editor at *City Journal*, and others. As would be expected from such professional writers, these are polished essays, free with the dropping of names and book titles. At the level of a lazy weekend afternoon, their essays about how they confronted

Originally published in *Intercollegiate Review*, October 8, 2014.

their mostly liberal upbringings and education and came to some type of conservatism make a pleasant read.

There are a few exceptional pieces. Joseph Bottum offers a thoughtful meditation on how abortion and family resulted in his rejecting the permissiveness liberalism of his youth. "[R]eal conservatism," he writes, "usually begins when you find in yourself a limit, a place beyond which you will not go," a truth that liberal society—which Bottum calls "the pleasure dome," home of "niceness" and "coolness"—tries to conceal. Bottum connects his rejection of the permissive society with a web of arguments rooted in constitutional history and traditional religious faith, and offers an interpretation of conservatism in America as a balance between "the Bible and the Enlightenment." He recognizes the paradox that "the Bible may help produce the ethics a modern state needs to allow [for] freedom, but the Bible didn't start out as the ethics of liberal democracy." Belief is independent of modern democratic politics, but may be necessary to it. Hence, liberal "civic religion" is likely to fail—as is an evangelizing Republican Party.

Todd Lindberg, editor of *Policy Review*, gives a moving account of his own journey, beginning with a parent's death. Lindberg's sensibilities seem always to have been on the right, though initially with more of a libertarian emphasis. He writes that while labels are less important to him now than in his youth, he does not "mind being called a conservative or neoconservative," so long as the importance of individualism within that tradition is recognized. His intellectual process of appreciating the freedom he valued as a younger man may resonate with some today. Lindberg also reminds us that the neoconservatives, an influence on him as he developed his ideas about politics and social change, were once known for their hard-nosed realism in confronting social reality, and their ideas served as a gathering point for young people seeking a way out of liberalism.

Overall, however, the collection reflects the problems of what now passes for mainstream conservatism, which is perhaps better termed anti-liberalism. The first clue to the book's direction is there in the subtitle. The political is really the last kind of journey a conservative should undertake; political positions are at root only reflections of philosophical and religious conviction. This deeper journey, though it no doubt occurred with some of these contributors, is largely absent. Instead, the flashpoints for these conservatives are restricted to the university, politics, or the small world of opinion journals. Not for them is Russell Kirk's reflections on the modern mind as he sat in the Great Salt Desert during the war, or the worldly and CIA veteran Willmoore Kendall's conviction that the constitutional order was designed to protect a specifically American form of self-government against its enemies. No, the model here (though he oddly goes unmentioned in the text) is Frank Meyer, whose great struggle against Communism was the spur to his becoming a conservative, and whose lasting contributions to conservatism were largely in strategy and tactics. Substitute "political correctness" for Communism, and the tenor of these essays becomes clear, though the danger less pendent.

Accordingly, we hear much about politics, campus radicals, and "left-wing" economics, but not much about hearth or home, neighborhood or culture—or at least not much as to why those things are (or should be) central to a conservative vision. In the closing essay, Rich Lowry tries to connect his family and faith to his conservatism, and his evocation of "filial piety" as grounding for his beliefs echoes Bottum's notion of a limit. But Lowry is a little younger than most of the other contributors, hinting perhaps at an intra-Boomer difference that is left unexplored, and this promising approach is not developed. Richard Starr, a managing editor at the *Weekly Standard*, mentions in passing his childhood on a farm and his respect for those who work outdoors with their hands, but he does not connect that background to the question of why he is a conservative now. Instead, we get a snub of Jimmy Carter's recognition of the limitations of national power. Far from being ridiculous, however, Carter's recognition is (or should be) a core conservative political insight, especially in light of the current adventures in the Middle East. That Carter was wrong about much else need not doom this insight. Indeed, Iraq is only occasionally mentioned here, and only positively when it is.

References to what were once considered rather humdrum conservative principles are now treated as punch lines. Some of the contributors, for example, explain that they got "really" conservative only after they had children. Fair enough, though that sounds like a line polished for Georgetown or Upper West Side cocktail parties as an excuse, not a defense, of their conservatism. But why? There is little sense, in other words, of what these contributors believe is worth conserving. For an earlier generation, conservation was the central issue: trying to convince themselves and others of the viability of the Western tradition against Communism abroad and liberalism at home. Of course, there were variations even then. Kirk, for example, thought liberalism had exhausted itself by the 1960s, and that Western civilization was moving into a new age whose identity had not been determined but whose content would be formed not through rational argumentation but through imaginative recreation of a tradition that would inspire loyalty and devotion and which was rooted in the permanent things of human existence.

Indeed, it is not even clear how far these putative conservative converts have really "journeyed" at all, despite the book's title. A few contributors are not shy about admitting that they are, in fact, not conservative. Brooks says he "drifts to the left on social issues" and calls the Iraq adventure "one of the noblest endeavors the United States, or any great power, has ever undertaken." Political theorist Peter Berkowitz believes "conserving liberalism itself is among our most pressing public tasks." Starr and Stanley Kurtz remain committed to versions of the "open minded" liberalism of their youth. MacDonald, scarred by her experiences with indoctrinating professors in the academy, wants a return to "old-fashioned liberal values" in academic life. And Satel proclaims she is "embarrassed to be in the same camp as moral conservatives and the religious right.... I am pro-choice, pro-Darwin, and pro-stem cell."

The tenor of such statements is not that their authors have become conservative, but rather that the older liberalism with which they are comfortable has moved on. If the Harvard faculty had not turned to postmodernism, or if the Democratic Party had not embraced multiculturalism, it seems, they would have remained contented liberals. In other words, to paraphrase Ronald Reagan: they have not changed, liberalism has.

Then why are they here, in a book marketed as a collection of conservative conversion stories? They are here, one can only conclude, because the kind of conservatism represented in this collection is a harmless one that does not actually threaten Brooks's editors at the *Times* or Eberstadt's publishers. These writers are for the most part deeply mortared into the New York–Washington political and cultural axes. They publish in mainstream liberal journals and differ from their liberal contemporaries mostly in their specific policy prescriptions. So these widely trumpeted "firebrands" are free to take their swipes at diversity-mongering in college admissions, feminist follies, and the like, while the corrosive cultural elites who loathe traditional values remain in power, their core commitments undisturbed by a genuine opposition.

Indeed, constructing so mild a "mainstream right" pushes other conservatives, whose claims are more pointed, farther to the cultural sidelines. Absent from this volume, for example, are positions such as Rod Dreher's "crunchy cons" or what they might mean to a conservative realignment. Nor are there mentions of other Boomer conservatives whose vision is sharply at odds with those presented here. Bill Kauffman's intellectual journey from Hill staffer for Senator Moynihan to the author of several books offering a wholesale reworking of an American tradition of regionalism—which directly challenges both the tenets of liberalism and of this kind of "mainstream conservatism"—would have been a perfect counterpoint to the potted histories presented here. The contrast of his roughly contemporaneous journey would have brought a little fire to this collection, and also reminded us that conservatives once heatedly disputed their commitments. Of course, the inclusion of a voice like that of Kauffman's is almost unimaginable in such a collection.

Ultimately, therefore, *Why I Turned Right* disappoints. Each personal journey is unique and worthy of respect—for who can see into another's mind and soul?—yet not all of them need be shared with the world. The contributions reflect an anodyne conservatism that differs in kind and not only in degree from the stronger stuff that animated the conservative movement since the end of World War II. These particular conversions, with few exceptions, are unlikely to capture the imagination of those young people forming their own conservative consciences today.

# *Authentic Conservative*

**I MET JAMES POULOS MANY YEARS AGO,** at a bar on K Street in Washington DC. He was studying political theory, but contemplating a move back to Los Angeles and away from graduate studies. He spoke in an intoxicating, discursive way about Tocqueville, Napoleon, and current conservatism. It was clear that academia was the wrong fit.

Poulos now writes for outlets as varied as VICE and Forbes, finding an audience in territory alien to the Right. He takes popular culture much more seriously than most conservatives, partly because our era is something new, he argues. As likely to quote Marilyn Manson or Lady Gaga as Descartes or Rousseau and sometimes all at once, alongside *The Big Lebowski* and the Kardashians, his prose has a distinctive voice. His residency in Los Angeles, a postmodern, low-culture city where individuals confront questions of what to *do* with their abundant freedom, is in this respect crucial.

Poulos first came to widespread attention through the blogs Culture11 and Postmodern Conservative. In an interview after Culture11's demise, Poulos reflected on the "predicament" of the individual: "convincing people—especially younger people—that a life in which political liberty has been readily surrendered in exchange for great cultural or 'personal' freedom is not a good life, either individually or socially." Surrendering political liberty, it turns out, releases new communal pathologies that transcend our usual left-right spectrum. Poulos edges toward a "postmodern conservatism" that wrestles with the decadence in contemporary life.

Originally published in *Claremont Review of Books*, January 27, 2017.

A series of essays in *The Federalist* in 2014 argued that we are living in "the pink police state"—not an Orwellian dystopia, or a Communist workers' paradise, or even a Tocquevillian soft despotism, but something new:

> a robust regulatory state that pursues health and safety at the expense of liberty in the context of a culture that demands robust interpersonal freedom. Rather than stamping out hedonistic pursuits and pleasure-centered living, 1984 style, the new statism creates a "safe" space for their "healthy" experience. Yet, rather than expanding the project limitlessly, Brave New World style, so as to make all pleasure official, the new statism tacitly acknowledges that our most potent appetites can never be fully domesticated, even with all the tools of force, surveillance, and coercion at the government's disposal.

For this new age, a new criticism is needed, one Poulos now presents in *The Art of Being Free: How Alexis de Tocqueville Can Save Us from Ourselves.*

Tocqueville is again Poulos's guide, because as the first and greatest interpreter of the new, democratic era, he understood the pernicious effect of equality. We, as the inheritors of American democracy, do not grasp the meaning of equality in our individual or collective lives. This era is *crazy*, in Poulos' terms, and threatens to drive us crazy as well. *Being Free* traces our insanity to the "Great Transformation" from an aristocratic age to a democratic one. Contrary to what we may think, the transition to the democratic age is not complete. Even though our personal lives change quickly and drastically, the larger culture's movement is a "slow fade-out of the first and slow fade-in of the second." Tocqueville is the perfect guide to this transformation because he "understood better than anyone how the dramatic craziness of life was a *constitutive*, baked-in part of Americans." Tocqueville's insight is that in this new age we believe that the quest for individual, personalized equality is more crucial than political inequalities.

Poulos understands the self not as a *what* but a *how*—an adverb rather than a noun or adjective. He wants us to explore how we are "crazily, selfishly, and melodramatically" at the core of our individuality, dimly aware that our being has a quality of arbitrariness. We are cast into "a kind of internal motion that feels beyond our power to control, not just because our relationships often have that effect on us but also because, deep down, we know that not really being in charge of ourselves is part and parcel of the life we live." We can no longer take comfort in the past's certainties, yet the wonders of the future promised by the Enlightenment have yet to arrive.

In other words, political freedom in a liberal democracy isn't enough. Poulos wants us to be "freely," that is, "experiencing our freedom, which is always already a part of all our relationships, chosen and unchosen, including with any of our supposed selves." Here Poulos draws a line between our over-medicalized identification of mental disorders to our longing to escape our craziness through identifying with others who are like ourselves. He argues: "[i]nstead of confronting us with the unsolvability of life, throwing our spread-thin selves back on our stretched-thin resources, disorders give us concrete problems that we can wrap our minds around—and that science in the form of prescriptions, can throw its massive resources into." Poulos contends that the diagnosing hinders rather than helps: "Allegedly, we Americans are more autonomous than ever. Many of us intuit that, in other ways, we're more tethered than ever to our debt, our baggage, our issues."

After setting up the problem of the self, Poulos confronts what it means to "live freely" when faced with questions such as change, money, God, sex, death, and love. This is not a political book, he stresses. He calls it sociology, but it's really more like social psychology.

Consider money, a common medium of exchange not only of goods but of values. In aristocratic ages, money was ignoble and disdained. But in democratic ages concentrated wealth causes cultural unease. As Tocqueville writes, rich democrats may try to ape their aristocratic forbears, making the rest of us feel insignificant by comparison. What "we fear most of all," writes Poulos, "is that money is so powerful that it can, by a horrible magic, *resurrect* the aristocratic age, returning the true and scary difference of human *kinds*, obliterating our diverse but united humankind with its equalized, nonthreatening multitude of superficial human equalities." But this would be a kind of oligarchy, since aristocracies are based on heritage and unchosen affiliations. Money reflects value in the age of equality, so oligarchic rule assumes that the rich are better than we are in obtaining the goods and values we would deserve...if only we worked harder or were more attractive. Money fuels our insanity. Fortunately, by acknowledging money's importance but also by requiring us to develop civic associations where we can live freely without succumbing the lures of the art of the deal, Tocqueville shows us a way out.

*The Art of Being Free* is not the standard conservative critique. Many conservatives want to go back, either to the autonomous self, uncontaminated by radical equality, or to some other imagined premodern world. Poulos's view to them is simply a surrender to the spirit of the age.

But Poulos is crafting a new way of reclaiming an authentic humanity in a world where the old certainties are fading or becoming only one choice among many. In the late Zygmunt Bauman's phrase, in a world of "liquid modernity," we must find a different path. But Poulos goes one step farther. Only by acknowledging that craziness can we begin to reclaim those things that make us human and free. He places the mystery of grace at the center of our experience of God, for example. That experience is important in an age suspicious of mystery. Mystery cannot be controlled. It allows us to deal with our uniqueness and commonality, our eternal destiny and cosmic insignificance.

*The Art of Being Free* is a book for our age: messy, a little crazy, and luminous.

# *Conservatism in the Time of Trump*

**The election of Donald Trump** has upended the expectations of what paleoconservatives and others have long called Conservatism, Inc. The influence of establishment conservatism all but evaporated during the primaries, as its chosen champions—Bush, Rubio, Cruz, Jindal, and the rest—fell one by one. As President-Elect, Trump moved away from an unthinking reliance on Republican lobbyists and cronies. And while his administration appointments have not reflected a uniform rejection of conventional Republicans, they have been better by a long shot than any Hillary Clinton (or any of Trump's Republican challengers) would have made. More importantly, he has changed the way the establishment must think about issues and about the voters whom they have treated with disdain for so long.

This election may have been the first one clearly to show that we no longer live in a free society: We are only choosing one style of authoritarian over another. Had Clinton been elected, the country would have had yet another president starting undeclared wars, authorizing drone strikes, continuing a policy of essentially unrestricted immigration, and forcing religious believers to violate their faith through the imposition of oppressive regulations. Trump, though he has broken the progressive hold on discourse, may prove to be an authoritarian of another kind, one who will make deals to keep companies in the United States and in this and other ways be more appealing to voters. Indeed, a case can be made that the erratic Trump might inadvertently convince Americans that perhaps the

Originally published in *Chronicles*, February 2017.

imperial presidency is no great idea, especially in the hands of people temperamentally unsuited to the power it confers on them. The conservative establishment's hold on voters may actually offer the country a chance to return to something like the republic the United States was formed to be.

It is notable, however, that Republican critics of Trump seem unaware that it is their own ideas which voters are rejecting. Conservatism, as distinct from the Republican Party, may thus be weaker than its political boosters have allowed. For example, the GOP-controlled Congress was unable to act to close down the corrupt Export-Import bank, defund Planned Parenthood, take a firm stand against U.S. military adventures abroad, or even to protect women from having to register for the draft. At the state level, several Republican governors have surrendered their position on transgender-rights bills after pressures were exerted on them by various interests including big business, a constituency establishment conservatives largely, though falsely, continue to believe is with them.

The old formulas don't work with an electorate that has seen economic opportunities disappear under financial capitalism, their culture and traditions ridiculed, and their children encouraged by state-funded schools to resent their own history. Ritual invocation of the Reaganite diptych of limited government and a strong national defense is increasingly anachronistic. After 15 years of war, most conservatives perceive that there is nothing limited about a government that wages those wars. The Republican establishment, still enthralled by obsolete Cold War tropes, recognized a great advantage to be gained in furthering a militarized state, which allowed them at once to assert their patriotism and to increase their power. Culturally and intellectually, conservatives have proved a dismal failure. While the country may not be as progressive today as it might have been absent resistance from the conservative establishment, it is surely not more conservative than it was a single generation ago.

Therefore, the age of Trump may be one of opportunity for a resurgence in true conservative thought. Indeed, the most interesting conservative commentary is coming from areas outside the mainstream Republican or conservative structure. Some, such as this magazine, *The American*

*Conservative*, and upstart websites like the (now defunct) *Journal of American Greatness* have considered "Trumpism" more seriously than his opponents, or even Trump himself, has. Those ideas—insofar as Trump can be said to have ideas—echo those of Pat Buchanan, the last major challenger to establishment-conservative dogma. Economic nationalism, restrictions on immigration, and an America First foreign policy were all brought into prominence by Buchanan in the early 1990's, though once they were pretty much a staple of American self-understanding. That they have been reanimated now by Donald Trump perhaps says more about how conservatives treat ideas than it does about Trump.

Thus, George Hawley's *Right-Wing Critics of American Conservatism* comes at an opportune time, and indeed Hawley, an assistant professor of political science at the University of Alabama, gained some prominence after the election as one of only a few academics who had considered even the possibility of a Trump victory. Since February of last year, he predicted that the Upper Midwest would be the key to a Republican presidential victory, and so it was. Nonetheless, in light of this election, Hawley's main thesis needs to be reworked.

The difficulty with his thesis is that Hawley treats the "conservatism" that has been the object of "right-wing" critiques as essentially the typical Republican nostrums crushed by Trump. Hawley begins with Paul Gottfried's definition of conservatism as whatever at any given moment opposes the left, which seeks above all else the imposition of an absolutist conception of equality. Like Sauron and his Ring, equality is the one principle to rule all others. Yet this raises a conceptual problem for Hawley, since he recognizes (as does Gottfried) that even the mainstream conservative movement embraces equality, just less stridently. Therefore, Hawley settles for a definition in which "the right will be defined as encompassing all those ideologies that, while not necessarily rejecting equality as a social good, do not rank it at the top of the hierarchy of values." But "mainstream conservatism" for Hawley is basically a constellation of think tanks, political columnists, and lobbying firms in Washington, D.C.—that is, the same groups that supported almost anyone other than Trump.

Of course, adjusting the definition turns this analysis upside down. Politics is downstream of culture, as most serious conservative thinkers have recognized. Russell Kirk, for his part, identified several elements that make up the conservative worldview, including the defense of variety and multiplicity, a respect for the moral order, a recognition of the need for hierarchy and order in society, localism, and a disdain for abstraction, including abstract economic man. If that is conservatism, who are the "right-wing" critics?

After two chapters that provide a serviceable introduction to some of the major themes of conservative history in the 1950's and 60's, Hawley devotes seven chapters to considering various critiques of conservatism, as he has defined it. Hawley is not an unsympathetic observer of conservative movements, and he tries to be straightforward even as he warns of the dangers some of these movements present. Yet the problem his thesis sets up is evident when one investigates these movements, especially in light of the election. Hawley gives libertarians two chapters (one for "mainstream" libertarians, another for "radical" ones), but he affords "localists" and paleoconservatives a chapter each, the same as he does "white nationalism." Yet this last chapter is not really an explanation of whether or how white nationalism makes a legitimate critique of mainstream conservatism. It seems to have been included because, in the progressive academic world Hawley inhabits, Bill Kauffman and his American localism, and Pat Buchanan and his economic nationalism, are on the same spectrum as racists, as all forms of conservatism are presumed to be tainted by racism and race hatred. This of course is nonsense, and indeed every other group in Hawley's book would rightly condemn anyone who tried to align white nationalists with conservatives.

This perspective makes the book less valuable than it might have been. Hawley does demonstrate a familiarity with conservative scholarly and primary sources, and he can see nuance among various positions. He notes accurately that "one could fairly argue that American conservatism has become calcified and lacks intellectual energy. Conservative talking points remain virtually unchanged since the 1980s." Many critics of conservatism would agree with that. But to get the fuller picture one must acknowledge that *liberal* talking points have also "calcified." Given Hawley's political focus, he could have noted in passing the collapse of the number of Democratic elected officials in Congress and state offices since 2008. Why is this happening? Is it because something new has been brewing in the Republican electorate—since 2008 surely, but also perhaps since Buchanan's run for the Republican nomination in 1996? Hawley doesn't ask this question, because his view appears to be that these other movements are no more than appendages to mainstream conservatism.

Hawley cautions conservatives against adopting "an anti-intellectual tone":

> Although a populism that pits ordinary Americans against out-of-touch intellectuals is politically useful, it will make it more difficult to advance a conservative political theory capable of solving twenty-first century problems.

It is true that a knee jerk anti-intellectualism is a weakness of the American right, but Hawley does not really consider that the program advocated obscurely by Trump but more clearly by men like Buchanan is in fact grounded in a political theory meant to address contemporary problems. Hawley is content instead to note that currently no "major think tanks or high-profile political figures advocat[e] substantive policies that would reverse" the trends toward greater globalization and centralization of economic and political power.

# *Can We Patch Up the Right?*

**Asking whether the Right** can be repaired seems strange; to some, the Right seems resurgent. There is a Republican in the White House, Senator Mitch McConnell is confirming judges as fast as his Republican majority can vote for them, the economy, while not without its problems, seems to be doing well, and some of the controversies of the Obama years (such as religious liberty) seem to be moving in a conservative direction. Indeed, given these factors, there are pretty good odds we will have another Trump term. Our friends on the left would also likely argue that the 2016 presidential election announced the triumph of the Right. The 1950s are here again, rights are being "rolled back," and the secular, progressive future cleansed of "deplorables" and enforced by bureaucrats wielding "dear colleague" letters, health regulations, and activist judges has been thrown into turmoil, if not jeopardy.

But as is well known now, inside the Right, the situation looks much different. The Trump presidency threw the "official" Right into turmoil. Establishment magazines such as *The Weekly Standard* and *National Review* took anti-Trump stances, while others were more cautious. After the demise of *The Weekly Standard*, several online sites arose to stake a claim as the anti-Trump right, while *National Review* pivoted to allow more favorable coverage of the president. But this foment is only partially about ideas.

The "Right" is a combination of the political movement embedded in the Republican Party, whose aim is to win elections, and the conservative

---

Originally published in *Law & Liberty*, April 1, 2020.

intellectual movement, which is supposed to explain why the elections are worth winning. Part of the current argument simply reflects the recognition that the conservative firmament—the well-funded ecosystem of think tanks, pundits, position papers, conferences, and the like that has grown up over the past thirty years—did not really foresee, and had little directly to do with, Trump's victory. That was a political failing, but that failing revealed more serious intellectual issues. The old unities have broken up, and hidden divisions, along economic, political, and cultural lines, are again in the open. Conservatives love to write think-pieces about the history of various factions, exploring the nature of conservatism and proposing new juxtapositions; I've written a few myself, and there have been such pieces as long as there has been a conservatism. But as evidenced by the repudiation of the mainstream conservative candidates in 2016, this work has become detached from the concerns of actual Americans.

Since at least the early 1990s, when I first became involved in conservative intellectual work, the Reagan collection of cultural conservatives, economic libertarians, and anticommunists lamented the lost three-legged stool that had brought conservatism to victories in 1980 and 1988, even as the world that created that coalition dissolved. The three Reagan-era groups were united by a common enemy. Communism was godless, so the cultural conservatives were on board. Communism was, well, communist, so the libertarians signed up to resist "big government" back home, and as for the anti-communists that speaks for itself, although the energy in defeating communism too often spilled over into expanding America's power (hard or "soft") abroad just because we could. After the Clinton years, a brief glimmer of hope arose in 2000 that George W. Bush, himself a believing Christian, would temper the country's foreign policy adventurism and cultural decay. But this was lost in the aftermath of September 11.

Roger Scruton in *The Meaning of Conservatism* discussed the relationship between conservative thinking and conservative practice in this way: "if it is true that conservatism becomes conscious only when it is forced to be so, then it is inevitable that the passage from practice to theory will not be rewarded by any immediate influence from theory back to what is done." A lot of the history of conservatism since is reflected in that sentence. There has been much conservative theorizing since the 1980s, but its success as translated back into conservative practice is disputable. For reasons Dan McCarthy spells out in his "A New Conservative Agenda," political elites, including conservative ones, have been sleepwalking through the twenty-first century and many had not, until the election of 2016, realized the world had changed. This rupture had been building way before Trump. In 2012, for example, I noted in *Perspectives on Political Science* that the emergence of the Tea Party may have represented a different type of conservative renascence, because the issues motivating them might cause them to avoid capture by Washington and Beltway conservatism.

So in different ways, conservatives have been trying to patch themselves up again for the better part of three decades. Even in the wake of Trump, traces of the old Reaganism survive. Some think the answer is to return to Reagan—this time as Democrats (the problem of rightwing pundits equating conservatism with presidential elections is a subject for another time). The 2020 National Conservatism conference, whose inaugural conference last year made such a splash as illustrative of the new conservative turn, invokes both Reagan and Pope St. John Paul II, a headline that could have been used for a DC conservative convention through the 1990s. Others want conservatives to avoid tribalism, but conclude conservatives are just being mean these days. And you can still find the occasional paean to global capitalism. Indeed, Jay Nordlinger threw up his hands in trying to find out "What Unites the Right?"

But the success of that postwar patchwork was always overstated, and one should be cautious in using that as an example of how conservatism should conduct itself today. There is perhaps a reasonable argument that government is smaller than it would have been had liberals won in 1980 or 1988, but one cannot argue that government is small as such or that its power has not grown to levels unimaginable to 1950s or 1960s conservatives (or liberals for that matter). But it is almost impossible to argue that culturally America is a more conservative place, in almost any sense of the term, than it was in 1980, which is simply a crushing blow to large parts of the conservative intellectual project. The progressive left has essentially won the culture war, although that victory was only cemented when corporations began (as Timothy Crimmins wrote recently in *American Affairs*) to "engage in progressive (rather than transgressive) culture-warring, to distract from rising discontent with rising inequality and dwindling wages." In other words, as Bruce Frohnen and Ted McAllister state in their recent book, *Coming Home*, "Cold War conservatism gained the world and lost its soul." The strains of conservative thought that stressed locality, hostility to militarism, and suspicion of "free markets" were submerged into a narrative that stressed instead global capitalism and democracy export.

We do not need to pause too long on the charge that patching up the Right would mean "going back." Entering into that argument is a progressive trap: sing the praises of the past, and one is a reactionary. But agree that settled political or cultural arrangements should be retained, and conservatism is accused of lacking principle and simply accepting whatever the current arrangements happen to be. Now, as Chesterton once said, the objection that one cannot turn back the clock is misplaced. A society, like a clock, is human-made, and we can turn it to wherever we like. But trying to patch together an alliance when the motivating forces that made that alliance worthwhile have dissipated or disappeared will end up being a fruitless enterprise. We need instead to think about what conservatism is for, before we can figure out who the allies may be. Conservatives would do well to focus once again on Scruton's "what is done," which I take to mean how Americans actually live today and what set of economic and political arrangements available in our constitutional system make the most sense. Some have already started to do that, but not all of them are conservatives in the expected sense.

So the old patchwork no longer works; it represents, as a group of *First Things* writers suggest, a "dead consensus." Is a new one worthwhile? As I have suggested, one positive thing about the (most recent) break-up of conservatism is that it has allowed some of the old profusion of conservative thought back into the conversation. The biggest example of this perhaps is the antiwar tradition that bloomed after the September 11 terrorist attacks and the ensuing endless wars in Iraq and Afghanistan, and reflected in the founding of *The American Conservative*. But that is not the only opportunity for a return to the rich sources of American conservatism. Kenneth Kersch, in his recent book *Conservatives and the Constitution*, cites a number of different ways conservatives of the 1950s and 1960s approached the Constitution. Not all conservative thinkers were what would today be considered originalists, for example, and some had a robust view of the connection between culture and the Constitution that differs from contemporary conservatives. And George Hawley discusses several groups, from paleoconservatives to radical libertarians, who have critiqued mainstream conservatives from the right. I would also note here the emergence of a more fully articulated black conservatism, which differs at crucial points from mainstream conservatism. This body of thought, I would argue, might very well have remained muted under the old dispensation, heavily indebted as conservative intellectual life was to white Southern influence. If there is one thing conservatism can do in this still-new century, it would be to integrate the African American experience into its defense of communities.

The role of government, for example, is rapidly shifting in conservative debate. Since the 1980s, if not before, the Right has been obsessed (with some exceptions) with reducing government, of any size, at every level, for any purpose, in order to counteract creeping socialism which in any event did not resonate with most Americans. But in fact, conservatives have often been just as interested in the power of government to coerce behavior as liberals have been, but too often have not really thought about what that means, except perhaps as an instrument to an ill-defined "liberty." "Law and order" conservatives, so popular in the 1980s of my youth, was simply another way of saying that power matters, and deciding what is legal and permissible, or illegal and prohibited, is in part a reflection of the common good of that community.

Russell Kirk often connected order in the individual with order in the commonwealth. As a localist—and a somewhat eccentric individual himself—Kirk primarily looked at this question from the bottom up; if individuals were well ordered, the commonwealth would also be. But he also understood the power of government, and knew that sometimes people come together to reflect the good they have in common through government. As Kirk wrote in his *Prospects for Conservatives*, he offered that this view of order, which he called Johnsonian, should be combined with what he called the Burkean. "Burke, however, though awake to the moral climate of opinion, believed that the particular system of social organization under which a people exist helps to shape their moral character, and therefore must receive the most sedulous attention." I had always understood this insight as part of the conservative critique of endless war. Conservatives opposed war, and especially the indeterminate occupation of various countries, not just because such wars were unjust and caused harm to the people in those countries at great cost to ours. Military occupation destroys the character of the people doing the occupying as well; the nation becomes militaristic, used to the casual cruelties of war and the solvent to family, locality, and culture such militarism brings.

Scruton similarly noted the intertwining of private society and the power of the state through the power of the law. Concepts like freedom do not exist in the abstract, and are embedded in the particular constitutions and customs of the particular nations in which they exist. Law is there to enforce and express the boundaries of those concepts in accordance with how the people see themselves and, ultimately, in accordance with their common good. Indeed, Scruton writes that contrary to a liberal individualistic view of the law, "the legitimate sphere of law will be all that matters to social continuity, all that can be taken as standing in need of state protection."

This fits nicely with the American federalist system properly understood; as Frohnen and McAllister recognize, Americans' dedication to local government "was prior to, and higher than, their love of individual freedom." Limited government need not be powerless government, and that at governmental levels closer to the people, government can do more. Now this claim has a natural objection: as someone on social media phrased it, the Shire needs Gondor. That is, for localities to be preserved or thrive, a strong state must stand above them. And that state must be run by people with the good of their people in mind; as political thinkers from Xenophon to James Burnham have written, the character of the regime is set by those who run it. A kind of nationalism, therefore, is not inconsistent with conservatism, but I suppose I am only a faint-hearted nationalist. Gondor only makes sense *because* it allows for Shires to thrive and it is even better that the Shire is only half aware of Gondor's protection.

Conservatives used to join the concept of nationalism with the countervailing factor of patriotism, which was more clearly articulated in the work of the late historian John Lukacs. He wrote that patriotism "is the love of one's land and its history," while "nationalism is a viscous cement that binds formless masses together." Nationalism faces outward, contrasting our nation with others, while patriotism at its best is inward. Moreover, although loyalty to one's nation in the abstract is one thing all Americans have in common, it must not be the only thing. Other loyalties need to be cultivated as well. Although many conservatives are finding nationalism attractive, more work needs to be done on developing a nationalism that puts America's interests first while reviving the country's heritage of devotion to and participation in local governments of real power. The patchwork between nationalists and localists needs to be a little more finely threaded.

The stolid Republican industrialists who did not want to rock the cultural boat have been replaced by Silicon Valley disruptors and woke global corporations. The anticommunists have had careers as Middle East experts and adjuncts to empire. The libertarians win victories, but are at risk of losing the war. Simply put, we need to cultivate new sources of conservative thinking, but conservative sentiment as well.

When I was writing my book on "postmodern conservatism," I found writers who shared conservative sentiments without adopting the Right's political commitments; indeed, one of the inspirations of the book was an essay by David Rieff on the easy alliance between multiculturalism (which conservatives are supposed to dislike) and capitalism (which conservatives were supposed to like). Some of these were also described in books like

Rod Dreher's *Crunchy Cons*. Since writing that book, there is now a large middle ground where people are feeling their way for new answers: they know community is dissolving but are trapped in a discourse (on both right and left) that assumes rights are prior to responsibilities, and are told to disdain obligations in favor of self-fulfillment. Looking at the contemporary situation, where writers like Peter Augustine Lawler landed was that modernity had, in a very real sense, ended, and that conservatism was the only worldview that could survive the transformation. Modernity was about transcending limits, but postmodernity will be about recognizing ourselves as bounded, relational individuals once again. The narrative and unifying principles for that "postmodern" world have yet to be developed, but would not likely replicate the political allegiances of the preceding periods.

Conservative intellectual work takes place on a number of levels, but too much of it has neglected Kirk's view that at times, change is the means to our preservation. The Reagan coalition thrived because it had an external enemy that was equally committed to the West's defeat. The post 9/11 conservative coalition, in retrospect, seems artificial. Americans wanted to fight terror, yes, but didn't want to be in the Middle East as an occupying force, and the cultural situation between 1950 and 2001 rendered the national unity of the former impracticable in the latter. The current conservative alignment has an adversary in progressivism but its proponents are, in fact, also Americans. So conservatives need to rediscover common ground as Americans. As Kirk and others knew, people naturally are drawn to tradition and continuity. Any conservative patchwork should include all those who recognize that common human drive.

# PART FOUR

## *Humanist Heroes*

# *Christopher Dawson: Christ in History*

**As one of the premier Catholic historians** in this century, Christopher Dawson sought to rehabilitate both the history of salvation and religion in Europe. Strongly embraced by conservatives today, Dawson was considered an innovative scholar among his peers. Even after Dawson's conversion in 1919, his interdisciplinary approach to history stirred controversy among Catholic scholars. Dawson drew on the emerging disciplines of anthropology and sociology to construct a fresh interpretation of the Christian past and incorporated popular culture and art into his historical analysis.

Dawson wrote with two different audiences in mind. He sought both to displace the bankrupt Victorian and Edwardian liberalism of his own day and to shake the complacency of his coreligionists who preferred to bask in the quickly fading light of false medievalism. His carefully crafted prose revealed a nuanced and original understanding of Western history.

To combat "scientific" theories of progress, Dawson argued that every civilization relies on those who most fully represent its ideals and shape the culture through their actions. Dawson maintained that "history is at once aristocratic and revolutionary. It allows the whole world situation to be suddenly transformed by the action of a single individual." It is this dynamic historical process that is fatal to a secular understanding of religious approaches to history. In the words of Edmund Burke that Dawson quoted with approval, at times a "common soldier, a child, a girl at the door of an inn have changed the face of the future and almost of Nature."

---

Originally published in *Crisis*, April 1996.

To the Christian, this understanding of historical development permits interpretation of past events in the light of divine will and spiritual forces that may be unknown even to the actors themselves.

Dawson set out for himself the task of explaining the twofold nature of Christian history: while the Christian faith embodies eternal values and the teachings of God, it nevertheless transforms utterly the cultures it contacts. When the Christian faith enters into a culture, as when it first burst upon an overcivilized and jaded Rome, it begins a spiritual regeneration that affects not only the material, external culture, but the interior constitution of its members. In an essay entitled "The Christian View of History," Dawson wrote:

> For the Christian doctrine of the Incarnation is not simply a theophany—a revelation of God to Man; it is a new creation—the introduction of a new spiritual principle which gradually leavens and transforms human nature into something new. The history of the human race hinges on this unique divine event which gives meaning to the whole historical process.

This new, world-transforming history overthrows its rivals, whether the Greek idea of an endless series of repeating cycles or the spiritless homogeneity of the "postmodern" era. The Incarnation gives shape to history and supplies a beginning, a middle, and an end: "the Christian view of history is a vision of history *sub specie aeternitatis*, an interpretation of time in terms of eternity and of human events in the light of divine revelation." This concentration on the physical substance of the Christian faith was a conscious counterweight to overly aesthetic theories of Christianity, such as the "super-Christianity" of Matthew Arnold, for example, which reduced the force of religious belief to a set of humanistic nostrums.

The figures whom Dawson chose to study highlight his interest in the transformative power of the Christian faith: St. Augustine, who formed Christian thought out of the ruins of the old world order; St. Thomas Aquinas, whose reception of the Greek-Arabic body of scientific knowledge created a new movement in Western thinking without compromising its integrity; and St. Ignatius Loyola, who inaugurated a new spirituality to confront the challenges of the Reformation. Dawson saw the present age as one similar to that of Augustine or Ignatius, and in need of saints who have the vision to lead the faithful into the next era. The Western world, he thought, was facing another of its "cultural discontinuities" that displace the old order and usher in a new social reality. The question that remained, for Dawson as for Eliot, was whether this new era was to be Christian or a "new civilization which recognizes neither moral laws nor human rights."

Dawson wished first to reassert the importance of a millennium of Christian belief to modern history. It is not necessary to be a Christian to recognize that Christianity has played a profound role in shaping European culture and that "there is no aspect of European life which has not been profoundly affected" by that faith. Dawson sought to counter the skeptics of his day who saw in Christianity at best a series of moral tales (and at worst mere pretexts) that had no lasting influence on Western social practice or political arrangements. This aspect of his writings won him many admirers, including T. S. Eliot and Arnold Toynbee.

A more basic issue for Dawson was the nature of the history to be taught once the importance of Christianity to Western history became established. In 1960 Dawson noted the rise during the previous decades of an extreme nationalism among the nations of Europe, a development that led "every European people to insist on what distinguished it from the rest, instead of what united it with them." This undue stress on national differences has been coupled with a denial of the spiritual foundations of European unity. We do not need to look far to see that nationalist and ethnic violence continue to threaten Europe and that the "wall of separation" remains as high as ever in the nations of the West.

Dawson's commitment to recover the moral basis of Christian society is an ambitious one. In a late work, *Understanding Europe*, Dawson describes the task in this way:

> If we are to make the ordinary man aware of the spiritual unity out of which all the separate activities of our civilization have arisen, it is necessary in the first place to look at Western civilization as a whole and to treat it with the same objective appreciation and respect which the humanists of the past devoted to the civilization of antiquity.

In contrast to a nation centered view of European history, Dawson advocated the study of Europe as a cultural whole, united by a common faith and moral standards. He focuses on Europe, but includes the other non-Western Christian societies, such as North Africa and the Orthodox churches. His point, in essence, is a simple one. One cannot understand the whole by studying only the parts, and if the whole is forgotten or explained away as unimportant, we condemn ourselves to ignorance. Dawson saw much of Europe's difficulty arising either out of a loss of historical memory, as in Dawson's own England, or from the Nazi and communist attempts to make Christianity into a stage along the road of Aryan domination or the classless society.

Dawson contended that it was precisely the gap between Christian principles and their realization that provides the drama of European history, a position that caused some tensions with more traditional Catholic historians. Drawing on St. Augustine, Dawson saw the conflict between the City of God and the City of Man in every age, from the simple dualism between Christian civilization and barbarism in the pages of Bede to the sharp inner tensions seen in the writings of Pascal. Although recognizing its divisiveness, Dawson had kind words for the reformers' zeal for the Gospel, as it provided an impetus for a reinterpretation of the Catholic faith that gave rise to the Baroque era and the great works of the counterreformation.

In a passage evocative of contemporary problems, Dawson described the fundamental challenge to Christian culture as "the revolt against the moral process of Western culture and the dethronement of the individual conscience from its dominant position at the heart of the cultural process."

The medieval insight concerning the central importance of the rationality and freedom of the individual personality, an insight that is a hallmark of Western thought, is in danger of being overwhelmed by a reabsorption of the individual person to a collective identity, whether it be based upon nationality, ethnicity, or gender.

When Western society no longer emphasizes moral effort and personal responsibility, Dawson questions the very survival of civilization as Christendom has known it for a thousand years. Modernity is not merely a return to a pre-Christian paradise, as some New Age adherents would claim; rather, it is a sudden wrenching of the course of history. Instead of a slow reversal of the past millennium, Dawson says, "Neo-paganism jumps out of the top-story window, and whether one jumps out of the right-hand window or the left makes very little difference by the time one reaches the pavement."

It was the Christian synthesis of freedom and community that made modern democracy and political liberty possible, a relation that was not well understood by the dominant Whig school of history in his day nor by the various critical theories of our own. Glenn Olsen has pointed out that Dawson's position implies that some components of Catholic thought came to fruition only after the Middle Ages, which was a sure departure from his contemporary Catholic history.

Dawson's understanding of the achievement of Christianity in creating a stable social structure based upon free membership in a spiritual supranational community is crucial. The extensive treatment of other cultures and their relationship with Christianity provided by Dawson is a model of a proper "multicultural" approach. As James Hitchcock has noted, it is ironic that the Catholic intellectuals who showed a deep respect for and sensitivity toward other cultures have been largely forgotten in this post-Vatican II age.

Dawson wrote a number of important essays and studies of these non-Western and non-Christian cultures and their relationship with the West. Dispensing with the simplistic notion of Western superiority that he thought marred the work of other historians, Dawson chose to dwell instead on the historical record. Put simply, it was the process of European exploration and discovery that shattered the relative isolation of the other world cultures and that brought every people into an international community of nations. This is a reflection of Europe's missionary character, a character that arises out of a sense of itself as the bearer of a universal and timeless message. Dawson does not dispute the baser reasons for Europe's expansion, but states that critics of colonialism and economic exploitation cannot "deny the existence of the Western missionary movement as a real factor in colonial expansion, nor even [can they] identify the two elements and regard the missionary as an agent of capitalism."

In his statements on colonialism and the relations of the West to the world, we see again Dawson's dual strategy. To other Europeans who seek to diminish the force of the Christian faith in the West, he presents the full historical record to give Christianity its due. To his fellow Catholics, Dawson supplies the reminder that there has been no perfect "Christian" society, only societies more or less devoted to the principles of the Gospel.

The contemporary value of Dawson's work lies in this recognition and explication of the continuing mission of the Church to use the present world situation of increased communication and ease of travel to bring about a new evangelization and to fill the great spiritual need that exists alongside of great wealth and technological advances. As Dawson wrote in *The Movement of World Revolution* (1959), they must fulfill the Church's "universal mission to bring the Gospel of Christ to all nations." He would be in full agreement with the late-Pope John Paul II's call to build a "Civilization of Love" and would perhaps have seen in him a present-day Augustine or Aquinas attempting to develop a new synthesis between the immense growth in human knowledge in the past century and Christianity.

During his own lifetime, Dawson supported the social teaching of the Church, which altered the traditional European tension between Church and state to the more important relationship between religion and culture. As Father Joseph Koterski, S.J., has written, the efforts of the papacy, as represented in a document like *Dignitatis Humanae*, are "an effort to ready the Church for the struggles of the next century and the new millennium, with a better vision than any current political regime or national culture shows." As early as 1942, Dawson discerned this shift in papal emphasis and himself announced a commitment to religious freedom as an essential step to the restoration of all things under the universal kingship of Christ.

The Church, by pressing ahead of secular regimes—even those of the West—in its defense of human rights and the inherent dignity of the human person, is preparing for a new stage of Christian culture, with new forms of Christian life. The body of work produced by Christopher Dawson gives us a glimpse of the possibilities.

# *Christopher Dawson and the Coming Conflict*

In 1938, fascism was on the rise in Europe, and Communism held a strong attraction for some Western intellectuals. Some believed that the establishment of totalitarian government in what is now called the Anglosphere was only a matter of time. The British historian Christopher Dawson disagreed. He thought that a different kind of state was more likely: equally authoritarian, perhaps, but backed by the coddling of a welfare state instead of brute force. Pure popular democracy presents the possibility of a different yet critical danger to the kind of free society that had been characteristic of Western political history: "It may be harder to resist a totalitarian state which relies on free milk and birth control clinics than one which relies on castor oil and concentration camps." Resistance would be even more difficult because such states use language that is comfortable to democratic ears, such as the rhetoric of equality and rights (or even "hope" and "change").

Like Alexis de Tocqueville, Dawson (1889–1970) saw the rise of equality as the signal development of the nineteenth and twentieth centuries. And Dawson had the advantage of the intervening decades to confirm what the Frenchman's work had anticipated. To be effective, equality must be joined to a state committed to enforcing egalitarianism: "if democracy means nothing more than the destruction of social equality and the reduction of our culture to the lowest common factor of intelligence, then the resultant mass society can be governed more simply and efficiently by a unified dictatorial system than by the relatively complicated and diffuse

Originally published in *The New Criterion*, March 2010.

methods of representative parliamentary government." That the system would be a soft despotism—for a time, anyway—would be small comfort to anyone concerned with preserving the traditional culture of the West, for two reasons. First, the mandarins of that new system, bearing politically correct weapons, would not ultimately be so gentle. And second, even that system, with whatever relics of the Western tradition it managed to retain, would not last without the traditional religious language and culture of the West.

Christopher Dawson lingers on the edges of two critical contemporary debates that have consumed the public life of America and Europe for the last two decades, and especially since the attacks of September 11. Given his opinions on the rise of liberalism and the importance of religion in human culture, it is not surprising that Dawson's reputation has been in and out of fashion: He was highly regarded in the 1920s and 1930s, but, as the historian Patrick Allitt has noted, by the time of the cultural revolutions of the 1960s, he was seen as simply another Catholic apologist, unsuited for the modern era. While that attitude surfaces even today, Dawson's insights into the importance of religion to culture and the nature of the West are, however, once again being noticed. Michael Burleigh, for example, has clearly been influenced by Dawson, as reflected in his studies of political utopianism, *Earthly Powers* and *Sacred Causes*. Dawson's books, many long out of print, are now being re-issued in a uniform edition, though, aside from a biographical memoir by his daughter, no full-length biography of Dawson exists.

The Welsh poet David Jones jokingly referred to Dawson as "the Tiger" because his placid and retiring demeanor was so at odds with his passionate prose and scholarly rigor. Born to mixed English and Welsh parentage, Dawson lived in a family castle on the English-Welsh border where he received private elementary education. This youthful experience of freedom and quiet learning strongly effected his historical imagination; in an autobiographical fragment, he writes that "it was then I acquired my love of history, my interest in the difference of cultures and my sense of the importance of religion in human life." He matriculated at Winchester and then Trinity College, Oxford. Among his tutors was Sir Ernest Barker, the great scholar of ancient political thought. Aside from brief post-graduate work in economics and sociology in Europe, Dawson pursued a course of private reading, leading to the publication of his first book, *The Age of the Gods*, in 1928. He spent most of his life as an independent scholar.

In 1914, Dawson converted to Catholicism, sponsored by his boyhood friend the writer Edward Watkin. The reasons for his conversion were mixed; one of the major factors was the strong influence and example of his wife Valery, who was Catholic. Another reason was the example of the Catholic saints upon him, both as a person and as a historian. Dawson appreciated them not only for their individual merits but also for what they said about the culture that produced them. He concluded that any "theory of life" that took no account of these religious exemplars lacked basic explanatory power and that the weakness of secular histories lay in their neglect of this significant cultural fact. These convictions are imperative to understanding Dawson as a historian: saints, prophets, and missionaries are real historical figures who shaped and reflected their culture and who actually believed in what they professed. His treatment is an explicit rebuke to the Marxists and "materialist" social historians of his era, and our own, who believe impersonal forces, rather than individual actions, create culture.

Dawson wrote fifteen books, in addition to several posthumous collections, the most famous being *Progress and Religion* (1929), *Europe and the Rise of Western Culture* (1950), and *Understanding Europe* (1952). His first publications, which formed the basis of his first work, were in sociological journals, but during the 1930s he became a more regular participant in the public debates of the time. He was a regular contributor to T. S. Eliot's journal, *The Criterion*, for example, and also served as editor of *The Dublin Review* in the early 1940s. From 1947–9, Dawson presented the prestigious Gifford Lectures. The range of his learning was enormous; his contributions ranged from the rise of Romanticism in Europe to the Native American peoples of the New World, from classical literature to the latest social science research, from medieval history to the Indian epics.

The combination of real passion with disciplined prose and a scholar's attention to detail and nuance won him accolades. Even William Inge, the Dean of St. Paul's in London and a fierce critic of the Catholic Church, found Dawson to be the only Catholic who did not annoy him.

In 1958, Dawson was asked to serve as the first holder of the Charles Chauncey Stillman Chair in Roman Catholic Studies at Harvard University, a post he retained until 1962. He and his wife spent their years in America traveling and giving lectures at colleges across the country. One result of his trip was his essay "America and the Secularization of Modern Culture." The essay places America at the center of the rising secularization he lamented, joined to a technological order in which "education and science and technology, industry, and business and government, all are coordinated with one another in a close organization." Nevertheless, he thought the country's intractable religiousness and its constitutional structure gave it a better hope than Europe for retaining both Christianity and the Western political heritage.

Most active from the 1930s through the late 1950s, Dawson anticipated the current debates over the future of Europe. Authors such as Christopher Caldwell, in his recent *Reflections on the Revolution in Europe*, have written the eulogy of the West: an aging population combined with an aggressive influx of non-European minorities and supported by a tolerant, secularized welfare state means that Europe, as it has been known since at least the early Middle Ages, will cease to exist. Caldwell is blunt—his book was written to ask "whether you can have the same Europe with different people. The answer is no." Dawson contended (in books like *The Making of Europe* [1932]) that Europe was a composite of different peoples, and that it was held together and defined by common belief and a common culture. A secular society struck at both roots, and made it vulnerable to other belief systems with a stronger hold on its adherents.

Yet another debate to which Dawson was an early contributor concerns religious belief and its connection to cultural development. Controversy over why humanity has always sought the divine has revivified recently, as evidenced by work from the "new atheists," whose arguments range from the tiresome (religion is a mass delusion) to the seemingly sophisticated (genes made us religious). Robert Wright, in his new book, *The Evolution of God,* tries a Marxian materialist analysis of religious belief that differs little in its overall arguments than those Dawson confronted eighty years ago. Wright wants to convince us that particular religions are converging on a higher moral sense, which transcends them all (and just coincidentally largely duplicates the moral sense of a former Christian living in Princeton, like Wright himself). As one reviewer noted, Wright's argument is basically "creationism for liberals," and it commits the same mistake that Dawson identified in the secularists of his time. They do not really believe that other people really believe what their faith teaches. So, for them, religion must be an explanation for something else and any "progress" must be in the secular-liberal direction.

As early as 1925, Dawson recognized that "modern writers on anthropology and primitive thought have tended to assume that religion is a secondary phenomenon and that man's earliest attitude to reality was a kind of empirical materialism." A student of the then-new discipline of anthropology might note sun worship among an agricultural people and conclude that the sun was worshipped because people did not know how to guarantee good crops year after year. In compensation, they sought to supplicate something they saw as beyond their power to control. Dawson contended, against its cultured despisers, that religion was not some "natural" outgrowth of primitive culture or an unsophisticated understanding of physical processes.

Dawson turned the argument of the anthropologist on its head: Religion is natural, to be sure, but it is also the core human experience from which culture, society, and even scientific analysis proceeded. It deserves to be analyzed in and of itself, and not as a byproduct of something else. Dawson contested the standard opinion of peoples like the Eskimo or Bushmen, whom the theorists of progress considered completely dominated by their physical surroundings. In fact, these cultures were the result "of a free and intelligent activity, and it expresses itself in an art and a folk-lore far richer and more original than that of many more advanced peoples." The spiritual resources of vibrant cultures, Dawson thought, enables them to subsume physical and social limitations into a transcendental vision of the cosmos.

One of the most significant of these tribes, for Western development, were the tribes of Israel. Buffeted by history and amidst hostile neighbors, they nevertheless carried their prophetic vision with them, creating in the process a strong and unique culture that survived its rivals. As the novelist Walker Percy once quipped, "Who now is a Hittite?"—meaning that many ancient cultures whose beliefs were not as strong have faded away, despite once having political and economic power. Dawson warned that this could the fate of Europe.

Religious faith has a political function in Dawson's thought. It enables believers to resist the ever-increasing power of the state, with its promises of paradise on earth. Christianity in particular has always contained the seeds of resistance to tyranny, from the first Christians refusing to worship the Roman Emperor, through the medieval doctrine of the "two swords," up to the present day. A secular mass-state must crush individual and corporate religious belief—if it is to succeed, it can brook no independent centers of authority. The subversion of the political order is often, unfortunately, helped by religious groups themselves, who mistake the state's secular humanitarianism for a common belief. The distinction between historical Christian witnesses, from the early martyrs all the way up through Martin Luther King, Jr., and, say, the devotees of Wicca or those who take their ethical principles from *Star Trek* could not be more stark. It is in the state's interest, in fact, to play up the equality of these faiths to put those with the psychological and social resources to present a threat at a disadvantage.

The total democratic state is, in the end, also an inhumane one. Dawson contended that a culture without a religious core must dissolve: it cannot survive on economic prosperity or political tolerance alone. Indeed, these would ultimately fail, too, either from the weak loyalties inspired by a secular culture and the concomitant mass-state or from outside pressures. The natural conclusion of this liberal secularizing process is totalitarianism, which elevates one idea—the concept of race, the class struggle, the state, or an undefined "tolerance"—over any others, and use the powers of government to enforce that idea. As Dawson wrote in *Judgment of the Nations* (1942), his book confronting the dark days of the 1930s, "The liberal movement in the wider sense transformed the world by an immense liberation of human energies, but liberalism in the narrower sense proved incapable of guiding the forces it had released."

The immense power and innovation of the Western economies should not blind us to the weaknesses beneath. Over the course of history, many cultures seemingly at the height of their power have disappeared. The drastic decline in birthrates and the full-scale retreat from defending Western society since the 1960s are expressions of a cultural decline, and it has had the unintended effect of allowing the adherents of another religion—Islam—to assume, in many instances, the place of Christianity as a cultural driver in Europe. Even secular philosophers such as Jürgen Habermas have come to recognize this reality, perhaps too late.

Dawson differs from Caldwell in one significant respect. Seeing the whole expanse of Christian history, Dawson argued that Christians in Europe must remember that Christianity is not a European religion: its teachings, "neither Eastern nor Western but universal," provide the true force for unity. It has been able to exist separately from individual European peoples even as it molded European culture as a whole. Indeed, Dawson attributes the largest portion of the creation of Western Christianity to the North African fathers, particularly Augustine. As Dawson wrote in his 1960 book, *The Historic Reality of Christian Culture*,

> The Church itself, though it bears a Greek name, *Ecclesia*, derived from the Greek civic assembly, and is ordered by the Roman spirit of authority and law, is the successor and heir of an Oriental people, set apart from all the peoples of the earth to be the bearer of a divine mission.
>
> Similarly, the mind of the Church, as expressed in the authoritative tradition of the teaching of the Fathers, is neither Eastern

> nor Western but universal. It is expressed in Western languages—in Greek and Latin—but it was in Africa and Asia rather than in Europe that it received its classical formulation. Greek theology was developed at Alexandria and Antioch and in Cappadocia, while Latin theology owes its terminology and distinctive character to the African Fathers—Tertullian, Cyprian and above all St. Augustine.
>
> While these men wrote in Latin, it was not the Latin of the Romans; it was a new form of Christian Latin which was developed, mainly in Tunisia, under strong Oriental influence. Christianity formed a new organizing principle, based not in birth or race, or even in nation, but in baptism.

The history of Christianity is, in other words, a universal history, open to all peoples. This argument has two consequences. First, "no historian can regard it as irrelevant that Christianity remains by far the strongest religious element in Western culture, and however far the process of secularization has gone, the influence of Christianity on culture, on ethics, in education, in literature and in social action is still strong." So the ridiculous spectacle of European politicians excising any mention of Christianity from the European Constitution is both bad history and suicidal politics. Christianity is not just some "Western" construct imposed on the world; it is the external belief system that created the West in the first place. Indeed, Dawson wrote an essay, "Is the Church Too Western?," that explodes this myth. Caldwell's book in particular is filled with the kind of examples that make one shudder, as they regularly demonstrate that the elites of most Western countries are actively at war with their culture's past and will make almost any compromise in order to efface historical reality.

The problem facing the West therefore is not, or is not only, demographic. It is also cultural in a very specific way: Christianity as a world-force, like the other major religions, can inhabit other cultures in other places, but without Christianity, Europe has no element binding it together. Multicultural directives, welfare, handwringing over "tolerance" and free-trade agreements will not win over people who have a rock-solid belief that their true destiny is a spiritual one. Where, in other words, were the Franciscans and Jesuits and Dominicans in the banlieus during the 2005 riots in France, evangelizing for—and being the example of—not just Western culture but the religious faith animating that culture? They were not there, of course, because, by and large, such orders no longer believe that they exist for such purposes, and the "tolerant" Western state would not look kindly upon such actions.

Dawson's answer to this new kind of total democratic state was clear. The engaged citizen must engage with the ideology that seeks to reject that civilization, either directly through secular politics or indirectly through allowing misguided multiculturalism or political correctness to run rampant. "No doubt this will involve conflict," he wrote, "but conflict is not a bad thing." A stereotypically tolerant citizen of the post-Christian West might seek to replace Dawson's "conflict" with "challenge." But perhaps only time will tell which is the proper word.

# *Progress and Religion*

**Not so long ago,** before the dot-com bubble burst and the September 11 terrorist attack, it seemed as if history would deliver all good things. The Dow was continuing its steady rise, and the nation seemingly faced no insurmountable problems. We were living at or near the end of history, with only a little tidying up to do at the rougher edges of the world before all would be permanently well. The events of last September compelled us to reconsider such rosy assumptions.

This pre-September 11 idyll was no anomaly. The belief in a perfect future has been a consistent feature of Western thought, emerging out of Christian hope of salvation in the next world. For the last two hundred years, however, this hope has been expressed usually in political or economic, rather than in religious, terms. This change has been so complete that the common presumption among elites, from the Davos World Economic Forum to the UN, is that this future path will entail the demise of religion. It is thus particularly appropriate that the Catholic University of America Press has reissued Christopher Dawson's *Progress and Religion* (originally published in 1929) as part of a planned series of Dawson volumes. Long before Francis Fukuyama's declaration of the end of history or Samuel Huntington's clash of civilizations, Dawson (1889–1970) proposed a very different foundation for the study of human society. With *Progress and Religion* as well as such other books as *The Age of the Gods* (1928) and *The Making of Europe* (1932), Dawson unapologetically placed religion at the center of culture rather than on the periphery.

Originally published in *First Things*, April 2002.

Dawson is one of those historians everyone should read but few actually do. It was not always so. In his lifetime, Arnold Toynbee and T. S. Eliot, among others, recognized his mastery of comparative history and religion and admired his crisp prose style. Almost alone in the 1920s and 1930s, he contended with those who denied religion any cultural significance. A young convert to Catholicism, Dawson was active for many years in ecumenical efforts in England. This experience had a clear impact on his awareness of cultural differences that is reflected in his sympathetic understanding of other cultures.

*Progress and Religion* is a direct attack on the nineteenth- and early twentieth-century social sciences and their understanding of progress. Now known as the "secularization thesis," the theory of progress proposes that civilizational development is directly proportional to a decline in religious belief and influence. In three chapters, one each devoted to sociology, anthropology, and history, Dawson examines the thought of such figures as Condorcet, Comte, Frazer, and LePlay. Drawing on their work, the social sciences excluded religion, either through Cartesian rationalism, Spenglerian theories of civilizational life cycles, or supposed general laws of anthropological development. They uniformly neglected "the study of religion in its fundamental social aspects." In the view of such thinkers, religion was "essentially a negative force like ignorance or tyranny" and so could not be a creative cultural influence.

Dawson overturned this entire way of thinking about culture. In passionate, disciplined prose, he demonstrated that materialist or environmental explanations of religious belief simply did not accord with the evidence. "Modern writers on anthropology and primitive thought have tended to assume that religion is a secondary phenomenon and that man's earliest attitude to reality was a kind of empirical materialism." On the contrary, as he wrote in 1925, the "great civilizations of the world do not produce the great religions as a kind of cultural by-product; in a very real sense the great religions are the foundations on which the great civilizations rest." In her introduction to the new edition of the book, the distinguished anthropologist Mary Douglas notes that Dawson "artfully stages a dialogue between the eighteenth-century philosophers, Condorcet, Rousseau, Kant, and Hegel, and the people they thought of as primitive." Religious faith takes on a different perspective if examined from the point of view of these people themselves, and not through the prism of anthropological theory. "The thin rationalism [of modern anthropology], which proceeded by arbitrarily separating one level of experience from the next, grossly distorted the subject matter and made a mockery of its pretensions to objectivity." These thinkers largely ignored the brute fact that "an obscure and confused intuition of transcendent being" was present in and influenced both so-called primitive cultures and more advanced ones.

*Progress and Religion* shows, moreover, that "the religious factor has had a far more important share in the development of human cultures than that which has usually been ascribed to it." Contrary to the assumptions of the progressive anthropologists, material and cultural progress need not go together. The early Christians in the Roman Empire, for example, created a more dynamic and vibrant culture than the dying, "higher" culture of the pagans. Likewise, Dawson notes peoples such as the Eskimo or Bushmen, whom the theorists of progress considered completely dominated by their physical surroundings. In fact, these cultures are the results "of a free and intelligent activity, and it expresses itself in an art and a folklore far richer and more original than that of many more advanced peoples." Dawson was no cultural relativist, but his analysis reveals that the secular scale of values simply does not capture the reality of human social life. The lesson he drew was that religious faith is the spark of culture, and external material success will not survive its being extinguished. That lesson is particularly important today, when some continue to describe complex world cultures in simple, undifferentiated terms and understand them using the same imprecise Enlightenment concepts.

Recent anthropological scholarship has confirmed Dawson's thesis about the religious basis of culture and cast serious doubt on the modern equation of progress with secularism. As such scholars as Rebecca French and David Hollinger have noted, religious ways of seeing the world remain the dominant interpretive tool for most people. Dawson anticipated this transition, insisting that progress "has begun to lose its hold on the mind of society...because the phase of civilization of which it was characteristic is already beginning to pass away." While a more positive assessment of religion's role has gained some ground, most of the academy and the wider circle of intellectuals and writers continue to ignore the formative role of religion, in the West and throughout the world.

Religion is a natural human impulse, and if it cannot be expressed in culture, it will find an outlet in ideology. In Dawson's time, the great temptations were the ideologies of fascism, communism, and Nazism. Today, our vulnerability is different. Elites in the West have become almost unable to understand religious motivations for conduct, even if the antiquated theory of progress no longer commands the scientific support it once did. This blindness has clear dangers not only with respect to our current efforts to understand Islam, but also in relation to other parts of the world, such as Tibet, and even in the United States itself, where the "culture wars" are largely motivated by a latent progressivism. The recent flare-up about evangelicals being "uneducated and easy to lead," not to mention the efforts to explain away certain strains of Islam as motivated by economic or other nonreligious factors, are recurring echoes of the problem Dawson originally diagnosed. Despite its claim to universality, the secularization thesis, no less than the "end of history" schema, contributes little to our understanding of the place of religion in the world today.

America, which Dawson did not visit until the late 1950s when he was appointed to the first Stillman Chair in Roman Catholic Studies at Harvard, initially seemed to be his worst-case scenario. The nation regarded itself as the culmination of the project of human freedom, where old loyalties were cast aside in favor of the *novus ordo seclorum*, and where self-invention was part of the national character. In the 1920s and '30s, Dawson thought that America could not resist becoming "a purely secular type of culture which subordinates the whole of life to practical and economic ends and leaves no room for independent spiritual activity." In *Progress and Religion*, American civilization was the embodiment of technology gone awry: life acquired meaning only through consumption and production, by "more cinemas, motor-cars for all, wireless installations, more elaborate methods of killing people, purchase on the hire system, preserved foods, and picture papers." (One can only wonder what Dawson would have made of the Internet.)

However, in an important lecture on "America and the Secularization of Modern Culture," presented in the same year that John Courtney Murray's *We Hold These Truths* was published (1960), Dawson set forth a more hopeful view. America's origins in the dissenting and pluralist tradition of Protestantism had established a realm of personal and communal freedom outside the power of the state. The nation's individualism clearly bore the imprint of the Christian focus on the sacredness of the person, despite occasional lapses into narcissism. Just as importantly, American culture had developed without the anticlericalism or antireligious character that was common among its European counterparts. Further, America had a clear, if legally unrecognized, role for religion in public life. While Dawson foresaw that the sometimes stark separation of the world of business and politics from that of religious belief threatened to produce what has been called a naked public square, he nevertheless thought that because the nation combined a deep religiosity with enormous material wealth and productivity, there "is great opportunity in America that may never be repeated."

Because of this heritage, Americans are able to understand religious belief. More importantly, at its best the nation can be a model of how to interpret modern political forms through the eyes of faith. The ability to hold strong religious convictions and to profess democratic principles is America's great contribution to the world, despite elite opinion about the "separation of church and state" on the one hand or a restricted "Christian America" on the other. This comfort with the modern mix of religion and politics may be of even greater importance in the coming century.

# *The Dynamics of World History*

**This new edition of** *Dynamics of World History* (John J. Mulloy, ed., with a new introduction by Dermot Quinn, ISI Books), first published by Sheed & Ward in 1958, is a welcome contribution to the burgeoning revival of interest in the work of Christopher Dawson (1889–1970), perhaps the greatest Catholic historian of the last century. It joins two recent collections of critical essays and the series of new editions being published by The Catholic University of America Press. *Dynamics* also includes a new introduction by Dermot Quinn, and an assessment of Dawson by his long-time commentator John Mulloy, which accompanied the earlier edition.

The title captures a central theme of Dawson's work. *Dunamis* means power or force in ancient Greek, and throughout his career Dawson focused on discovering the motivating forces of history, the hydraulics hidden beneath the surface of events. There were many supposed dynamics to choose from: Enlightenment rationalism, the civilizational cycles of Spengler or Toynbee, the Hegelian World-Spirit, the Marxist class struggle and, more recently, the global marketplace. From his wide reading in theology, political history and the newer disciplines of sociology and anthropology, Dawson found each of these wanting. Instead, he concluded that religious faith moves cultures and it was spiritual forces that provided the true "key to history."

It has been many years since T.S. Eliot named Dawson one of the most influential thinkers in England, and he is not much read by academics

Originally published in *The Chesterton Review*, XXIX, 1–2, 2003.

these days. Yet this collection reminds us of his prescience. Long before Samuel Huntington proclaimed the "clash of civilizations," Dawson was writing appreciatively of the different world-cultures and against a universalist view of history that flattened real cultural differences, ignorance of which could prove disastrous. Long before David Brooks discovered the "Bobos in Paradise," Dawson was confronting in the 1930s the challenge bourgeois civilization presents to traditional Christian culture. Dawson speaks to us precisely because he was not a "mediaevalist," a label his calumniators tried to pin on him. Writing in journals like *The Sociological Review* and Eliot's *Criterion*, he demonstrated in much of his work a preoccupation with modern problems, and he saw more clearly than his contemporaries the trials that were approaching.

Dawson reminded his audience that cultural growth was not the same as political power or economic wealth. "The fact is," as Dawson wrote in "The Eclipse of Europe," an essay included here, "that the fate of civilization is not determined solely, or even predominantly, by political and economic causes. The decline of the Roman Empire was also an age of spiritual rebirth, which prepared the way, not only for the coming of mediaeval Christendom, but also for the civilizations of Byzantium and Islam." Secularism and progress need not go together, as a new generation of scholars, such as Rebecca French, are discovering, confirming Dawson's work and exploding the "secularization thesis."

In contrast to the ideological blinders of the secularist, Dawson saw complexities: the Jewish people, among the poorest of the Middle Eastern tribes, nevertheless carried a higher spiritual culture as their pagan neighbors disappeared from history. Rome fell because it had lost its spiritual roots, only to be restored with the rise of Christianity. The Reformation destroyed the unity of Western Christendom, but this led to the glories of the Baroque, the exploration of globe and the rediscovery, through Protestant scholars, of the Hebraic roots of Christianity. And after some early hesitation, Dawson also came to believe America, despite its secularism and commercialism, could represent a new hope for Christian history in light of the exhaustion of Europe.

*Dynamics* is divided into five sections, covering more than three decades of Dawson's career. The selections include his important essays on "Civilization and Morals," "Stages in Mankind's Religious Experience," "The Christian View of History," "History and the Christian Revelation," and "Catholicism and the Bourgeois Mind." The final section collects Dawson's assessments of other historians. Here, Dawson assesses Toynbee, H.G. Wells, Marx, Gibbon, Spengler, and St. Augustine. It was Augustine who persuaded Dawson of the interaction between the Two Cities, and that the real truths of history in fact transcend temporal boundaries.

The dual citizenship of the Christian had dramatic political effects that remain important to this day in the political self-conception of the West and its preservation of freedom in contrast to elsewhere in the world. Indeed, it is the failure to recognize the Christian roots of this freedom that has rendered the West vulnerable to those who would destroy it. The West was able to carve out a political sphere that was able to remain connected with the religious basis for Western culture. The combination proved extremely successful. "[I]t is not the business of the Church to do the same thing as the State;" rather, it exists within and apart from the State, and serves a different function. The historical analysis of the dramatic consequences for Christendom of this compromise prefigures arguments made by philosopher Roger Scruton in his recent book, *The West and the Rest*, and speak directly to our current confrontation with Islamic militarism.

Dawson wrote his most important works, such as *Progress and Religion* and *Religion and the Rise of Western Culture*, explicitly to correct the anti-religion bias of the great historians of the previous century, especially Gibbon. Nevertheless, in his Essay "Edward Gibbon and the Fall of Rome," Dawson is generous to the historian of the Roman Empire: "Few historians have possessed so high a degree as Gibbon the power of transforming the chaos of the past into an intelligible order," despite his "limitations of spiritual vision and historical imagination." In *Dynamics* we have further proof that Dawson possessed both of those qualities.

# *Chesterton and the Leopard*

❧

**In 1957,** Giuseppe Tomasi di Lampedusa, the last Prince of an ancient Sicilian house that traced its ancestry back to the imperial household of Tiberius, published his first and only novel: *Il Gattopardo (The Leopard).* Not long after its publication, it was recognized internationally as a classic and as one of the great works of modern literature. The Prince, however, did not live to receive any acclaim for his brilliant and eccentric work, dying just before the book was published after his work had been refused by several publishing houses. The story is based loosely on the events and personalities of Lampedusa's own family and recounts the emergence of democracy in Sicily and the destruction of the old order in the days of Garibaldi. Richness of prose and thought is here in abundance, and to discover how the age of the *ancien régime* ended and to observe its successor as it slouched to its birth one cannot do better than this fictional, but not false, account of the advent of modernity in Italy. This book haunts and succors by turns, and its achingly beautiful descriptions remain lasting monuments to a vanished time.

Lampedusa's novel was the culmination of a lifetime of reading and reflection. With the benefits of wealth and leisure, the Prince lived a life immersed in literature. While a wide-ranging reader in many Continental literatures—in addition to his native Italian, the Prince was fluent in French, Spanish and German—Lampedusa had a special place in his heart for the literature of the British Isles, in whose language he was also adept. Indeed, he considered himself to have less a Sicilian than an "English"

---

Originally published in *The Chesterton Review*, XXI, 3, 1995.

temperament.[1] Lampedusa spent long periods of time in England, visiting and gathering books; and, when home in Sicily, he absorbed the body of English literature almost in its entirety.[2] The Prince did not confine himself to the classic works of the various national literatures; he delighted in the "minor" writers as well, finding in them the foundations upon which the masters built their work.[3] This lifetime of reading resulted in a unique perspective upon the purpose and place of letters in the English tradition, a perspective memorialized in a set of commentaries Lampedusa composed on the major and minor writers of the English tradition, from its beginnings up to his own day. Through these commentaries, the Prince passed on his love and knowledge of the English in a series of lessons that he gave to a young poet, Francesco Orlando, in order to provide him with a broader education.[4] These lessons, in two volumes, have recently been published,[5] and they furnish fascinating insights into our own tradition through the eyes of an erudite foreigner. The volumes are filled with wise insights and observations, and provide new interpretations to some of the giants of the English canon.

The volumes are arranged chronologically; and, toward the end of the second volume, Lampedusa devotes an entire section to Chesterton, whom he treats as one of the important figures of modern English literature. As an introduction, Lampedusa lays out for his audience his opinions about the character of the English Catholic writer, as opposed to the Catholic

1. For this and other biographical information, the indispensable source is David Gilmour, *The Last Leopard: A Life of Giuseppe Tomasi di Lampedusa* (Pantheon, 1991), which is the only full-length study of the Prince in English.
2. It seems the only major work in English that the Prince did not read was the epic *Beowulf.* See Stephen Sartarelli, trans., "Reflections on English Literature, by Giuseppe Tomasi di Lampedusa," *The New Criterion* (September 1993), p. 27.
3. Sartarelli, "An Amateur's Love of the English: Lampedusa's *Letteratura Inglese*," *The New Criterion* (September 1993), p. 24.
4. The Prince also set out to compose a similar survey of French literature, but this was never finished because of his concentration on completing *The Leopard.*
5. *Letteratura Inglese,* Nicoletta Pollo, ed. *Volume I: Daile origine alla Settecento* (Arnoldo Mondadori Editore, Milan, 1990) and *Volume II: L'Ottocento e il Novecento* (Mondadori, 1991), both with introductions by Gioacchino Lanza Tomasi, who is the cousin and adopted son of the Prince. Except for the Sartarelli selections, no parts of the Letteratura have been translated into English.

writers of Italy. Lampedusa credits the former with resoluteness in the face of adversity. He writes:

> The English Catholics think to themselves that the long centuries of persecution have removed all the lukewarm Catholics and those Catholic "by habit." You realize that to be an English Catholic is a very different matter, almost an opposite to being an Italian Catholic. The clergy are scarce but magnificent [in England], and below their clothing they bear around with them authentic Christian virtue. And their writers follow their example.[6]

Lampedusa speaks poorly of the Italian Catholic writers of his own day, seeing their faults with the eyes of a native, but he admits that the mediocrity which he finds is not entirely because of their lack of skill or conviction. Quite simply, Italian Catholics did not suffer from the same sort of persecution as their English counterparts, and thus an indigenous tradition of apologetic writing did not develop. Where the English Catholics had minority status and few privileges; and French Catholics had, as the Prince says, "various shades of unbelief," with which to contend, the Catholic Italian is at the very heart of Christendom; enemies are sparse, and consequently the need for defenders of the faith (in the manner of a Chesterton or a Bernanos) is not as great. Add to this the Prince's own preference for things English, and his aristocratic disdain for much of modern Italian life, and the criticism, while still harsh, becomes more understandable. After providing his Italian listeners with this short comparison of Catholic authors from different countries, Lampedusa proceeds to his study of the work of Chesterton. The discussion of authors in the *Letteratura* is not strictly biographical. Lampedusa means to furnish a literary portrait of his subjects and thus he does not dwell long on details external to the intrinsic merits of the works that he considers. Indeed, the

6. *Letteratura Inglese, Volume II*, p. 340. Unless otherwise indicated, all translations are my own.

Prince was known on occasion to compose historical details himself in order to assist the flow of his narrative.[7]

Lampedusa's examination of Chesterton begins with the poems. He calls Chesterton a "poet of worth," and a novelist of the highest order. The Prince also recognizes that the source of Chesterton's literary power lay not only in his talent, but in the convictions that shaped that talent. Lampedusa especially notes his "respect for tradition, defense of the individual person [and] defense of a Catholic charity opposed to every form of hypocritical largesse."[8] Lampedusa lists some of Chesterton's books of poems, and singles out *Lepanto*, *The Ballad of St. Barbara* and *The Ballad of the White Horse* as the best. Among the prose works, Lampedusa sets *The Man Who Was Thursday* apart from the rest of Chesterton's novels. Lampedusa names the book a masterpiece, and cites as evidence its "constant good humor, the bent toward caricature and the sudden phrases revealing profound theological insight."[9] He sees the book as a counterpoint to the philosophy of Voltaire, and deems Chesterton a better stylist: "There cannot be two styles more different than those of Chesterton and Voltaire: the latter's style is as meager and thin as the former's is dense and full of dialect."[10] He praises Chesterton's ability to embody abstract philosophical positions in living and believable characters. The Prince finds the Father Brown detective stories also worthy of attention. Aside from Sherlock Holmes, "Father Brown…is the only character in detective fiction who approaches art."[11] This *pretepoliziotto* ("priest-policeman") seeks not just the crime but the sin that lay at its root. Each novel ends, says the Prince, with the discovery not only of the criminal, but of a subtle truth as well. The remainder of the section is concerned with a series of works outside Chesterton's poems and prose pieces. Lampedusa almost despairs

7. For example, Lampedusa gives an account of Belloc's dispute with Oman over military tactics during the Napoleonic Wars. The account, included in the Chesterton section, is embellished for the sake of narrative flow.

8. Ibid., 340.

9. Ibid., 342.

10. Ibid., 342.

11. Ibid., 342.

of being able to characterize them and writes, "I don't know what to call them, 'theoretical works,' or some such."[12] Included in this category are the periodical pieces that Chesterton wrote throughout his career, the apologetics and the biographies. The Prince gives the other fiction—*The Club of Queer Trades*, *The Man Who Knew Too Much*, *The Return of Don Quixote*—high marks, but he finds a decrease in the quality of the later periodical pieces, which he attributes to a sort of spiritual fatigue.

The Prince discusses *Orthodoxy* at some length, a work which he calls "absolutely the best" of Chesterton's works. He tells his Italian listeners that it is a book concerned with a life of *buon costume*, good morals, and represents not a specific religious orthodoxy, but an orthodoxy of life. Lampedusa writes:

> The argument may seem a little gray, but open the volume to any page and continue through to the end—you will be captivated. The spirit of the author presents to us the truth. In contrast to the paradoxes, jokes and flutterings of the poetry, the themes of this work in favor of traditional morality, the old way of life and the simplicity of existence are clear.[13]

In Chesterton, the Prince states, the old England can still be discovered. Indeed, the Prince says that Chesterton is indispensable for those who refuse to believe that the materialism and positivism and the "witty yet arid" mentality of Shaw hold undisputed sway in England. Chesterton's writings begin the revolution against the desiccated modern philosophies. Here Lampedusa points to Chesterton's study of "*ii romanziere*," Charles Dickens, and the Introductions to the latter's works that Chesterton wrote for the Everyman Library series as evidence of this new movement in favor of the old traditions of England.

12. Ibid., 343.
13. Ibid., 343.

The Prince closes his study of Chesterton with a short summary of his opinion of the Chestertonian corpus. He says that there is "much that is interesting, entertaining and fortifying" in Chesterton's works,[14] and he gives the following advice to his audience: "A set of good Chestertonian readings will be a great benefit to you."[15] We should do well to follow that advice.

14. Ibid., 343.
15. Ibid., 342.

# *What's Right with the World*

❧

**This year** marks the centenary of G. K. Chesterton's *What's Wrong with the World*. The book continues to inspire and surprise with its prophetic insights on issues from economics and property, to its bracing defense of the "wildness of domesticity."

And what is wrong with the world for Chesterton? "What is wrong with the world is that we do not ask what is right." In other words, the evils are plain, but to solve them we must know what is the good that will correct these evils. As Chesterton put it in his opening chapter, "The Homelessness of Man":

> We agree about the evil; it is about the good that we should tear each other's eyes out. We all admit that a lazy aristocracy is a bad thing. We should not by any means all admit that an active aristocracy would be a good thing. We all feel angry with an irreligious priesthood; but some of us would go mad with disgust at a really religious one. Everyone is indignant if our army is weak, including the people who would be even more indignant if it were strong. The social case is exactly the opposite of the medical case. We do not disagree, like doctors, about the precise nature of the illness, while agreeing about the nature of health. On the contrary, we all agree that England is unhealthy, but half of us would not look at her in what the other half would call blooming health.

Originally published in *Crisis*, July 9, 2010.

At a stroke, Chesterton anticipates—and refutes—the proponents of what is sometimes called the neutrality of liberalism. Such a program focuses on means, rather than ends; process, rather than substance. Thus, American political culture is inundated with talk of rights but little discussion of what rights might be for. We have built remarkable bureaucracies to solve problems, but without providing a description of what solutions to those problems would look like.

Joined to this lack of what may be called (but Chesterton does not) teleology is an ideology of innovation. The reformers in Chesterton's day were convinced that the future held endless possibility, and was to be preferred over the dysfunctional present or the boring past. He writes:

> We often read nowadays of the valor or audacity with which some rebel attacks a hoary tyranny or an antiquated superstition. There is not really any courage at all in attacking hoary or antiquated things, any more than in offering to fight one's grandmother. The really courageous man is he who defies tyrannies young as the morning and superstitions fresh as the first flowers. The only true free-thinker is he whose intellect is as much free from the future as from the past. He cares as little for what will be as for what has been; he cares only for what ought to be.

Chesterton applies his analysis to mistakes modern reformers make about man, woman, and child, and concludes with "the Home of Man." His focus on the family unit is crucial, because for Chesterton the family is the center of human society, and we must understand what the family is before we can help it. He defends the family both against the socialists who would end the family in favor of the state as well as the capitalists who would destroy it in the name of individualism. Indeed, in his incisive parable about Hudge the socialist and Gudge the capitalist, they amount to the same thing in terms of their damage to the family.

Chesterton confronted liberalism in its heyday, when progressives thought they were at the vanguard of a new world. Tradition and religion were hidebound and destined to disappear. The American writer and critic Russell Kirk faced a different world: When Kirk was writing his great books and essays in the 1950s and 1960s, such as *The Conservative Mind*, he had already begun to discern the end of liberal hegemony and an opportunity to renew enduring norms.

However, Kirk was left to contend with the results of the same mistakes concerning human nature that Chesterton had identified. They both criticized the illusions of social engineers, capitalist economic redistribution, a fetish for technology, and a misplaced reliance on the moral authority of science. But where Chesterton could at least invoke the common history and morals of the West in his debates with progressives, today that kind of common language has almost been lost.

With Chesterton, however, Kirk realized that imagination would be the most important tool in any cultural renewal. Kirk saw coming an Age of Sentiments, spurred by new technologies that rely on image, not on rational argumentation that was characteristic of the age of liberalism. "The immense majority of human beings will feel with the projected images they behold upon the television screen; and in those viewers that screen will rouse sentiments rather than reflections. Waves of emotion will sweep back and forth, so long as the Age of Sentiments endures. And whether those emotions are low or high must depend upon the folk who determine the tone and temper of television programming." And those folk must be infused with the moral imagination, or else the tone of the ever-present images will be low indeed.

Chesterton used his amazing facility for paradox and wordplay, on display in every page of *What's Wrong with the World*, to showcase the flaws in modern ideology. Kirk created an alternative thought-world for those seeking refuge from liberalism's death throes. But each served the same cause of reminding the West that it is as important to know what is right with the world as it is to know what is wrong.

# *Seeking the Truth with Orestes Brownson*

**Historian Arthur Schlesinger, Jr.**, among others, thought highly of Orestes Brownson—indeed, Russell Kirk, who led the Brownson revival in the last century, placed him "in the first rank of American men of ideas," and his work is of more than historical interest. Reflections on American society as good as Tocqueville? Check. Addressing a devastating critique of socialism before Marx even writes *Capital*? Check. Produces the central work of post-Civil War political theory? Check. Friend of Emerson and Cardinal Newman? And finally, native Vermonter and burned-over district preacher who became a Catholic? Check indeed.

Yet despite this high level of respect, there is an Orestes Brownson sized hole in American intellectual history. In this handsome anthology titled *Seeking the Truth: An Orestes Brownson Anthology*, Richard Reinsch reminds us why all Americans, but especially Catholics, should care what Brownson has to say. He provides a powerful intellectual argument for the complementarity of our democratic experiment with Catholic thought. This argument is needed far more than ever. With the recent meltdown of American evangelicalism over support for Trump, the influence of the "religious right" is at an all-time low. Ross Douthat has recently argued that "some kind of religious conservatism must be rebuilt," because a right-wing without the formative power of religious belief would be "very dark indeed." Yet that reborn religious conservatism must also reject the easy identification of America with the Kingdom of Gods, which has been a besetting weakness even of the non-Trump religious right. Brownson may offer a way through.

Originally published in *Crisis*, October 19, 2016.

The typical dismissal of Brownson (1803–1876) is that his mind was undisciplined. He allowed his powerful intellect to get pushed by the winds of doctrine and politics this way and that and so his opinions, which changed drastically over time, can be safely ignored. But as Reinsch notes in his excellent introduction, that view fails to appreciate the underlying unity of Brownson's work. Brownson was searching for the truth, and our modern relativism—that since he changed his opinions, none of them could be true—says more about us than about him. He rejected a pragmatism that measured truth only by utility or material comfort, and engaged with modern philosophical thought from a perspective open to supernatural as well as natural evidence. "Brownson's writings, born from his existential wrangling, were addressed to our authentic human longings to know the truth about ourselves. To study Brownson is to learn from a man whose first concern was to be open to the truth about what it means to be a human person." And what it means to be human is to live in relationship (what Brownson called *communion*) with others, with the world, and ultimately with God.

Only a relational God, one who loves us and whom we also love, makes our human experience of reality comprehensible. Modernity had sidetracked political society because it tried to ground that society on incomplete ideas, like the social contract (a topic Brownson excoriated in his essays), the popular will, or, more recently, an authoritarian "tolerance." Rather, the conclusion about our human experience should lead, "Brownson held, to a profoundly different ground for a liberal politics precisely because the person found his authentic freedom in love of man and God. Politics is transcended by and must support these truths of human freedom and existence." This does not mean a confessional state. Brownson was too much the American for that, and as we will discuss shortly, contested with Rome over the proper relations between religious belief and politics. However, it does mean that politics is derivative of our beliefs about the human person, and so will have consequences for how we organize our political life.

Reinsch discusses the biographical details of Brownson's life to set the stage for his work. Brownson was born in Vermont and raised by neighbors after his father's death when Brownson was six. Although raised in a Congregationalist household, at eighteen he made a public profession of Presbyterianism, which he soon left because he was frustrated by the rejection of reason in Protestant theology. Thus began a lifelong journey through various American denominations; along the way Brownson married, had eight children (two sons died in the Civil War), and taught himself Latin, Greek, Spanish, German, Italian, and French. He was deeply involved in both philosophical debate with current European trends, as well as argument about federal power and political favor in America. For much of his life he supported himself by his writing, and his prose is a distillation of elaborate Victorian sentences punctuated by sharp denunciations or affirmations.

In 1840, while in the throes of a secular progressivism that sought to create a "Church of the Future," Brownson wrote one of his most famous essays, included in this collection. Titled "The Laboring Classes," the essay reflected both his deep empathy for workers and concern for inequality, as well as a description of a socialist utopia before Marx wrote his *Capital*, which came out in 1867. He is critical of the bourgeois middle class: "The middle class is always a firm champion of equality, when it concerns humbling a class above it; but is its inveterate foe, when it concerns elevating a class below it."

However, the reaction to the essay had a sobering effect on Brownson's thinking. The essay was seized upon by the Whigs against Brownson's Democrats in the election of 1840, and Brownson was devastated by having to defend himself against charges of radicalism. This shook his faith in the revolutionary majority, and brought to the fore themes he had been exploring, including "his deep-seated disagreement with the notion that the sovereign people were the masters of government," and the "ease with which democracy can become authoritarian." At the same time, the years after "The Laboring Classes" saw Brownson reflect more deeply on the nature of God, which brought him to Catholicism in 1844.

It is his work on religious liberty and the American polity that may be more important today. Upon becoming a Catholic, Brownson argued on two fronts. The first was simple American nativism. Brownson became a

Catholic when the Church of Rome was under deep suspicion of dual loyalty, superstition, and the general charge that Catholics could not be good Americans. Brownson turned that argument on its head and demonstrates that Catholicism reflects a better grounding than secular Deism or Protestantism for the American Founding. He makes this argument in an essay called "Catholicity Necessary to Sustain Popular Liberty." As Brownson understood, and argued in his classic 1865 work, *The American Republic*, generous portions of which are included here, philosophy cannot demonstrate the truths, for example, of the Declaration of independence that all men are created equal. And because of that, society must degenerate unless sustained by religious foundations, specifically Christianity's notion of a relational, personal God. Democracy, he writes, "is a beautiful theory, and would work admirably, if it were not for one little difficulty, namely,—the people are fallible, both individually and collectively, and governed by their passions and interest, which not infrequently lead them far astray, and produce much mischief." Something outside its own will must sustain the people.

> We know of but one solution to the difficulty, and that is in *religion*. There is no foundation for virtue but in religion, and it is only religion that can command the degree of popular virtue and intelligence requisite to insure to popular government the right direction and a wise and just administration. A people without religion, however successful they may be in throwing off old institutions, or in introducing new ones, have no power to secure the free, orderly, and wholesome working of any institutions. For the people can bring to the support of institutions only the degree of virtue and intelligence they have.... We say, then, if democracy commits the government of the people to be taken care of, religion is to take care that they take proper care of the government, rightly direct and wisely administer it.

Brownson thought the best religious support to democracy was Catholicism, precisely because it was supposedly immune from the democratic or individualistic temptations of both secularism and certain forms of Protestantism. But Brownson did not think this meant a confessional state. Because of this, Brownson also had adversaries among his fellow Catholics. Some European Catholics argued that religious liberty was acceptable only until Catholics could support a confessional state. Brownson responded that the constitutional protection of all faiths allowed Catholicism to grow; moreover, the First Amendment reflected a better understanding of the human person. In this, Reinsch argues, he anticipates some of the arguments made decades later by John Courtney Murray, S.J. and reflected in Vatican II's declaration of religious freedom, *Dignitatis Humanae*.

In his essay, "Religion and Liberty," Brownson distinguished between theological tolerance and civil tolerance. The Church has authority of discipline over the former, but not the latter. "Error has no rights, but the man who errs has equal rights with him who errs not." The Church's authority in a civil social order is moral and spiritual, not temporal. But this also means that the state cannot interfere in spiritual matters or the exercise of one's faith, and for the same reason. Each individual must follow his own faith without compulsion to violate it. "The enemies of religion must understand that if they require the state to use its power against religion, or to suppress it, they violate the first principle of civil and religious liberty.... The state, under the control of infidelity, and establishing atheism, is, to say the least, as hostile to religious and civil liberty as the state under the control of the clergy, and establishing the Roman Catholic Church."

Alas, that consequence may be coming to pass, as the "enemies of religion" interpret the First Amendment as prohibiting any expression of religion in public life and through the government's extensive involvement in social services, in effect banning theistic expression in things like healthcare. If Catholics in the nineteenth century were beset by the larger Protestant culture, now they are under threat by a secular culture hostile even to the very idea of religious liberty. Brownson saw the weakness in establishing a social order on mere consent of flawed individuals, without transcendent warrant. Only by recognizing that our destiny transcends the political, can we hope to have a stable political order.

# *Barzun at* 100

**Remember the culture wars?** In light of September 11 and the continuing War on Terror, it seems hard to believe that there was a time when Jesse Jackson chanting with Stanford undergraduates seemed like a real threat. The fight still rages on in some quarters, however, generating, as it did two decades ago, more heat than light. Writers like Christopher Hitchens have written that, once the war against terrorism here and abroad has been won, the world will enter a new era of liberal secularist progress, while others mutter darkly about "American fundamentalism." Meanwhile, conservatives too have their divisions. Some, like David Brooks, see the future largely as a pleasant bourgeois paradise; others, such as Russell Kirk, were less optimistic about the benefits of technology and consumer culture.

Nevertheless, those years raised a question that remains critical in a time that presents real enemies. Is there a thing called Western culture, and can we determine whether it was declining or progressing? One of the last of the generation of critics that included Edmund Wilson, Irving Howe, and Lionel Trilling, Barzun developed a historically informed critical approach that was designed to answer these questions without descending into polemic. For Barzun, "the historian can only show, not prove; persuade, not convince." To do that required both sureness of judgment as well as respect for the unpredictability and vagaries of history.

Like only a few others—his longtime Columbia colleague Trilling, for example, or the late Philip Rieff—Barzun inspired respect both as a

Originally published in *First Things*, December 31, 2007.

critic beyond the academy and as a scholar within it. While now generally viewed as a conservative, in that he defended a series of values that were superior to others, and (more important) could be distinguished from them, Barzun evades neat description. He certainly has avoided the vilification poured upon others, such as Allan Bloom, when offering his critiques of popular culture and modern education, which he criticized for credential inflation and failure to maintain its proper object, the removal of ignorance, in favor of networking and "life skills." For example, Barzun helped invent the area of study now known as cultural history, which has been derided (often rightly) by conservatives as a hotbed of leftist agitprop, poor scholarship, and political correctness. This was a world away from Barzun's view, which stressed the importance for the historian to use cultural materials to identify the "makers of culture" from the mass of humanity, a focus that has now largely been reversed in contemporary academia.

Given the struggles the West now faces before a resurgent Islam, it may be worth returning again to Barzun's work. It was not that long ago when certain elites saw the West to be backward, if not hopelessly oppressive. Barzun, writing before September 11, did not share this opinion, though he was not shy about his assessment of the weaknesses of Western culture. In the magisterial *From Dawn to Decadence*, published in 2000, Barzun opens his study of the last half-millennium survey of Western culture as follows:

> All that is meant by Decadence is "falling off." It implies in those who live in such a time no loss of energy or talent or moral sense. On the contrary, it is a very active time, full of deep concerns, but peculiarly restless, for it sees no clear lines of advance. The loss it faces is that of Possibility. The forms of art as of life seem exhausted; the stages of development have been run through. Institutions function painfully. Repetition and frustration are the intolerable result. Boredom and fatigue are great historical forces.

This sketch, of course, is a generalization. Ages are hardly so neat, as Barzun recognizes, and what appears to be stagnation in one era may appear to be something else to another. Religious belief, in particular, was not afflicted by boredom; indeed, "fundamentalisms are vocal everywhere; religious issues and personalities occupy the media as never before." Islam "is again fighting the West, and where it conquers it is much more intolerable than it was in the sixteenth century." In light of these contradictions, Barzun explores what it may mean to live at the close of a cultural epoch and what may be worth fighting for. The result is a nuanced and innovative look at Western culture. Contra the left, Barzun does not believe that all cultures are equal, and contra the right, a culture of Birkenstocks may still better than one of burqas. What is needed is an understanding of what it means when a society adopts, say, athletes and pop stars as role models and how we can distinguish those models of legitimacy and authority from those of other times and places. Further, Barzun's analysis can help tell us whether, in the face of our new threat, decadence can be halted.

*From Dawn to Decadence* capped a remarkable career in academic and public life that has spanned seven decades. The subjects Barzun chose to write about comprise an unmatched resource of cultural reflection and analysis, and their subjects remain touchstones of our contemporary obsessions. It seems Barzun had astute comments about almost everything. Race? *Race: A Study in Superstition* (1936), in which he wrote that the "race question" "defaces every type of mental activity." The role of science? *Science: The Glorious Entertainment* (1964). Evolution? *Darwin, Marx, Wagner: Critique of a Heritage* (1958). America and its role in the world? *God's Country and Mine* (1959). All told, Barzun has some three dozen books edited, translated, or written by him to his credit, in addition to hundreds of essays and reviews on everything from neglected American critics such as John Jay Chapman to the delights of detective fiction, and from Berlioz to baseball.

His biography reads like a classic American immigrant success story. Barzun's parental household was affluent and artistic, friendly with the artistic classes of Paris but traumatized by visions of the First World War. He arrived from France in 1920, and matriculated at Columbia at fifteen. He was to spend the next five decades there, eventually becoming provost in

1958, a post he held through the mid-1960s. While there, Barzun taught a famous seminar with Trilling on the great books. After retiring from Columbia in 1975, Barzun became an adviser to Charles Scribner and Sons. Since his retirement some years ago, he has been living in San Antonio, all the while writing and publishing polished, crafted articles and books detailing the life of a culture.

Reading through Barzun's work today is fruitful on any number of issues, but, seen as a whole, three consistent themes emerge. The first is the role of the critic. Barzun wrote much of his best work during a time when public intellectuals had not yet morphed into full-time talking heads. Journals like *Partisan Review* explored issues that even correcting for nostalgia now seem remarkably serious and that are carried on today in fewer places. Most critics are increasingly unable to escape from the preoccupations of the postmodern ivory tower, with its endless theorizing and pretensions to "subversion." The rest are stuck in the pop culture whirlwind, reluctant to criticize too harshly and who often confuse simple description with analysis; the puff reviews in *Vanity Fair*, where advertising masquerades as critique, are a classic example of the genre. Indeed, the critic Sven Birkerts complained recently that criticism has been threatened by blogging, which turns everyone into a critic and destroys what he describes as the "architecture" of criticism, where some elite critics wrote what they thought about ideas and literature, and the rest of us read about it.

He has it half-right; what has been lost is the *hierarchy* of criticism, where some cultural products can be assessed and judged according to common standards of judgment. This loss, however, is no fault of bloggers; instead, it is the result of a half-century of higher education that has eliminated all such critical distinctions.

Barzun, whom *Time* featured on its cover in 1956, was from a different era. For him, a critic had a serious role to play; he rejected the method of the New Critics, for example, because simply interpreting a work from the inside was not the work of a critic. If a work of art or literature required explication, "then something has to be brought from the outside, even if only the beholder's experience of life and residue of education." Other than in the most skilled hands, the New Critics' method becomes a sort of postmodernism *avant la letter*, where "everyone could preach and contemn, no one could argue or refute, for symbols were ambiguous and elusive and each vaunted method was at bottom arbitrary."

Barzun applied this method to science and its role in shaping public life and public opinion, which forms a second major theme. Indeed, he named science, or, rather, a misunderstanding about the nature of scientific inquiry, as one of the enemies of Intellect. The prestige of scientists carried over into nonscientific fields, disrupting the authority of those disciplines and investing the public with a false credulity over its claims. In *Science*, Barzun subjects the claims of science to rigorous analysis not as claims about physical reality but on the claims made then (and made now) that science somehow can address nonscientific problems. He was not pining for a prescientific past, which Barzun called the "Fallacy of Utopian Addition." Those subjected to the fallacy "enjoy the lost blessings they discern in the past with the advantages we now enjoy and take for granted." Science does not exist in a vacuum, set apart by its methods in a separate culture, the famous "two cultures" theory advanced at the time by C.P. Snow and others. Culture was one, not two, and science could not be "a way of life," Barzun wrote, "any more than art of war or maritime law. Nothing is quite good enough to be made a way of life, and all attempts fail."

These themes converge in his writings on his adopted country. America was filled with intelligence but lacked respect for intellect; open to new ideas but therefore vulnerable to "scientific" quackery; manic about making money yet unsure of the culture that could result. There are some false notes; his essay on New York, in *God's Country*, is an uncharacteristically cranky reflection on crowds and dirt, though acknowledging in passing the city's "spectacle of grandeur." Other points are much stronger. His essays on advertising, for example, offer a critique of its shallow stoking of desire that could have been written yesterday, while not without some glimpse of appreciation for the verve of good advertising prose. Never a simple cheerleader, Barzun nevertheless warmed to the nation's ideals and tried to incorporate them into his larger reflections on culture. In a celebrated essay on "Lincoln the Literary Artist," Barzun credits Lincoln with a "style that is unique in English prose and doubly astonishing in the history of American literature." Lincoln was an original. Lincoln's precision and empathy were his alone, but his "workaday style is the American style par excellence." That American style was defined by the large expanse of country that softened the edges of the Old World, giving everyone a place to settle. Moreover, Barzun writes, our mad dash of industrialization forced everyone to get along, so that "[i]n Europe a thousand years of war, pogroms and massacres settle nothing. Here two generations of common schooling, intermarriage, ward politics, and labor unions create social peace." This process has been messy, and with some serious failings, but nonetheless it represented a new type of social order "unplanned, but ultimately wildly successful.

Despite the legion of admirers, there are no Barzunian schools, and certainly no one with the erudition and longevity to claim a place as his successor. One hopes that Barzun will be with us another century, long enough to write a sequel to *From Decadence to Dawn*, reversing the sequence in the title as the tradition of the critic and historian is rediscovered. Failing that happy eventuality, his work is the best illustration of the culture that he explicated so artfully.

# *David Jones and the Sacrament of Art*

**Shy, retiring, religious, and physically frail,** David Jones (1895–1974) considered art a "sacrament," an act of co-creation that connects us to God. In a 1962 BBC address, Jones warned that "the nature of man demands the sacramental. If he's denied the deep and the real, he'll fall for the trivial, even for the ersatz." But Jones's reputation has not been as brilliant as his contemporaries thought it promised. Although *In Parenthesis* (1937), Jones's first major work, won the Hawthornden Prize in 1938, joining works by Robert Graves and Evelyn Waugh, this pitch-perfect poem about the infantryman's Great War came years after the war poetry of Wilfred Owen and Siegfried Sassoon, and it recorded a war receding into the past when the world was busy preparing for the next. Almost twenty years after *In Parenthesis*, Jones published *The Anathémata* (1952), meant to serve as sort of a creation story for Britain and overlay Christian salvation history onto island mythology. Like his friend the historian Christopher Dawson, who used the then-emerging disciplines of anthropology and sociology to understand Western culture, Jones used modernist poetry to reinterpret Western myth. While a critical success in some quarters (Auden, for example, considered it one of the finest long poems in English), *The Anathémata* never achieved iconic status.

Both *In Parenthesis* and *The Anathémata* are dense, allusive, demotic experiments, written to reflect what Jones called the "nowness" of poetry. "The poet, of whatever century," he wrote in 1952, "is concerned only with how he can use a current notion to express a permanent mythos." The

Originally published in *The New Criterion*, November 2006.

world emerging from the trenches of France had, to Jones, seemingly abandoned the traditional stories—the Grail Quest, *Roland*, not to mention the Good Samaritan and the Passion—which were becoming incomprehensible to modern man. Without a sure grounding in what Jones called the *materia* of the background culture, poetry becomes either a private joke or a vehicle for political or social activism. Jones called this the "objective problem" of the modern artist, who must work with images and signs after language has faded.

Jones was an established visual artist long before he was recognized as a poet. His paintings moved between the naturalistic and the allegorical, and avoided abstraction: "While the beauty of form and line can be appreciated without [a] common background...if the allusions are outside the comprehension of the reader or listener, clearly a sense of what is said is immeasurably blunted." Here, too, Jones had his admirers, including Kenneth Clark.

Jones was born in Brockley, Kent, to parents split between the low and high wings of the Church of England. His Welsh father, James, an evangelical, worked as a printer. His English-Italian mother, Alice, preferred the Oxford Movement's Edward Pusey and High Church. Although his father did not speak Welsh, the young Jones took up the Welsh culture his father largely had left behind. At the early age of fourteen, so young that the tutors would not allow him to draw the model from life, Jones entered the Camberwell Art School in London. He was there for five years, during which he was exposed not only to the traditional art-schooling of the day, but also to the work of the pre-Raphaelites and Pierre Bonnard, whose influences (especially in some of Jones's interiors) reappear in his own work.

In January 1915, just shy of twenty, Jones enlisted in the London Welsh Battalion of the Royal Welch Fusiliers. This was the same regiment in which Graves and Sassoon served as officers. Jones fought on the Western Front and was wounded at Mametz Wood, experiences he called "a parenthesis" between his early training and later career.

After the war, Jones continued his studies at the Westminster Art School, where he discovered the Post-Impressionists, whom he believed did more than make representations: "what is implicit in the notion of abstract art is that men make things which exist in their own right and... not 'impressions' of other things." The painting becomes a thing itself.

Jones had been on a religious quest even prior to his infantry service, and Christian symbols became Jones's materials after he returned from the war. As early as 1917, we see a crucifixion scene among Jones's sketches, though one that focuses not on Christ but on the Roman soldiers at the foot of the Cross, who are dressed like British tommies. After some period of hesitation, Jones converted to Roman Catholicism in 1921 under the direction of Father John O'Connor, the model for G. K. Chesterton's "Father Brown." His conversion fused his emerging sense of purpose as an artist with longing for a symbol-laden religion.

After a time at Ditchling Common, a community of craftsmen and artisans in Sussex founded by the woodworker and writer Eric Gill, Jones lived the life of a (sometimes almost literally) starving artist, largely relying on his network of friends for support, and moving constantly between his parents' home in Brockley, the Gills' various camps, and Rock Hall, the home of his long-time patron, Helen Sutherland. He also became involved with the interwar London literary scene, meeting Eliot in the late 1920s and congregating around a group of young Catholic artists, writers, and publishers. These relationships reinforced ideas about art Jones had developed in Ditchling. Jones was much taken with the French Thomist Jacques Maritain, whose *Art and Scholasticism* Jones read in 1923, and his conviction that art is a sacramental discipline devoted to representing the real.

In the 1920s and early 1930s, Jones provided woodcuts for editions of Coleridge's "Rime of the Ancient Mariner," Aesop's fables, and other works for the Golden Cockerel Press. And he began exhibiting in London with the 7&5 Society of painters and sculptors formed by Ben Nicholson, with whom Jones later broke because of their devotion to abstract painting. But overwork from efforts to express the Thomistic representation of reality in art resulted in a mental collapse in 1932, which did not lift until 1936; for the rest of his life, Jones struggled with depression, which led to the inability to work for long periods.

Jones completed *In Parenthesis*, which Eliot deemed a "work of genius," in 1932, but was unable to fine tune it for publication until his recovery four years later. Jones wrote snatches of the poem while on a painting trip to Brighton, and then was encouraged by friends to expand it into a poem. Keith Alldritt, a recent biographer, identifies the poem as one of a handful of works that define British modernism, along with *The Waste Land* and *Ulysses*. The text, a mixture of poetry and prose, recounts the fate of a British infantry unit, whose members come "from Islington and Hackney/ and the purlieus of Walworth/ flashers from Surbiton/ men of the stock of Abraham/ from Bromley-by-Bow." The poem follows them through training to an attack on the German lines somewhere in France, combining the banality of military life (soldiers "sucked Mackintosh's toffee where they lay/ and littered the narrow burrow with tiny grease-proof paper twists") with the terror of infantry warfare ("When the shivered rowan fell/you couldn't hear the fall of it./ Barrage and counter-barrage shockt/ deprive all several sounds of their identity").

A tone of Celtic wildness gives this work a distinctive, bardic tincture. Merlin and Guinevere seem to hover just beyond the trenches. Here is the Welsh soldier Dai Great Coat proclaiming his ancestry, in the manner of traditional Celtic boasts:

> My fathers were with the Black Prince of Wales
> At the passion of the blind Bohemian king.
> * * *
> I was the spear in Balin's hand
> That made waste King Pellam's land.
> I took the smooth stones of the brook,
> I was with Saul
> playing before him.
> I saw him armed like Derfel Gatheren.

Jones thought that only when the war was placed in a literary context, beginning with the Welsh epic *Y Goddodin*, could it make any sense at all.

Jones was not, as we now use the terms, "pro-" or "anti-" war; combat for him was a basic fact of human existence, and for him a searing experience, to be understood and explained in the context of tradition. The historian Paul Fussell, who nevertheless called Jones an "unclassifiable genius" in his *Great War and Modern Memory*, thought this strategy a failure. The Great War was so completely new and "other," Fussell argued, that Jones's attempts to link it with the soldiers of Western cultural memory were misguided.

After the publication of *In Parenthesis*, Jones returned to painting, for which he achieved increasing recognition. He was included as one of "Nine British Contemporaries" in a November 1945 exhibition on the Champs-Elysées, and his sales were steady through the 1940s. But Jones continued to work on what he called an "uncompleted writing," which became *The Anathémata*, subtitled "fragments of an attempted writing." Its subject is the Christianization of the West in general and Britain in particular. Jones starts twenty millennia before Christ, in the Paleolithic age, and mixes anthropology and geology with his reinterpretation of Welsh myth and Roman history. The poem is heavily annotated, covering Bronze Age archeology to obscure points of theology, and its diction veers from Old Welsh, Latin, and Greek, to various specialized vocabularies of shipbuilding and soldiering.

Jones sets the stage in the first few lines of the poem:

> the cult-man stands alone in Pellam's land:
>   more precariously than he
> knows he guards the *signa*: the pontifex
>   among his house
> treasures (the twin-*urbes* his house is) he can
>   fetch things new
> and old...the things come down
>   from heaven together with the
> kept memorials, the things lifted up and
>   the venerated trinkets.

All these—memorials and trinkets—are part of what Jones referred to as the "deposit" of myth and artifacts that constitutes the Western tradition. Jones mixes the iconography of England and Christianity through images that render the two together. A ship, for example, is not only a symbol of England, but, being made of wood, also a symbol of the Cross. When Jones writes of the domestication of the dog as man's companion, he brings in Cerberus, the dog of the New Testament who comforted Lazarus, Odysseus's dog Argos, and the myriad hounds in Welsh and Arthurian myth. The extensive notes that accompany *The Anathémata* refer to multiple meanings of particular words, as if Jones was afraid to let any resonance pass unnoticed.

The second section, "Middle-Sea and Lear-Sea," places Christ's birth in the sweep of Western history, as Christianity spread from the Mediterranean to England, a theme that returns in the penultimate section, "Mabinog's Liturgy," which refers to the "seven hundred and eighty-third year," since the founding of Rome, and the thirty-fourth since "his Leda/ said to his messenger/ (his bright *talaria* on)/ *fiat mihi*." This is the story of the Nativity, which Jones will bring forward to the Resurrection. Jones again invokes the Celtic boast, this time that of Christ:

> *Alpha es et O*
> That which the whole world cannot hold.
> Atheling to the heaven-king.
> Shepherd of Greekland
> Harrower of Annwn
> Freer of the Waters
> Chief Physician, and
> *Dux et pontifex.*

Jones closes the poem at the altar of the Mass, where the priest performs the sacrifice "after the mode/ of what has always been done... . What did he do yet other/ riding the Axile Tree?" The mode Jones used—highly idiosyncratic, non-chronological, and mixing common speech with profound reflections on the divine in history—was meant to express the "nowness" that he deemed essential to poetry. As Jones wrote in a fragment first published in 1967, "I have been on my guard/ not to condemn the unfamiliar. For it is easy to miss Him/ at the turn of a civilization." Civilization had turned, but *The Anathémata* was to serve as a kind of guidebook for those who could no longer see the past straight behind them.

At first blush, all this may be, and sometimes is, too much. Jones himself thought the poem "damned obscure" and he complained that it had "barely registered" with its intended audience. Most of the early reviews concentrated on the sources of Jones's allusions, and few on his poetic attempt to recreate a new source-text that incorporates all that went before. Around the time of the poem's publication, Jones became even more despondent about the success of his type of poetry:

> I'm becoming more and more doubtful as to the validity of this way of carrying on. It's not just names or being able to pronounce them: it involves a whole complex of associations. So far classical allusions and biblical ones and (in my case) liturgical ones still more or less work, but only more or less, because the whole of the past, as far as I can make out, is down the drain.

His paintings during this period reflect the same compression of symbols. A 1947 watercolor, *Vexilla Regis*, for example, is crowded with a checklist of Roman and Christian symbols and does not quite work to convey any living symbolic heritage.

Beginning in the 1940s and 1950s, Jones focused more on inscriptions, which allowed him to construct word-pictures that themselves act as symbols. Since Ditchling, Jones had experimented with inscriptions, but they were clearly secondary to painting and poetry. After a second bout with depression in the 1940s, for which he was treated with drugs and electroshock therapy, he came back to this form. His 1956 watercolor inscription, *Arbor Decora*, mixes Greek, Roman, and Anglo-Saxon lettering in various colors. Similarly, his brilliant 1958 inscription *nam Sibyllam* replaces Anglo-Saxon with Welsh, and adds Middle French and a passage from *The Waste Land* running vertically along the side.

In the 1950s and 1960s, Jones began to enjoy some level of literary celebrity, receiving the CBE in 1955 and the Bollingen Prize in 1959, but his cultural influence remains opaque. Today there are no Jones disciples, and he is eclipsed by the other British modernists. It is perhaps tempting to see, especially in the inscriptions, a connection with our hyperlinked world—words and images fused together in one multimedia spectacle. But this comparison misses a crucial distinction. Contrary to too many ironic-hip critics, Jones believed that words have meaning, that symbols point the way, and that the artist should direct them to uncovering an ultimate unity.

# *The Poet, the Great War, and "The Break"*

❧

**The centenary of World War I** has occasioned numerous commemorations of the generation of poets who wrote about the war. The work of Rupert Brooke, Siegfried Sassoon, Robert Graves, Edmund Blunden, Julian Grenfell, Wilfred Owen, and many others define the experience of the Great War in a way different from almost any other conflict. If the post-World War II era is defined by reportage, and current conflicts by YouTube videos and Twitter accounts, the first real world war remains defined and understood by its poetry.

However, one poet of that generation has not received similar attention, even though his experiences as a British soldier in France became a poem praised by T. S. Eliot and W. B. Yeats. In 1937, David Jones published a long narrative poem titled *In Parenthesis*. Born in Brockley, Kent, in 1895, Jones (1895–1974) was the son of a Welsh father and an English-Italian mother. It was the Welsh heritage that Jones warmed to above all others. He was just short of twenty years old, a promising art school student, when he entered the British Army. He was a soldier in the Royal Welsh Fusiliers (as was fellow war-poet Graves), and went on to become a well-known painter and engraver and a convert to Catholicism. The central events of *In Parenthesis* arose out of Jones' searing memories of the War, especially the attack by the British on German-held Mametz Wood in 1916. In his adult life he suffered severe bouts of depression and inactivity, and it was not until later in life, in the 1950s and 1960s, when he achieved

---

Originally published in *Catholic World Report*, December 11, 2014.

some level of renown. Even that was short-lived, however, and he again is threatened with being forgotten.

*The Times Literary Supplement* called *In Parenthesis* "one of the most remarkable literary achievements of our time," and it ended up winning the prestigious Hawthornden Prize in 1937. Jones' biographer Keith Alldritt lists it alongside James Joyce's *Ulysses* and Eliot's *The Wasteland* as one of the great modernist literary works. Like many modernist masterpieces, the poem is not conventionally structured and it has long semi-prose passages with lots of military argot and slang, not all of which is explained at once. Like Eliot with his 1922 poem, *The Wasteland*, Jones appended notes to the poem to explain some of the more obscure references and allusions. But that structure gives the poem much of its power. The poem carries readers into the training grounds and battlefield, and the shifting voices and perspectives Jones uses gives some sense of the confusion and complexity of battle.

But *In Parenthesis* is also a war poem in the tradition of the *Iliad*, the *Aeneid*, and the warrior legends of Jones' native Wales. He begins *in medias res*, as any epic must, with the mustering of soldiers already organized into companies and regiments to face battle on the continent. "Heavy jolting and sideways jostling, the noise of liquid shaken in a small vessel by a regular jogging movement, a certain clinking ending in a shuffling of the feet sidelong—all clear and distinct in that silence peculiar to parade grounds and refectories" goes a typical passage, the sounds of the words invoking the sounds on that parade-ground. The poem is divided into seven parts, following the actions of several soldiers, but centered around John Ball and Aneirin Lewis. Ball is the personification of Britain; Lewis and others, including the mysterious Dai Greatcoat, of Wales.

Jones worked for years after the War to finish *In Parenthesis*, but did not publish it until dark clouds were already forming in advance of the next European, and world, war. That timing perhaps partially explains its relative neglect; the poem was seen as explaining the last war, when all eyes were on the one coming. But there is also a difference in tone between Jones' work and those of the other poets during this centenary. Many of the war poets who have perhaps been better remembered convey their elegiac tone in their poetry, of a world lost in a mad rush to war, and the tragic death of so many young men. Thus Owen famously wrote poems like "Dulce et Decorum Est," which dwelled on the ugliness and waste of modern warfare, and that was meant to counteract what some saw as the more straightforward war poetry of others, such as Brooke. That antiwar mood largely suits our own, comparatively peaceful era, where the governing classes are further away from the fighting classes than they were a century ago. And there is an added difficulty: much of the poetry in the war focuses on individual experience and on individual suffering and pain, and so is more easily understandable in our individualist age.

Jones fits in neither camp, and indeed in his later years despaired that his poetry would be understood because the past he meant to capture was disappearing. He does not discount the disaster and sorrow of war, which are there throughout the poem, along with the boredom and endless waiting. Jones can convey the fierceness of war in short phrases: "When the shivered rowan fell/you couldn't hear the fall of it./Barrage and counter-barrage shockt/deprive all several sounds of their identity.") In the last part of the poem, for example, the British and Welsh soldiers are pinned down, and can hear the cannon fire around them.

> And the surfeit of fear steadies to dumb incognition, so that when they give the order to move upward…hugged already just under the lip of the acclivity inches below where his traversing machine-guns perforate to powder white—
>
> white creatures of chalk pounded
> and the world crumbled away
> and get ready to advance
> you have no capacity for added fear only the limbs are leaden
> to negotiate the slope and rifles all out of balance, clumsied
> with long auxiliary steel

For Jones, war was simply a fact, and it was a horror unless it could be understood, and for Jones the scarring experience of fighting could be understood only through the cultural traditions in which it took place. Thus the Roman legions and the Round Table, crusading knights and medieval Welsh warriors, haunt this poem and enrich its language. But he nevertheless contended that there was something noble about the profession of soldiering amidst the violence, tedium, and tragedy. In his own introduction to the poem, Jones marvels at the experience of different men being thrown together in common experience and to a shared purpose; Jones speaks of it as a place of dark "enchantment." His soldiers come from a variety of backgrounds, from "Islington and Hackney/and the purlieus of Walworth/flashers from Surbiton/men of the stock of Abraham/from Bromley-by-Bow." As a Catholic, Jones knew that war was an inevitable result of the Fall; but because of grace even fallen activities can be redeemed. Indeed, in his preface to the poem, he writes he was not necessarily intending to write a "war poem" at all. Rather, he wanted it to be about "a certain kind of peace... We search how we may see formal goodness in a life singularly inimical, hateful, to us."

During the 1920s and 1930s, Jones, who converted to Catholicism in 1921, was among a group of Catholic writers and intellectuals who were exploring a world that seemed to be falling apart. At that time, the threats were from the materialist ideologies of communism, Nazism, and fascism; more broadly, the West was faced with a general rejection of religious belief and with it a rupture from its cultural past, what Jones and others at the time called "the Break." Those figures, including the historian Christopher Dawson, confronted what they saw as a real challenge to religious artists and writers. If the culture no longer spoke in the language of the Gospel, literature or art invoking that language was at risk of being incomprehensible. Like the early Christian engagement with the pagan Roman Empire, Christianity—and the art used to express it—needed to be familiar and yet also completely new.

*In Parenthesis* was one attempt to repair that break; so in another way was Jones's visual work, as he was an accomplished painter and illustrator even before he achieved prominence as a poet. The danger for Jones was that an entire way of seeing and understanding that world lay on the other side of that widening space; he feared that and once it was gone, art as it had been known in the West, with a shared symbolic language and references, would be gone as well. Without what he called the *materia* of the larger culture, poetry becomes either simple narcissism or empty word games, a fate many would say has already befallen contemporary poetry. So his work is tightly wrapped with allusion and citation to the great tradition of the West, both Christian and pagan, in an effort to connect the experiences of the soldiers in the trenches with the larger martial tradition.

This gives his poetry a completely different feel from that of the other war-poets, even those with a then-typical classical education. *In Parenthesis* ends, for example, with a passage combining the ancient legends of Europe such as King Arthur, and Christendom's tales of heroism, such as the Song of Roland. The complexity of the poem, therefore, was not, as it became in some works of the period, simply for its own sake. It was meant to point outside of itself toward the truths of human nature and the story of salvation.

In his work, Jones was trying to compress the history of his culture into an account of the war that brought that culture to an end. He continued this project in later, even more challenging works such as his long poem called *The Anathemata*, published in 1952, which combined the Christian story of salvation with the unique history of the British Isles. These poems, and his visual art, remain a kind of guidebook to the history of the West, and to the world without end to which he believed that history points.

# *Hildebrand's Aesthetic of the Universal*

**The vociferous reaction** from the usual suspects to the proposed executive order, drafted this past February by the non-profit National Civic Art Society, that the federal government build "with special regard for the classical architectural style" was unsurprising. Opponents claimed that the proposal was "weaponizing" classical architecture and was "borderline totalitarian." *The New Republic* wrote that the move "would stifle architecture and violate the free thought and artistic expression that are essential to a democracy." But of course, to these skeptics, architects should be free to impose their "vision" on a public space at taxpayers' expense. Whatever the merits of the proposal, it is hard not to see in the opposition a dedication to a certain view of aesthetics, one that caricatures the notion of objectively beautiful public buildings as a tool of oppression or political tyranny, or more simply a postmodern position that "impl[ies] the complete rejection of beauty in any positive sense," as Dana Gioia describes it in a foreword to one of the volumes reviewed here. But having the ability to recognize what is good or beautiful is central to a culture, something the West is in danger of losing completely.

In his monumental two-volume *Aesthetics*, the German philosopher Dietrich von Hildebrand (1889–1977) rejects the notion that beauty is unimportant to nurturing civilization or is somehow reserved only for the elite or privileged: "One should not make the mistake of assuming that because many people today apparently lack any sensitivity to beauty, beauty is not a fundamental source of happiness, even for the simplest people....

Originally published in *The New Criterion*, September 2020.

The atrophy of this sensitivity is a terrible loss, and this ought not to be interpreted as a progress that modern man has made in the industrialized world." As a consequence of our rejection of beauty, we have confused our understanding of aesthetic experience. Now everything is "art" if it expresses some feeling, no matter how vulgar or ugly, and it seems we must promote—and pay for—anything designated as art.

Hildebrand is receiving renewed interest as his major works have been translated (or re-translated) in the last few years, thanks largely to the efforts of the Hildebrand Institute and his wife Alice, a philosopher herself and a close collaborator. More recognized in Europe, Hildebrand has had admirers such as Pope John Paul II and figures such as Gioia, Roger Scruton, and John Finnis, who provide forewords to these volumes that help introduce Dietrich to the Anglophone world. Hildebrand's work ranges widely but was primarily focused on aesthetics, ethics, and moral philosophy.

A son of Adolf von Hildebrand, a well-known sculptor who himself penned an influential aesthetic treatise, Dietrich was born and raised in Florence in a cultured household focused on art. The Hildebrand villa was something of a regular stop among German artists, composers, and writers as they toured Italy. As a young man, Dietrich made the reverse trip, visiting Bayreuth at the request of Wagner's widow, then (in 1907) beginning studies in Munich under Max Scheler and Edmund Husserl, both of whom remained significant influences on his work. Scheler ultimately was perhaps the stronger influence. He introduced Hildebrand to the idea that holiness could also be beautiful, and it was Scheler who was the crucial factor in Hildebrand's conversion to Catholicism in 1914. As John F. Crosby, Hildebrand's most astute American interpreter, writes in the introduction to *Aesthetics*, Scheler combined for Hildebrand aesthetics and philosophical beauty through the examples of the saints. The moral values these figures express, "though not themselves aesthetic values...have a certain radiance or splendor of beauty and thus have aesthetic value. They are not in the first place aesthetic values, but they *also* have aesthetic value." Hildebrand expands upon this insight in his work, and ultimately concludes that moral values such as generosity, courage, and purity, among others, have aesthetic value as well.

Hildebrand remained in Germany and by 1921 had already been targeted by the Nazis for his opposition to their program. He left Germany for Austria, where he continued to write and speak against Hitler's party. No less a figure than Franz von Papen, the German ambassador in Vienna, complained that the "damned Hildebrand is the greatest obstacle for National Socialism in Austria. No one causes more harm." Hitler himself, in the years before the *Anschluss*, demanded that the Austrian government shut down the opposition paper Hildebrand was publishing. Later in life, Hildebrand wrote an account of his anti-Nazi work at the request of his wife Alice, titled *My Battle with Hitler*. After much difficulty, Hildebrand, his first wife (who died in 1957), son, and daughter-in-law had fled Europe and landed in New York City in 1940. He taught at Fordham University until 1960, when he retired from teaching, though not from writing: several dozen more books appeared before his death in 1977.

Phenomenology is focused on understanding experience from a philosophical perspective. At a very general level, rather than deducing from initial, perhaps abstract truths, phenomenologists of Hildebrand's sort start instead with our experiential knowledge. This approach has its dangers. Deriving philosophical truths from any situation may lead to the conclusion that the right action is simply based on what one *feels* to be right in that situation. Indeed, a kind of degraded phenomenology is the ethical currency of our age. Everyone must live "their truth," we are told, because no one can really understand the other's actions or judge them according to some external, objective standard. Hildebrand rejected this easy relativism. We may be particular actors faced with specific factual situations, with our own unique life histories, but that experience can still be subjected to a moral framework. In *Morality and Situation Ethics*, first published in 1966, Hildebrand addresses those "champions of situation ethics [who] would do away with every bond. Because of their idol of freedom, they interpret the intrinsic 'oughtness' character of the moral sphere as being an adaptation of morality to the juridical sphere"—in other words, the proponents of simple legalism. As Finnis notes, this book was a full-scale assault on the philosophers and theologians who were beginning to develop what became known as "proportionalism" or other kinds of situationism, which placed much more emphasis on the interior, subjective state of the actor, and less on whether there was an external standard to which that actor must conform.

As Rocco Buttiglione writes in his foreword to *Graven Images*, Hildebrand "was convinced that an accurate phenomenological analysis can clearly distinguish values as they present themselves in human experience from the psychological and emotional phenomena that accompany and very often distort them." One of the great strengths of Hildebrand's approach is that he writes clearly about the differences between the experience of art and the objective reality of the art object itself. In an essay titled "Aestheticism and the True Disposition to Art," he opposes the idea that "content can exist only in subjective, emotional effects that are of no importance." To the contrary: "I really grasp the autonomy and intrinsic importance of art only when I see that it possesses not only its own language but also a content of its own, which is thoroughly objective and must be distinguished from subjective emotional effects."

*The Aesthetics*, which has, surprisingly, never before been translated into English, tries to draw out those distinctions across numerous media. The first volume sets out the difference between moral values (which Hildebrand calls "metaphysical beauty") and aesthetic values that have no separate moral content ("audible and visual beauty"). Thus a bad person can have a pretty face. Aristophanes can be funny but also obscene. The pretty face has visual beauty, but that tells us nothing about the person's moral value; Hildebrand writes that "the sublime spiritual beauty of the visible and the audible is clearly distinct from expressed metaphysical beauty." A physically unsightly saint's holiness, however, radiates from them in a way we appreciate as beautiful—not only morally but also, in a way, aesthetically. (Note that this is different from the belief that a saint who works as an artist must be a great artist: "[A] saint who works as an artist need not produce any great works of art.")

But how does that interplay work in everyday aesthetic experience? Hildebrand does not say simply that art serves a didactic purpose, as a channel to the transcendent. He starts with the experiential fact that audible or visual beauty—a piece of music, a striking sunset—has, as Crosby phrases it, a "beauty that does not seem to be proper to, or proportioned to, the light and colors and spatial expanse from which it arises." That is, we are struck more deeply by the view of a majestic mountain than the mountain itself would seem able to bear. This "excess" aesthetic experience is not an illusion, nor does it need to mean that the experience is some kind of divine interpolation on a natural event. Rather, Hildebrand keeps the two phenomena—natural beauty on the one hand and internal experience of excess on the other—in a "sacramental" balance. In a section called "The Solution to the Riddle," Hildebrand calls this contrast a *mirandum*, a wonder. The key distinction is this: a person possessed of moral values becomes transfigured so that the bearer and what is borne (metaphysical beauty) are the same. For Hildebrand's "audible and visual beauty," however, a mountain that evokes in us an experience of sublime visual beauty, is still a mountain: the bearer and the borne are not quite the same. Rather, that experience "proclaims much higher realities," a framework that Hildebrand puts to use in examining the Catholic doctrine of the sacraments.

Hildebrand has an undeniably elevated and cultivated taste, and one might feel on an initial read that his approaches to aesthetic value have little resonance in a world of high-definition movies, video games, and graphic novels. But that impression does not do justice to Hildebrand's analyses, which categorize and enumerate the differences among aesthetic experiences. Hildebrand is precise and careful in delineating how we experience art. The *Aesthetics* include discussions of "The Role of the Senses in Apprehending Beauty," "The Three Antitheses to Beauty: Ugliness, Triviality, and Boringness," and "Beauty and Truth," among other topics.

In the second volume, Hildebrand uses his overall approach to examine several different forms of art, including painting, music, and architecture. But the philosopher does not look at these media generically. He distinguishes among types of visual styles—image, representation, the difference between a "copy" and a "replica"—across types of media such as painting, drawing, and photography. The existence of the visual, representative arts is a mark of our humanity: "The ability to recognize and understand a representation also presupposes the human being as a spiritual person. A dog will not recognize its master in a photograph or portrait." Hildebrand does not, as one might expect, denigrate photography in favor of painting. Instead he tries definitively to articulate what each is able to achieve. Photography, as well as figurative painting and drawing, is the representation of visible reality. In the former, however, we get something "fully present. This is not a link that passes via the intellect, as with the word." The insertion, however, of the camera and the related technical process, makes photographic representation different from that expressed by paint or pencil. It is not the thoughtless work of a machine; photography still involves the "leading role" of the photographer that "determines the whole photograph in its quality, in its effectiveness, and so on." Still, Hildebrand finds this different in kind from a painting or most drawings because a photograph is a type of "perception": we see the object in its fullness and "perceive its essence. This is more than a mere acquisition of knowledge." But it is also different from the representation of a painting. There, the fullness of presentation is absent, so we must supply what Hildebrand calls "imaginative perception" to account for the immediacy of perception he finds in photography, which in turn calls for an interplay between artist, object, and viewer.

He subjects music to the same treatment and distinguishes the folk song—which invites us in to sing along as part of a community, which grows organically and from a deep tradition—from what we would call pop music. This latter category, Hildebrand says, is "generated artificially," has "a frivolous tone," and is a "typical child of fashion" that is destined to be short-lived. Neither need be great art, nor "bad" art. But each should be understood for what it is, before we can apply a moral framework to it.

Similarly with architecture. How can we tell what a "good" (note the combination of morality and usefulness implied in that word) building is? Scruton, in his foreword, notes that Hildebrand takes care to focus on a range of examples of building, such as fountains, towers, and staircases; Hildebrand recognizes "the inescapable nature of the art of building, which is exhibited in all our attempts to settle.... We understand architecture not merely as a structure that encloses, but also as a way of shaping, decorating, and opening all the spaces where we conduct our lives." Architecture is a public art, and a builder must be sensitive to the context in which the building is to be added. Unlike most other arts, architecture has what Hildebrand calls two themes: the practical, in that buildings have purposes, from shelter to religious worship, and the artistic, the beauty of the structure itself.

Of course, as Hildebrand recognized, beauty can itself become a god, and worship of beauty a morality of sorts. His own upbringing was in a kind of nonsectarian Protestantism, but really it was a culture of beauty-worship. Hildebrand's *Graven Images* explores what it means for an individual and a culture to exchange other idols for true moral understanding. His chapter on the "main substitutes" of morality is required reading for anyone trying to make sense of the current moral landscape—even though it was first published in 1957. His paragraph on "liberalism" could be written today about the average "social justice warrior":

> Moral goodness is identified with broad-mindedness, desire of progress, tolerance. Several fundamental amoral values such as purity, reverence, humility are not included in morality. Other moral values such as justice, veracity, generosity are seen in the light of the open-minded liberalism, erroneously interpreted as consequences of this morality.

It is noteworthy that Hildebrand focuses on purity here, as a large part of his work is also about interpersonal ethics, including sexual morality. The progressivism that Hildebrand discusses is often joined with the idea that morality is simply what one desires: "any law that imposes a control on the spontaneous impulses of our heart is seen as the expression of a monstrous rigidity, a bureaucratic pharasisim." The Italian philosopher Augusto del Noce, writing also around this time, focused on the elimination of modesty and purity as the opening for an ethics of "pure animalism."

In contrast, Hildebrand sets out the Christian view of morality, which is neither legalistic in the sense in which situationists believe nor committed to a boundless individualism. Nor is it simply loyalty to abstractions like "progress," in the way of the contemporary Left. Rather, the grounding of a Christian ethic is that we must conform ourselves to the objective moral order, and model ourselves *similitudo Dei.* "The fundamental obligations of the moral law are based on the essence and the nature of man, and on his essential relationships, and thus they have force wherever we find man," in each of our unique circumstances. This is precisely why we can talk about "universal" truths or recognize virtues across times and events. Hildebrand's aesthetic and philosophical work is perfectly suited to meet the particular challenge of our age—the primacy of individual feeling—because it makes the connection between that individuality and the universal.

# *Mr. Eliot's Double Life*

THE LETTERS OF T. S. ELIOT, *Volume 1:* 1898–1922; *Volume* 2: 1923–1925—the first published originally in 1988, the second now joining it with much fanfare—chronicle the period during which T.S. Eliot developed from the scion of a prosperous Midwestern family to the poet of *The Waste Land* and "Prufrock," but also to a banker and one-man editorial staff of a fledgling new journal of "cosmopolitan tendencies and international standards," The Criterion, which would attract writers across Europe.

Perhaps the most notable of these early letters includes the draft of a poem that did not see publication until long after the poet's death, in *Inventions of the March Hare* (1997). The poem, a slightly erotic reverie called "The Love Song of St. Sebastian," was later included in a notebook given to John Quinn, a lawyer and early supporter of Eliot who makes frequent appearances in these letters. Eliot sent the draft in July 1914 to his friend the poet Conrad Aiken, whom he had met when they were undergraduates at Harvard, and wrote that he was glad that "the war danger was over"—though that, of course, was not to be. A letter written to his mother the following month recounts Eliot's hastily leaving Marburg, where he was studying, for Rotterdam on the eve of World War I. Although Eliot does not seem ever to have been particularly happy, these early letters contain drawings and lighthearted sketches, the likes of which largely disappear as he gets older.

His subsequent stay at Oxford lasted only a year, and he gave some thought to returning to America, perhaps to teach philosophy. Instead,

---

Originally published in *Chronicles*, March 2013.

that year settled him in England for the remainder of his life. In 1915, he married Vivienne Haigh-Wood, whom he had known only a short time, an event unbeknownst to both their parents. The union was spectacularly unhappy, but Eliot later credited Vivienne at least with keeping him away from America and thus preserving him for poetry. The few of her letters included here show a flighty, troubled person but one with some humor, talent, and a measure of devotion to Eliot.

By and large, these volumes do not lend much insight into Eliot the poet or prose critic. *The Waste Land*, for example, is mentioned almost in passing, except to discuss its publishing details. And amid the encomia that accompanied the poem in the memory of the contemporary reader lay Eliot's own throwaway judgment in November 1922 to Richard Aldington, an Imagist poet and friend of Pound's, that the poem "is a thing of the past so far as I'm concerned and am now feeling toward a new form and style." He does not elaborate, and new concerns, including *The Criterion*, emerged to draw him away from regular writing.

The letters are an account of Eliot's two emerging lives. The first is that of Eliot the husband, who needs to find secure employment to take care of his wife. Vivienne began ailing from a number of illnesses almost from the beginning of their marriage, and her poor health is a constant refrain in these letters. Eliot, too, was often sick, and the letters are filled with descriptions of treatments and doctors' visits. Eliot has long been criticized for his treatment of Vivienne—in the 1930's she was admitted to a psychiatric hospital, where Eliot never visited—but his letters make his concern for her health quite evident. The expense necessary to allay those concerns added to the Eliots' already precarious financial situation.

The second is the Eliot who came to London to participate in the literary life away from an America he thought provincial and vulgar; as he wrote shortly after his wedding, "if one is to do anything in literature [London] is the best place to be." He had important friends, most notably Ezra Pound, who wrote to Eliot's father about the prospects of a literary life in London and to defend Eliot's decision to remain. Eliot's parents seem to have been extraordinarily generous and supportive of this quixotic effort by their son, who soon got himself a job at Lloyd's of London and wrote when he could.

In these volumes, Eliot's champion Pound comes across as a combination of preening self-confidence ("I have engineered a new school of verse") and generosity. It was Pound who tried to gin up a fund among wealthy admirers to support Eliot. Called Bel Esprit, the effort was to release Eliot from the bank. The stress of writing poetry and criticism (Eliot was writing reviews in order to make extra money), working, and caring for Vivienne was too much for him. The idea first appears in a letter from Pound to Eliot in 1922, though Pound had discussed such a thing with Quinn at least two years earlier.

Eliot was grateful for the effort but cautious, in particular because did not want the fund to become public knowledge. He was working at Lloyd's, after all, and talk of independent support could threaten his job prospects and his ability to care for Vivienne. Eliot seems in fact to have been quite good at his job; by 1923 he was writing his brother Henry of his management of a department of clerks, with a recently raised salary of 500 pounds and "a position of responsibility." This was his situation after the publication of *The Waste Land* in 1922 had confirmed his talent and attracted notice on both sides of the Atlantic. Even then, he was writing Pound that he could not leave the bank unless he received "such guarantees—for my life or *for Vivien's life*—as would satisfy a solicitor." In the event, the scheme went nowhere, and he remained at Lloyd's until 1925, when he joined the new publishing firm of Faber and Gwyn.

The second volume shows Eliot hard at work on his journal, which was supported first by Eliot's longtime patron Lady Rothermere and later by Faber itself. He is tirelessly writing, in several languages, to the luminaries of the age, and many lesser lights, in furtherance of the publication and his own work: Herman Hesse, Robert Graves, Virginia Woolf, W.B. Yeats, Owen Barfield, and E.R. Curtius are among those with whom Eliot corresponded to generate copy for the magazine. It ends with Eliot (in December 1925) praising *The Great Gatsby* and asking Fitzgerald whether he would be interested in being published in England by Faber—and would he happen to have any stories lying around for *The New Criterion*? (Eliot always had the keen sense of salesmanship and business acumen needed to run a cultural enterprise of this sort.)

But that effort, too, produced great strains. In March 1923, Eliot writes that his work for the journal and for Lloyd's has brought him to near exhaustion. It was only the transfer to Faber in 1925 that eased, a little, his personal and financial pressures. And not a moment too soon. The pressure was so great that, in an exchange in April of that year with the critic John Middleton Murry, Eliot confides that "I have made myself into a machine. I have done it deliberately—in order to endure, in order not to feel—but it has killed V." His words have been interpreted as a sign of Eliot's disdain for Vivienne, but in context it is better understood as an expression of a protracted agony by a young man in a challenging marriage. Murry gives what words of support he can, being a friend to both husband and wife, but in the end he sided with Eliot. First forcefully in a private letter ("There is a point at which the choice really is: she may die, I must die. Then you must say: I will not die"), next less so in a letter meant for Vivienne's eyes ("But, if you will really lead, take the decision and the responsibility, V. will follow.") What is clear is that during this period Eliot took his marriage very seriously and was shaken to his core by the difficulties his wife was enduring.

These volumes chronicle, almost daily, the tireless effort Eliot put into satisfying his obligations—literary, professional, and personal. They shed new light on the person and on the age, but it may be the role of later volumes to throw new light on the works itself.

# PART FIVE

## *The Catholic Thing*

# *Catholics in America: An Uneasy Alliance*

AT FIRST, it may seem Catholicism contributed little to the American founding. The Founding Fathers were Protestants or deists and had themselves mostly arrived from the formerly Catholic kingdoms of England and Scotland, many as dissenters from the initial dissent of King Henry VIII. They had little obvious sympathy for Catholic doctrine or political thought.

Among the Founders in 1776, only Charles Carroll of Carrollton was Catholic. The Acton Institute's Samuel Gregg has invoked Carroll as an example of a Founding-era Catholic who sought to integrate his faith with the secular republic of the young United States, even though at the time Catholics labored under significant civic restrictions. But Carroll was an outlier, both in terms of his faith and his influence, owing to the fact that he was one of the richest men in the Colonies at the time of independence.

Catholics were a minority in the Colonies and initially of little political significance. There was a further problem. In Europe, the Church was facing the inferno of the French Revolution and was in no mood to endorse or support a government across the Atlantic that rejected the Church and, instead, literally deified reason. The government the Founders instituted in the United States, with its religious freedom, popular sovereignty, and individual liberty, seemed quite far from that of Catholic states such as Spain or the Holy Roman Empire. The invocation of "Nature's God" in the Declaration of Independence, and the separation at the federal level between ecclesial and political authority, was foreign to much of the Catholic

---

Originally published in *Chronicles*, September 2020.

experience of political life. Moreover, the placement of sovereignty with the people and the absence, for example, of clear references to the common good or to the obligations of citizens to God in the founding documents were likewise foreign. At base, it seemed, America was a Protestant nation, in which Catholics could not feel welcome.

But that is not the whole story. America, as it happens, is larger than the original 13 Colonies. The history of Catholics in America is older than the nation itself and older even than the British Colonies. St. Augustine, Florida, was founded by the Spanish in 1565, and the French were in parts of Maine by the first years of the seventeenth century, followed by the Spanish again in Texas and the West. The Louisiana Purchase is an early example of the new nation absorbing a large land mass settled and populated by Catholics, with a different political and legal tradition.

Like many progressive political impulses, outrages like the recent toppling of statues of Saint Junípero Serra in California may have the opposite effect by erasing even further the non-white, non-Anglo-Saxon, non-Protestant history of the country, eliminating the Spanish and indigenous settlements that were there by the time the "Americans" arrived. On the other hand, if this iconoclasm is appropriately resisted by those who care about the nation's admittedly complicated history, it may herald a return to the larger history of contributions of Catholic settlements to the American story. Indeed, some "postliberal" Catholic writers half-jokingly refer to the "Empire of Our Lady of Guadalupe" as a successor to America.

Even that is not the whole story. Since the founding, America has proven to be a congenial home for millions of Catholics, especially as they began to arrive in greater numbers in the nineteenth century. These Catholics were unrelated to French or Spanish efforts at empire building, but were instead fleeing the poverty of the Old World. They embraced the "American way of life," sometimes without knowing it, and the tensions between the Catholic and "American" understandings of political life grew less severe.

Sure, the Know Nothings made life difficult for Catholics, and the last of the anti-Catholic Blaine Amendments was overruled by the Supreme Court just this year. But in spite of these hurdles, Catholics built up a network of their own social and political structures within America. By the early twentieth century, Catholics were well-established in most urban centers across the country. World War II and the Cold War gave them the opportunity to prove their loyalty. By the 1980s, Catholic writers like George Weigel and Michael Novak were quite happy to harmonize neo-conservative economics and foreign policy with Catholic thought.

Nevertheless, the basic conundrum of Catholics in America, evident from Carroll's time, remained: there was much to be celebrated and supported in the Founding, but it remained somewhat incomplete. Catholics could not shake the fact that there seemed to be something not quite right about America. In 1864, papal statements such as *Quanta cura* and the *Syllabus of Errors* condemned various theses that seemed awfully analogous to the American experience of religious liberty and personal freedom. They were a challenge to Catholics, who tried to find some common ground between the papal condemnations and the flourishing Catholic culture in America during the late nineteenth and twentieth centuries.

The writer Orestes Brownson, for example, ultimately interpreted these documents in accordance with what he saw as the true spirit of American liberty as well as Catholic teaching. But he also saw that the coming "liberalism" of post-Civil War America meant more than simply providing for the freedom of conscience and of the Church. It was rather "a total rejection of authority in church or in state, an absolutizing of individual conscience, a complete independence of church from the state (that is, political atheism)," and other factors.

Two things were happening at the same time. Catholics were becoming integrated into American society; also, Catholic thinkers were looking at the arc of liberalism and trying to shore up defenses against it. More recently, beginning in the 1950s, Catholic writers began to argue that in fact there were connections between the Founding and the older philosophical and religious traditions of the West. This connection was based on the idea of natural law. The Christian man formed over 2,000 years was a certain kind of being, and one different from the communist citizen or the emerging secular citizen.

Russell Kirk saw in the Constitution the glimmers not only of John Locke, but of the Anglican divine Richard Hooker, and through Hooker to Saint Thomas Aquinas and the scholastic tradition. Kirk saw in the provisions of the Constitution a reflection of the natural law tradition. Indeed his great work, *The Roots of American Order* (1974), was written to make precisely this point. America derived from the ideas of Montesquieu, Edmund Burke, David Hume, and William Blackstone. From these four, one could find a good portion of the intellectual heritage of the West.

In Kirk's view, this heritage was reflected by, but not fully contained in, the Constitution, whose framers "took it for granted that a moral order, founded on religious beliefs, supports and parallels the political order." For generations of Catholics, this was a close enough alignment to Pope Saint Gelasius I's Two Swords theory, positing the autonomy of the temporal and spiritual powers, for them not to worry too much about the niceties of political theory.

Kirk also argued that religion could not be separated from politics, though politics could not dominate religion. He wrote:

> Religion in America has never been a private concern merely. It is religious faith, indeed, that has made the American democracy successful; the lack of religious foundation has been the ruin of other democracies.

John Courtney Murray, S.J., in his famous book *We Hold These Truths* (1960), held that the First Amendment was meant to form a structure amenable to most of the Christian sects. They generally sidestepped the questions raised in *Quanta cura* by arguing that American constitutionalism was not substantive, like the philosophes' France.

One should not take these arguments too far, of course. No important Catholic writer thought that the Constitution permitted a confessional state, for example, or that it secretly imported Catholic theological concepts, despite rumblings by writers like Paul Blanshard. Murray believed that religious liberty was recognized in the Constitution because it was a good thing. Moreover, because religious faith—as well as its institutional and practical expressions—was a good thing, the country could prefer religious belief over nonbelief. Thus Catholics could have a seat at the table, because the Founders, in Murray's words, "built better than they knew," and reflected the natural law in their constitutional design.

Murray and Kirk caught a glimpse of what was coming, with Murray identifying the "post-modern" as the Cartesian dream of reason's mastery over the world and ourselves becoming, in fact, a nightmare. However, the speed of the rise of the "woke" brigades and the accelerated abandonment of America's Christian heritage has once again caused Catholics to doubt the compatibility of their faith with the American experiment. We see this in challenges to Catholic judicial nominees such as Amy Coney Barrett or Brian Buescher, as well as in more intentional attacks such as the Obama administration's attempt to coerce Catholic nuns into complying with its contraceptive mandate.

In response, a number of scholars dubbed "integralists" have argued that liberalism, arising out of the Protestant ground of the founding, cannot be reconciled with the Catholic understanding of the common good or the citizen. Patrick Deneen, Gladden Pappin, and Adrian Vermeule, for example, have in recent years mounted substantive critiques of liberalism that in general seem to take the position that the American experiment had to end in failure, that Lockean man inevitably leads to the woke activist. Economic liberalism is a dead end of exploitation and inequality that destroys the common good.

More important, the value of religious freedom is a Trojan horse: religious authority and government need to work together to support virtue. The famous story of Benjamin Franklin expressing the government's disinterest in whomever the Church appointed as bishops in the new nation—to the astonishment of the Vatican, accustomed as it was to negotiating with secular powers for ecclesiastical appointments—is turned on its head. Where it used to be a sign that Catholics, like others, could worship freely, in the integralist view the lack of sensitivity toward the mission of the Roman Church becomes an ultimately fatal weakness.

As a Catholic, I have some sympathy for the integralists, and would be very happy to live under the Catholic Habsburgs, for example. In particular, I appreciate their central insight that cultures are always animated by religious faith even if it is not recognized as such. Kirk himself, drawing on Christopher Dawson, for example, said much the same about secular replacements for religion. So yes, progressivism is a religion for some, with its own heroes and villains, saints and martyrs, holidays and rituals. And it is a secular religion, hostile to Christianity. Vermeule notes there is now a hierarchy of speech, where protests for acceptable, progressive causes are permitted despite the pandemic risk, but funerals and church services are prohibited.

What the integralists have done is to reveal the "neutral liberalism" of the aging baby boomers was a fantasy. For a generation, intellectuals on the right internalized the idea that so long as the economy was thriving and judges set out a level legal playing field, they could leave Hollywood, the media, and Silicon Valley to their own cultural devices. This was incorrect. The founding generation did not believe it, and the progressive, post-Christian elites do not believe it, and these latter are not afraid to use government power to enforce their beliefs.

The liberal consensus of the 1950s and 1960s broke, in part because elites forgot the connection between religious belief and public order. But those wishing for a Guadalupean Catholic empire in America also must face a similar problem. Taking the woke elites and the dispirited or misguided populace into an integralist state is inconsistent with the pluralist American tradition, and is unlikely to succeed—at least in a peaceful way. Moreover, as Richard Reinsch and others have written, Catholic contributions to political thought support the federal constitutional system and should be used to do so. Brownson, Murray, and Kirk realized that the Catholic contribution to the founding was to recast the combination of reason and faith that made it possible in the first place.

# *A Catholic Defense of Freedom*

❧

**For a generation,** some Catholics in America believed that the Gospel injunction to help the poor meant to help them through government. Joined to that was a distaste for the WASP-dominated business culture of postwar American prosperity, even though Catholics had enjoyed the fruits of that prosperity along with other Americans. The long tradition of Catholic reflection on the need for limited government and the licitness of a robust free market, was obscured.

Samuel Gregg, director of research at the Acton Institute, has written a vigorous defense of that tradition in the face of fresh threats to liberty. He represents a second wave of thinkers reflecting on Catholicism and the American experiment since Vatican II. The first generation, dominated by thinkers such as Michael Novak, returned to Catholic thought a favorable view of limited government and the free market. This was no easy sell. On the one hand, there were still groups of traditionalist Catholics who, disdaining modernity, thought that the better—indeed, the only proper—relationship between the state and church was a premodern one in which the Church controlled the excesses of the state from an official position, and the state controlled the excesses of the market. This may have made sense in a premodern world where the apparatus of state control was undeveloped, and where improvements in trade and finance made free-market exchanges difficult. But that had not been the case for some centuries, and a residual distaste among some Catholics for bourgeois society was not

---

Originally published in *Crisis*, September 5, 2013.

a sufficient basis to reject the unprecedented prosperity the free market brought to the world, rich and poor alike.

On the other hand, there were significant numbers of Catholics and other Christians who also believed the state needed to intervene and control the economy, but with less emphasis on any formal union between church and state. These advocates of 'social justice" were more than willing to let the Church take a backseat to political planners and a centralized economy. Thus an older generation of Catholic leaders, including bishops, equated the welfare state with Catholic teaching, and argued (for example, even recently against Congressman Paul Ryan and the United States Catholic Bishops Conference) that reduction of such programs was somehow contrary to Catholic teaching.

Gregg has three competing stories to tell. First, he wants to explain how a Catholic can responsibly defend limited government and the free market in accordance with Catholic teaching. This remains a crucial argument to make; since the 1980s, the welfare state has only expanded. As the financial and housing crises of 2008 show, many still look to government to control the economy, and bail out entire industries. Second, he wants to defend the substance of those teachings against both liberal Catholics and other sorts such as libertarians. Catholicism is not capitalism, and its defense of free-market exchanges and limited government is rooted in a certain view of the human person that is not the same as a secular liberal one. The Catholic view promotes human flourishing, but holds that flourishing must be consistent with the natural law and the ends of human life, such as the cultivation of virtue and the common good. Third, he wants to reconcile Catholicism specifically with the American form of republicanism. Gregg argues that the example of Catholics in America shows that the two are compatible, and that indeed the American experiment is consistent with the long tradition of Western liberty inaugurated by the Church.

That first battle, in some sense, has been won. The collapse of the Soviet Union and the socialist dreams it inspired persuaded a generation of young Catholics that freedom, not control, was not only the future but also was more in accord with human nature. In America, as Gregg writes, "these Catholics were proudly and unambiguously *American*, though not in a narrow parochial sense. They were Catholics *and* Americans, and American *and* Catholic. Not only did they believe that Catholicism, as the fullest expression of religious truth, had an indispensable contribution to make to the shaping and uplifting of American culture; they also believed American Catholicism had gifts to offer global Catholicism.... And for many such Catholics, part of their 'Americanness involved affirmation of what John Paul II called 'the business economy,' 'market economy,' or simply 'free economy.'" This new generation, Gregg argues, needs to apply Catholic historical and moral insights to the market economy as they have to other aspects of life. "[T]he central thesis of this book is that Catholics who underscore the cause of economic liberty can—nay, must—invest the cause for limited government with the same moral depth that Catholics have brought to other issues." Being in favor of limited government, of course, does not mean favoring no government; Catholics are not anarchists or radical libertarians, and recognize that government can and should do certain things. But government's tasks should "normally have a small number of clearly-defined functions limited in their scope and impact, including with regard to the economy." How and to what extent the government should intervene are prudential judgments, to be made by politicians and voters in good faith. There is no requirement of any particular set of policies, except that such policies must lead to the common good of all and work no moral evil on the citizens subject to them.

To tie this argument together for Catholics, Gregg invokes Charles Carroll of Carrollton. Carroll (1737–1832) was a successful merchant and the only Catholic signer of the Declaration of Independence. Gregg reminds us that in Carroll's day, Catholics faced significant political and social restrictions. Nevertheless, Carroll embodied a combination of economic virtue and civic-mindedness that may prove an example for contemporary Catholics in America. Young Charles returned to his family's vast Maryland estates in 1765 after almost twenty years abroad, educated largely by the Jesuits, and trained also as a British barrister. Gregg recounts the liberal education provided to Catholics in those days, deeply infused with medieval and classical learning. These lessons, capped by Carroll by his studies of the European civil and British common law traditions, provided the intellectual backdrop for his defense of the colonies and their traditional liberties.

Charles Carroll enmeshed himself in public life, even though Catholics were prohibited from basic civil activities such as voting or holding political office. Under the pseudonym "First Citizen," Carroll became a prominent voice in a debate over the proper powers of government. As Gregg explains, Carroll was deeply educated in the Western intellectual and political tradition, and he drew upon this deep learning to defend a tolerant, liberal government in the face of vicious anti-Catholic attacks and in a state that denied Catholics their participation in public life. Moreover, Carroll was a prosperous businessman who saw no problem in cultivating virtue in his private life. Carroll, like many of the Founders, believed that virtue was the basis for government, and liberty meant, first and foremost, government of the self before self-government as a community could occur. Those habits of virtue were only partially, if at all, able to be fostered by the state. Rather, small communities, and the family above all, were the source of those habits.

Drawing on the so-called "new natural law" of John Finnis, Germain Grisez and others, Gregg describes the Catholic view of the human person as deeply intertwined with the concept of free choice. Our "choices about ourselves last until they are negated by a contrary choice.... For better or worse, we become the content of our choices." Thus Catholic freedom is the process in part of learning to choose wisely. This view Gregg astutely contrasts with the Enlightenment view that the individual is a self-contained unit, whose choices do not affect who he truly is. The Catholic tradition knows better, and knows that choice is not the same as willfulness. A centralized state, which tells us what is good for us, and promises to provide for us, corrodes that habit of learning and exercising wise choices.

The determination of how government should act and to what extent has long roots as well in Catholic thought, and Gregg devotes some space to a consideration of subsidiarity. This concept should be familiar to Americans under the name of federalism. In its briefest sense, it means activity should be conducted and governed as close to the people affected by it as possible. It is therefore exactly at odds with the modern notion that experts located in Washington can understand and improve the varied circumstances of 300 million people, and more. Tocqueville recognized the vast profusion of private groups and associations Americans formed in the 1830s, and are still doing so today. Those groups must be the primary sources of engagement and civil renewal, not government. If government is to be involved, the lowest possible levels should be engaged first before moving up to the state or the national government. However, more work needs to be done in this area by defenders of the free market. It is all well and good to say government should be involved at the lowest level, or restricted to certain activities, but those details are too often left vague, which permits those favoring state intervention to step in.

Moreover, not all government activities are treated equally. It is true that welfare programs can decay the work ethic and harm individual dignity, including replacing the family with the state, and Catholics are right to oppose all such efforts. However, an excessive and extensive military is also a danger. It destroys local communities, puts strains on families, engages in social engineering opposed at times to Christian understanding, and places ordinary citizens into morally hazardous situations, usually far from home. Moreover, it suffers from potentially disastrous overreach, such as with the recent revelations about NSA spying. Opposition to such a bloated bureaucracy should not have a home only on the Catholic left. It can be opposed based on the same Catholic principles Gregg outlines here, while still preserving the role of the state in providing national defense.

*Tea Party Catholic* therefore does a good job in updating the reason why Catholics should support the free market and limited government, and showing it is in line with both Vatican II and the more recent teachings of Popes John Paul II and Benedict XVI. However, more importantly, Gregg goes further. One possible criticism of the first generation of Catholic free market defenders had been that their criticisms of excessive government involvement had not been matched by criticism of consumerism, which has also drawn the ire of Catholic teaching. Gregg recognizes this issue, and notes that Catholic teaching, by stressing that the material world is good but not final, and that we are shaped by our moral choices, can serve as a bulwark against the equation of material good with moral worth.

Gregg would also do well, in future work, to consider how the union of consumerism and government regulation has evolved. The current HHS mandate, which Gregg rightly discusses as the threat to religious liberty that it is, represents the government taking a side in a battle, and asserting its own secular values (for a certain view of "health" or "equality") against the religious freedom enshrined in the Constitution. This insertion of government as a participant on one side of a debate rather than an umpire in imposing regulations is different from the fights of the 1970s or 1980s, and the arguments of free-market Catholics, while still applicable, need to address this new threat, which combines consumerism and a false individualism with government power. That is the next front in the battle to preserve both the Catholic view of the person and the American tradition of pluralism and religious freedom, where thinkers like Gregg will serve a critical role.

# *Subsidy or Subsidiarity?*

❧

**Individualism and community** are the opposite halves of the American character. For every myth of the self-made man, there is the image of the closely knit New England small town. For every lone cowboy on the frontier, there are the social, political, and cultural groups that Americans have formed since the beginning of the Republic. Yet while individualism remains as ingrained as ever, the impulse toward community has weakened. As Robert Putnam has pointed out in his influential book *Bowling Alone*, participation in groups of all sorts has dropped dramatically. The informal social capital that develops from community life and that is critical to democracy is in danger of dissipating.

The Catholic principle of subsidiarity, first set forth in its modern form by Pope Leo XIII in his social encyclicals, provides a political template for reinterpreting the balance between community and individual. Subsidiarity proposes a series of nested communities, beginning with the family and extending up through the national state; it encompasses not just "public" or governmental institutions but also private institutions, such as churches, corporations, and civic groups, that make up society. Social problems should be addressed at the most local level able to solve them, which has the result of increasing community attachments. More generally, Catholic social thought is grounded in a conception of the human person that is relational rather than individualistic. That is to say, Catholicism emphasizes the bonds persons have with one another as created beings and asserts that these bonds create reciprocal duties and responsibilities.

---

Originally published in *Crisis*, July 2002.

In *The Catholic Ethic and the Spirit of Community*, John E. Tropman, a professor of social welfare and business at the University of Michigan, asks whether this Catholic ethic exists as more than an intellectual ideal. Taking his title, of course, from Max Weber's famous book on the Protestant ethic and the spirit of capitalism, Tropman's thesis is that something called "the Catholic ethic" conditions attitudes on subjects ranging from community to forgiveness, and that this ethic differs from a "Protestant" ethic in significant ways.

The book is divided into five parts. The first introduces the concept of a Catholic ethic in contrast to a "Protestant" ethic. Part 2 lays out what Tropman calls the "Pillars of the Catholic Ethic." These include assumptions about what the Catholic ethic teaches about work, money, family, forgiveness, and the otherworldly focus of life, which Tropman summarizes as a "helping ethic." Part 3 supplies a "Cultural and Structural History of the Catholic Ethic and Community Helping," in which Tropman examines both values and institutions that have shaped the Catholic ethic, from monasteries to Catholic Charities USA. Part 4 focuses on America. Here Tropman uses surveys and other sociological data to discover whether the principles described earlier have contemporary resonance. The final part, "The Long View," offers concluding observations about possible applications of the Catholic ethic.

Tropman finds, generally, that Catholics are different. The available surveys of members of particular religious groups show that Catholics come to different conclusions about economics, the family, social life, and politics than their Protestant counterparts. In general, the Catholic ethic stresses family more than work, community more than the individual, other values rather than wealth, and takes a more favorable attitude toward the poor. Catholics also have a more favorable view of government, in general, than Protestants (with the exception of African American Protestants, whose views on some issues are closely aligned with those of Catholics).

The "helping ethic" Tropman finds at the heart of Catholicism, however, is not without problems. He arbitrarily separates his Catholic ethic into "dominant" and "subdominant" strands. In most cases, Tropman simply equates a pro-welfare state attitude with the Catholic social ethic. Indeed, Tropman concludes that the "helping elements" of the Catholic ethic "were politically important…in establishing the social acceptance necessary for the New Deal and the Social Security Act to succeed" and that "the Catholic ethic directly supports welfare state activities." Any approach that diverges from this pro-welfare position—such as that of Michael Novak, whom he mentions only in passing—is presented as a Protestant intrusion into "mainstream" Catholic social thought.

This dichotomy is too simplistic; it distorts important nuances of the Catholic ethic. While Catholics may not as a matter of principle oppose the concept of government aid to the needy, a secular welfare state that usurps rather than supports the role of family and local communities is not the same thing as a social welfare system animated by Christian charity and operated through local communities. And while Catholics may not stigmatize the poor because of their poverty—as Tropman finds characteristic of a Protestant ethic—that does not mean that Catholicism absolves individuals of responsibility as persons. It means only that Catholicism does not assign a theological status to anyone on the basis of his economic position.

The connections between the theological understanding of humanity and the duties flowing from that understanding are lost in Tropman's interpretation of the data. Too often, Tropman simply assumes that the welfare state is derived from a watered-down Catholicism or that the Catholic ethic is a sacralized New Deal. (Tellingly, Tropman offers no sustained discussion of subsidiarity.) This conclusion makes the Catholic ethic merely the *praeparatio evangelii* of the liberal welfare state and does not further any discussion of Catholicism's unique contribution to social thought.

These problems aside, Tropman is generally a fair-minded scholar, and *The Catholic Ethic* performs the valuable service of showing that Catholics do think differently. More work needs to be done on the question of what Catholics think the role of private welfare institutions should be and on their attitudes toward poverty. Nevertheless, Tropman sheds needed light on the present expression of some of the values that have shaped Catholics for two millennia.

# *The Real Myth*

**Conservatives,** argues David Sehat in *The Myth of American Religious Freedom*, profess religious freedom, but only to secretly assert the coercive power of law to force people to live under a particular religious establishment. Liberals, in turn, are afraid to acknowledge the conservatives' plot, lest they lose power at the ballot box. Instead, they argue that America has always separated church and state. That, Sehat insists, is the dangerous "myth" that has caused deep confusion about America's heritage of religious liberty.

Nor is this coercive assertion of religion of only antiquarian interest. Sehat, a professor of history at Georgia State University, argues that, as recently as the 1987 confirmation process in connection with Judge Robert Bork's nomination to the Supreme Court, "it soon became apparent, if it had not been obvious all along, [that] conservatives were not interested in equally maximizing religious liberty for all—just those of Judeo-Christian heritage." Rather than correct the myth of religious freedom, liberals have played along, "reluctant to acknowledge past religious power for fear that it would strengthen conservative jurisprudence."

Contrary to Sehat, however, religious freedom has been a contested ideal since the beginning of the nation, and it is just as American to run a "heretic" out of town on a rail as to let him speak and worship freely. It is true that there have been close links between the Christian faith of a majority of Americans and the country's legal and cultural underpinnings. In 1811, for example, Chancellor James Kent of New York, in *The People*

Originally published in *First Things*, February 2011.

*v. Ruggles*, declared Christianity a part of the common law, and even as late as 1952 the Supreme Court declared, in *Zorach v. Clausen*, that "we are a religious people whose institutions presuppose a Supreme Being."

Yet the great paradox of American religious freedom is how a nation, overwhelmingly Protestant, that enacted laws against blasphemy, required religious tests for public office, and generally assumed that Christianity provided a base for democratic government welcomed people of every religion (and none) even before there arose what Sehat describes as "the Liberal Moment": the slow, primarily judge-driven dissolution of any formal connections between religion and the state.

This "moment" extended from the end of the Second World War through the early 1960s, although Sehat finds precursors even in the 1920s. The moment began with decisions such as that in the famous 1941 case *West Virginia Board of Education v. Barnette*, in which the Court held that the state could not force Jehovah's Witnesses to salute the flag. By the 1960s the liberal moment had triumphed with decisions such as *Torcaso v. Watkins*, which declared that freedom of religion included the freedom not to believe. Such decisions, and the larger tumult of the 1960s, dismantled the formal "moral establishment," yet that establishment continued through what Sehat calls a "proxy religious establishment," which, while not enshrined in law, was nevertheless effective in coercing nonbelievers.

With a Roberts Court presumably favorable to that proxy establishment, Sehat thinks it now is time for a "judicial minimalism" that will seek to adjudicate competing moral and religious claims. He does not describe this minimalism in detail, but, again presumably, it will consolidate the gains of the liberal moment. He argues that a "morality that is enforced by law must be tied to reason and subject to argumentation about how moral standards advance good in a way that is agreeable to many different groups." How judges would articulate the content of that reason, or what *agreeable* might mean in this context, he leaves vague, but he suggests that a "defense of individual rights made democracy possible, and the only unity required was a shared agreement to protect the rights of all."

And therein lies part of the problem. The "shared agreement" Sehat wishes for a post-religious America is precisely what Europe carved out over the eighteen centuries before America's founding generation got around to drafting the First Amendment. What Sehat misses is that what he calls the moral establishment, which roughly corresponds to the mainline Protestant cultural hegemony that existed through the early 1960s, was common to all sides of the debate and made the conversation over religious liberty possible in the first place. Indeed, because, as he concedes, religious believers still constitute a majority of Americans (and Christians a majority of those), his argument amounts to the demand that believers agree to exclude religious reasons from the public square and allow only secular reasoning as an acceptable basis for any "shared agreement."

Sehat describes at least four kinds of developments in American religious history. First are decisions, such as the *Barnette* case, that help one religious group express its beliefs against the opposition of other groups. Second are those in which religion in general, or a specific faith in particular, is favored against other beliefs, as in the older requirement at the state level that officeholders believe in God, or in the nineteenth-century practice of supporting some churches with taxes. Third is "the preferential treatment of Christianity in the legal system," which is sometimes extended to cultural preference in general. The fourth, emerging primarily from that liberal moment, is a secular worldview that interposes itself between individuals and the state or adjudicates on behalf of a secular state between private individuals. These four are not the same, and not all are inconsistent with a notion of religious freedom (indeed, only the fourth presents a true and lasting threat to religious belief), but Sehat confuses these narratives as he tries to fit them into his story of "dissenters" (such as William Lloyd Garrison and Elizabeth Cady Stanton) fighting against conservative oppression.

Even Sehat's thesis that the American heritage of religious freedom is a myth is not a new one. A decade ago Kenneth Craycraft argued in *The American Myth of Religious Freedom* that the myth was that the government could neutrally adjudicate moral claims among religions. Instead, Craycraft contended, the structure James Madison and others wrought always placed the interests of the government above those of religious people. Craycraft argues that the solution is to trust, not in the Supreme Court or in national elites to protect religious liberty, but in a divided federal government and strong state governments, which will allow the people to form smaller political communities that express how they choose to live.

In the end, Sehat fails to acknowledge, as do Craycraft and other astute observers of the public scene, that the square does not remain naked. The judicial minimalism enforcing abstract individual rights that Sehat thinks would protect religious liberty is a fantasy; in an empty public square, the state inevitably will assert its own beliefs. And those beliefs likely will not be favorable to anyone's religious expression. Indeed, in some ways, Sehat's minimalist state is already here: Courts at the state and federal levels have used expansive government "interests" as reasons to trump protected religious exercise. Conversely, the state now tolerates express religious bigotry; the United States Court of Appeals for the Ninth Circuit recently upheld a declaration by the San Francisco Board of Supervisors that attacked the Catholic Church as an improper "foreign" influence in the public square. Further, as legal scholars such as Rob Vischer have pointed out, under the auspices of a secular state, individual religious liberty is morphing into an open-ended right to individual autonomy, which a secular state favors in otherwise private disputes between private parties.

The historical antecedents that led to this intellectual landscape make up the more interesting development, but it is not one that is readily accessible in Sehat's account. Sehat's reliance on individual "rights" as protectors of religious freedom is unpersuasive when these "rights" are divorced from their historical"—largely Christian—context. Unfortunately, Madison and the other Founders, whom Sehat discusses in his opening sections, can be of little help here. While Madison did call for a centralized, "godless" state to protect minority groups and individual rights, he did not foresee the consequences of a political culture in which there was no intermediary between the individual and the state.

Indeed, for all its faults, the moral establishment recognized a central tenet of the Western tradition: The state does not have total power over the individual. Public acknowledgment of religion's claims is a recognition of the limits of state power. Even now, Americans rely on an attenuated Christian understanding of individual dignity to navigate the separation between law and faith. The real myth, in other words, may be that there can be religious freedom at all in the modern state without a strong religious tradition acting both as a curb to the state's power on behalf of believers and nonbelievers alike and also as an alternative narrative within which people can work out their individual visions of the good life.

# *A Different Discipline: The American Catholic Novel*

❧

I. Consider the following hypothetical. X has just published the most recent in a series of novels based loosely on his own life. X is widely recognized as a fine practitioner of his craft and has won several awards for his work. Although formally raised a Catholic, he has not practiced the faith since reaching adulthood. His work in general does not portray Catholicism favorably. The main character in the current novel is presented with a choice of whether to return to the Catholic faith of his childhood. He rejects that option, however, and prefers instead to "outgrow" his religious upbringing. Our second author Y, on the other hand, has also published a novel, her first. It is a thinly disguised autobiography that concerns a young woman who, after experiencing a number of trials that test her secular beliefs, has a transformative experience and formally embraces Catholicism. The novel, however, is rough and disjointed in places, and its emotion sometimes overcomes its structure.

How do we assess each of these novels as examples of "Catholic fiction"? Are their creators "Catholic writers"? While we may agree with the substance of Y's story, and applaud her efforts to present Catholicism as a viable option for individuals in the modern world, we may also agree, however reluctantly, that she is the lesser novelist. X is the stronger writer, yet we hesitate before naming him a "Catholic novelist," because of the ambiguity about his faith. Somehow, we may feel, a Catholic novelist should not do that sort of thing. This confused response is the result of the two parallel approaches that have been used to interpret Catholic authors.

---

Originally published in *Renascence*, 51.3, Spring 1999.

Catholic authors are judged, at least implicitly, both by the technical quality of their work as well as by the extent to which their work confirms or repudiates a certain vision of Catholicism, all too often, the vision held by the critics themselves. The work of Andrew Greeley, for example, presents a comforting image of the Church in a time when many Catholics were doubting the Church's ability to provide guidance in the modern world. As Anita Gandolfo has argued in a recent book, contemporary Catholic fiction represents an attempt to distinguish itself from apologetics, and to create a new paradigm of the Church that would incorporate modern elements.[1] Whether the connection between Catholic writing and orthodoxy has ever been as strong as it is perceived is itself a question open to debate; as early as the 1930s and 1940s, Catholic critics derided simplistic tales of virtue's triumph over vice.[2]

This article argues that these conflicting positions on the role of Catholic writers grant too much and too little power to Catholic novelists. The "orthodox" standard of judging Catholic authors is a remnant of an earlier age of Catholic devotional piety, when artists were thought to be ciphers, useful only to transmit the truths of the faith. Such a view deprives authors of their own creative voice. The "new paradigm" stance, on the other hand, cedes to the more recent authors a power that is difficult to gauge with any accuracy. The post-Vatican II writers, even more than their preconciliar counterparts, are a varied lot, and each occupies his own artistic plane. Their influence has not all been in the same direction, even when that influence can be traced. In fact, however, Catholic novelists occupy a middle ground between the two camps: they can shape the cultural landscape of Catholicism in ways that reflect their individual perceptions but cannot in the end replace the traditional teaching methods of the Church.

---

1. Anita Gandolfo, *Testing the Faith: The New Catholic Fiction in America* (Westport, CT: Greenwood Press, 1992), 208–209.
2. Arnold Sparr, *To Promote, Defend and Redeem: The Catholic Literary Revival and the Cultural Transformation of American Catholicism,* 1920–1960 (New York: Greenwood Press, 1990), 143.

**II.** Dispute over the "Catholic novel" has existed from the genre's inception in the last century. Early critics, such as Andre Gide, charged that the Catholic novelist could do no more than rehearse the standard pieties, because the outcome—the triumph of goodness over evil—was known from the outset. Therefore, the criticism argued, the drama necessary for a successful novel could not be supplied. In a famous essay, "Inside the Whale," George Orwell stated bluntly that Roman Catholicism is not compatible with good fiction.[3] Orwell himself, however, was not consistent in his assessment of religious writing, as he in fact praised several Catholic novelists of his day. These criticisms are less common now, in part because novelists like George Bernanos in France and Flannery O'Connor in the United States have demonstrated the inherently dramatic nature of the story of grace.

However, new objections to the possibility of Catholic fiction have arisen. Kieran Quinlan, examining the work of Walker Percy, argues that modern developments in philosophy have made the truths Catholics like Percy relied on obsolete, making fiction exploring those truths ultimately incredible.[4] Likewise, Theodore Fraser, in his recent study of the Catholic novel in Europe, argues that the future of Catholic fiction is unclear because of the vast changes that have occurred in the Church in the past thirty years.[5] Others take the opposite view and argue that it is the wider culture that cannot understand the complexities of the Catholic novel. They contend that the reading public (especially in the United States) prefers instead either "sentimental" fiction with happy endings or, if the novel touches on religious themes at all, hyper-religious thrillers weighted down with supernaturalism.[6] Still others see a more robust Catholic presence in contemporary culture. In a thoughtful study, Giles has argued that

3. George Orwell, "Inside the Whale," in *Collected Essays, Journalism and Letters of George Orwell*, Volume I (London: Secker and Warburg, 1961), 148.

4. Kieran Quinlan, *Walker Percy: The Last Catholic Novelist* (Baton Rouge: Louisiana State University Press, 1995), 219–220.

5. Theodore Fraser, *The Modern Catholic Novel in Europe* (New York: Twayne, 1994), 150–151.

6. Vince Passaro, "Dragon Fiction," *Harper's* 293:17 (September, 1996), 65.

Catholicism has long been and remains a strong cultural influence in the United States, not only in literature but also in other arts such as film. This Catholic influence, however, has not all been of the same sort, nor always to the same effect. The lives and work of the "lost generation" of American Catholics who left the faith, such as F. Scott Fitzgerald, have a complex and not wholly orthodox relationship with the faith of their more insulated ancestors.[7] If, as Thomas Woodman has argued in the context of British Catholics, there "is more than one way of being a Catholic," that variety surely holds among American Catholics as well.[8]

Scholars of the Catholic novel have generally recognized the difficulties in categorizing authors who either are no longer Catholic or who have been influenced by Catholicism and have limited the scope of their work accordingly. Labrie, for example, in his generally excellent survey of the Catholic imagination in American literature, concentrates on practicing Catholics, and only on their works that concern Catholic themes.[9] This type of focused approach is useful, because it highlights for the reader a tight range of issues, but its very precision is problematic. It cuts off Catholic authors from the wider culture of which they thought themselves to be a part, even though some of them sought refuge in the Church against that culture's uglier features. The Catholic literary establishment, even in its most isolationist phases, was conscious of Catholicism as a force that could influence the wider culture.[10] In addition to an understandable desire to have their works widely read, many of the most prominent Catholic authors saw themselves as engaged in an apostolate not only among their fellow Catholics, but towards the wider American reading public as well.

The early Catholic novel seemed readily identifiable. The "classic" Catholic novel had a set of stock features derived from the pioneering

7. James T. Fisher, "Clearing the Streets of the Catholic Lost Generation," *South Atlantic Quarterly* 93.3 (Summer 1994), 625.
8. Thomas Woodman, *Faithful Fictions: The Catholic Novel in British Literature* (Philadelphia: Open University Press, 1991), 163.
9. Ross Labrie, *The Catholic Imagination in American Literature* (Columbia: University of Missouri Press, 1997), ix.
10. Sparr, *To Promote, Defend and Redeem*, 145.

fiction of Mauriac, Bloy and Bernanos: a critique of materialism, a belief in the holiness of poverty and the idea (adopted from Charles Peguy) that the sinner is at the heart of Christianity.[11] In the years following Vatican II, practitioners of the Catholic novel have moved from a strictly theological to a more general literary or sociological orientation. The postconciliar novels—for example, Lodge's *Souls and Bodies*—have focused on the reactions of individual Catholics to the changes that have occurred in the Catholic worldview, which have disrupted their childhood image of the Church. No longer were Catholic novels expected to present affirmations of the truth of that worldview, with an eye to influencing nonCatholics. Instead they explored perceived discontinuities between doctrine and ordinary life.

Defining a set of common features overstates the case, however: attempts to fit together such disparate figures as J. F. Powers and Leon Bloy, Evelyn Waugh and Sigrid Undset, David Lodge and Walker Percy stretch the definition of the "canonical" form of the Catholic novel almost beyond recognition. Fraser does not discuss *The Hobbit*, for example, yet in that consciously anachronistic tale could be found a number of themes that occupied Catholic writers of the time, such as the nostalgia for a medieval past. Nor does he discuss *The Leopard*, arguably a Catholic novel of a different sort, by the Sicilian noble Giuseppe Tomasi di Lampedusa. The novel depicts, through the life of the title character, the transition from an aristocratic, Catholic Sicily to a democratic, modern Italy. It illustrates a number of themes touching on Catholic life and the modern world.

The provenance of Catholic fiction lay in the work of Chateaubriand and Baudelaire.[12] More important to its development was Dostoyevsky, who, although no friend to Roman Catholicism, altered the realist form of Flaubert and Zola to allow the introduction of spiritual elements. The Catholic novel therefore has its roots both in Romanticism and in realism.[13] This dual source causes a certain amount of tension, because neither tradition is

11. Fraser, *The Modern Catholic Novel in Europe*, xv.

12. Ibid., 5.

13. Bernard Bergonzi, *The Myth of Modernism and Twentieth-Century Literature* (New York: St. Martin's Press. 1986), 175.

fully compatible with Catholicism. The romantics suffered from an excessive subjectivism and (for some of them) intimations of pantheism, while the realists were burdened by their empiricism and naturalism. Realism and romanticism are unsuitable modes in which to convey the principles of Catholic incarnational theology. Either approach, from a Roman Catholic perspective, represents only a partial truth that must exist in balance with other valid truths. Neither alone, or even in combination, is sufficient.

These conflicted beginnings point to a central difficulty in understanding Catholic fiction, a point perceived by Orwell. Essentially, the novel is not an appropriate forum for transmitting the doctrines of the Catholic faith. That is not to say that Catholic authors cannot pursue a Catholic message or Catholic themes in their writings. Indeed, it would be almost absurd to assert that proposition. But Catholic authors cannot support or create a new vision of the Church in the modern world. Fiction, in short, is not apologetics, nor do writers represent the *magisterium.* Through their work, writers can explore and interpret the faith; they can present striking images of the life of the Church (both positive and negative) or delve into the religious faith of their characters and its impact upon their lives. Sometimes they can even defend their faith or lead their readers to it. Catholic writers, however, cannot elaborate upon or teach it in a formal sense.

This does not mean that artists' work should be judged only by the criteria of art, although the adage does have some relevance. As T. S. Eliot noted, the religious perspective can comment upon the greatness of literature; but we can determine whether a work is literature only by literary standards.[14] Both literary and religious critiques are necessary to a proper understanding of a work's merit. There was much bad Catholic writing during the "golden age" of Catholic fiction. Didacticism is the perennial temptation in Catholic literature. Rather, my point is that the novel, representing as it does the view of one artist put forth in a peculiarly modern form, cannot substitute for the view of the Church. The presence of an

14. T.S. Eliot, "Religion and Literature," in *Selected Prose of T. S. Eliot*, ed. Frank Kermode (New York: Farrar. Straus and Giroux, 1975), 97.

authoritative teaching body, which claims the right to pronounce definitive answers to a wide variety of questions, limits an author's ability to advance convincing alternatives from Church practice that would be valuable for a universal Church.

This conclusion is supported by the example of the greatest Catholic authors themselves. Most Catholic writers themselves have shied away from the label and considered themselves as writers who happened to be Catholic rather than Catholic writers. The tension between the Catholic writer and the Church is the reason why "Catholic fiction" has developed into such a contentious category; writers from other faiths do not have this problem to the same extent. At their best, the works of Catholic authors can serve the same function as the old collections of saints' lives, without the latter group's occasional lapses into preachiness. They demonstrate the presence of God in everyday life, which redeems the world along with (or even despite) the workings of the visible Church.

**III.** Defining Catholic fiction, then, is difficult enough; to identify a peculiarly American subset is even more so. The term "American Catholic novel" has numerous meanings, depending on the identity of the speaker as well as that of the audience. The standard story of the emergence of American Catholic fiction goes something like the following. Before the Second World War, there was a frantic search to find one or more native writers who could compete with the European masters; Catholic anthologies and literary magazines flourished in an attempt to discover the authors who would lead American Catholics out of their intellectual provinciality.[15] The obsession with finding American analogues to Bernanos or Mauriac reached its height in the 1930s and 1940s, as more American Catholics were educated and desired a place in the intellectual world equal to both American Protestants and European Catholics.

This attitude changed after the War, and especially after Vatican II; Catholic fiction began to focus on a Church that seemed to be dysfunc-

15. Sparr, *To Promote, Defend and Redeem*, 144–145.

tional and unresponsive to contemporary problems. The desire for a cadre of Catholic intellectuals decreased in the 1950s and 1960s, as integration of Catholics with the larger population accelerated and the self-image of a ghettoized minority faded. (In interesting ways, this pattern parallels the controversy among Catholic political theorists as to whether Catholicism was compatible with democracy.) The past two decades have witnessed a flourishing of new American Catholic writing that has attempted to find a proper model for the Church in the modern world.[16] This has coincided with increased scholarship on that pre-Vatican II generation of intellectuals.[17] The contemporary Church is composed of many voices, who advance different conceptions of the Church's role. Novelists and other artists are among the most influential participants in this discourse.

Part of the difficulty in definition stems from the appropriation of European examples and categories, and their transportation to the United States. The Church in America has developed along different lines from the Church in Europe. While Catholics in America have suffered from a not insignificant amount of discrimination, the fierce institutional anti-Catholicism present in some European countries has been relatively absent. Additionally, the American Church was not linked to a ruling class or *ancien régime*, as in parts of Europe, and so had enjoyed comparatively freer movement and independence. From its very beginnings in the new nation, the Church in the United States was influenced by the democratic spirit of the American character. Dolan identifies three critical periods in the American Church's development; each one involved a conscious attempt to conform Catholicism with the larger currents in American culture. These influences impacted such features of Catholic life as the system of parish governance, which was self-consciously different from the European practice.[18]

16. Gandolfo, *Testing the Faith*, 209.

17. James Hitchcock, "Postmortem on a Rebirth: The Catholic Intellectual Renaissance," *The American Scholar* 49:2 (1980), 211.

18. Jay Dolan, "The Search for an American Catholicism," *The Catholic Historical Review* 82.2 (1996), 174.

Among the writers themselves, of course, there were affinities between American Catholic novelists and their European counterparts. Literary modernism, for example, which was largely a European-inspired movement, attracted many members of the American Catholic "renaissance," which flourished during the decades prior to Vatican II. As Flannery O'Connor said of herself, she was peculiarly possessed by a "modern consciousness," which meant being "unhistorical, solitary, and guilty."[19] Of course, this modernism was not peculiarly American; similar expressions of the modern dilemma can be found in the work of Graham Greene or David Jones. In the United States, however, this broader tradition combined with native traditions including, paradoxically, an indigenous anti-modernism. Yet even as they employed a modernist vocabulary, some Catholic writers identified flaws in modernism. Allen Tate in the United States, perhaps the most prominent example of an American convert comfortable with new European intellectual trends, employed his Southern and Catholic heritages to great effect in his work. The Catholic converts advocated, in Tate's phrase, the "right kind of modernism," that is, one supported by spiritual underpinnings.[20] These underpinnings many converts found in the antimodern stance of Catholicism.

**IV.** American Catholicism, then, is heir to several traditions by way of its European models (which may have led to superficial comparisons of American Catholic writers with their European counterparts), as well as native traditions of nonsectarian Protestantism, individualism, progressivism and a strong belief in individual rights. These influences have given rise to several differences between the development of American Catholic and European Catholic writing. Of course, even among the European countries, as Lampedusa noted in the 1950s in a series of commentaries on English literature, the quality and vigor of Catholic writing varied widely.[21]

19. Flannery O'Connor, *The Habit of Being*, ed. Sally Fitzgerald (New York: Farrar, Straus and Giroux, 1979), 90.

20. Peter A. Huff, *Allen Tate and the Catholic Revival: Trace of the Fugitive Gods* (New York: Paulist Press, 1996), 34.

American Catholic writers, especially the converts, internalized their mixed cultural inheritance and expressed it in their writings.[22] Catholic writers like Mary Gordon or Thomas Merton have drawn on their experience as Americans in separating themselves from the formal hierarchy. Although informed by her Catholicism, Gordon's feminism has clear connections with the larger American movement for women's rights. Likewise, Merton's work is indebted to the example of the great American individualist Henry David Thoreau. There are further complications even within the general framework of American thought. The anti-modernism of some Catholics during the 1930s through the 1950s has roots both in a traditional Catholic disdain for modernity as well as a native tradition of criticism dating from Henry Adams and (the Catholic convert) Orestes Brownson.

These intellectual influences are compounded by geographical ones. The United States is a large country, larger of course than most of the individual European nations. This characteristic has added to the richness of American Catholic writing, but also has made discovery of common features more challenging. An East Coast Catholic reading Jon Hassler's novels, for example, which are largely set in rural Minnesota, may know little of the context or history of the faith in that part of the country. Contrast that example with the novels of Bernanos. His work can be placed within the context of the larger controversies between French Catholics and royalists and their adversaries that gripped France for decades. Despite this complex matrix of influences, however, we can still speak of a universal Catholic imagination in which American writers share. The work of O'Connor, Fitzgerald and Hassler, for example, share a definite worldview that separates them even from other American writers who may share their regional background.

There is a subsidiary complication. We should be cautious in combining the literature of born American Catholics with converts, and those who grew up in the traditional Catholic setting with those who did not. The born Catholic writer approaches the faith from the inside out; its rituals,

21. Giuseppe Tomasi di Lampedusa, *Letteratura Inglese, Volume II: L'Ottocento e il Novecento* (Milano: A. Mondadori, 1991), 339–340.

22. Labrie, *The Catholic Imagination in American Literature*, 9.

beliefs and social structures are the material with which the writer can work. Moreover, the expression of faith is generally a social phenomenon: everyone is Catholic. The convert, on the other hand, even if she knows this to be true, nevertheless must take the first step alone. Of course, even after their conversion, these converts are still living with their pre-conversion experiences, and their fiction represents this prior experience. While some native Catholic authors, such as Paul Horgan or J. F. Powers, examine the impact of the worldly Church upon its redemptive mission in their novels, converts are more self-consciously reflecting on the lucidity and power that the Church presents to the individual as an instrument of God's grace.[23]

Although obviously influential, the "ghetto" image of American Catholicism was strongest only in the Northeastern Irish-dominated Church. It represents a small part of the development of the Church in America, and the term itself has fallen out of academic favor.[24] In terms of literary development, recent studies by Huff and Labrie highlight the academic movement away from the ghetto model as an analytical tool for American Catholic literature. Many of the most accomplished practitioners of American Catholic literature were not part of this culture, such as Flannery O'Connor, Robert Lowell or Caroline Gordon. Even though the security of the ghetto may have been a source of initial attraction, in general the insular cultural and intellectual life of the twentieth-century American Church had little effect on the development of the work of the more distinguished Catholic converts.[25] Indeed, the pattern of influence worked in reverse: once these converts, drawn in some cases by the example of the living Church around them but just as often by the Church's anti-modern stance or aesthetic appeal, began to write and speak on behalf of their beliefs, the intellectual life of American Catholicism raced to meet them.

The direction of the next stage in scholarship has already been indicated by scholars such as Giles and Gandolfo. We should inquire whether the

23. Ibid., 269–270.

24. Fisher, "Clearing the Streets of the Catholic Lost Generation," 608.

25. Huff, *Allen Tate and the Catholic Revival*, 17.

influence of Catholic writers extends beyond Catholic circles, and whether that influence has caused an integration between the Catholic imagination and American cultural life. In other words, can we trace elements of the "Catholic imagination" through aspects of American intellectual life other than the writings of Catholics? In addition to looking for traces of Thoreau in Merton, perhaps we should also be scanning contemporary authors for traces of Catholicism. Literature is essential to explain and elaborate the universal Catholic message anew for each generation through the prism of individual stories, but it is less useful to establish the limits and substance of that message in the first instance.

As Allen Tate noted in a 1958 lecture, the sacramental life calls for a discipline different from that of the literary life, and someone who excels in the one should not be assumed to excel in the other.[26] O'Connor, for example, disputed Waugh's contention that Catholic authors should treat only problems of the faith. She preferred instead to make the category "generous," and considered as proper definition to be "Catholic mind looking at anything."[27] Even after all the difficulties of definition are admitted, we remain convinced that there is a distinctive Catholic way of seeing reality and interpreting experience, which blends "natural feeling, sentiment, and insight with what is believed in faith."[28]

The title character of Hassler's novel *Dear James*, an Irish priest, marvels at the ignorance of Americans of the Catholic faith as compared with their Irish counterparts. "Was there a teenager anywhere in Ireland, James wondered, who didn't know the difference between Popes and saints? How foreign America must be. How pagan. How mysterious."[29] Introducing foreign, pagan America to the sometimes equally mysterious Catholic Church is a role to which the Catholic novelist who reflects that faith through fiction is ideally suited.

26. Ibid., 95.

27. O'Connor, *The Habit of Being*, 236.

28. Robert Sokolowski, *The God of Faith and Reason* (Washington DC: The Catholic University of America Press, 1995), 140–141.

29. Jon Hassler, *Dear James* (New York: Ballantine Books, 1993), 30.

# *Catholicism Before and After* 1963: *Two Novels*

IN TRYING TO UNDERSTAND the extraordinary changes the Catholic Church underwent in the middle of the twentieth century, I recently came across two illuminating novels. The first was the last novel in Evelyn Waugh's Sword of Honor trilogy, *Unconditional Surrender*. The three novels loosely trace Waugh's own military experience, darkly satirizing the military and more broadly modern society. Specifically, Waugh uses the war as a backdrop against which to lay out a different battle, this one between Catholicism and the modern world. The trilogy is widely regarded as Waugh's masterwork.

Piers Paul Read's *Monk Dawson* was the other novel, drawn from his own experience at Ampleforth, a British Catholic boarding school. It was Read's third novel, and it follows the life of young Edward Dawson from Catholic boarding school through seminary, chronicling his loss of faith and disillusionment, laicization, and a kind of return and reconciliation. The novel was an immediate hit, winning several prizes and appearing a year later in the United States.

As it happens, the books were published only eight years apart. *Unconditional Surrender* came out in 1961, *Monk Dawson* in 1969. A Catholic born in Britain in 1941, like Read himself, would have encountered Waugh's book at age twenty and Read's at twenty-eight. Between those two dates was a revolution so complete it is hard to imagine now that both these books are of the same decade. Waugh and Read portray starkly

Originally published in *First Things*, January 19, 2015.

different social and religious worlds, even though, according to the timelines of the novels, both main characters live at the same time.

Waugh recounts the life and war career of Guy Crouchback, scion of an ancient Recusant family. Guy's wife Virginia has left him, and he has returned from self-imposed exile in Italy to find some worthy purpose to his life. He is therefore triply removed from traditional British society, as a divorcee, Catholic, and exile. Britain is on the verge of war, and he finds some direction in the military and in joining the great cause of freedom. After several episodes, including the disastrous evacuation from Crete and the abandonment of Jews in the Balkans, Guy becomes disillusioned when the war for Christendom he hoped to be fighting turns out to be rather sordid and, with the betrayal of Catholics in Yugoslavia for Britain's short-term interests, ultimately disappointing. Yet his faith remains a ground for Crouchback's existence. Even when stranded in bombed-out Italy, Crouchback finds a church to attend. During the war, Guy's father dies and in one of the novel's great set-pieces, he is laid to rest witnessed by the family's servants and townspeople in the family crypt. With him, Waugh implies, British Catholicism disappears.

Although Waugh has been rightly criticized for his snobbishness and focus on the upper classes he so admired, *Unconditional Surrender* points out a Catholic outlook that truly was different and that people believed to be different. Much of the book's central subplot revolves around the fact that Guy is still, according to the Church, married to his (non-Catholic) wife, despite their civil divorce and her infidelity. Waugh portrays the real pain of Guy's situation, but in his portrayal of the faith, the Church's views on marriage and the importance of individual charity are woven into Guy's life and make emotional and rational sense. Confession is something Catholics "have to do now and then," and marriage is a theological fact, regardless of civil niceties.

Before his death, the senior Crouchback tells his son to act as he can for others; reflecting on this at his father's funeral, Guy thinks, "One day he would get the chance to do some small service which only he could perform, for which he was created. Even he must have his function in the divine plan. He did not expect a heroic destiny. Quantitative judgments did not apply. All that mattered was to recognize the chance when it was offered." And the chance does come. After his father's burial, Virginia, now pregnant by another, returns to him. Her motives are mixed, at first. Yet Guy feels the call of charity. He takes back his wife, even after (or, as he says, because of) the news that she is pregnant. How could he do this? "It was no business of yours," says a concerned friend. "It was made my business for being offered," he responds. Amidst the misery of a world at war, he adds, "This is just one case where I can help. And only I, really. I was Virginia's last resort." He reflects, "If only one soul was saved, that is full compensation for any amount of 'loss of face.'" Thus the last heir of an ancient line, full of social and ecclesiastical privilege, humbles himself for another, and in doing so fulfills his vocation.

*Monk Dawson*, in contrast, was written with the heady ideas of liberation theology and social justice in the air after Vatican II. Its title character wants to do good, but confuses a desire for social justice with a religious vocation. Once ordained, Dawson is led astray by quasi-Marxist politics and sexual temptation. First, he believes the parish would be better for his social conscience than the monastery because parish life is more attuned to "real" problems of injustice, but he is overwhelmed by the problems of his individual parishioners, and thinks the Church should be doing good works on a broader scale. He leaves his vocation entirely, enters into a couple of affairs and begins a new life as a writer, taking the *nom de plume* "Monk" Dawson to add authority to his attacks on the Church and traditional morality that he now disdains. Another brief fling with Communism ensues, as he wonders whether he could "change again? Could he say...that he had found the answer for a third time?" But the answers do not come. The book's narrator, a friend named Robert Winterman who lost his faith much earlier, thinks their common Catholic schooling and the Church herself "mucked" Dawson, and its outdated notions serve merely to provide false hopes for the ignorant.

Read shows how the Catholic understanding of life that undergirds Crouchback's internal drama was shattered during the postwar years, especially in the late-1950s into the 1960s. In the enthusiasm for social justice, quantitative judgments were all; large-scale programs or revolution preoccupy Dawson, for whom the seemingly meaningless monastic rounds of prayer and the retail salvation of a parish church are not enough. Recusant Catholics are portrayed, offhandedly, as faintly ridiculous and tawdry. Thus Jenny, a woman with whom Dawson takes up after he leaves the priesthood, has an affair with Jack, whose "family had been Catholic since before the Reformation." Indeed, Read calls him simply the Recusant. Dawson himself seems to have lost all faith or residual fear of God; he presides over a mock Black Mass and it is Jenny rather than he who considers their affair adulterous.

Although it is unclear whether Read endorses Dawson's path, the book is filled with complaints against the Church that one still hears: Prayer is useless in an unjust world; the Church is too rigid, or too rich, or does not understand human sexuality. Arguments from the Church ring hollow in the face of Dawson's anger at injustice. As Theresa, the daughter of a parishioner with whom Dawson has an affair, states, "I just don't seem to need Faith.... There are so many straight-forward, intelligent people who don't believe a word of it, honestly, who think that believing a bit of bread is the body of Jesus Christ is like thinking that babies are brought by storks." Dawson, and the novel, has no response for her. Unlike the Crouchbacks, who move within a world touched by divine grace and separate from the secular society, Dawson's England is a search for status and a rejection of the moral language and framework that Guy would have understood. At the novel's end, Dawson has retreated into a monastery, though from real faith or simple exhaustion at the world is unclear. One atheist commentator wrote to Read that his conclusion successfully portrayed the "insanity" of a religious vocation. Winterman, however, who still repeats the arguments against the Church, seems to have suffered no ill effects himself in casting off traditional doctrine, though he is almost the only one. The other characters in the novel, including Dawson's two lovers, are broken people; Jenny loses herself in violent revolution and Theresa is a suicide.

Roger Scruton has written in these pages of the social and moral changes wrought by what is called "the 1960s," which in fact extended past the *annus terribilis* of 1968 through the mid-1970s. These two books portray the impact of those changes for Catholics not just in the United Kingdom, but throughout the West. Waugh's protagonist knows himself, and learns to look for the purpose for which he was made. Read's Dawson thinks he knows the causes of all our social ills, but does not—except, perhaps, at the end—know himself. Some believe that the revolutions of the 1960s were not revolutions at all, that they merely stripped off a false veneer and showed us what people "really" were like. These books, taken together, offer a sharp critique of that view.

# *The Fellowship: The Literary Lives of the Inklings*

"A FEELING FOR LITERATURE WHICH UNITED, in an unusual way, scholarship and imagination." Thus David Cecil described an Oxford literary club that midwifed books that have become classics of fantasy literature, apologetics, and poetry. C. S. Lewis, the engine behind the group known as the Inklings, described it more earthily: "We smoked, talked, argued, and drank together." This they did, despite professional setbacks, personal disputes, and a world war, for almost three decades—until the death of Lewis. There was nothing fashionable or avant-garde about the Inklings: they were a small group of white men who got together to talk about religion, literature, and philology while smoking and eating unhealthy pub food. Yet Tolkien remains the most important writer in Britain according to polls, Lewis continues to command attention, and their influence remains across a range of genres and scholarship. In *The Fellowship: The Literary Lives of the Inklings: J.R.R. Tolkien, C. S. Lewis, Owen Barfield, Charles Williams*, Philip and Carol Zaleski try to discern both why the Inklings lasted and why they still capture our imagination.

Meeting on Tuesday mornings at Lewis's rooms in Oxford's Magdalen College and Thursday nights at the Eagle and Child pub (the famous "Bird and Baby" in Inkling parlance), the group was dedicated to reading and critiquing one another's work. From these meetings came the work that made them famous: *The Lord of the Rings*, *Out of the Silent Planet*, fiction by Charles Williams, and work by the fourth figure profiled here, the lawyer and philosopher Owen Barfield, who has been called the "first and last

Originally published in *Commonweal*, May 27, 2016.

Inkling." Other figures fill out the portrait, such as Lewis's brother Warnie, Dom Bede Griffiths, David Cecil, and Henry "Hugo" Dyson. The details of the meetings are not known, but the Zaleskis dig deep into archives, letters, and other sources to provide in-depth biographies, summaries of popular and critical reception, and insight into the group's creative process. We get to know Tolkien, a fecund source of languages and mythic tales who tended to mumble at the group's meetings. The Lewis presented here is jovial and in command, ready with a sharp barb or remembered quote form his copious store of British literature. There is constant talk among the Inklings about work in progress, work contemplated, or work abandoned.

As with any good myth, there is an origin story—or rather, there are two. One was a literary club established by an Oxford undergraduate, Edward Lean, in 1932–33; he called it the Inklings. Lewis and Tolkien became members, continuing an acquaintance that had begun in 1926, when Lewis met the "smooth, pale fluent little chap" at a tea. The two formed a strong bond over beef, beer, English literature and, at least initially, a common interest in their Christian faith. The second origin story involves the long walks that Lewis took along with Barfield and Cecil Harwood in the 1920s, which combined enjoyment of the countryside with rigorous evening philosophical discussions.

It is easy to think of the group as a model of intellectual fellowship and mutual support, but over the course of their long career together the Inklings had a number of disputes and arguments. In particular, Tolkien, as a Catholic, took a critical view of his friend's "mere Christian" apologetics. Lewis, for his part, harbored a residual Protestant distaste for Rome. Dyson, whose career was overshadowed by Tolkien and Lewis, seemed after some years to favor conflict and rivalry over fellowship.

Williams does not appear until about two hundred pages in, and dies about a hundred pages before the book ends, but in some ways he is the magnetic and mysterious core of the story. Although previously acquainted with the Inklings, Williams began to attend their meetings regularly only after his offices at the Oxford University Press, where he worked his entire career, were relocated to Oxford proper at the outset of the war. His arrival changed the group's dynamic. Lewis thought highly of him, and praised his work at almost every chance. Tolkien saw him as a rival for Lewis's attention, and Williams's lectures at Oxford drew some of Tolkien's audience away. But most of Williams's books were, and remain, neglected, ever on the brink of rediscovery, though a new biography might finally introduce him to a wider audience.

In a way, Williams's obscurity makes sense: his occult interests (membership, for example, in the esoteric Fellowship of the Rosy Cross) and idiosyncratic religious doctrines did not travel well outside of the England of his time, and much of his Arthurian poetry sounds odd to contemporary ears. Williams was perhaps one of those whose qualities are easiest to appreciate in person—a man whose agile and restless mind mesmerized students and companions with its play of words and ideas. The Zaleskis rightly focus on his strangeness. Williams really did, for a while at least, believe in magical and occult practices, and he seems to have had odd and sadomasochistic (but also seemingly chaste) relationships with some of his more ardent female admirers. Certainly Tolkien did not fully take to him, even though some of the details of Williams's stranger practices were unknown to him or the other Inklings. Still, the Zaleskis give Williams his due; his "doctrine of co-inherence," and the informal community he established to live it, is strongly related to his interpretation of Christian doctrine. And they note that Lewis thought highly of Williams's unusual fiction, a series of supernatural (or better, transcendental) novels, some of which might make very interesting movies.

Barfield was another important member of the group, but one whose orbit was eccentric. He spent much of his life as a solicitor in London, which he generally regretted since it took so much time away from what he considered his more important literary and philosophical labors. Although among the earliest members of the Inklings, his devotion to Anthroposophy, a school now as exotic as Williams's occultism, kept him at a distance from the increasingly orthodox Christianity of Lewis and Tolkien—so much so that Barfield would not discuss his theological ideas at meetings. He suffered a series of disappointments, both personal and literary, and he seemed for a time the least distinguished of the Inklings. But that is not the whole story; in the 1960s and '70s, as the other Inklings passed away—Lewis died in 1963, Tolkien and Dyson in 1975—Barfield kept going, an inspiration to those who have not spent their lives in intellectual pursuits but still wish they could. He arrived for the first time in the United States, less than a year after Lewis's death, for a stint of lectures at Drew University.

In his book *Surprised by Joy*, Lewis had famously described Barfield as the Second Friend, the one with whom "you go at it, hammer and tongs, far into the night, night after night.... Out of this perpetual dogfight a community of mind and a deep affection emerge." American audiences in part wanted to see who had drawn such respect from the master, and Barfield was more than willing to oblige. He lectured and wrote about his early friendship with Lewis, and their philosophical disputes (which they called, semi-seriously, "the Great War"), as well as his own work. His lectures were well attended and he entered into a remarkably vital and creative phase of his life. He wrote a well-received book on Coleridge, and two other books, *Poetic Diction* and *Studies in Words*, have attained cult classic status. He never became a household name like Lewis and Tolkien, but in his areas of interest he is now considered as accomplished as any other member of the group.

The Inklings lasted for as long as they did, the Zaleskis believe, because they were serious about their work and the critiques of their fellows, and they were serious about a certain kind of (male) friendship. They shared convictions about the power of story, including that True Story of creation and redemption they believed was reflected, obscurely, in literary creation. But what about their lasting influence? The enduring popularity of Lewis and Tolkien, in particular, has inspired critics (like the feminist Germaine Greer) to discount them as mere tellers of just-so stories. But Tolkien's philological scholarship is still important. Barfield continues to inspire more than just Christians (or Anthroposophists). And Lewis's apologetical work and literary scholarship is widely read and respected, even if most people know him for his Narnia stories.

The Zaleskis highlight what perhaps really discomfits some modern readers about the Inklings: they believed in redemption, in what the Zaleskis call the Happy Ending—not an ending without sorrow or wounds, but salvation all the same. They believed that Western culture had lost the image of salvation, which was expressed in story, legend, and myth (including what Lewis called the Truth Myth, Christianity). But they were not really nostalgists; their work was directed not "simply to restore the discarded image, but to refresh it and bring it to life for the present and the future."

# *Faith, Doubt, and Fiction in a Secular Time*

THE WORLDVIEW Nick Ripatrazone portrays in *Longing for an Absent God: Faith and Doubt in Great American Fiction* is sorely needed in these days of social distancing filled with concern that physical closeness could breed infection. The Catholic literary tradition, like its religious traditions, is deeply tactile. As Ripatrazone writes, "Catholicism is an assault on the senses." Its practices, both inside churches and in the daily lives of the faithful, surround us in the conviction that God is among us—here, now.

And as this marvelous book shows, even writers who have fallen away from the Faith feel God's absence. Their fiction is in some cases just as charged with an incarnational sense of God, but they wrestle with the implications of what a world without God, but needing belief, would look like.

Ripatrazone, himself a poet and essayist who has been able to cross back and forth between the Catholic and secular press, has essays here on a number of writers, including Thomas Pynchon, Louise Erdich, and Toni Morrison, who reflect their faith in various ways. He also, quite interestingly, pairs writers—Walker Percy with Andre Dubus, for example, Graham Greene with Flannery O'Connor, or Don DeLillo and Ron Hansen—as a way to explore how those with a living faith differ in their writing from those with vestigial or no faith.

As he writes in comparing the work of Don DeLillo (whose work he describes as "Catholicism without belief") and that of Ron Hansen (author of *Mariette in Ecstasy*), their work would please neither "readers wishing

Originally published in *Catholic World Report*, April 16, 2020.

for fully atheistic writing or those craving purely devotional work." For DeLillo, "the miraculous is artifice. His fiction attempts to manipulate the mysteries of God, to label signs. For Hansen, God is mysterious and complicated, resistant to control." Ironically, it is the non-believing novelist who is more dogmatic, who wants to control God and life's vagaries, while the believer inserts into the story an element of mystery and the possibility of the miraculous.

*Longing for an Absent God* is at the center of two different but overlapping arguments. The first is whether religious faith in general, or Catholicism in particular, even has a place in fiction. Ripatrazone recognizes that in our contemporary secular world, religious writers receive less serious attention than they once did. Part of this is because the nation once was, culturally at least, more Christian and so religious themes in serious fiction was not unacceptable for elite literary culture. But it was also the case that Catholicism was different. Its images, rituals, and doctrines were a rich source of narrative that appealed to Catholics who grew up in that world as well as those who did not. That relationship has changed significantly, and now even writers of "doubt" are lumped together with the writers of "faith" in attempting to break through to the wider culture.

The second debate is over the role of the Catholic novelist. All the writers in Ripatrazone's collection would, he argues, qualify, despite the complicated relationship some of these writers have to their faith. They are all Catholic writers because the Catholic sensibility invades their work. For the lapsed writers, their work "reveals a Catholic milieu, but also a cultural one devoid of any transcendent faith, [but a] discerning reader will notice the vestiges of their former belief."

The believing writers have different challenges. O'Connor, a literary giant whose style was inimitable, still remains influential in her conviction that believing writers could not be didactic, but had to shock the reader into receptivity toward God. She had little patience for pious fiction; her "messy sermons" were part of a larger understanding of a writer's role. She thought that in a world without God, the religious novelist had to "bend the whole novel—its language, structure, its action" in a compelling way.

In his last chapter, "Literary Faith in a Secular Age," Ripatrazone surveys the current crop of younger Catholic writers and sees cause for hope. He notes, rightly, that the sense of Catholicism as a "separate" world waned significantly after Vatican II. The generation of Catholic writers who came of age in the 1980s live in an imaginative world much closer to their Protestant and secular neighbors than those in the golden age of Catholic life, with its close-knit ethnic communities, Latin Mass, and Friday fish frys.

Ripatrazone focuses on Alice McDermott and Phil Klay, both contemporary writers who are also practicing Catholics. Both have been recognized as significant voices—McDermott's *Charming Billy* won the National Book Award in 1989, and Klay's *Redeployment*, a collection of short stories arising from his military service, in 2014. Both, but especially Klay, are writing for a post-Catholic world and see a need to integrate their faith in a different way than earlier Catholic writers. For Klay, that means (as a character in one of his stories puts it), the writer needs to find a "crack" in the sufferings of others through which to communicate. For McDermott, it is a recognition that the ground spring of her faith and her writing is the astonishing fact that "out of love—love—for such troubled, flawed, struggling human beings, the Creator, the First Cause, became flesh that we, every one of us, would not perish."

Ripatrazone shows how this message continues to be played out in dialogue between the Catholic writers of faith, and those of doubt.

# *Telling the Truth about the Church*

THE BASIS for U.S. church-state jurisprudence has its roots in anti-Catholic prejudice. How we got here is a theme of Rodney Stark's new book, *Bearing False Witness: Debunking Centuries of Anti-Catholic* History, which traces and debunks a number of falsehoods about the Church that have made deep roots in our culture. As Stark, a historian who is not Catholic and teaches at Baylor University, a Baptist institution, recounts, his historical research uncovered one lie after another about the Church. And sometimes these lies persist in the culture long after professional historians no longer believe they are true.

Stark wrote that he began to realize that "the issue of distinguished anti-Catholic history is too important and its consequences too pervasive to ignore." If one does not accurately understand the Church, one will not understand Western, or indeed much of world, culture. Stark's chapter on religion and science is alone worth the book, since the Church has done so much to foster real scientific advancement; indeed, some have argued that it is Christian belief in an objective order supported by natural law that makes science even possible.

Stark divides the book into ten chapters, which cover subjects such as anti-Semitism, the Crusades, the Inquisition and the supposed "suppression" of lost scriptures. He does not ignore the sometimes-ugly episodes of Church history, but he is interested in clearly setting out the lies about the Church that remain current, even if false.

---

Originally published in *National Catholic Register*, May 29–June 11, 2016.

Thus, in response to the announcement of another "lost gospel" that supposedly shows Jesus acting in ways contrary to Church teaching, Stark, after thorough review, states simply that "these gospels were not so much suppressed as they were discarded as obvious forgeries and nonsense."

The idea of a Church crushing dissent with the aid of civil authorities surfaces with the Inquisition and again during the French Revolution, and again, the facts are otherwise. Stark probably claims a little too strongly that the Church favored the revolution—in fact, the Church did support significant reforms, but not overturning the monarchy; but he is exactly right that the war against the Church was started by the revolutionaries who could not abide by the nuance of the Church's teaching: that there are two spheres of authority, one spiritual and one temporal. That same government hostility to religious faith is echoed in the Obama administration's attack on the Church today.

These lies all serve a similar purpose, of course: to denigrate the Church's teaching authority and moral standing, and thus remain useful to those who want to see the Church as "backward" or needlessly punitive. Stark writes as an historian, not an apologist; but the truth is not only good history, but also the best defense of the Church.

# Cui bono? *Bringing Thomistic Thought to Bear on Modern Economics*

LAST JANUARY, the Vatican issued a "Bolletino" titled *Oeconomicae et pecuniariae quaestiones*, subtitled "Considerations for an ethical discernment regarding some aspects of the present economic-financial system." Like many such Vatican documents on complicated social questions, the *Bolletino* is a mixed bag. There are clear statements of longstanding Catholic principles, such as that "markets do not regulate themselves," and a recognition that despite gains in wealth, inequality and poverty still remain, and in some places remain extreme. Further, the document notes that economics relies on a vision of the human person at odds with modern tendencies to define people as consumers or customers. So far so good. But the *Bolletino* also contains too-brief analyses of very abstruse financial instruments and a capsule summary of the "financial crisis" of a decade ago; it is likely that this is the first time the phrase "credit default swaps" has appeared in a Vatican document.

The *Bolletino* comes at an important time. Catholics, especially in America but throughout the West and the world, are rethinking once again the relationship between economics—particularly in its "global capital" or "neoliberal" varieties—and Catholic social thought. Until very recently, in the American or more generally Western context that debate was thought to have been settled. Communism was the enemy of the Church; it was also the enemy of capitalism. Some Catholic thinkers then thought that because communism opposed both, capitalism and Catholicism must be compatible with one another. Further, this "capitalism" was one of worldwide free

Originally published in *Catholic World Report*, April 25, 2019.

markets with an emphasis on financial instruments and abstract forms of wealth, rather than industry or farming. The 1991 papal encyclical *Centesimus Annus* can be thought of as the high-water mark by proponents of this line of thought, since that document praised private property and seemed to condemn centralized planning and what it called "real socialism."

But more recently a generation of Catholic critics has emphasized other parts of Catholic teaching, also evident in *Centesimus* and other papal writings. This teaching promotes ideas like the just wage, rights of workers against oppression, and a suspicion generally that economics is a standalone "science" separate from ethical concerns. More generally, this school of thought suggests that "capitalism" may itself inscribe patterns of behavior and injustice hostile to Catholicism.

Unfortunately, this important debate has been hindered by the fact that so few of the participants have the facility with both economics and theology to make sense of their commonalities and differences, or to think of the former in light of the latter. Theologians too often condemned the mere notion of business or profit-seeking as immoral; economists thought theology irrelevant to the hard facts of buying and selling. Now comes Mary Hirschfeld, who received her economics doctorate before her conversion, and her theology one afterwards. She knows economics as a discipline, and more importantly she knows how and where it diverted from Catholic thought and where it is the same. Her new book from Harvard University Press, *Aquinas and the Market: Toward a Humane Economy*, is a welcome contribution to returning to a distinctive, Catholic way of looking at economics, but one that does not rest on unrealistic abstractions or misunderstandings.

Hirschfeld identifies one critical commonality between Catholic teaching on economics, seen through the lens of St. Thomas Aquinas, and that of academic economists: both seek to explain human choices. For the economist, the dominant model is what is called "rational" choice theory. Now—and this is the first of Hirschfeld's helpful correctives—rational choice theory is not the same as the concept of *homo economicus*, a being with no end other than the material. The rational choice model "simply says that people efficiently calculate how best to achieve their desired ends but is silent about the nature of those ends. Rational agents can pursue a range of ends, ruthlessly furthering their narrow self-interest in making as much money as possible, say, even if they were running a slave market, but the rational choice model can also account for a Mother Teresa, so long as she efficiently deploys her resources to succor the poor as well as possible." That model is often reduced to complicated mathematical formulas that tend to marginalize the most important question: does it matter what those ends are, which people are so efficiently pursuing? Without them, those models tend to treat all ends as equal, and material ends as the only ones that count. Enter Aquinas.

Aquinas, too, knows that people make choices, but for Aquinas people are oriented toward happiness, not maximizing utility. That is, Aquinas sees a substantive good against which people's choice can be measured. This difference in what Hirschfeld calls "metaphysical assumptions" about human wants "has important ramifications for how we understand human rationality, the role of economic activity, and the relationships between ethics and economic issues." Moving from this basic commonality of human choice and core disagreement about the ends of our choices, Hirschfeld draws out the implications of a Thomist economics. In the traditional Thomist view "the good of economic efficiency carries no weight in its own right." Rather, "neither markets nor natural wealth have value independent of their role in servicing the higher goods they support," such as happiness. And as Hirschfeld shows, the abstractions of rational choice are fading before new kinds of thinking about economics that share the empirical and non-material interests of Catholic economics. Indeed, contemporary economics has even begun to recognize the role of happiness in economic decision-making, and that efficiency tells only part of the story.

Because modern economic theory places such emphasis on efficiency, the use of money as a means of exchange can threaten to replace the substantive goods represented by that exchange. That was one problem with the financial crisis: the complexity of the instruments being used was one thing, but the greater problem was that the market for these instruments had lost connection to reality and the goods those instruments were intended to serve. For Hirschfeld, as for Aquinas, economics is a matter of justice as well as exchange: for persons to demand the "lowest" price as determined by a formula can deny the fact that those in the other side of the exchange have their just needs as well. The emphasis is wrongly placed on squeezing out the greatest advantage against another, rather than seeking out the most just arrangement. Hirschfeld skips the vexed question of usury, but notes that Thomas' focus on justice and substantial goods could support certain interest-bearing transactions.

It is when she considers the consumer economy that Hirschfeld's analysis becomes even more radical. An economy is not only efficient to the extent possible, but *well-ordered*; "rational choice, in contrast, invites us to make our choices in a piecemeal fashion without thinking carefully about how various goods and services fit into the overall pattern of our lives." If we believe that some goods are not served by efficiency, then an economy which stresses them (through the price mechanism) may themselves be harmful for human flourishing. Hirschfeld takes the example of household chores such as dishwashing. Modern appliances make work easier and quicker; but because our demand for convenience can be boundless, we make repeated choices for more and more such devices, which may lead us to remodel our homes, which then may cause a family to have to work harder to afford such and to spend less time together. A series of choices seen only from the vantage point of efficient time-usage, without being ordered to the substantive good (here, of family life), may very well result in less well being, not more.

A Thomistic economics teaches us that economic goods are, and are always, simply instrumental goods to assist us in human flourishing and ultimately in getting to Heaven. His teaching on private property, charity, and economic justice can help erode the emphases modern economic life places on measuring income as happiness and efficiency as an end goal, even if that goal crushes workers and results in less happiness. Hirschfeld has provided a new starting point for a discussion of what economics should be for.

# *Blaine Strikes Again*

A CASE NOW PENDING before the Supreme Court of Arizona shows that it will take a long time to rid state law of a pervasive symbol of anti-Catholic bigotry: the so-called Blaine amendments.

A "Blaine amendment" is a state law that bars public aid to "sectarian" schools. Some of these laws are embedded in a state's constitution itself. The name comes from the Maine Congressman James G. Blaine who tried to add such an amendment to the federal Constitution in the late nineteenth century. That attempt failed, but many states went ahead with their own laws. The historical record is unequivocal that "sectarian" in these laws really means "Catholic."

The Blaine amendments were passed during a wave of anti-Catholic sentiment that swept through the country in the last years of the nineteenth century and which continues in some circles today. The Supreme Court in 2000 said that the history of the Blaine amendments represents a "shameful pedigree that we do not hesitate to disavow." Unfortunately, many of the 35 states that still maintain such amendments have not followed the Supreme Court's lead. In a case called *Cain v. Horne*, the Arizona court is faced with whether its version of the Blaine amendment should withstand scrutiny. The amendment, called the Aid Clause, provides that "No tax shall be laid or appropriation of money made in aid of any church, or private or sectarian school, or any public service corporation."

In 2006, the Arizona Legislature enacted a state scholarship program under which public school students with a disability who transfer to a

Originally published in *National Catholic Register*, January 16, 2009.

private primary or secondary school will be paid a scholarship by the state up to the amount of basic state aid the student would have received if the student had remained in the public school.

Cain challenged this program, claiming that it violated the Aid Clause because some of the students who could receive this aid would use it in "sectarian" schools. The lower court rejected these claims and upheld the scholarship program, but the Arizona Court of Appeals reversed and found that the scholarship program did violate the Aid Clause. The appellate court concluded that the scholarship program provided impermissible support for private or sectarian schools. Now the case is before the Arizona Supreme Court.

A brief filed in support of the program by the Becket Fund for Religious Liberty, a nonprofit organization devoted to protecting religious freedom, argues that the court should look behind the words of the statute to recognize that the Aid Clause, like so many other similar statutes, has a history tainted with anti-Catholic and, in some cases, racist baggage and so should be rejected.

The appellate court did not seriously consider the background and purpose of the Aid Clause. The court reasoned that it had to uphold the Aid Clause even if it "may have been tainted by questionable motives," if the language of the law itself seemed neutral and not discriminatory.

This argument makes no sense, as it is an invitation to write laws that seem "neutral" but are designed to target particular groups. The Supreme Court, in a case called *Hunter v. Underwood* did just that. Hunter declared unconstitutional a seemingly neutral law that had the purpose of disenfranchising African American voters. The same situation presents itself in Arizona.

So, in other words, if there is evidence for a discriminatory purpose against religion, a court should be allowed to consider it in assessing the validity of a statute. Moreover, a law may be discriminatory in effect, even if the law's drafters did not intend that effect. As the Becket Fund brief notes, most of the students attending private religious schools attend Catholic schools, and so the denial of funds under the program would disproportionately affect Catholic schoolchildren. Given this history, one can only hope that the Arizona Supreme Court will prevent the discriminatory Aid Clause from prohibiting assistance to disabled children who wish to go to a religious school.

The continued existence of Blaine amendments, given their history in anti-Catholic bias, is troubling. But more troubling than this case, or even the unfortunate history of anti-Catholicism that fostered the Blaine amendments in the first place, is how such laws distort our understanding of religious liberty.

Such laws imply that there is no place for mutual support between public aid and private religious schools and that the relationship between religious faith and secular government must be adversarial rather than cooperative. Therefore, they help to disrupt the delicate balance between a religiously neutral public space with a vibrant and diverse religious life.

In other words, the Blaine amendments are a problem not only for Catholics but for all who care about religious liberty.

# *Catholic Social Thought and the Large Multinational Corporation*

❧

**Over the past several years,** scholars have employed the principles of Catholic Social Thought ("CST") to examine corporate behavior and organization.[1] According to its exponents, CST espouses an ethic that is "rooted in human nature rather than either corporate power or national identity" and may provide an alternative vision of the person and economic activity different from underlying contemporary global capitalism.[2] In particular, CST offers a critique of classical liberal economics and its conception of persons as autonomous consumers or shareholders seeking to maximize their preferences.[3] CST places economic concerns within the larger framework of the Catholic Church's teaching about the meaning and purpose of human life. Developing such an approach is important because "a Christian social theology that lacks a theology of the large corporation will have no effective means of inspiring those Christians who do work within large corporations to meet the highest practicable Christian standards."[4]

The recent *Compendium of the Social Doctrine of the Church* and other Church documents are replete with references to the corporation and the boundaries of economic conduct.[5] They are, however, only one aspect of the engagement between Catholic thought and the multinational corporation.[6] CST has spoken with more than one voice on the question of appropriate corporate structure and conduct; even the practitioners of CST acknowledge that the working out of the implications of CST for corporations is in the beginning stages.[7] On the one hand, CST principles do not propose any one type of economic structure. Yet on the other hand,

Originally published in *Journal of Catholic Legal Studies*, 46.1, 2007.

they clearly pose limits to economic activity, by state action if necessary, to further other commitments, such as defending the poor.[8]

This paper will outline three major components of the Catholic understanding of economic life, as set out in the recent *Compendium of the Social Doctrine of the Church* and other documents: the common good, solidarity, and "subsidiarity."[9] Next, the paper will examine whether subsidiarity offers a way for CST to address the challenges of the multinational form. In particular, the paper will break down subsidiarity into three characteristics—size, structure, and purpose—as the analytic framework to see whether CST can offer any guidelines for the multinational.

CST's serious engagement with the social and moral issues raised by corporate and multinational conduct can be traced to the American theologian Michael Novak whose 1990 book, *Toward a Theology of the Corporation,* sets out a case for understanding corporations in general, and the large corporation in particular, in the light of Catholic teaching.[10] Novak's argument is twofold.[11] First, he argues that the corporation is a private institution that can protect individuals from the corrosive powers of the state. "Corporations...are a useful instrument of social justice, a

1. See generally Mark Sargent, "Competing Visions of the Corporation in Catholic Social Thought," *Journal of Catholic Social Thought,* 1 (2): 561–593 (2004).
2. Kenneth E. Goodpaster, Foreword to *Rethinking the Purpose of Business: Interdisciplinary Essays from the Catholic Social Tradition*, eds. S. A. Cortright and Michael J. Naughton [hereafter *Rethinking the Purpose of Business*], xi.
3. See Mark Sargent, "Utility, the Good and Civic Happiness: A Catholic Critique of Law and Economics," *Journal of Catholic Legal Studies*, 44.1 (2005).
4. Michael Novak, *Toward a Theology of the Corporation* (AEI Press, 1990).
5. See *Compendium of the Social Doctrine of the Church* (hereafter CSD).
6. See Diarmuid Martin, "Globalisation in the Social Teaching of the Church," in *The Social Dimensions of Globalization*, ed. Louis Sabourin (2000) [hereafter *Social Dimensions*], 82 (noting that, until recently, globalization, including economic globalization, was not a theme of Church teaching).
7. *Rethinking the Purpose of Business*, xv (noting "relative silen[ce]" from Catholic universities on questions of business practice).
8. CSD §351.
9. See generally ibid.
10. See generally Novak, *supra* note 4.
11. Sargent, *supra* note 3, at 43–44.

mediating institution between isolated individuals and the omnipotent state."[12] Novak first wrote this in 1981, and his analysis is in part a defense of capitalism against the "anticapitalist bias" he saw in many Western intellectuals during the Cold War.[13] He proposed "for the consideration of theologians the notion that the prevailing moral threat in our era may not be the power of the corporations but the growing power and irresponsibility of the state."[14] The large corporation, in other words, is a barrier to socialism. Others have taken up Novak's argument, and today represent what Mark Sargent has called the "right wing" of CST scholars.[15] They have argued that the principle of subsidiarity is the CST principle that clearly expresses this anti-state bias. Legal scholar Stephen Bainbridge has written that subsidiarity is the means of protecting individual liberty from the power of the state by carving out a private sphere beyond the government's reach.[16] Corporations also provide an environment for people to exercise virtues such as industriousness, thrift, and creativity.[17] In particular, some scholars have argued that the history of the corporation provides evidence that it was envisioned as a tool to encourage the growth of small businesses.[18] For example, beginning with New York in 1822, states concluded that limited liability should be adopted as policy because this structure serves "democratic goals" by acting "as a means of encouraging the small-scale entrepreneur, and of keeping entry into business markets competitive and democratic."[19] Father Robert Sirico has written

12. Novak, *supra* note 4, at 3.
13. Ibid. at 15.
14. Ibid. at 34.
15. Sargent, *supra* note 3, at 4.
16. See Stephen M. Bainbridge, "Catholic Social Thought and the Corporation," 3 *UCLA School of Law Research Paper Series*, Paper No. 03–20 (2003).
17. Ibid. ("Put another way, subsidiarity logically implies that subordination of economic institutions to the state poses a grave threat to both communal and personal liberty"); see also Stephen M. Bainbridge, "Law and Economics: An Apologia," in *Christian Perspectives on Legal Thought*, Michael W. McConnell et al., eds. (2001).
18. Bainbridge, *supra* note 16, at 3.
19. Stephen B. Presser, "Thwarting the Killing of the Corporation: Limited Liability, Democracy, and Economics," 87 *Northwestern University Law Review*, 148, 153–56 (1992).

that subsidiarity is a necessary bulwark of the entrepreneurial economy, and its primary purpose is to "set limits for state intervention" in order to allow for more voluntary business and social action.[20] This argument has support in official Church documents. For example, the recent *Catechism of the Catholic Church* provides that "subsidiarity is opposed to all forms of collectivism [and it] sets limits for state intervention."[21] If left unchecked, the state "tends to absorb within itself other institutions, such as the family and religious bodies."[22]

Novak's second argument is theological. He argues that corporations can be "instruments of redemption...[and] of God's grace."[23] As the corporation is where many people spend their working lives, a religious critique should consider the possibility that there are "signs of grace in the corporation," such as creativity and the protection of liberty.[24] Indeed, in a later article Novak writes that "[b]usiness is a noble Christian vocation, a work of social justice, and the single greatest institutional hope of the poor of the world."[25] Accordingly, theologians should not reject the corporation, but should instead embrace its possibility as a channel of grace for those working within it. In *Theology*, Novak discusses the multinational only briefly, primarily noting that most American corporations are in fact *not* multinationals, and identifying four contributions multinationals make to their host countries: capital facilities, technological innovations, easing the host country's balance of payments, and wages paid to the host country's workers which remain in that country and are available for saving or investment.[26] He deals with general arguments against the

20. Robert A. Sirico, "Subsidiarity, Society, and Entitlements: Understanding and Application," 11 *Notre Dame Journal of Law, Ethics and Public Policy*, 549, 551 (1997).
21. *Catechism of the Catholic Church* [hereafter CCC], 2nd ed. (1997), §1885.
22. John Paul II, Encyclical Letter *Centesimus Annus* [hereafter *Centesimus Annus*], 45.
23. Novak, *supra* note 4, at 60; see also ibid. at 7 (stating that corporation is also a metaphor for "the ecclesial community").
24. Ibid. at 43–49.
25. Michael Novak, "A Philosophy of Economics," Vol. 1, *University of St. Thomas Law Journal*, 791 (2004).
26. Novak, *supra* note 4, at 40–42.

potential dangers that corporations pose, but not specifically with those of multinationals.

While influential, these arguments have not completely carried the day. Some CST scholars—Sargent's "left wing"—have given up hope in the corporate form, considering it a mere shell for human greed that lacks the moral compass that should guide a human decision-maker.[27] As Quigley has argued, "[t]hough there has been much discussion about making corporations moral or socially responsible, their legal DNA prevents them from acting like humans and having the chance to act in moral ways."[28] Therefore, the argument goes, the corporate form should be abolished to allow "the full panoply of ethical and social responsibility" embodied in CST to act directly upon the individuals who engage in business conduct, rather than indirectly through the corporate form.[29] Others have disputed Novak's claims that corporations, considered as themselves, have any theological status.[30]

This pessimistic view of the corporation in general, and the multinational in particular, has also found occasional expression in official Catholic teaching. The 1981 Papal Encyclical *Laborem Exercens*, for example, attributed the exploitation of poorer nations to "the companies referred to as multinational or transnational [that] fix the highest possible prices for their products, while trying at the same time to fix the lowest possible prices for raw materials or semi-manufactured goods."[31] A second encyclical, *Solicitudo Rei Socialis*, which appeared in 1987, echoed this criticism. In it, the Pope asserted that

27. See, e.g., William Quigley, "Catholic Social Thought and the Amorality of Large Corporations: Time to Abolish Corporate Personhood," Vol. 5, *Loyola Journal of International Public Law*, 109, 125–28 (2004) (noting that there is no realistic proposal that would remedy the lack of social responsibility that has characterized corporations).

28. Ibid. at 109.

29. Ibid. at 128.

30. See Sargent, *supra* note 3, at 22 ("At times, such is his enthusiasm that his 'theology of the corporation' verges on an idolatry of the corporation that does not even admit the possibility of critique.").

31. John Paul II, Encyclical Letter *Laborem Exercens* [hereafter *Laborem Exercens*], 17.

> The international trade system today frequently discriminates against the products of the young industries of the developing countries and discourages the producers of raw materials. There exists, too, a kind of international division of labor, whereby the low-cost products of certain countries which lack effective labor laws or which are too weak to apply them are sold in other parts of the world at considerable profit for the companies engaged in this form of production, which knows no frontiers.[32]

## I. The Multinational Today

As Micklethwait and Wooldridge recount in their history of the corporation, the multinational is now perhaps the largest force in the world economy; in 2001 there were approximately 65,000 "transnational corporations" employing fifty-four million people, with nineteen trillion dollars in revenues.[33] The largest of them dwarf, by some estimates, the GDP of some nations.[34] While international economic concerns have existed in Europe since the early Middle Ages,[35] developments in technology, information processing, and political decentralization have all contributed to the growth of a new kind of multinational firm: flexible, powerful, and quickly able to move its workforce, production, and managerial assets from one geographic region to another.[36] The growth of the multinational relative to state power is especially noteworthy now, when the power and autonomy of individual states have arguably been diminished by the ease of movement possessed by capital and labor; "nation-states can no longer

32. John Paul II, Encyclical Letter *Solicitudo Rei Socialis* [hereafter *Solicitudo Rei Socialis*], 43.
33. John Mickelthwait and Adrian Wooldridge, *The Company: A Short History of a Revolutionary Idea* (Modern Library Chronicles Series, 2005), 173.
34. See Sakiko Fulcuda-Parr, "Human Development Report: Deepening Democracy in a Fragmented World," TBL.1 (2002), 149 (available at http://hdr.undp.org/reports/global/2002/en/).
35. A. W. Clausen, "The International Corporation: An Executive's View," 403, *Annals of the American Academy of Political and Social Science*, 12, 13–14 (1972).
36. Ibid. at 14.

avoid coming to terms with the expectations of the international capital markets."[37] Indeed, the globalization of markets would not be possible without them: "Multinational firms form the institutional structure through which most of the global economic integration takes place," especially in the finance sector.[38] This paper will define the multinational as a corporate entity with its legal existence and significant shareholders located primarily within one country, but that has operations, either directly or in the form of subsidiaries, in other countries.

Yet, perhaps not surprisingly, the growth of the multinational has coincided with an increasing sensitivity toward its potential dangers. These entities possess great economic and legal power through means such as lobbying, high-quality legal and other professional support, as well as other means.[39] Developing countries especially may not have countervailing political or economic force sufficient to counter this power.[40] The intense competition among multinationals for relative advantage in wages, taxes, and government subsidies makes the location of any particular facility precarious, and increases the pressure these companies can place on governments for favorable terms. This in turn can lead to a breakdown of community norms and exposure of the workforce (especially in less developed nations) to economic hardship if a particular company were to relocate.[41] The Papal Encyclical *Quadragesimo Anno* speaks to the damage

37. Stefano Zamagni, "Globalisation and Local Particularities: Globalisation Processes and Transnational Civil Society Between Universality and Particularism," in *Social Dimensions, supra* note 6, at 72, 74.

38. Lee Tavis, "Corporate Governance and the Global Social Void," 35 *Vanderbilt Journal of Transnational Law*, 487, 492 (2002). For an excellent study of the rise of American multinational firms, see Mira Wilkins, *The Emergence of Multinational Enterprise* (1970), ix (examining the rise of American multinational manufacturing corporations with "direct investments in more than just sales abroad" prior to 1914).

39. See Martha T. McCluskey, "The Substantive Politics of Formal Corporate Power," 53 *Buffalo Law Review*, 1453, 1453–54 (2006) (discussing the increasingly privileged position that corporations have in the American legal system).

40. Sergio Bernal Restrepo, "The Social and Cultural Dimensions of Globalisation," in *Social Dimensions, supra* note 6, at 56, 61.

41. See Giuseppe C. Ruggeri, *The Catholic Social Tradition and Business in the Age of the Worker-Capitalist* 14 (2003), available at http://www.stthomas.edu/cathstudies/cst/mgmt/Bilbao/papers/Ruggeri.pdf.

wrought by unscrupulous corporate activity as a result of "the individualist spirit in economic life": a "deadly and accursed internationalism of finance or international imperialism whose country is where profit is."[42]

There is also the question of accountability. Numerous instances of multinational misconduct, such as Nestle's disastrous marketing of baby formula in developing countries in the late 1970s and early 1980s[43] or the Union Carbide Bhopal disaster in 1984 to Royal Shell's political conduct in Nigeria and the environmental damage its operations caused in the North Sea,[44] have highlighted the dangers posed by improper multinational conduct in developing nations. Disasters like these have resulted in calls to reform and rein in the multinationals through codes of corporate conduct and international regulation.[45] The activities of ITT in Chile in the 1970s, for example, led the United Nations to condemn the political activity of multinationals in developing nations, and the 2002 OECD Guidelines for Multinational Enterprises prohibited multinationals from "any improper involvement in local political activities."[46]

## II. CST and Economic Life

The Church's understanding of economic life is centered on the principle that work is a basic part of the individual human vocation.[47] Indeed, Catholic teaching accords the existence of work as a confirmation of the "profound identity of men and women created in the image and likeness

42. Pius XI, Encyclical Letter *Quadragesimo Anno* [hereafter *Quadragesimo Anno*], 109.
43. See James E. Post, "Global Codes of Conduct: Activists, Lawyers, and Managers in Search of a Solution," in *Global Codes of Conduct: An Idea Whose Time Has Come*, Oliver F. Williams, ed. (2000), 103, 108–109.
44. See Thomas Donaldson and Thomas W. Dunfee, *Ties that Bind: A Social Contracts Approach to Business Ethics* 1–9 (1999).
45. See, e.g., Paolo N. Rogers, "Multinational Corporations: A European View," 403 *Annals of the American Academy of Political and Social Science*, 58, 65 (1972). See generally Post, *supra* note 43 (discussing the development of international codes of conduct).
46. Organization for Economic Co-operation and Development, "The OECD Guidelines for Multinational Enterprises," 19 (2000).
47. CSD, *supra* note 5, §270.

of God."[48] Economic life is merely this principle writ large: "[M]an is the source, the center, and the purpose of all economic and social life."[49] This has been a particularly prominent theme in the social encyclicals of Pope John Paul II, for whom "the principal purpose of work is the shaping and development of the laborer's humanity."[50] Two foundational principles relevant to the organization of work through business forms flow from this conviction: First, businesses should serve the common good,[51] and second, in pursuing its objectives, businesses must not neglect "the authentic values that bring about the...development of the person and society."[52]

This understanding of the purpose of economic life differs from that offered by contemporary economics. Stefano Zamagni has characterized conventional economic thinking as embodying "a limited conception of personal well-being and the common good and which takes little account of human capacities for moral sentiments going well beyond the limited accounting of personal and immediate gains."[53] By focusing strictly on market relationships, economics ignores other economically significant transactions, such as altruism or reciprocity.[54] In short, "economics...neglects something important which affects people's happiness."[55] In contrast, CST proposes to integrate economic life into an anthropology that focuses

48. Ibid., §275.

49. Second Vatican Council, Constitution *Gaudium et Spes* [Hereafter *Gaudium et Spes*], 63.

50. Anthony Scaperlanda, "John Paul II's Vision of the Role of Multinational Enterprise Expansion in Building the Social Economy," 25 *International Journal of Social Economics*, 1764, 1765 (1998).

51. CSD, *supra* note 5, §338.

52. Ibid.

53. Stefano Zamagni, "Happiness and Individualism: An Impossible Marriage," 1 (2003) (unpublished draft, on file with author). See generally Stefano Zamagni, "Happiness and Individualism: A Very Difficult Union," in *Economics and Happiness: Framing the Analysis*, Luigino Bruni and Pier Luigi Porta, eds. (2005), 303.

54. *See* Pier Luigi Sacco et al., "The Economics of Human Relationships," in 1 *Handbook of the Economics of Giving, Altruism, and Reciprocity*, Serge-Christophe Kolm and Jean Mercier Ythier, eds. (2006), 697–98; see also Robert G. Kennedy, "The Virtue of Solidarity and the Purpose of the Firm," in *Rethinking the Purpose of Business, supra* note 2, at 51–52 (distinguishing the "economic paradigm" from CST).

55. Luigino Bruni, "The 'Technology of Happiness' and the Tradition of Economic Science," 26 *Journal of the History of Economic Thought*, 19, 22 (2004).

on satisfying the fulfillment of the whole person, who is "the source, the center, and the purpose of all economic and social life."[56] That person is necessarily social, that is, defined by relationships that transcend market connections: Solidarity with others should enable persons to

> see the "other"—whether a person, people or nation—not just as some kind of instrument, with a work capacity and physical strength to be exploited at low cost and then discarded when no longer useful, but as our "neighbor"...to be made a sharer, on a par with ourselves, in the banquet of life to which all are equally invited by God.[57]

In his encyclicals, Pope John Paul II emphasized that business associations, no less than other kinds of associations, represent one aspect of the naturally social nature of the human person. The encyclical *Centesimus Annus*, for example, describes both business and family with the term "community." A business is a "community" formed for the sake of filling the needs of society; the family is, among other things, a "community of work."[58] This term implicitly rejects the model of the business corporation based solely on voluntary contracts or maximizing profits. A business, though formed with the end of profit, is still a community of persons. Those working within it, therefore, have obligations of solidarity toward those with whom their work brings them into contact. In particular, the new multinational economy rests upon a radical change in the way we understand economic power. This is the "information revolution," and the recognition that human skill and ingenuity, and not land or even raw materials, is now the moving force in international economics.

*Centesimus Annus*, though without explicitly referring to multinationals, saw this development as the new basis for economic strength:

56. *Gaudium et Spes*, 63.
57. *Solicitudo Rei Socialis*, 39.
58. *Centesimus Annus*, 49.

> Whereas at one time the decisive factor of production was *the land*, and later capital—understood as a total complex of the instruments of production—today the decisive factor is increasingly *man himself*, that is, his knowledge, especially his scientific knowledge, his capacity for interrelated and compact organization, as well as his ability to perceive the needs of others and to satisfy them.[59]

The encyclical goes on, in detail, to describe the risks and problems with this new state of affairs, as well as its potential advantages. In particular, the encyclical points out that the emphasis on human capital places at a disadvantage those societies where education and other resources are inadequately developed, which could lead to exploitative relationships by more advanced societies.[60] The encyclical goes on to state that among the "new things" in the economy is the appreciation of business as a "society of persons" in which each person "collaborates in the work of his fellow employees, as well as in the work of suppliers and in the customers' use of goods, in a progressively expanding chain of solidarity."[61]

### A. *The Common Good*

The "common good" is one of the "permanent principles of the Church's social doctrine."[62] It is "the sum total of social conditions which allow people, either as groups or as individuals, to reach their fulfillment more fully and more easily."[63] This common good, however, is not a simple utilitarian calculation equaling the sum of all individual goods. It is instead "indivisible," and such individual good can only be attained together.[64] Preserving

---

59. Ibid., 32.
60. Ibid., 33.
61. Ibid., 43; see also Giuseppe C. Ruggeri, "The Catholic Social Tradition and Business in the Age of the Worker-Capitalist," 15, 17–18 (July 2003) (unpublished manuscript, prepared for the Fifth International Symposium on Catholic Social Thought and Management Education, noting increased emphasis on, and opportunities for, the individual in post-capitalist societies).
62. CSD, §160.
63. Ibid., §164, quoting *Gaudium et Spes*, 26.
64. CSD, §164.

and furthering the common good "is a central principle of Catholic Social Thought and therefore must be the starting point for defining a Catholic vision of the corporation."[65]

The common good in an economic context speaks to the proper uses of private property, including corporate property. In the Catholic tradition, the principle of private property is not "absolute and untouchable."[66] Rather, because individuals achieve their own good in common with others, property itself has a "universal destination"; that is, the earth was given by God to the whole human race "without excluding or favouring anyone."[67] Therefore, any one institution or generation is merely a custodian of property that belongs to humanity as a whole. Such an institution or generation remains, in part, an instrument to help others attain and sustain the common good.

For business organizations, profit is a legitimate component of this common good, and a determination to make a profit is not an improper goal for business. Profit, however, is "insufficient" to measure its success.[68] Multinationals are no less bound than other business organizations by the statement in *Centesimus Annus* that:

> the purpose of a business firm is not simply to make a profit, but is to be found in its very existence as a *community of persons* who in various ways are endeavouring to satisfy their basic needs, and who form a particular group at the service of the whole of society.[69]

This conclusion derives from the teaching that the "subjective" value of work—the value and dignity of those who work—outweighs its "objective"

65. Susan J. Stabile, "A Catholic Vision of the Corporation," 4 *Seattle Journal for Social Justice*, 181, 184 (2005).
66. CSD, §177.
67. Ibid., §171 (emphasis omitted).
68. Jean-Yves Calvez and Michael J. Naughton, "Catholic Social Teaching and the Purpose of the Business Organization: A Developing Tradition," *supra* note 2, at 3, 11 (emphasis omitted); see also *Centesimus Annus*, 35.
69. *Centesimus Annus*, 35.

dimension, the resources and production that go into work.[70] In other words, profit is not the end of the analysis as to whether corporations are serving the common good.

What constitutes a corporation's common good? Is it "the whole of society," as *Centesimus Annus* suggests, just those to whom it has clear legal obligations, or some other grouping? Traditional corporate law in the United States is quite explicit in holding that company directors are responsible only to the shareholders, and that their primary duty is to increase shareholder value rather than to some larger "common good." The classic statement is that of *Dodge v. Ford Motor Co.*, in which the court declared that "[a] business corporation is organized and carried on primarily for the profit of the stockholders."[71] As Kenneth Davis has written: "The bedrock principle of U.S. corporate law remains that maximization of shareholder value is the polestar for managerial decision making."[72] Behind this settled legal doctrine, however, are a number of assumptions about the corporate form, including whether this doctrine is in fact a doctrine.[73] Namely, the model assumes that the corporation is designed to increase shareholder value, which as a consequence increases efficiency and lowers social costs for all. Accordingly, there need be no distinct obligation on the corporation or its managers to serve other interests or the society

---

70. CSD, §270–271.
71. Dodge v. Ford Motor Co., 170 N.W. 668, 684 (Mich. 1919).
72. Kenneth B. Davis, Jr., "Discretion of Corporate Management to Do Good at the Expense of Shareholder Gain—A Survey of, and Commentary on, the U.S. Corporate Law," 13 CAN.-U.S. L.J. 7, 8 (1988). Some scholars have questioned whether the stark separation of ownership and control in a publicly held corporation serves the interest of shareholders. See Lucian A. Bebchuk, "Letting Shareholders Set the Rules," 119 *Harvard Law Review*, 1784, 1792–94 (2006) ("Effective centralized management does not require boards to retain absolute power").
73. See Leo L. Clarke, Bruce P. Frohnen and Edward C. Lyons, "The Practical Soul of Business Ethics: The Corporate Manager's Dilemma and the Social Teaching of the Catholic Church," 29 *Seattle University Law Review*, 139, 150–52 (2005) (questioning the dominance of the shareholder-maximization theory); see also Stefano Zamagni, "Religious Values and Corporate Decision Making: An Economist's Perspective," 11 *Fordham Journal of Corporate and Financial Law*, 573, 577–78 (2006) (noting that businesses "may be efficient and generate value even if the objectives include, in addition to profit maximization, other variables which take into consideration broader collective interests").

as a whole. As scholars such as Martha McClusky have argued, however, these conclusions need not go together. There is no precise "scientific economic measure" that can "separate a necessary cost in a transaction (i.e., a price)...from the peripheral, unnecessary, 'transaction costs'—like moral hazard—that get in the way of efficient market transactions."[74] The question of costs and benefits is inseparable from a consideration of what level of benefit can be accepted at what level of cost, and to whom.[75]

The 1986 United States Bishops' Pastoral Letter, *Economic Justice for All*, explicitly supported a so-called "stakeholder" model of corporate governance as an alternative to shareholder-maximization.[76] The usual definition of stakeholders is "those groups without whose support the organization would cease to exist."[77] The bishops stated that "[e]very business, from the smallest to the largest...depends on many different persons and groups for its success...customers, creditors, the local community, and the wider society. Each makes a contribution to the enterprise, and each has a stake in its growth or decline."[78] The bishops implied that it was the obligation of the business community to develop "new institutional mechanisms for accountability" to take into account the interests of these

74. Martha T. McClusky, "The Substantive Politics of Formal Corporate Power," 53 *Buffalo Law Review*, 1453, 1471–72 (2006).

75. See ibid. at 1472–1473.

76. See National Conference of Catholic Bishops, Pastoral Letter *Economic Justice for All: Catholic Social Teaching and the U.S. Economy*, 298, 305–306 (Washington, DC, November 18, 1986) [hereafter *Economic Justice*]. But see Lynda J. Oswald, "Shareholders v. Stakeholders: Evaluating Corporate Constituency Statutes Under the Takings Clause," 24 *Journal of Corporation Law*, 1, 4, 7 (1998) (noting that the effectiveness of stakeholder statutes has been mixed); A.A. Sommer, Jr., "Whom Should the Corporation Serve? The Berle-Dodd Debate Revisited Sixty Years Later," 16 *Delaware Journal of Corporate Law*, 33, 54–55 (1991) (concluding that it "is difficult to predict" whether stakeholder statutes will withstand the traditional emphasis on the duty to shareholders).

77. R. Edward Freeman and David L. Reed, "Stockholders and Stakeholders: A New Perspective on Corporate Governance," 25 *California Management Review*, 88, 89 (1983).

78. *Economic Justice*, 298; see also Trevor S. Norwitz, "'The Metaphysics of Time': A Radical Corporate Vision," 46 *Business Lawyer*, 377, 384–86 (1991) ("A company exists to make a profit, but it also exists to provide goods and services, create employment and thereby to promote the social welfare generally").

groups.[79] In particular, the bishops recommended increased partnerships between labor and management, especially in making significant corporate decisions such as plant closings.[80]

Shareholder primacy presents its own problems for CST. First, as Bruce Frohnen and others have argued, such a position is untenable in light of corporate statements that indicate corporations themselves seek goals other than shareholdermaximized profits, as well as economic realities that the shareholder-maximization model cannot explain.[81] In the modern financial world, the existence of an identifiable group of "shareholders" is almost as difficult as defining a set group of stakeholders. Shareholders always must be defined as shareholders as of a particular time. Given the fluid financial markets, shareholders today may not be shareholders tomorrow. Placing their sometimes-transitory interest, therefore, above others, such as long-term workers or the community in which an office or plant is located, may be problematic for CST. Indeed, sophisticated investors such as hedge funds have developed investment strategies that permit them to obtain the legal benefits of shareholders (such as voting) without the economic risks of ownership. For example, purchasing a block of stock while at the same time "shorting" an equal amount of stock protects the investor from economic loss (because if the stock drops in value, the short position increases in value), but also allows the investor to vote the shares it has purchased.[82] Under the shareholder primacy model, even nakedly short-term interests must be favored over the accumulated interests of workers, suppliers, and even the localities in which a long-term company may be based.

But also, the stakeholder model is not an exact fit for CST. First, the stakeholder/shareholder discussion is itself rooted in a conception that

79. *Economic Justice*, 298.

80. Ibid., 303. See generally Jeffrey R. Gates, *Democracy at Risk: Rescuing Main Street from Wall Street* (2001), 7–10 (outlining proposals designed to give employees and other stakeholders more involvement in corporate decision-making).

81. See Clarke et al., *supra* note 73, at 151–52.

82. See Ianthe Jeanne Dugan, "Hedge Funds Draw Scrutiny Over Merger Play," *Wall Street Journal*, January 11, 2006, (describing the "hedging strategy" used by a hedge fund seeking to influence a merger vote while eliminating economic risk).

reduces human relationships to an environment defined solely by satisfaction of preferences and voluntary agreements in order to attain those preferences.[83] Even when defining stakeholders more loosely, as any group that contributes to the corporation's existence, it seems difficult to imagine that it would be practicable to define such groups of stakeholders—say, "customers"—of an entity with far-flung global operations. Simply determining the wishes of such groups might be prohibitively expensive or otherwise impracticable.[84] Additionally, forcing the corporation to have legally enforceable duties towards these varied groups would place an extreme burden on the entity and its management.[85]

The fluidity of the identity of individual shareholders has led to the increased influence of institutional investors, such as mutual funds or pension plans, in the area of corporate governance and shareholder involvement. By 2002, for example, more than half of publicly available shares were held by institutional investors such as mutual funds or pension plans.[86] Such entities invest in securities on behalf of a changing class of individual investors, but may themselves remain shareholders of a particular corporation over a period of time. But, the mutual fund investor is "essentially a customer of the fund's management," and looks at the mutual fund as a means of managing investments rather than as a means of asserting their identity as voting shareholders in an identifiable corporation.[87] The mutual fund votes on their behalf and the shareholders of the fund are

83. See S. A. Cortright, Ernest S. Pierucci, and Michael J. Naughton, "A Social Property Ethic for the Corporation in Light of Catholic Social Thought," 2 *Logos* 138, 144–45 (1999).

84. See Timothy L. Fort, "Business as a Mediating Institution," in *Rethinking the Purpose of Business*, *supra* note 2, at 237, 247–250 (outlining the three major problems with stakeholder theory).

85. See Stephen M. Bainbridge, "The Bishops and the Corporate Stakeholder Debate," 4 *Villanova Journal of Law and Investment Management*, 2 (2002).

86. See "Institutional Investors as a Force for Change," November 6, 2002, available at http://www.upenn.edu/pennnews/researchatpenn/articleprint.php?506&bus; cf. Presser, *supra* note 19, at 152–53 (criticizing contemporary theories of corporate law for focusing on current dominance of institutional investors and neglecting history).

87. David J. Carter, Mutual Fund Boards and Shareholder Action, 3 *Villanova Journal of Law and Investment Management*, 6, 10 (2001).

more interested in the returns on the particular portfolios in which they are invested rather than the underlying companies. Even if shareholder-maximization is the proper goal, it is not clear whether corporate action that raises the value of the mutual fund company's shares always directly translates to the value of the shareholder's shares.

The problems with either the shareholder or stakeholder model are simply magnified in the multinational context. Their shares are held either directly or, in the case of a foreign corporation whose stock trades on an American exchange, in the form of (on the New York Stock Exchange, for example) American Depositary Receipts.[88] Determining the common good is therefore particularly difficult for multinational managers, who face a series of conflicting loyalties: that of guest, citizen, employee, and foreign and domestic shareholders, among others.[89] A multinational comprises many communities:

> Many of the business units can be located in different and often disparate societies. As communities overlap and nest within one another, societies are formed...with institutions that reflect the particular values of that society.... The issue is which cultural characteristics of which society should be established as the standard for the multinational network and which should be a part of local managerial discretion for the local business unit.[90]

88. "An American Depositary Receipt (ADR) is a share of stock of an investment in shares of a non-US corporation." The Investment FAQ, Subject: Stocks-American Depository Receipts (ADRs), available at http://invest-faq.com/articles/stock-adrs.html (last visited February 13, 2007).

89. See Bernard Mennis and Karl P. Sauvant, "Multinational Corporations, Managers, and the Development of Regional Identification in Western Europe," 403 *Annals of the American Academy of Political and Social Science*, 22, 23 (1972).

90. Timothy M. Tavis and Lee A. Tavis, "Managing the Corporation as Community" 12 (July 2003) (unpublished manuscript, prepared for the Fifth International Symposium on Catholic Social Thought and Management Education), available at http://www.stthomas.edu/cathstudies/cst/conferences/bilbao/papers/Tavis.pdf [hereafter Tavis and Tavis].

A different way to analyze the corporation is to combine a view of the corporation as a network or a corporate enterprise group[91] with a notion of the firm's "common good." Corporate enterprise groups differ from the usual understanding of corporate personality in that the concept recognizes that, although there may be many different legal entities within a corporate organization, they are all working for the end of the organization as a whole. Therefore, they should be treated as coordinate parts of one entity, even if the various subsidiaries or affiliates are organized as legally separate entities. The multinational has been characterized itself as a community, as a network of related entities, and as a "mediating institution" that enables individuals to develop themselves as human beings.[92] Further, CST recognizes the multinational's public dimension, in which "corporate activity has broad social and political ramifications that justify a body of corporate law that is deliberately responsive to public interest concerns."[93]

Utilizing a notion of "the common good" of the firm allows consideration of the interests of other groups in management decision-making in the light of extra-economic or religious values, and changes the calculus of decision making to include factors other than maximizing profits.[94] Like a politician who has responsibility not just for those who voted for him, but for all the voters, "the manager of a large firm is not only the agent of those who employed him…but also the fiduciary of those who work under his leadership…."[95] Indeed, the manager has a "precise duty" to care for and promote the human dignity of those working for the manager.[96] As Calvez

91. See Phillip I. Blumberg, *The Multinational Challenge to Corporation Law*, 231–32 (1993).
92. See Tavis and Tavis, *supra* note 90, at 12.
93. David Millon, "Theories of the Corporation," 1990 *Duke Law Journal*, 201, 201 (1990).
94. See, e.g., Luigino Bruni and Amelia J. Uelmen, *Religious Values and Corporate Decision Making: The Economy of Communion Project*, 11 *Fordham Journal of Corporate & Financial Law*, 645, 652 (2006).
95. Peter Koslowski, "The Common Good of the Firm as the Fiduciary Duty of the Manager," in *Business and Religion: A Clash of Civilizations?*, Nicholas Capaldi, ed., 301, 306 (2005) [hereafter *Business and Religion*].
96. CSD, §344.

and Naughton have argued, this requires "employers and entrepreneurs to create workplace conditions that allow employees to develop."[97] While, significantly, American managerial theory and practice have incorporated what Eugene McCarraher has called "a sacralized ideal of the corporation" in its reflections on human personhood, too often the results of that incorporation have been a shallow vision of the human person and has not placed corporate activity in the service of human dignity.[98]

## B. *Solidarity and Human Flourishing*

At root, solidarity is a "firm and persevering determination to commit oneself to the common good."[99] Solidarity recognizes that all people are united by virtue of their basic humanity, that by nature man is a social being, and that people express the fullness of personality only in and through communities that recognize this social dimension.[100] Those conclusions derive from the recognition of "the intrinsic social nature of the human person, the equality of all in dignity and rights and the common path of individuals...towards an ever more committed unity."[101] This sociality is even more pronounced in a globalized age, where the ability to form relationships with others who live at great distances has been made extremely easy due to new technology and where the "interdependence between individuals and peoples" is growing.[102] Due to this recognition of interdependence, solidarity demands action to "determine the order of institutions" to correct the imbalances of equality.[103] The *Compendium* identifies two particular areas

97. Jean-Yves Calvez and Michael J. Naughton, "Catholic Social Teaching and the Purpose of Business Organization: A Developing Tradition," in *Rethinking the Purpose of Business, supra* note 2, at 7.

98. Eugene McCarraher, "Me, Myself, and Inc.: 'Social Selfhood,' Corporate Humanism, and Religious Longing in American Management Theory, 1908–1956," in *Figures in the Carpet: Finding the Human Person in the American Past*, Wilfred M. McClay, ed., 185, 189 (2007).

99. CSD, §193.

100. See Lee A. Tavis, "Modern Contract Theory and the Purpose of the Firm," in *Rethinking the Purpose of Business, supra* note 2, at 224.

101. CSD, §192.

102. Ibid.

103. Ibid., §193.

of solidarity that must be safeguarded in the globalized economy—that between generations and respect for other cultures.[104] Private property or some ownership of external goods affords each person the scope needed for personal and family autonomy, and should be regarded as an extension of human freedom. "By its very nature private property also has a social quality which is based on the law of the common destination of earthly goods."[105]

Solidarity, therefore, affects economics, including corporate structures and governance. Solidarity and economic efficiency must be examined together, for efficiency at the cost of human flourishing is not acceptable.[106] Corporations are institutions that must be ordered according to recognition of this interdependence. "[A] business cannot be considered only as a 'society of capital goods'; it is also a 'society of persons' in which people participate in different ways and with specific responsibilities...."[107] Therefore, a corporation cannot be content with seeking only the intermediate goods of, for example, efficiency or wealth creation alone. Because it is composed of individuals whose flourishing is dependent upon everyone working together towards achieving the good of each, a company must also "contribute to the genuine development of the persons who participate in its activities."[108] Individuals have an affirmative duty to recognize their interdependence in their working lives:

> Therefore political leaders, and citizens of rich countries...have the moral obligation, according to the degree of each one's responsibility, to take into consideration, in personal decisions and decisions of government, this relationship of universality, this interdependence which exists between their conduct and the poverty and underdevelopment of so many millions of people.[109]

104. Ibid., §366–367.
105. *Gaudium et Spes*, 71.
106. CSD, §332.
107. Ibid., §368.
108. Kennedy, *supra* note 54, at 59.
109. *Solicitudo Rei Socialis*, 9. One aspect of this solidarity is a devotion to truth-telling in language and not "selling dreams" that provide a distorted view of the human

## C. *Subsidiarity*

Subsidiarity is primarily a principle of governance and organization that has received much attention from CST scholars across a range of issues.[110] As Robert Vischer notes, subsidiarity represents a longstanding Catholic social vision rooted in a "complex web of family, social, religious, and governmental ties" that serves to support the exercise of the individual's responsibility in society.[111] Making its first explicit appearance in *Quadragesimo Anno*, as summarized in *Centesimus Annus*, subsidiarity posits that:

> A community of a higher order should not interfere in the internal life of a community of a lower order, depriving the latter of its functions, but rather should support it in case of need and help to coordinate its activity with the activities of the rest of society, always with a view to the common good.[112]

The principle is still most often used to describe decentralized government authority. The European Union, for example, has explicitly adopted a form of subsidiarity for its political arrangements.[113]

---

person. See Raymond N. MacKenzie, "Selling Dreams: Catholicism and the Business Communicator," 2 *Logos* 118, 136–37 (1999).

110. Cf. Scott Fitzgibbon, "'True Human Community': Catholic Social Thought, Aristotelean Ethics, and the Moral Order of the Business Community," 45 *St. Louis University Law Journal*, 1243, 1244 (2001) (discussing Catholic social thought, Aristotle, and the corporations); Susan J. Stabile, "Using Religion to Promote Corporate Responsibility," 39 *Wake Forest Law Review*, 839, 846 (2004) (proposing "an alternative view of the person and her relation to the world, one rooted in religion, in an effort to influence how academics and others think and talk about the social obligations of corporations"); Amelia J. Uelmen, "Toward a Trinitarian Theory of Products Liability," 1 *Journal of Catholic Social Thought*, 603 (2004).

111. See Robert K. Vischer, "Subsidiarity as a Principle of Governance: Beyond Devolution," 35 *Indiana Law Review*, 103, 109 (2001).

112. *Centesimus Annus*, 48.

113. See Paul D. Marquardt, "Subsidiarity and Sovereignty in the European Union," 18 *Fordham International Law Journal*, 616, 617–18 (1994). It also posits a role for multinational institutions and cooperation among nations in those situations where the resources of a single nation are insufficient. *Pacem in Terris* explicitly endorsed cooperation among nation-states through international organizations to solve problems that may be beyond the scope of any one nation to solve. See John XXIII, *Encyclical Letter Pacem in Terris*, 140. The encyclical cites "[t]he same principle of

As a political concept, and as Paolo Carozza has pointed out, subsidiarity envisions both a positive and negative role for the state.[114] Pope John Paul II has written that the state

> has the task of determining the juridical framework within which economic affairs are to be conducted, and thus of safeguarding the prerequisites of a free economy, which presumes a certain equality between the parties, such that one party would not be so powerful as practically to reduce the other to subservience.[115]

Indeed, as corporations are themselves traditionally understood as creatures of corporate charter, their early existence in American law may be seen as an example of subsidiarity in action because governments permitted the existence of private actors to accomplish functions that were not appropriate for the government to do itself. But subsidiarity also has a negative or protective aspect. Robert Vischer describes this as subsidiarity's "radical edge," based in a "substantive anthropological vision of solidarity."[116] This vision is opposed not simply to state power as such, because subsidiarity supports "the prudent devolution of government authority."[117] Rather, on this view, subsidiarity opposes the use of state power to enforce norms that

subsidiarity which governs the relations between public authorities and individuals, families and intermediate societies in a single State, must also apply to the relations between the public authority of the world community and the public authorities of each political community. The special function of this universal authority must be to evaluate and find a solution to economic, social, political and cultural problems which affect the universal common good."

114. See Paolo G. Carozza, "Subsidiarity as a Structural Principle of International Human Rights Law," 97 *American Journal of International Law*, 38, 44 (2003).

115. *Centesimus Annus*, 15.

116. Robert K. Vischer, "Subsidiarity as Subversion: Local Power, Legal Norms, and the Liberal State," 2 *Journal of Catholic Social Thought*, 277, 278 (2005); see also Simona Beretta, "Wealth Creation in the Global Economy," in *Rediscovering Abundance: Interdisciplinary Essays on Wealth, Income, and their Distribution in the Catholic Social Tradition*, Helen Alford et al., eds., 129, 149–50 (2006) [hereafter *Rediscovering Abundance*] (referring to subsidiarity as an "ontological" principle).

117. Ibid., 290.

are hostile to Catholic notions of the common good or solidarity, such as collectivism or liberal individualistic norms.[118]

A kind of subsidiarity has been adopted by a number of companies and is now becoming a dominant mode of organizing multinationals. "Today's multinational organization consists of multiple business units—subsidiaries and affiliates—with greater authority and responsibility, tightly linked through computerized information networks," with success measured by the subsidiary's ability to meet production goals and not its ability to take direction from a far-off, centralized headquarters.[119] Many corporations have become "heterarchical," where "resources, managerial capabilities, and decision-making are dispersed throughout the organization rather than concentrated at the top."[120] This new kind of multinational makes a proper understanding of subsidiarity even more important.

Subsidiarity can be understood as comprising three (at least) characteristics that can be applied to corporate governance and organization: size, structure, and purpose.[121] Structure means how to understand the nature of the corporate *person* in a way that maximizes the flourishing of those who work with and in it. Scope is concerned with how to consider whether a corporation or business association is the *right size* for the task it is organized to perform. Finally, purpose is concerned with what the corporation is supposed to be doing; does its size and structure serve a legitimate end?

❧

118. See CCC, §1885.

119. Tavis, *supra* note 38, at 494.

120. Lee A. Tavis, "Modern Contract Theory and the Purpose of the Firm," in *Rethinking the Purpose of Business*, *supra* note 2, at 230.

121. Gerald J. Russello, "Subsidiarity as Business Model," in *Business and Religion*, *supra* note 95, at 313, 318–319.

## III. Multinational Corporate Governance and Subsidiarity

### A. *Do the Principles of CST Limit the Size of Multinationals?*

Are multinationals *too big*? Can they be? Size becomes, in the words of *Quadragesimo Anno*, a "disturbance of right order" only when a larger collectivity assumes the functions of lesser entities or, implicitly, when its size becomes a hindrance to its own functions.[122] Where that dividing line may be is sometimes unclear, and requires the exercise of prudence by managers in making decisions with regard to expansion or growth opportunities. According to *Centesimus Annus*, people jointly pursuing projects share in a "community of work."[123] To be a community of work means treating individuals as persons, and not solely as means to profit for the shareholders or corporate managers. Therefore, there may be stages in an organization's growth where it can no longer respond, or even recognize, the needs of the members of the overlapping communities that make up its existence. So while CST may not oppose large business associations on the basis of their size alone, the sheer size of an activity poses unique problems from a CST perspective, because solidarity and the common good may become harder to achieve or maintain.

At the one extreme, a multinational may violate subsidiarity in circumstances where it becomes so big it assumes the properties of a state. The clearest examples of this may be the company town, or where a large multinational dominates the politics of a small or underdeveloped host country. In such circumstances, the corporation has assumed responsibilities that do not properly belong to it, such as governing the nonemployment aspects of employee lives, assuming traditional governmental functions (such as control over the legitimate use of force or the creation of currency), or interfering with the legitimate government of a nation.[124] In CST, the State does

122. *Quadragesimo Anno*, 79.

123. *Centesimus Annus*, 32.

124. This conclusion is complicated in cases in which a multinational's actions increase sensitivity toward disadvantaged groups, for example by influencing a totalitarian

have a role to play in protecting rights and ordering social life and especially in ensuring that those goods that "are not and cannot be mere commodities" are preserved.[125] To have an economic institution replace the social functions of the State would violate the subsidiarity principle.

In less extreme cases, however, considering size includes examining whether particular industries or economic sectors are at a greater risk of interfering with the "internal life" of a multinational's constituent parts or with the communities it serves. High-tech industries or industries where logistics are complex and multifaceted, such as petroleum or automobile production, have been most hospitable to multinational growth.[126] The ability to transfer technology or expertise, or the ready access to capital markets, enable such multinationals to bring to bear financial resources that are necessary to create the infrastructure and facilities for their operations. In such instances, subsidiarity can foster entrepreneurship as well, not just in the classic economic sense of wealth creation, but also in a context that cultivates the virtues that are "the nexus between effective business activity, including wealth creation, and effective and just forms of wealth distribution."[127]

Conversely, other industries that have possibly conflicting goals may find inclusion in the same multinational problematic. Such circumstances

---

state, therefore furthering solidarity or the common good. In the context of international law, subsidiarity "necessarily goes beyond the rigid dualism of states on one side and international community on the other, and includes in its ambit a variety of sub and supranational levels of association and authority in human rights." Carozza, *supra* note 114, at 67. Indeed, *Centesimus Annus* lays the primary responsibility on preserving human rights in the economic sector "not [on] the state but to individuals and to the various groups and associations which make up society." *Centesimus Annus*, 48. This responsibility bears further scrutiny today, since multinationals in some cases are stronger than the governments of the nations in which they operate. At the same time, as international institutions such as the UN, WTO, and others have increased their roles, multinational corporations have also grown in influence. See Renata Buarque Goulart Coutinho and Helene Bertrand, "Global...Business Ethics? Challenges and Paradoxes," 4–5 (2003) (unpublished manuscript), available at http://www.sase.org/oldsite/conf2003/papers/coutinho-bertrand.pdf.

125. CSD, §349.

126. John Fayerweather, "The Internationalization of Business," 403 *Annals of the American Academy of Political and Social Science*, 1, 5 (1972).

127. Francis T. Hannafey, "Entrepreneurship in Papal Thought: Creation of Wealth and the Distribution of Justice," in *Rediscovering Abundance*, *supra* note 116, at 102, 119.

require a careful consideration of the details of the relevant businesses that compose the multinational, and whether the businesses conflict in such a way as to hamper their individual flourishing. For example, the ownership of news organizations by an entertainment conglomerate may pose difficulties for the proper functioning of the news organizations. The ability of the latter to carry out its function of gathering and reporting news may be restricted by its inclusion within the larger entity, which may be concerned with the impact of negative news reports about its advertisers or clients. Or one could look to the growth of law firms and accounting firms from small, city-based partnerships to multinational limited liability structures with global clients. There is a growing literature that such growth has harmed not only the practice of those professions, but also the emotional and professional lives of those working within such institutions.[128]

## B. *Do the Principles of CST Dictate the Structure of the Multinational Corporate Form?*

CST does not require any particular form of business organization so long as the organization shapes economic activities by the principles of solidarity, subsidiarity, and the common good. American corporate law in general treats the corporation as a "legal fiction," that is, as a legal personality separate from its owners and directors, in which the directors act as custodians for shareholder value. The shareholders, in turn, have risked their equity in the corporation in exchange for the possibility of a return on their investment. The corporate entity has all the basic legal rights of owning and disposing of property, suing and being sued, and similar rights that mark it as a legal "person,"[129] unlike, for example, a partnership or unincorporated association. Changes in law and business practice in the early twentieth century changed the understanding of the corporation

128. See, e.g., M. Cathleen Kaveny, "Living the Fullness of Ordinary Time: A Theological Critique of the Instrumentalization of Time in Professional Life," 28 *Communio*, 771, 773–74 (2001) (discussing the detrimental effects of large law firm life on the meaning and purpose of a lawyer's life).

129. Blumberg, *supra* note 91, at 209–10 (1993).

from a state-chartered entity towards a view that understood the corporation as a "natural entity" established by the incorporators and shareholders, with only minimal state involvement.[130] This movement permitted early proponents of corporate autonomy to downplay the public nature of the corporate charter, and to assert that its "private" character relieved the corporation of public responsibilities.[131]

That conception, however, has been partially displaced by the "nexus-of-contracts" theory,[132] which provides that "most organizations are simply legal fictions which serve as a nexus for a set of contracting relationships among individuals."[133] On the contractual view, therefore, there is no separate "corporation": there are only individual contractual relationships that exist for the benefit of the contracting parties. Therefore, we should not expect the corporation to have any duties or responsibilities—public or otherwise—not set out in the relevant contracts and that do not contribute to the increase of shareholder value. Contractarian theory posits autonomous individuals who seek to make the most advantageous bargain. If the corporation is not a separate entity and exists only to serve the profit-maximizing interests of the contracting parties, it cannot have any independent responsibilities to do anything else.[134] This move to a contractual theory had the same rhetorical effect as the earlier move to the "private entity" theory: to eliminate any obligations of the corporation, other than shareholder profit.[135]

---

130. Millon, *supra* note 93, at 214–16.

131. Ibid., at 211–12.

132. See Stephen M. Bainbridge, "Community and Statism: A Conservative Contractarian Critique of Progressive Corporate Law Scholarship," 82 *Cornell Law Review*, 856, 859–60 (1997) ("As a matter of intellectual interest, the debate over the contractual nature of the firm is over").

133. Michael C. Jensen and William H. Meckling, "Theory of the Firm: Managerial Behavior, Agency Costs, and Ownership Structure," 3 *Journal of Financial Economics*, 305, 310 (1976). This insight derives from the work of Ronald Coase. See R. H. Coase, "The Nature of the Firm," 4 *Economica*, 386, 387 (1937).

134. See Stabile, *supra* note 65, at 188–89 (noting that the contractarian theory represents an "impoverished vision of the human person" at odds with CST).

135. See Millon, *supra* note 93, at 230–31.

Neither of these conceptions is completely satisfactory from a CST perspective. At the outset, it is unclear whether the model of the corporate person—as either a separate legal person or a nexus of contracts maximizing efficiency—need be accepted as arising from basic economic rules. There has been, for example, a large body of critical legal work on the corporation that bases its success not on economic efficiency, but on political maneuvering, or self-interest.[136] As a general matter, arguments in favor of the classic corporate form too often assume arguments that instead should be proven, such as whose efficiency is being maximized, and to what purpose, and what other costs are being ignored or accepted. Some strong versions of the corporation as fully separate from the managers who run it can serve to shield otherwise unethical behavior by corporate managers, who have no personal responsibility for the decisions.[137]

Both conceptions share the same flaw: treating the corporation as an instrument for profit or wealth creation and not—as CST understands it—as a community oriented toward the common good and devoted to the solidarity and flourishing of its members. For its part, the nexus theory treats questions of culture or extra-economic obligations as extrinsic to the life of the business. Corporations do, however, have their own unique histories, cultures, and identities. Indeed, many corporations tout such cultures in their advertising or public relations materials. As John Paul II has emphasized, human activity always occurs within a particular cultural context.[138] Any analysis of subsidiarity in a multinational, therefore, must also take into account the different cultural circumstances in which the multinational operates. Because multinationals encompass multiple communities across many nations, subsidiarity must be utilized to preserve the autonomy of these communities as centers of human flourishing, within the overall community of the multinational organization. These identities arise from the traditions and customs of the people working within a

136. See McCluskey, *supra* note 39, at 1456n19.

137. See Clarke et al., *supra* note 73, at 144.

138. *Centesimus Annus*, 51.

particular business division or unit. For example, there may be craft traditions at a car company, or ways of solving problems customary at an engineering firm. Corporations, in other words, have "cultures" that are not reflected in any nexus of contracts, and which have weight and exist through time.[139] A corporation—even when it is formally considered a combination of contracts—does not absolve the individuals who executed the contracts from their social obligations, even though they are acting through the corporate form.

Accordingly, a multinational should strive to combine solidarity with subsidiarity to avoid either a deadening centralization (solidarity without subsidiarity) or a disjointed and unwieldy collection of autonomous unity that has no conception of the common good to be served (subsidiarity without solidarity). Further, a multinational will have to handle these dangers while at the same time being sensitive to the varied local communities in which it operates, each of which may have their own ways of translating solidarity, the common good, and subsidiarity. Any multinational structure should develop a framework for handling inter-cultural issues, as well as a decision-making process for determining which practices or principles should take precedence in which circumstances.[140]

## C. *What Can CST Say about Multinational Purposes?*

The next aspect of the multinational that subsidiarity impacts is purpose. CST—given its rich view of the human person—"rejects the idea that social welfare is merely a question of giving people what they want without regard to what it is that people want."[141] CST restricts what businesses a corporation may pursue; that is, some purposes may be improper aside from any question of making a legitimate profit.

139. See, e.g., Clarke et al., *supra* note 73, at 151nn31–32, 152n35 (citing corporate statements, including Ford Motor Company, Whole Foods, and Target); Timothy L. Fort, "Business as a Mediating Institution," in *Rethinking the Purpose of Business*, *supra* note 2, at 237, 242–43 (discussing the "communal" nature of the corporation).

140. See, e.g., Donaldson and Dunfee, *supra* note 44, at 27, 49 (developing a theory of "hypernorms" to govern corporate decision-making).

141. Stabile, *supra* note 65, at 189.

Understanding a corporation's purpose has two aspects. First, there is the business purpose of the corporation; at the most general level, the purpose of every corporation is to make a profit for its shareholders or management. But, as Frohnen shows, many corporations have more specific purposes. Forming a corporate purpose is the responsibility of all levels of the organization, especially the senior managers.

> Fulfillment comes through service to a cause, an idea, a mission, or others external to ourselves; best a purpose with a transcendent character. Each of us has the right to the dignity that comes from a job with real purpose. The role of the leader is to create this purpose for the unskilled worker as well as for the highly skilled technical workers or the executives in the organization.[142]

As Goodpaster shows in his study of Medtronic, Inc., it is possible to imbue an organization with purpose that extends not only through, but beyond, the company's products. Goodpaster identifies several features of the corporate environment, including witness, frequent emphasis on the corporate mission of healing, and taking into consideration the firm's mission when considering acquisitions or other corporate action. *Laborem Exercens* is quite clear on the importance of fostering individual initiative and virtue. The encyclical warned that "excessive bureaucratic centralization" can extinguish the meaning that people put into their work.[143] Such centralization can engender the feeling in employees that they are mere "production instrument[s]" rather than human persons. "It is possible for the financial accounts to be in order, and yet for the people—who make up the firm's most valuable asset—to be humiliated and their dignity offended."[144]

---

142. Kenneth E. Goodpaster and Thomas E. Halloran, "Anatomy of Corporate Spiritual and Social Awareness: The Case of Medtronic, Inc.," (1999) (unpublished manuscript, on file with author).

143. *Laborem Exercens*, 15.

144. *Centesimus Annus*, 35.

More generally, corporations have as a purpose serving the common good. Multinationals especially are enjoined to act for the benefit of others. "One of the fundamental tasks of those actively involved in international economic matters is to achieve for mankind an integral development in solidarity…[which] requires a vision of the economy that…guarantees an equitable distribution of resources" and is responsive to the interdependence of peoples.[145] This vision may take a number of forms, from direct aid to underdeveloped communities in which the multinational operates, to other methods.

## Conclusion

The influence and power of multinationals in the globalized economy make them prime subjects to consider in light of CST. Even though the "turn to subsidiarity" among some multinationals has occurred primarily because profits today seem to come from decentralization, rather than any awakening interest in CST, multinationals now are in a closer position to being "communities of work" than a generation ago, with the potential for better understanding of their public and internal responsibilities. Accordingly, CST can contribute to explicating what a truly "subsidiarized" multinational might look like, considered along the axes of scope, structure, and purpose. As explained above, on certain questions, such as profit maximization, devotion to shareholders, and sensitivity to local norms, a CST-inflected approach may lead to diverging conclusions from other contemporary theories of corporate conduct. Further, multinationals may now be evolving toward a form in which subsidiarity plays a prominent role. Therefore, there is a possibility that their ability to instantiate solidarity and other principles of CST in other countries, and to exercise their role, in cooperation with the state, of preserving human dignity, may be enhanced.

There is at least one reservation, however, in assessing the multinational role. While the disparities between labor and capital may be disappearing

145. CSD, §373.

in the developed world, the evils of economic rapacity that Popes Leo XIII and Pius XI warned against are far from vestigial in the developing world. Multinationals too often act like the extractive corporations of old, and the market pressure described above limits significant progress in forming lasting communities of work that would help developing nations lift themselves out of poverty. Just as importantly, the rich social context embedded in the principle of subsidiarity can fit uneasily with the market-driven model based on an individualistic view of the person, either in the form of worker, consumer, or shareholder.

# PART SIX

## *The Power of the Law*

# *The Prisoners' Dilemma*

❧

THE RECENTLY ENACTED Military Commissions Act and the Supreme Court Hamdi and Hamdan decisions, which tried to limit the suspension of the protections of habeas corpus, have spurred a new series of debates on the somewhat technical legal area of habeas corpus. The Great Writ, as it was known, stands for a very simple principle: power does not trump. A government may wish to detain someone secretly, perhaps indefinitely, and may believe it has good reasons to do so, but in the Anglo-American legal tradition, that is not good enough. As the Supreme Court stated in 1969, the writ is "the fundamental instrument for safeguarding individual freedom against arbitrary and lawless state action." The government therefore has to "produce the body for examination," as the translation of the full Latin tag put it, before a magistrate and justify the reasons for the person's detention.

The position announced in the MCA and its related statutes may or may not be bad policy for defeating terrorism, but it certainly undermines a key component of free government. Government must in the normal course act in the open and must be held to a standard of reasonableness as to its actions, including being forced to explain why it has decided to detain someone. In the American legal tradition, and more broadly that of the West in general, providing the protections of habeas corpus has been a mark of civilizational achievement and we rightly consider those countries that do not do this to be less developed.

Americans across the political spectrum support the general principle of habeas corpus, but the war on terror has created opposing views about

Originally published in *The American Conservative*, December 18, 2006.

its application. On the one hand, some, mostly conservatives, have supported the government's authority to hold possible enemy combatants in foreign countries or at home without charge or judicial process. For them, the exigencies of the new threats to our safety justify reconsideration of traditional civil liberties. Others, generally liberals, have sought to extend the Constitution's guarantee of habeas corpus to anyone brought within the power of the American government, even non-citizens captured in military operations abroad. For this side, the war on terror is analogized to the civil-rights movement and seen as another area for expansion of rights beyond their traditional scope.

While both sides are playing to their respective bases, the dispute is real, and each side has legitimate arguments to which it can turn. It is clear, however, that no one had thought out the situation that has led to the MCA beforehand. This is especially the case for those supporting the war, for whom the conquest would be a "cakewalk" and the possibility of holding persons for over three years in military facilities, if ever considered, was never stated publicly. As a result of its invasions of Iraq and Afghanistan, the United States is now presented with thousands of people of uncertain status who have been transported far from their homes, who have been collected into facilities indefinitely, and who have no real redress in either American courts or through the military justice process. The Hamdan decision does not solve this: the case merely holds that for those people determined by a tribunal to be enemy combatants, habeas protections apply to a degree; however, the government has no obligation to ever determine when someone is an enemy combatant, casting these individuals into jurisprudential no-man's land. This situation has no real precedent in American history, and one can feel some sympathy for those trying to wrestle with the legal and political issues the war on terror has caused and the strain it has put on constitutional government.

With its actions in Guantanamo Bay, Abu Ghraib, and elsewhere, the United States has entered unknown territory, and is walking the knife edge between retaining the clear characteristics of a free republic and becoming something else. Some people have taken to calling this new entity an empire, but that is true only in certain respects. Because of its refusal to acknowledge any intent to occupy or govern conquered territories as its own possessions, preferring a policy of democratizing "rogue states," what may be emerging is more of a perpetual war state, preparing for and engaging endless combat against "terror."

Whatever it is called, one of the features of this emerging entity is the stratification within it of individuals based on their status—from full citizens down to those awaiting "enemy combatant" designations who are basically at the whim of the government. That too is an unfortunate side effect of imperial ambition—and one, perhaps not coincidentally, reflected in the maze of classifications and status designations in the immigration law. In one case, there is a class of guest workers abroad, who are not citizens but are useful for domestic policy; the other is a class of guest detainees serving a similar purpose for foreign policy.

But here is the tricky part: a state action can be "lawless," in the language of the Supreme Court, only if it violates some law. In American jurisprudence that means statutory law or the Constitution. So if the law does not apply to foreigners, as respectable conservative argument might propose, what is the big deal? The Constitution provides that the right of habeas corpus may be abrogated only "when in cases of Rebellion or Invasion the Public Safety may require it." This language was clearly intended to cover a limited crisis whose end could be determined with some certainty. Rebellion and invasion have commonsense, widely understood meanings. It is obviously far from clear how this limited exception may interact with an endless war on terror, with no clear guideposts or defined enemies. The Constitution does not directly address the question of what to do with these detainees.

Habeas corpus is not a universal right protecting one from being hauled up and locked away. Nor is it some irrevocable principle like the law of gravity. But that is not the end of the story. As conservatives well know, historical experience and development, even with its recognized flaws, is a surer safeguard of liberty than an appeal to vague or expansive "rights" and must be sustained by the customs, conventions, and beliefs of a people. This is where those advocating universal application of habeas fall short: their "rights talk" ignores the flaws of that theory of rights as it has been applied to areas ranging from criminal procedure to religious freedom: endless assertion of right against right (here, the right of habeas corpus against that of national self-defense) makes political life impossible. And their rush to support the Hamdan Court's reliance on the Geneva Conventions or international law is clearly only a fig leaf for their own preferred outcomes. If the Conventions permitted slavery or torture, they would not be considered so persuasive.

But in pushing for limitations on habeas corpus, conservatives are ignoring their own best traditions. Conservatives are rightly suspicious of government, or at least they are with respect to the efficient provision of health care or welfare; it has been less so recently on issue of war. But the Hamdi decision perfectly illustrates the reasons for conservative suspicion: there the government wanted to detain a citizen without habeas corpus simply because it determined he was an "enemy combatant." The Supreme Court, in a set of divided opinions, put a stop to that nonsense, but the fact that the case had to come before the Court at all should serve as a reminder to conservatives that the nature of a centralizing power is to strengthen itself.

The debate over extending habeas protections is echoed in the debate over torture. The debate over torture is basically on utilitarian terms: how many terrorists are worth torturing, and to what degree, in exchange for saving how many lives? A form of this utilitarian calculus is at play as well in the habeas corpus debate. The thinking seems to be that the greater the number of detainees, the less harm will come to us. But this is the wrong approach. The practice of torture is corrupting to us, as well as damaging to those we torture, because the practice degrades us. Once a society starts arguing about when such coercive methods are "appropriate," it has already begun to condone permitting its own citizens to brutalize and debase themselves as well as harm their victims. Similarly with habeas corpus: while those subject to the MCA are being ill served, getting citizens used to the having large numbers of foreigners held at our mercy is corrosive and corruptive of our liberty. Once a nation grows accustomed to the idea that it may hold some people without trial indefinitely, it is easier to dissolve the characteristic—citizenship—that is marked out as the reason for different treatment.

The habeas corpus debate, much like our debate over the uses of torture, betrays the absolutist mind lurking beneath much of American idealism. According to this mindset, recognized by conservatives such as Robert Nisbet over 40 years ago, the "moral and political aspirations" of foreign policy blind us to realities on the ground. Here a great injustice is being done to many people within the direct power of the United States to help, and all the talk of promoting democracy or defeating the terror masters will not hide that.

# *Who Are You? The Law of Status*

WHAT DO veterans, drug users, children, and suspected terrorists have in common? They all have specialized courts to deal with them and their legal issues. Illinois has become the latest state to set up a special "veterans' court" to handle veterans charged with nonviolent crimes. (New York has had a similar program in place since early last year.) The court will not only adjudicate offenses but connect veterans to a range of services and programs that are meant to prevent them from becoming repeat offenders. The judge organizing this court has even selected veterans to serve as prosecutors and defense attorneys.

The first family courts date from the 1960s and Great Society-like initiatives meant to address "root causes" of dysfunctional behavior. Their origins, however, stretch back a century or more to the orphans' courts and reform houses established by the community organizers of the Gilded Age. Rather than simply punish, their advocates thought, courts should rehabilitate those offenders who were thought to be reformable.

The existence of such specialized courts raises some interesting questions for American law. Equality before the law is supposed to be a protection against the assertion of arbitrary power. At its most banal, there is the enforced frustration of waiting around in a courthouse all day while being considered for jury duty. Everyone there is at the same level, and 12 (in the classic formulation) will be randomly selected to judge whatever is on the docket. But specialized courts explicitly assign people a forum based on who they are, a forum denied other people because of who they are. A

Originally published in *Chronicles*, November 2009.

nonveteran, in other words, is out of luck, at least with regard to the attention the law will give him. In a world of increasingly straitened resources, favored status may come to mean better treatment by the legal system.

The old common-law system was comfortable with different laws for different folks. The British common law, for example, had long made room for ecclesiastical courts, which dealt with a range of offenses and controversies. The defense known as "benefit of the clergy," for example, lasted in the United Kingdom until the early nineteenth century. Although eventually available to anyone who could read, this defense was originally meant to keep clergy from the harsher penalties of the secular courts. It was, in other words, a classic type of status-based court. In the Middle Ages conflicts between feudal tribunals were presided over by the local noble, with a king's justice seeking to impose uniformity over the nation.

The common characteristics of these courts are secrecy, a lack of what we would usually consider due process, and a wide scope within which the judge can act. The Foreign Intelligence Surveillance Court, known as FISC, conducts its proceedings, like the Star Chamber, in secrecy. Generally, only the government gets to present its case before the FISC. While these courts do not fit with our culture's current hyperegalitarian rhetoric, as they are quite clearly institutions that promise unequal treatment based on either variable (veteran) or temporarily invariable (child) status, they do square nicely with our obsession with identity politics. If the government can pull you over for being of a certain "type," then maybe you should be able to demand your own court to see if the action was justified.

A libertarian might scoff at this and note that, so long as entry into one of these specialized courts is voluntary—as some of them are, at least for now—all is well. Why not allow every identity its own court? This is essentially what happens with private systems of resolving disputes, such as arbitration, which has its status-based variations. Rabbinical courts, called battei din, are not uncommon in certain parts of the country. And the archbishop of Canterbury has suggested that *sharia* be introduced into England for those Muslims who wish to be bound by it, although it may be impolitic to ask whether Muslim women have much of a choice in the matter.

Universal rights and top-down legalism have never been conservative causes, and the classic knock on traditionalist conservatives is that they prefer a hierarchical society. On this view, establishing a range of courts might provide a step back to a premodern set of arrangements and reinforce a stratified society. Indeed, the archbishop's suggestion of "overlapping jurisdictions" sounds quaintly old-fashioned, as if he were an apologist for the polyglot Austro-Hungarian Empire rather than a vanguard of the post-multicultural society of modern Britain. These objections miss the point. The world is different, and those conceptions of the self that accompanied the complex relationships in premodern worlds (described with great skill in Charles Taylor's *A Secular Age*, for example) are no longer possible.

In the older system, the existence of Church courts was at base a recognition that the state was not the only power, and that it did not have exclusive dominion over justice (much less mercy). The Church had Her own ends and jurisdiction, and the state was bound to recognize Her autonomy, at least in some areas. A cleric could assert his status against the power of the state; that claim might be rejected by the state, but such an action would at least be recognized as a transgression of its boundaries.

Now, it is the state itself that sets the boundaries. Today's specialized courts might have advantages in terms of efficiency, by doing away with the protections of the typical common-law court, but these mechanisms not only reinforce the importance of status but place enormous powers in the hands of the judge and, by derivation, those of the state. And we have a developing jurisprudence that focuses exactly on what happens when the state determines status. In a number of recent cases, religious groups have been forced to accept laws that make them act contrary to their beliefs, such as forcing pharmacists with religious objections to dispense the "morning-after" pill or requiring Catholic Charities to place foster children with same-sex couples. In such cases, the state has denied rights based on these parties' status and has ruled instead that other groups' status (as consumer or nonbeliever) should be vindicated. The example of religious groups or individuals is important because religious identity is the only status recognized in the Constitution as deserving of special consideration.

Your status now promises (or threatens) to become one more weapon in the identity-politics arsenal. There is no easily recognizable way to divvy up one's status, and it is a postmodern trope (not completely true, but true enough) that one's identity is forever malleable. An individual could conceivably claim a different identity every day. The malleable rhetoric of the law could easily accommodate these identities, and clever lawyers could make a case for special access or treatment. If veterans get their own court, one of these talented lawyers might say, why not others? One does not have to think very hard to come up with other groups in contemporary America who might enjoy courts that are sensitive to their special needs and circumstances.

# *Some Dissents Are More Equal Than Others*

**Anyone who has clerked** for an appellate judge knows that assisting in writing a dissent is one of the better parts of the job. While a majority opinion, however important it is, almost always involves compromise, a dissenting opinion allows a judge the full range of rhetorical devices, unhindered by the need to cobble together a majority or to convince colleagues to vote the same way. As Adam White has written in a piece on Justice Samuel Alito, dissents "offer the best opportunity to peer into [a justice's] judicial philosophy." And as the encomia for the late Justice Antonin Scalia attest, a judge's dissents can stand on their own as a kind of counter-history to the course of constitutional jurisprudence.

At their best, they are guidance—or warning—to future generations. So a study of judicial dissents makes sense.

In an opening chapter of his new book, *Dissent and the Supreme Court: Its Role in the Court's History and the Nation's Constitutional Dialogue*, Melvin I. Urofsky skillfully explains the different considerations in writing a majority opinion as opposed to a dissent, and explains how Court practice has changed over time.

John Marshall, the first Chief Justice of the Supreme Court, famously tried to provide a uniform "opinion of the Court," and for many decades dissents, even when they occurred, were relatively rare and looked down upon in favor of consistency and unanimity. But the consensus that these were the highest judicial virtues has broken down. In the modern era, dissents are an important part of what Urofsky calls our "constitutional dialogue."

Originally published in *Law & Liberty*, April 21, 2016.

Unfortunately, although Urofsky provides some good insights and useful information about many important cases, he adopts a simplistic Progressive view of the law. In this book, liberal dissents move the law "forward," and the less said about conservative dissents, the better. Urofsky uses his concept of the constitutional dialogue to find the "so-called canonical or prophetic" dissents. This statement early in the book gives the game away about the author's view of what dissents should do: The "great" dissents show "a justice trying to limn how the Constitution should be interpreted in light of changing social conditions."

*Dissent and the Supreme Court* could serve as the basic constitutional law narrative in your average elite law school (oxymoron intended). And there is a distinctly generational feel to this book. Urofsky (born in 1939) covers a range of issues, but the main event is the civil rights revolution of the 1960s and its aftermath. For Urofsky's cohort, the Constitution is mostly about "equality" and expanding rights; and despite some rough spots, the best justices have advanced that concept in the face of social and political resistance, until we arrive where we are today, with that view of the Constitution (and the Court) being simply assumed as the right one. Other, contrasting, views of the Constitution are interesting, so long as they remain in the minority. This is a backward look at elite opinion coming around to obviously correct interpretations of the Constitution.

The book would have been strengthened immeasurably had the author looked forward. For example, what if Justice Scalia's critiques, expressed largely through dissent, that the Supreme Court has become an arbiter and ruler of an undemocratic system that reflects not an abstract "justice," but the provincial views of the contemporary elite, are correct? Some indeed think those dissents were and are "prophetic." But if you assume dissents must be busy "limning" under changing social conditions, then such comparisons don't even present themselves.

To be fair, the constitutional dialogue for Urofsky expands beyond the judiciary and includes other branches of government and the general public. Court decisions can move public opinion, and sometimes dissents provoke more action than majority opinions. Urofsky points, for example, to Justice William O. Douglas' dissent in *Sierra Club v. Morton* (1972), which denied that environmental organization standing to challenge development in the Sequoia National Forest. This dissent helped spark the modern environmental movement to protect nature preserves through legislation and other action. Another example he gives is the powerful dissents in *Dred Scott* (1857) that eclipsed the reasoning in Chief Justice Taney's majority opinion.

Urofsky spends a significant amount of time on the first John Marshall Harlan, who sat on the Court from 1877 to 1911, and who was known as the Great Dissenter. Justice Harlan wrote 703 majority opinions, but over 300 dissenting ones. For Urofsky, he is the author of numerous prophetic dissents, especially on the Fourteenth Amendment and racial segregation, but on other issues as well. Although Harlan was out of favor after his death in 1911, in the latter half of the last century Harlan's reputation saw a rebirth when "the Court began to undo the legacy of apartheid created in the latter nineteenth century against which Harlan had protested."

The author rightly focuses on the *Civil Rights Cases* (1883), in which Harlan, as the lone dissenter, wrote to protest the Court's striking down of a federal antidiscrimination law as beyond the powers of the Fourteenth Amendment. Harlan likewise dissented in *Plessy v. Ferguson* (1896). These dissents reemerged as authoritative accounts of the constitutional understanding of equal protection in the 1960s, and into today, with conservative and liberal justices alike citing Harlan's dictum that the Constitution does not permit the classification of citizens by race.

There is, according to Urofsky, a "certain irony" in Justice Clarence Thomas' quoting the Harlan dissents in defense of a colorblind Constitution, because carried to its logical end, he writes, "a color-blind Constitution would not allow racial classification even for benign purposes." If it is unclear where Urofsky stands on whether he prefers the Constitution as an all-purpose weapon against "classification," he endorses the extension of Harlan's reasoning to *Romer v. Evans* (1996), which had nothing to do with race.

After Harlan, Urofsky dates the permanent change in Court behavior to the Judiciary Act of 1925, known as the Judges' Bill. This law opened the way for the Supreme Court to move from simply a court of last resort to a more of a constitutional court. It gave the Court more control over its docket, which in turn helped the justices focus on cases with constitutional importance. Writes Urofsky:

> As judges heard more constitutional questions, they found themselves developing jurisprudential theories that carried over from one case to another. Not only did they stop acquiescing, but they also felt it important to explain why they disagreed.

The number of dissents began to increase, and the stigma of being a repeat dissenter declined. Explaining a dissent became a way to initially influence the majority opinion. Justice Ginsburg, for example, has said her majority opinion in the gender-discrimination case concerning the Virginia Military Institute (*United States v. Virginia*, 1996) was stronger for reading an advance copy of Justice Scalia's dissent. But the writing of a dissent also became a way to build a foundation for later legal change in the dissenter's favor.

As noted, Urofsky has little time for dissents from the conservative side of the judiciary, prophetic or otherwise. Justice Scalia, for example, is grudgingly granted one dissent that, after polling academic colleagues, Urofsky concluded might gain entrance into the "canon." It is Scalia's brilliant dissent in the 1988 decision in *Morrison v. Olson*, the independent counsel case.

This dissent sets out Scalia's approach to and defense of separation of powers in his arguments against the position of independent counsel. Written only a couple of years into Scalia's tenure on the Court, it immediately set him apart as a unique voice.

But even there, Urofsky cannot help but critique. He likes the dissent, but notes that its reach might be limited because of Scalia's "unbending adherence to a literal reading of the text and his insistence that a document drafted in 1787 will provide all the answers necessary" to resolve contemporary issues.

There are too many errors in this summation of Justice Scalia's jurisprudence to be worth mentioning. Not the least of them is that Scalia did not see the Constitution as a box of answers for every problem; rather, he preferred actual representative government to decide how the people should govern themselves.

Just as noteworthy is that the other two top dissents proposed here for canonical status—Justice Ginsburg's in *Federation of Independent Business v. Sebelius* (2012), and Justice Brennan's in *McClesky v. Kemp* (1987)—receive no similar criticism.

Urofsky's contention that dissent is a positive good that furthers a constitutional dialogue is not unreasonable and could be interesting, indeed. Unfortunately, this book gives us only a vision of liberalism admiring itself.

# *The Right Unwritten Constitution*

**Beneath its cool blue cover,** *Constitutional Morality and the Rise of Quasi-Law* is an explosive book. The thesis of coauthors Bruce Frohnen and George W. Carey is that constitutional government as was once known in the United States is in fact a memory.

They define what we have instead—a realm of "quasi law"—as:

> a series of directives with the force of law that lack the crucial characteristics of genuine law. Emanating from all three branches of government, quasi-laws create rights and duties like laws but lack essential legal attributes such as promulgation through prescribed means and provision of predictable rules rather than mere delegation of discretionary power.

This regime is recognizable to citizens who have had to make their way through the myriad of regulatory structures that comprise most individuals' contact with "the law." Not incidentally, this realm of discretion, unclear directives, and lack of accountability privileges a lawyer-priest class who know how to negotiate this dangerous landscape and guide the hapless ordinary American through it.

The use of executive orders and presidential "signing statements" is another example of the rise of quasi-law. Such actions do not share most of the characteristics of law in the American tradition, and indeed for many

---

Originally published in *Law & Liberty*, March 9, 2017.

decades were restricted, in practice if not by law, because of how American understood the nature of their self-governing republic.

Frohnen and Carey contrast quasi-law with an older understanding of "constitutional morality." By this term they mean "the felt duty of government officials in particular to abide by the restrictions and imperatives imposed on them by a constitution." Constitutional morality was a concept developed largely through the work of Carey (1934–2013), who taught political science at Georgetown University for over half a century. In books like *Basic Symbols of the American Political Tradition*, first published in 1970 (a classic work that he coauthored with Willmoore Kendall), Carey placed our political life within the larger context of the nation's historical and cultural experience. *Basic Symbols* argued that Americans have understood themselves as a self-governing people with a particular history, in which events such as the Mayflower Compact serve as symbols of that experience.

The work of Frohnen, who is a professor of law at Ohio Northern University College of Law, can be seen as continuing that important project. Commenting on *Basic Symb*ols, Frohnen described

> the cluster of symbols of self-government by a virtuous people deliberating under God was forged by acts of word and deed, but most especially by public documents such as the Constitution. These words and deeds shaped a tradition that flourished for centuries and was not seriously questioned among the people until the 1960s.

The duty to abide by the limits enshrined in the Constitution, says Frohnen, is bound up in "the notion of an 'American way,'"—it is both example and important part of the nation's larger constitutional morality.

Constitutional morality is different from, but overlaps with, that often-misused phrase, the "unwritten Constitution." The great American thinker Orestes Brownson popularized the latter term, which Brownson defined as:

> the real or actual constitution of a people as a state or sovereign community, and constituting them such and such a state. It is Providential, not made by the nation but born with it. The written constitution is made and ordained by the sovereign power, and presupposes that power as already existing and constituted.

This is a definition that obviously clashes with that found in mainstream liberal constitutional scholarship. "We the People" made the Constitution to reflect that people's current existence as a cultural and political unity of American communities developed over time, and "the form of union they chose—their written constitution—by its nature depends for its character and its efficacy on the institutions, beliefs, and practices that preceded and helped produce it," write Frohnen and Carey.

The current volume takes apart the argument put forward by thinkers like Akhil Amar, whose unwritten constitution is of a very different kind. According to Professor Amar, an unwritten constitution merely provides guideposts for a Progressive future. Such an understanding is transformative of, rather than faithful to, the actual constitutional text or supporting tradition.

Frohnen and Carey here trace the roots of quasi-law to the Progressive era. This is not surprising. Indeed the Progressive mentality of the early twentieth century is the root in many ways of our currently flowering leftism: misguided reliance on experts and displacement of the will of the people onto an unelected bureaucracy. The authors discuss some of the more important works developing the justifications for the administrative state, such as those by Frank Goodnow, Herbert Croly, Woodrow Wilson, and Pendleton Herring. The quest to reflect the popular will ends, in the hands of these writers, in the conclusion that a bureaucracy insulated from popular pressures and controlled by experts is the purest expression of what is "best for the people."

The result of the Progressive revolution was in essence a new government. Progressivism would, as Frohnen and Carey write, "in essence, blur the separation of powers, creating a fourth branch of government in which the powers of the other three would be mixed." And it would "substantially increase the powers the president would be called to exercise."

What the Progressive constitution signally lacks is restraint, which was a key element of the Founders' constitution, and which was definitively cast aside with the New Deal in the 1930s and 1940s. In a distinction critical to understanding Frohnen and Carey's argument, Progressives espouse what they term a "commanding," not a "mediating," constitution. The "command constitution" demands action, and has little patience for the deliberately slow pace of the American constitutional design. The discretion of the executive—and through the executive, the bureaucracy—to act, becomes so great as to efface not only the separation of powers but even the recognition of different political units such as the states.

But what is wrong with that? The Progressives would say that such a "living" constitutionalism is exactly what is required for a changing social and political system, and many do not even bother pretending that fidelity to the written text is a relevant criterion. But for Frohnen and Carey, this use of the law, and of quasi-law such as regulations and executive acts, destroys rather than supports free government. Law for the Progressive is a tool to further social progress and end perceived evils. Because the Progressives believe that their good intentions are what matter most, the written text of the Constitution and the settled practice and customs of a people can be disregarded. But as the authors point out, the law "is not, in fact, a tool in any meaningful, practical sense. Laws are not discrete objects capable of achieving narrowly defined ends. Law rests on common, cultural assumptions relating to our common identities."

To force the law to upset those common assumptions can result in conflict—even violent conflict. Thus, the expanse of the regulatory state into areas of religious belief, for example, in the interest of "health" potentially harm our traditions of religious liberty.

Frohnen acknowledges that we may have come too far to return to a mediating constitution of the kind that guided the nation from its Founding through the 1960s. Our settled practices and understandings, in the sense of Brownson's unwritten constitution—especially in the four decades since Carey and Willmoore were writing—may have frayed too much to recover. New understandings of rights, government structure, and a disregard for restraint in the pursuit of socially transformative goals have taken their place.

Recovery in any event must first be cultural and not political, a project Frohnen and Carey think would take decades if it is to occur at all. Nevertheless, the authors propose a recognition of the limits of law, and a return to what they call "associational pluralism." The array of formal and informal groups that provide meaning to people, and that also provide multiple sources of political power, are places to begin.

*Constitutional Morality* is a subtle, sophisticated work that covers a lot of ground, including the nature of common law, judicial reasoning, and much else. But it is not without polemical bite, since Frohnen and Carey address with deep concern the fracturing cultural and philosophical principles and assumptions that gave birth to our republic and whether any nation so conceived can endure.

# *Judicial Democracy*

**The problem** with Justice Breyer's recent book begins at the second sentence: "The Constitution's framers and history itself have made the Court the ultimate arbiter of the Constitution's meaning as well as the source of answers to as multitude of questions about how this vast, complex country will be governed."

There is a lot to unpack in that extraordinary claim, including the meaning of "history itself" and how the Court became not only an interpreter of the Constitution but also the "source of answers" for how we live together as citizens of a republic. But first, a little background. Justice Breyer has served on the Supreme Court since 1994, when he was nominated by President Clinton and subsequently confirmed. Prior to that he served for almost fifteen years as an appellate judge on the First Circuit Court of Appeals, which covers parts of the Northeast. Although he never practiced in business or in a private law firm (a norm increasingly common across the federal judiciary), he has authored influential works on administrative law, and has become known for a flexible pragmatic approach to judging.

Breyer quickly took a position on the liberal side of the Court, and is often contrasted with Justice Scalia as providing intellectual heft for liberal judges. An earlier book, *Active Liberty*, which was published in 2005, advanced the thesis that the goal of courts, especially the Supreme Court, should be to promote democracy, a term he leaves frustratingly undefined. He continues that theme in *Making Our Democracy Work*, which tries to

---

Originally published in *Law & Liberty*, February 8, 2012.

explain, largely in layman's terms, how the Court works and how his own pragmatic approach explains the best traditions of the Court.

*Making* is divided into three broad sections. "The People's Trust" sets out Breyer's case for holding the Supreme Court as the only institutional organ charged with definitive interpretations of the Constitution; "Decisions that Work" lays out examples of areas in which Breyer believes his theory of judicial review have successfully worked; and the last chapter, "Protecting Individuals" raises questions of individual liberty and government power.

Breyer writes in clear prose, and his book is structured, mostly, around discussion of individual cases for a common reader unused to legal arcana or technical language. And he wants to address a central point: how can the Court maintain the confidence of the American people? He notes for example, that there have been instances in the past, such as the Cherokee displacement cases, where the people did not listen to the Court's decision. In others, such as *Brown v. Board of Education*, other arms of the government needed to enforce the Court's decision.

The cases he selects are, in some sense, the regular canon of liberal law professors; *Dred Scott*, *Brown v. Board of Education*, and *Korematsu*, for example, and ending with recent cases surrounding holding suspected terrorists or enemy combatants at Guantánamo. There is no mention of *Roe v. Wade* or *Planned Parenthood v. Casey*, and no sustained discussion of the Court's religious liberty jurisprudence or its holdings regarding corporations or substantive due process. Breyer uses his case examples in a way anyone who went to a liberal law school will recognize: the nation slowly unfolded to a recognition of the Court's central role in American legal and political culture, and although *Dred* is bad (and Lincoln's opposition to it ultimately bad as well, because it undermines the final authority of the Court), *Brown* is good and therefore we can take comfort in justifying ever after the Court's exercises in social engineering. The difficulty is that Breyer does not explain why—other than appealing to a vague sense of liberal morality—we should choose one decision over the other, or why, more important, such wrenching cases need to be precedential for the proposition that the Court is the ultimate "source" for all answers regarding how we live in America. As Breyer realizes, the Court cannot enforce decisions on its own, and the Court does make mistakes, as in *Dred*. Breyer simply seems to take as evident that a modern liberal court will be more right than wrong, and so we should continue to abide by all its decisions lest national disaster strike.

Breyer argues that

> American public officials and the American public have come to accept as legitimate not only the Court's decisions but also its interpretations of the Constitution. The public has developed the habit of following the Court's constitutional interpretations, even those with which it disagrees. Today we find it as normal to respect the Court's decisions as to breathe the air around us.

Breyer considers this subservience to nine unelected officials a step forward for democracy and liberty, and argues that each generation, through proper education, must learn how "our constitutional government works." But this assumes too much: every year millions of people gather to protest one particular decision of the Court that they consider not only unconstitutional but also deeply immoral. That decision, as Hadley Arkes and others have argued, has actually reduced respect for the Court and its opinions. This challenge goes unmentioned by Breyer.

To show that the Court must also do its part, Breyer sets out a "pragmatic approach" that focuses on a statute's purpose and consequences (rather than its text and history) to assist judges. He distinguishes this from an "originalist" approach because he finds that history gives no true answers and that even if it did, sometimes our (that is, the Court's) understanding of the underlying values of the Constitution should trump. But too often a simple preference for government action seeps in. Breyer would have upheld the Washington DC gun prohibition the Court rejected in *Heller* because the value ostensibly protected, "life itself," was too compelling even though as Breyer stated, he could not tell if the ban actually worked. On the other hand, opponents of *Roe* equally argue "life itself" is at stake, yet Breyer in this book is silent on how a judge would rule in that case. Similarly, Breyer dissented from the Court's 1995 *Lopez* decision, in which it overruled a law banning guns near schools, the first rejection of Congress's power under the Commerce Clause in decades. Although most treated that decision as a victory for federalism and therefore for a system of ordered liberty, Breyer would have deferred to Congress to make the "empirical" determinations of whether such laws affected interstate commerce. From his study of administrative law, Breyer surely knows the compromises and lobbying that go into such legislation, so his simple trust in Congressional "experts" seems quaintly misplaced here.

Anticipating the objection that no one can assume which values or purposes might have motivated the actual Congress, Breyer posits a "reasonable member of Congress" to which the Court can attribute purpose. Although Breyer is correct that sometimes Congress will avoid its responsibility to write clear legislation in the hope that the Court will interpret the law for them by deriving some purpose or knowledge of consequences, Breyer's approach simply agrees to take that responsibility from them, which does not advance either liberty or representative government. Forcing Congress to write clear statutes might force them to consider the flood of legislation they do pass, which would increase the sphere of liberty for ordinary citizens. Breyer's having the Court step in, although beneficial perhaps in individual cases, is not helpful in the long term.

*Making* presents a vigorous case for a kind of liberal jurisprudence that is perhaps less ideological than that evident in the Warren Court or law school seminars in the 1980s. However, it does not answer the central question, upon which that liberal jurisprudence is based, as to how deferring to the Court's decisions advances the cause of liberty or democracy.

# *Tool, Mirror, Goad: What Is Christian Legal Thought For?*

**Does Christianity** have a place in the law? Many American jurists said it did, and most Americans would have had that general impression until the 1960s, or even the 1970s. And they would not have been wrong. If the Founding generation was overwhelmingly Christian (and it was), and if the legal system they imported was from a Christian country (as it was), then why wouldn't that legal system reflect Christianity, not as a protected class of beliefs but as part of the architecture of the legal system itself? Almost every colonist in 1787 would have understood the Constitution only as embedded within their larger, religious society.

As early as the 1811 case, *People v. Ruggles*, Chief Justice Kent upheld a blasphemy prosecution under New York law in part because such prosecutions were appropriate under English common law, despite the state constitution's guarantee of religious freedom. He wrote that "the people of this state, in common with the people of this country, profess the general doctrines of Christianity, as the rule of their faith and practice; and to scandalize the author of these doctrines is not only, in a religious point of view, extremely impious, but, even in respect to the obligations due to society, is a gross violation of decency and good order." As Russell Kirk explained in his *Rights and Duties*, American jurists did not seek to impose the full Christian revelation upon the nation, but they also did not forget that the system of laws already in place was inspired from a very particular religious tradition. And of course many states had established churches into the 1830s.

Originally published in *The University Bookman*, April 5, 2020.

But what would applying "Christian legal thought" mean in our current society? Historically, the law was widely assumed to have some role in public morality, and because the majority of people were Christian, that meant a Christian moral baseline. That in turn meant laws restricting "sinful" practices or furthering virtuous ones were not seen as beyond the bounds of public discussion. A common good was reflected, even if implicitly and oftentimes imperfectly, in divorce laws, "blue laws" regulating liquor or other sales on Sundays, obscenity laws, and corporate laws. The congruence was not complete, and there was plenty of room for debate, and one cannot forget that minorities such as the Amish, African Americans, and Catholics might demur from this picture of Christianity and the law. However, the idea that Christianity should mean *something* in the law was a common view among religious believers of all kinds.

This is, to be clear, a different question than the constitutional protection of Christianity under the First Amendment. A generation of legal theorists and judges, working mostly under various versions of originalism, have provided a bulwark against an assault limiting the protections of the religion clauses; as Richard Garnett has noted, there is ample authority to support the view that the Constitution can protect religion generally as against irreligion. But those actions, as important as they are, ultimately are rearguard protections for those interested in whether the law should have moral content of any kind, Christian or otherwise. One can easily (perhaps too easily!) imagine a pagan society where churches get to pick their ministers and worship in peace but are otherwise sidelined from public life through a mixture of legal action and social opprobrium. Such a society might still be very hostile to Christians and the natural law principles Christians believe should order political society.

The larger problem with originalism (as Adrian Vermeule recounts in *Common Good Constitutionalism*) is that it is largely focused on method, while progressivism is primarily substantive. Whether the law is conducive to the common good, for example, is not generally the primary goal of the originalist judge (though not always: some originalist scholars believe, for example, there should be a "default to liberty" in constitutional interpretation). Progressives, on the other hand, are all in on results. These methods vary because they are concerned with being democratic (or not), but they align in furthering a set of substantive goals such as equality, secularism, or non-judgmentalism against those they perceive as their enemies. One proof that this might be the case is the example of the fifty state constitutions: they contain all sorts of guarantees and protections that reflect substantive commitments to a common good.

The law is increasingly subject to the "dominion" of liberalism. Court decisions and regulatory agencies are often hostile specifically to Christianity. The controversies over the Obama administration's "contraceptive mandate," which pitted religious belief against assertions of equality and healthcare, are just one recent example. And some law professors have begun a cottage industry by asking what is so special about religious freedom anyway (short answer: not much).

We seem now to be at a tipping point between a legal society with embedded Christian understandings of the person, the family, and such mundane legal topics as contract or finance, and one with (sometimes very different) understandings. Law still both imposes and reflects morality; at the moment it is simply a confused and mixed morality. The "woke" legal subject is different from the citizen or the Christian, and the law would necessarily reflect that difference. We can see these fissures in cases like 1989's *Michael H. v. Gerald D.* Justice Scalia's discussion in that case to fundamental rights as being those generally recognized in our tradition or at common law only make sense as part of a Christian tradition; that is where the tradition and common law come from in our society. But if you think, for example, that that tradition is motivated by a Justice Kennedy-like "animus," then whether a right was not considered fundamental at a Christian-inflected common law is not that relevant.

This is part of the reason why *Christian Legal Thought*, by Patrick M. Brennan and William S. Brewbaker III, is so important. Drawing on significant scholarly work that has been done in the past couple of decades on what "Christian legal thought" might look like, the book provides an overview of various Christian traditions with a rich selection of readings, ranging from extensive sections of the Bible to Mary Ann Glendon, Oliver O'Donovan, various papal texts, Protestant thinkers such as Abraham Kuyper, Reinhold Niebuhr, Dietrich Bonhoeffer, and Karl Barth, as well as texts that form part of the American civil religion, such as Lincoln's Second Inaugural, Martin Luther King Jr.'s Letter from a Birmingham Jail, and the Massachusetts Body of Liberties.

As the authors write, "Christian theology sometimes reinforces the standard jurisprudential accounts, sometimes supplements them, and sometimes even corrects them." The book reminds us that Christianity remains embedded in the background of the law, both statutory and common, but that these traces can be hard to see. However, it also shows us where that background is dissolving. Brennan and Brewbaker include the 1934 decision permitting the distribution of James Joyce's *Ulysses*, as well as *Obergefell*, as examples of the new relationships between larger cultural forces and the law. In *Ulysses*, Judge Augustus Hand determined that because the "dominant effect" of the novel was not obscene, then it could be imported into the United States despite a federal law to the contrary. That led the way to a more general judicial approach that so long as some artistic artifact has "merit" it should be allowed, even if it is otherwise obscene. This has had expanding effects, for example, rendering most local restrictions on activities or performances deemed obscene more difficult to enforce except on a seemingly neutral "health and safety" ground. *Obergefell* is an example of a case establishing open-ended liberty interests based on application of the principle of equality.

But those are only the most contested areas. McKinley and Brewbaker address a range of other topics such as property, environmental law, and corporate and business law to either illustrate how we still, at times, operate within a Christian framework and at other times how Christian concepts may serve as a critique. As a current example, officials in California and Tennessee have both recently enforced anti-price-gouging or anti-hoarding laws. Such laws have a clear goal of maintaining a "just price" (though the laws don't use that term) in a state of emergency. One could easily imagine a state where such laws did not exist, so that every person was at the mercy of the "market."

As the authors discuss, contract law includes similar protections for those at a disadvantage. A contract can have terms that are simply unfair, even if the parties willingly entered into its terms. In *Jones v. Star Credit* (1969), included here, a New York state court invalidated a contract that, while not fraudulent, took advantage of poor people to their detriment. The idea that there could be an "unconscionable" contract implies, well, a conscience, and implies as well a set of objective criteria to which that conscience must adhere. Indeed, as contract theorist James Gordley has argued, such cases are congruent with natural law arguments for a "just price," since the doctrine is based on the unfairness of the terms, not (as in modern law and economics) whether both parties bargained in good faith and in the absence of fraud. Recognizing the roots of those contractual doctrines is a way for Christian legal theorists to show how different premises about how the law should protect those at a disadvantage would result in very different legal regimes.

The financial system is another example. Here, however, the pressure on Christian legal thought comes from a different direction: not progressive wokeness but a sort of stripped-down profit-maximizing individualism. Take usury. Lending at interest has long been condemned by Christian authorities, even as it has become increasingly common: "[t]he Christian prohibition of [usury], however, is clear and unequivocal (even if the particulars of what constitutes usury admit of legitimately wide disagreement among Christian sources)." But these arguments fall on deaf financial ears without adequate alternatives, even though some residual usury laws are on the books.

Numerous types of financing instruments and arrangements look like loans but may not be, but there has been little analysis of which instruments are appropriate in a Christian framework. That framework offers a critique of some financial practices not as rooted as each party trying to get the greatest profit from the other but conceptualizing lending as a relationship in which one shares in the project rather than an individualistic enterprise that "make[s] a return on a loan possible without there being an ongoing relationship between the parties, or a connection between a return on the loan and the use of the money." Compare that gap to the extensive work major financial institutions have done on developing financial instruments consistent with Islamic principles. There is no reason why such instruments cannot be developed or promoted, and then made legally enforceable.

Similarly with even drier areas of the law such as property. William Blackstone's celebrated definition of property rights as "sole and exclusive dominion" is deeply embedded in Anglo-American law; indeed, defense of absolute property rights is something of a mark of American conservatism. And modern property law does have a strong bias toward the power to dispose of property at will (what the law calls its alienability), But this concept, without further glossing, is in tension with the more permeable treatment of property rights in the Christian tradition. The Church Fathers, Aquinas, and more recent statements such as the *Catechism* insist on a "universal destination of goods" that limits private property rights. And here, too, American law echoes that tradition. The authors include cases where absolute alienability has been restricted for a number of reasons, including where adhering to the wishes of the property owner would harm neighbors, a community, or the owner's family.

So what does this mean for our current situation? Well first, that Christian concepts remain important, and can be used as an instrument to move the law in particular ways. Although constitutional law has taken up most of the attention, as this casebook shows the law is a vast and still-to-be contested battleground.

Second, this scholarship could serve to show how these embedded principles of the law reflect a certain kind of legal person, which is different than the person imagined under a different kind of jurisprudence. Interested lawyers should focus on explaining and preserving some of these concepts from contracts, from property, from environmental law, and so on. This would involve more historical, scholarly work of a kind, perhaps, that Ofir Haivry has done with John Selden and, in a different way, Richard Reinsch has done with Orestes Brownson. There are judges whose biographies need to be written, doctrines whose histories need further uncovering.

The third aspect of Christian legal thought should be as goad. The law is constantly pushing and pulling those subject to it in certain directions. It is not wrong for Christian legal thought to acknowledge that one of its purposes may very well be to get us closer to the Kingdom of God; it is prescriptive as much as liberalism is. But what these materials show is that the Christian tradition also encapsulates a lot of what people think they like about secular legal culture. There is room, in a Brownsonian fashion, to find common ground with believers of different faiths, or of none, in a way that liberalism, in its current woke form, does not permit. Moreover, the American federalist structure allows for a lot of flexibility in particular expressions of property, contract, family law, and other areas, so that even within a broad common acceptance variations are still possible. Christian lawyers can infuse these concepts as well.

This project need not be sectarian—the authors here are refreshingly ecumenical, again in contrast to current legal academia. One theme that comes through from these materials is simply that people have thought about the law differently, and that secular or progressive assumptions can be questioned. At the same time, lawyers should be developing strategies to identify and use these resources, as the Becket Fund has used the law guaranteeing religious liberty. Some ideas are starting to ferment, especially in the areas of finance and securities law. More is waiting to be done.

# *For This Employer, Faith Is No Hobby*

❧

**The conscience wars** have now expanded beyond Catholic hospitals and religiously affiliated colleges.

A couple of weeks ago, the Becket Fund for Religious Liberty filed a case challenging the U.S. Department of Health and Human Services insurance mandate on behalf of Hobby Lobby, a family-run Christian business, and its owners. This case, which has not yet garnered the attention it deserves, represents a new dimension in the struggle to overturn the mandate.

Hobby Lobby, based in Oklahoma and founded in 1970, has hundreds of stores and thousands of employees throughout the country. It was founded by David Green and is still owned and operated by the Green family, which has made a conscious effort to run the business according to Christian principles.

Indeed, the company's statement of purpose reads, in part, that the Green family wishes to run the business "in a manner consistent with biblical principles." The stores are closed on Sundays, for example, to give employees time at home with their families, and the company has clergy on staff for those employees who want pastoral counseling.

The owners are opposing the HHS mandate because of their opposition to abortion and the HHS mandate requirement to include abortifacient drugs in their company's health-insurance coverage. They feel they simply cannot abide by that requirement and act consistently with their beliefs.

---

Originally published in *National Catholic Register*, September 28, 2012.

The complaint, filed in federal district court in Oklahoma, is part of a second wave of cases challenging the HHS mandate. The first wave was filed largely on behalf of Catholic social-service institutions and religiously affiliated educational establishments. Those complaints made the simple case that such entities were founded to act on their beliefs, and forcing them to act contrary to those beliefs has clearly violated their rights under the First Amendment.

These cases made the point that the mandate, and the secular viewpoint behind it, simply misunderstood religious freedom. According to secularists, religion is something you believe in your own mind with the door closed, but the moment you acted on it, the government could stop you.

Not so. The First Amendment and the full Western tradition holds that religious liberty is also (in the words of the amendment) free exercise, and religious believers and institutions must be permitted to worship and act in the public square as they see fit.

In bowing to the intense pressure challenging the constitutionality of their actions, the HHS has given more time to some employers before they are required to comply with the mandate. However, the HHS has not changed the fundamental problem with the mandate, which is that it forces employers and religious believers to act contrary to their religious beliefs.

But as the Hobby Lobby case shows, religious institutions are not the only entities that will be affected by the HHS mandate. Even companies that are run for-profit, and which do not offer social services like Catholic charities, have First Amendment rights to religious liberty, including free exercise. Companies like Hobby Lobby should be permitted to decide the kind of insurance coverage they wish to offer that is consistent with their beliefs, even as it can decide whether to close on Sundays or other religious holidays.

This second generation of cases focuses not only on the religious-discrimination aspect of the mandate, but the arbitrary bureaucratic discrimination the mandate represents. For the truth is: The mandate is not a blanket requirement, and it is being implemented unequally. As the Hobby Lobby complaint alleges, "Millions of employers may escape the mandate because of the age of their plans or because of the number of people they employ." HHS itself may have already granted thousands of waivers to the policy, and more than 50 million Americans will be covered by grandfathered plans, and therefore not subject to the mandate, through 2014.

However, HHS has adamantly refused to grant blanket exemption based on religious belief, neither for social-service organizations such as charities or Catholic hospitals, and even less so for for-profit business like that of the Greens. This practice gives the lie to the statements by the government on the importance of forcing the mandate on religious institutions as a matter of national "health," and, indeed, in another case regarding the mandate (involving Hercules Industries), one court has already found the government's protestations on this point of little merit.

In some respects, the Hobby Lobby case is just as important as those earlier cases. More Americans, after all, work in private or family-owned companies like Hobby Lobby than in social-service organizations. This case makes it clear that the HHS mandate will reach into every corner of our public life, making the religious liberty of all Americans less secure.

# *Victory for the Ground Zero Cross*

❧

SYMBOLS MATTER. What we remember and how a society explains and understands tragedy is of crucial importance. A federal court has recently held that the government can acknowledge the importance of Christianity in reacting to September 11 and that a cross can stand at Ground Zero.

As we have previously reported, Franciscan Father Brian Jordan was sued for violating the First Amendment for his efforts to preserve the so-called World Trade Center Cross. The cross—a cruciform piece of metal discovered in the ruins of the Twin Towers after September 11, 2001—quickly became for many a meaningful symbol of God's presence among the wreckage. It has long been considered a historic artifact from the World Trade Center site, and, in 2011, the Port Authority, a quasi-governmental agency, donated the cross to the museum being built at Ground Zero.

During and after the discovery of the cross, Father Jordan and others conducted worship services in front of it, and it was blessed during those services. Indeed, for five years before the donation, the cross was housed at St. Peter's Church in Lower Manhattan.

The case was resolved in the priest's favor—the plaintiffs made the ridiculous argument that he was acting as an agent of the state when he blessed the cross—but the controversy continued.

Last July, the reverence for the cross, and the symbolism it represented, caused the American Atheists Inc. to sue the memorial foundation

---

Originally published in *National Catholic Register*, May 1, 2013.

and others, allegedly for violating the (constitutionally imaginary) "wall of separation" between church and state. Having the cross at the site, the atheists argued, amounted to an endorsement of religion in general, and Christianity in particular. Therefore, the placement of the cross was unconstitutional.

The case of the cross represents one example of the larger fight over religious liberty, which includes the HHS cases as well. In both instances, the goal of the forces campaigning against religious liberty is to restrict religion's place in the public sphere and in national memory. Those who control the past control the present, according to George Orwell.

One way to control the past in a secular direction is to deny religion's large historic role. For the atheists and their allies, the ultimate goal is essentially to eliminate references to Christians and the importance of Christianity to Americans. If successful, it then becomes easier to downplay Christianity's formative role in Western civilization and religion's importance more generally.

One sees a glimpse of this ideology at work in cultural projects as well, like the recent Jackie Robinson movie *42*. The film unfairly downplays the strong religious beliefs of Robinson, as well as those of his supporter Branch Rickey (whose deep Christian faith earned him the nickname "The Mahatma").

In an opinion released at the end of March, the court rightly dismissed the atheists' case and indeed made short work of their arguments. The court found that the cross and its presence at the memorial did not "endorse" religion and its presence at the memorial in no way violated the First Amendment.

The court considered a number of factors to reach its conclusion. It first determined that the mere inclusion of the cross in a museum commemorating a national tragedy does not mean the government "endorses" that particular religion or means to exclude those of other faiths. The judge's opinion noted that, "because a reasonable observer would be aware of the history and context of the cross and the museum—especially given that the cross...will be accompanied by placards explaining its meaning and the reason for its inclusion, and surrounded by secular artifacts—no reasonable observer would view the (cross) as endorsing Christianity."

In other words, religious objects that are significant to an historical event can be displayed without running afoul of the Constitution.

Similarly, the court dismissed the atheists' argument that placing the cross at the museum "entangled" the state with religious belief—and for the same reason. Any rational person understands why the cross is included in the museum, which is displayed in an exhibit explicitly about how those affected by the Sept. 11 attacks responded. Some turned to patriotism or working with victims; others turned to faith. The state can acknowledge such facts.

In a contemporary culture where so much effort has been devoted to excluding religion, this decision is a welcome bit of good news for people of faith.

# *Debating the Constitution*

❧

**DURING THE RECENT DEBT-CEILING STANDOFF** in Washington, some observers debated what role, if any, the Constitution might play. An obscure provision of the Fourteenth Amendment states that the "validity of the public debt of the United States, authorized by law, including debts incurred for payment of pensions...shall not be questioned." Some argued that this provision required that the debt ceiling be raised, so as to avoid a government default. Others said that the clause didn't require raising the debt ceiling if resort to other means (such as higher taxes or reduced spending) could service the obligations. Also at issue was the question of who could make this determination—Congress or the president. Lawrence Solum and Robert Bennett have built careers exploring such questions. In their new book, *Constitutional Originalism: A Debate*, they build state-of-the-art cases for the two main schools of constitutional interpretation. Each contributes a generous essay presenting the merits of his own approach and offering a thoughtful rebuttal to the other's argument. If you've been seeking a concise introduction to the central debate in American constitutional theory, this is the book for you.

Solum advocates originalism, which he summarizes in four key precepts: that the Constitution has a fixed meaning; that this meaning is the "original public meaning" as understood at the time of enactment; that that public meaning has the force of law; and finally, that constitutional interpretation (figuring out what the words mean) and constitutional

---

Originally published in *City Journal*, a publication of the Manhattan Institute for Public Policy, Inc., on August 5, 2011.

construction (applying those words to a particular set of facts) are not the same thing. He is careful to distinguish this kind of originalism from its previous incarnation, which first emerged in the 1970s and 1980s and focused on "intention" rather than "meaning." Since determining intention is problematic and cannot provide the clarity that originalists hope to find, contemporary originalists look instead for evidence of the public meaning of the Constitution's language.

Bennett, meanwhile, argues for what is often called "living constitutionalism," which insists that "understanding of the document must keep up with a world that does not stand still." On this view, the amendment process set out in Article V of the Constitution is "both too difficult and insufficiently supple to do the job, with the result that the judiciary has stepped into the breach, making the Constitution a living one in an ongoing process of interpretation in the adjudication of cases over time." Bennett, like Solum, shares a desire for constraints on judicial review. But he argues that originalism doesn't provide that constraint, because the reliance on some "public understanding" of the constitutional text is too vague and shifting to provide the fixed meaning that originalism demands.

In arguing for their approaches, both Solum and Bennett discuss the 2008 case *District of Columbia* v. *Heller*, in which the Supreme Court banned a D.C. law regulating handguns. The majority decision in *Heller*, which concludes that bearing arms is an individual right, explicitly depends on the eighteenth-century public meaning of the phrase "the right of the people to keep and bear arms" in the Second Amendment. Solum argues that the amendment's opening words, which mention a "well-regulated militia," describe a *purpose* served by the right to bear arms but do not limit that right. Bennett, in turn, notes that all of the opinions in *Heller*, including the dissent, rely on historical arguments that are, to him, equally plausible in interpreting the text.

Intuitively, originalism seems to possess greater appeal. Great Britain has no constitution, for example, and so the interpretation of its basic laws rests with Parliament. The United States instead places sovereignty in a document, and it seems reasonable, therefore, to insist on fidelity to that document, at least in some generally understood way. The disregard for such an understanding, beginning in the 1960s, wrought great changes in the law with little public deliberation and long-term unintended consequences. Most Americans, even today, seem comfortable with the idea that some conception of the "original" understanding of the Constitution must govern as a way to limit governmental overreach.

Yet originalism has seen decades of judicial decisions antithetical to this philosophy. It's no coincidence that originalism saw its first wave of intellectual interest in the 1970s, in part as a reaction to the decisions of the Warren Court. Solum does not advocate a wholesale rejection of these decisions, acknowledging that the precedents now serve as the basis for vast areas of law, even if wrongly decided. Instead, he believes that the Supreme Court should embark on a years- or decades-long process of slow reversals of such decisions. (A sustained project like this isn't likely to happen.) Solum also suggests repeatedly that originalism is "evolving" into more sophisticated forms. That won't be much help, however, to judges today who seek to rule in a manner consistent with originalism as currently understood.

The United States has certainly changed enormously since 1787, 1865, and even 1932. Rather than seeing the changes as an argument for a living constitutionalism, however, we should see them as an argument for broadening the scope of constitutional interpretation from the courts to the rest of the government. No eighteenth-century "public meaning" existed for the kind of government we have now, with dozens of unaccountable federal agencies regulating vast areas of personal and consumer transactions. Originalism's next evolution might focus on persuading not just the judicial branch, but the legislative and executive branches as well, to recognize their constitutional obligations. One awaits a companion volume exploring those issues from Solum and Bennett.

# PART SEVEN

## *Lingua Latina Non Mortua Est*

# *The Fall of Rome: Season Two*

❧

**What was perhaps** the most pro-Christian show on television did not have a single Christian character in it—and there was no way it could have. *Rome*, the hit series that has just completed its second (and for now final) season on the cable channel HBO, turned out to be a surprising affirmation of the Western religious tradition. While it is packed with sex and violence, its message—intended or no—is that the Roman world was desperate for Christianity.

Neo-pagan life before Christianity does not come off well. Against a Gibbon-centered historical approach that placed primary responsibility for the decline of the classical world at Christianity's rise and the concomitant loss of traditional Roman virtues, historians such as Christopher Dawson argued earlier in the last century that Christianity had a revolutionary, and positive, effect on the pagan Roman world. It turned slaves into serfs, wedding contracts into sacramental marriages, and placed limits on the unjust use of authority. The show's depiction of the commonplaces of Roman life—even if a bit exaggerated at times, in keeping with the Rome-as-soap-opera marketing—gives us the reasons why.

The show is set in the closing days of the Roman Republic; the first season ended with the assassination of Julius Caesar on the floor of the senate by his friends Brutus and Cassius. The second season was concerned with the emergence of the empire under Octavian, Caesar's nephew and adopted son, who becomes Caesar Augustus and who reigned as *de facto* emperor from about 27 B.C. to his death in 14 A.D; his rule ended the

Originally published in *First Things*, April 9, 2007.

republic and brought about the Roman Empire. The series ends with a triumphal procession of Augustus after his return from defeating the forces of Cleopatra and Marc Antony in the Battle of Actium.

Along the way we see the fighting between Julius Caesar and Pompey Magnus for control of Rome, the death of Cicero, the Battle of Philippi, where Brutus and Cassius are defeated by the combined forces of Octavian and Marc Antony before their own falling out over, among other things, Antony's affair with Cleopatra (at the time he was married to Octavian's sister). Tracking their more famous fellow Romans are the centurions Lucius Vorenus and Titus Pullo, who are actual historical figures mentioned in passing in Caesar's *Gallic Wars*, but about whom little else is known. Their more normal lives allow the directors to explore sides of Roman life not often seen in the history books.

Three features stand out amid the thrilling story lines. The first is slavery. The casual cruelty of the Roman world as it is portrayed here is striking, and this is especially so in its treatment of slaves. Rome was, after all, a slave society, and slaves had no rights—indeed, almost no recognized existence except as property. They are everywhere in the show, sometimes as trusted servants (such as Cicero's amanuensis), sometimes treated like commodities (such as when Atia, Julius Caesar's niece and also Octavian's mother, offers her female slaves to Marc Antony, with whom she is having an affair) and sometimes just as the constant source of labor and menial service. They are routinely brutalized (as shown in a sequence set in a slave farm to which Vorenus goes to find his children). The show treats this aspect of Roman life matter of factly and not for shock value or with a false sentimentality. Life in the ancient world could be rough for anyone; it was just worse for slaves.

This is not to deny that Roman law is one of the great inheritances of the West or to demean the real virtues that Rome bequeathed to the West. The Romans did develop a legal culture that included notions of natural law and rights, and our language and procedures still echo their Roman forebears. But that system, we should not fail to remember, was harsh. Testimony from slaves in court, for example, was not admitted absent torture, a fact which is noted in one particularly gruesome scene. The legal system, in other words, had not yet been enlightened through the principles of equity that would make their appearance with the Catholic Church's canon law and admonitions of charity.

The second notable feature of the show is its treatment of family. Husbands could, and did, beat their wives with impunity, and children, even into adulthood, were only extensions of the father's will. Roman fathers could choose not to recognize their offspring and could expose them to the elements or offer them to strangers (often slave traders). In the first episode, when Vorenus returns after years campaigning with Caesar, his wife (who had thought him dead) hides from him an illegitimate child; otherwise, she says to her other children, "He will kill us all"—including the child, with, we are given to understand, hardly any risk of punishment. And indeed, by the end of the series, Vorenus does discover the child and goes at his wife in a murderous rage.

The portrayals of the upper classes are no better. Octavian marries his sister to Marc Antony for reasons of politics, rather than let him be with his mother, and orders another woman to divorce her husband in order to become his wife. There are exceptions to this otherwise depressing treatment: Vorenus and his wife do have reconciliation after his return, and Pullo marries a slave (whom he first frees), but the overall impression is one of family as a function of power.

Finally, there is religion. Rome is saturated with it—there are prayers and oaths, offerings made to deities known and unknown, and religious processions and priestly orders. One of the strengths of the show is that, as with other aspects of daily life, the naturalness of religious belief is treated soberly and as a normal way to behave. But these gods rarely provide a guide to conduct or right behavior. At most, they serve to confirm the honor and shame-driven culture of the time. When Vorenus' daughter is forced to work as a prostitute before she is rescued, Vorenus brings them before a priest to cleanse her and the other children of their shame. And, of course, there is always suicide as an honorable way out of dishonorable situations, a recourse several characters take during the series. A pagan world, in other words, is not one in which we control the gods, as trendy neo-pagans suppose, but a world in which we are ever at risk of offending some god for failure to make the right offering or sacrifice.

Some may quibble with the historical accuracy of this or that detail, but in the main the show has it right. The picture presented by *Rome* is provocative, troubling, and at times downright strange. Despite how well we know the story of the fall of Rome, and despite our clear debts to the Romans as a constituent part of our own culture, they are not us and we are not them, in large measure because of the interposition of Christianity. Indeed, the most recognizable people in the series are perhaps the Jewish characters, whose ethical structure is clearly recognizable as our own from the brief glimpses we are given of it.

From the account the series presents of life in Rome, it is no wonder that the message of Christianity, building perhaps on other mystery cults emerging around this time, would be so appealing to slaves, women, and others whose participation in Roman life was partial at best. As Walter Pater wrote in 1885, the revelation of the Christian message must have been seen as fresh air in a suffocating world:

> Penetrating the whole atmosphere, touching everything around with its peculiar sentiment, it seemed to make all this visible mortality, death itself, more beautiful than any fantastic dream of old mythology had ever hoped to make it; and that, in a simple sincerity of feeling about a supposed actual fact. The thought, the word, *Pax—Pax Tecum!*—was put forth everywhere, with images of hope, snatched sometimes even from that jaded pagan world, which had really afforded men so little of it from first to last.

This breath of air was revolutionary, and we should do well to remember it in the context of our own resurgences into barbarism in the areas, for example, of family life and treatment of the poor.

All this is not, of course, to say that in some respects the ancient world improved immediately upon the rise of Christianity, or that, for example, marriages, even into the modern age, were not done for convenience or for reasons of power politics. But the point is that the intellectual and moral climate that made any improvement possible would not have been possible at all within the classical pagan world.

These days, some contend that a world without Christian restraints would be more egalitarian, less violent, and more individualistic. But for those with a historical sense, *Rome* shows that another alternative is more likely. The classical world was not all marble columns and noble rhetoric. It was a world where the strong ruled, and those who could not conquer were themselves conquered. Far from being egalitarian, the only clear rule was inequality: between masters and slaves, husbands and wives, or plebeians and patricians. Those wishing to reject the West's Christian heritage should take a hard look at what that world was like.

# *Latin Lives*

G. K. CHESTERTON once responded to the charge that Latin was a "dead" language by stating, "Every living language is a dying language, even if it does not die. Parts of it are perpetually perishing or changing their sense; there is only one escape from that flux; and a language must die to be immortal." So if Latin has died, it still remains present in our culture and it represents a repository of historical knowledge that cannot be accessed without that linguistic ability. The classical texts are only the very topmost layer of a vast edifice. As Jurgen Leonhardt notes in his provocative *Latin: Story of a World Language*, the amount of material in Latin published after the classical era, even into the late nineteenth and early twentieth centuries, is many times greater than what we have recovered from the classical period. Leonhardt estimates that "the quantity of postclassical Latin texts is so extensive that it exceeds the total of all extant classical Latin texts by a factor of ten thousand." This fact alone should cause us to reconsider our cultural relationship with Latin, since it extends geographically and temporally well beyond classical Rome.

In this book, originally in German but recently translated, Leonhardt comes out in roughly the same place as Chesterton, and his *Latin* provides us with a deeper way of understanding the relationship between European culture and the language that sustained it for more than a thousand years. Leonhardt is a professor of classical philology at the University of Tübingen, and he wants to rescue Latin from what he sees as its mausoleum. To do this, he handily discredits the notion that Latin is "dead." Drawing on

Originally published in *The New Criterion*, March 2014.

linguistic scholarship, he distinguishes between a language that is fluid and one that is "fixed." Fixed does not mean dead, but rather that the language has developed stable components that do not change. A fixed "language is therefore not a language that is closed and can no longer develop but a language in which several core components remain unchangeable, while other parts continue to evolve as in any other normal language." Latin is such a fixed language, and not a dead one in the sense that no one uses Latin any longer or that the language does not change. Latin is still used in some communications (unlike, say, Etruscan or Hittite), and Latin can change, and has changed over time while still remaining itself. Indeed, Latin continued to evolve through the late Middle Ages, and continues in some respects to do so through the present. Thus, for example, the Vatican, whose official language is Latin, has on its website a Parvum Verborum Novatorum Lexicum and, as Leonhardt notes in one of several examples that demonstrates Latin's enduring hold on the Western imagination, between 1999 and 2006 Finland regularly published reports in Latin during that nation's service in the presidency of the Council of the European Union.

Leonhardt's book has two further aims. The first is to make a claim for Latin as one of a very few fixed languages with global reach. Latin is a "world language," in that, like ancient Greek and Sanskrit, it survived the initial circumstances of its creation to become a second, adopted language with heightened cultural and intellectual weight. Latin lasted and even flourished long after the seven-hundred-year Roman Empire ended. Unlike Arabic, which tended to crush local languages in the wake of Muslim military victories, imperial Rome cared less about its own linguistic superiority. To be a Roman citizen, Latin was essential, but so long as the people could also communicate in Latin, the Empire was otherwise largely indifferent to the "native" language.

Further, its reach is not solely coterminous with military conquest. Many parts of Europe, such as Poland or Ireland, which were never part of the Roman Empire, nevertheless adopted Latin as the language of theology, intellectual activity, and diplomacy. After the end of the Empire, the peoples of Europe were of course very comfortable speaking their "mother tongues," yet the pull of Latin remained. There was no clear reason, for example, for Charlemagne to have selected Latin as the court language rather than his native Frankish, yet he did so.

Rather, Latin existed as a common cultural backdrop, along with the common Christian faith, to unite the continent during the millennium from the fall of Rome in the fifth century through the early Renaissance in the fifteenth century:

> One of the key characteristics of this multilingualism is that these languages coexisted within a primarily Latin culture. These were not different, isolated written cultures; rather, they were new written cultures that developed out of largely unwritten European vernaculars, all of which set their sights on Latin, with its stylistic possibilities, literary forms, and intellectual legacy.

Another noteworthy example of a developing grammar in the shadow of lingua Romana was the Old English program of King Alfred the Great, who commissioned a set of translations from Latin into Old English to jumpstart that language's literature from Latin models.

This common backdrop lasted into the very recent past, and shows how important Latin was until almost yesterday. In his masterful *A Time of Gifts*, the great British writer Patrick Leigh Fermor includes an account from his time as a commando in Cyprus, when he captured the German General Heinrich Kreipe. Taking the captive to the shore to be transported back to England, Fermor and the general were crossing Mount Ida, famous in myth as the birthplace of Zeus. Upon seeing the mountain, the general quoted a line, in Latin, from Horace's ode Ad Thaliarchum; Fermor finished it for him, as well as the remaining stanzas, also in the original.

That is what Leonhardt means when he says that knowledge of Latin opens up not only the classical world, but also the entire history of Europe, in a way that no other European language can match. English has come perhaps the closest as Latin's successor, but Leonhardt (perhaps expressing some German pride) does not think it will overcome the various European languages as Latin once did.

Having saved Latin from the charge that it is dead, Leonhardt's second purpose is more complex. He wants to investigate why it is that much of postclassical Latin has been ignored in favor of a "pure" classical Latin. This is not the fault of the medieval scholastics, or even of the Renaissance masters who brought classic Latin prose back into vogue. It is really the fault of ideology. First came the nationalists, then the academic pedants. Together, they served to inter Latin, and especially any Latin written or spoken after the classical era. There was no "natural" reason, Leonhardt argues, for Latin to have disappeared as a lingua franca across Europe at the close of the Middle Ages. Other cultures have had two languages at the same time, one for formal or political communications, the other in more common use. Instead, Leonhardt argues, Latin was doomed because "the nationalism that developed during the early modern era also brought national languages, which were consciously elaborated and constructed between the fifteenth and the nineteenth [centuries], to the fore." These national languages acquired a prestige and a high literature of their own, and Latin began to be displaced.

The second reason is joined to the first; nationalism rendered the idea of a common cultural unity, moderated in Latin, increasingly unpalatable. Because of that development, Latin as a common language lost its hold, and the notion then arose that Latin should simply be ignored because it was "dead." There had long been a school of thought that equated Latin only with its classical forms, so all words and their variants must have a classical antecedent to be considered valid. By definition, this left much of medieval Latin—both spoken and written—subpar. This school triumphed over the approach taken by humanists such as Erasmus, who argued for a more modest approach that would "not only have retained Latin's openness to innovation but might very well have also become the basis for a wholly new European Latin standard." That was not to be, however, and so Latin gradually got shunted off, first to only highly specialized areas, then discarded as a common language entirely. Whereas Latin until this time had been an actual means of diplomatic, intellectual, and literary communication, now it became simply a "measure of human self-perfection." This legacy has resulted in the overly scientific and schematic approach to teaching Latin that those of us remember, some with joy, some with dread, and some with both. But having learned Latin in this way, recovering it as a living historical thing is both difficult and refreshing.

Leonhardt closes the book by calling for a new appreciation of Latin, one "that is aware of its exclusively historical point of reference but does not retreat into a purely observational and analytical 'scientific' approach, which is what Latin teaching at schools and Latin philology at universities have done for 200 years." He is no nostalgist, wishing that Latin can return to the dominant place it once had over the various European languages. Nevertheless, he notes that the age of linguistic nationalism may be over. Even as regionalism, especially in Europe, has been on the rise—and along with it sub-national languages such as Catalan or Umbrian—still the European Union continues to move forward as a pan-regional governing body. Latin has endured such linguistic and cultural circumstances before, and *Latin* reminds us that understanding our past can help to shape our future.

# *Defensor Linguae*

❧

**At the Jesuit high school** in Manhattan that I attended, my freshman year, 1985, was the first in which Latin was no longer the language required for the first two years. Father Headmaster wrote to explain that the school nevertheless still strongly encouraged its young charges to take Latin, in keeping with Jesuit tradition and as an introduction to Western culture. Most of the entering class followed his advice, and we immersed ourselves, unselfconsciously for middle-class adolescents, in the campaigns of Caesar and the conjugations of irregular verbs. Without knowing exactly why, we had a sense that Latin still had something significant to say to us. Since that time, the situation has changed dramatically; such encouraging letters are no longer written, and Latin is much less emphasized.

We did not know then that we were part of a long intellectual tradition, now almost extinct, that had placed Latin at its center. Françoise Waquet, director of research at the Centre National de la Recherche Scientifique in Paris, traces this tradition, as well as the possibilities of its revival, in her richly researched and delightful *Latin: Or the Empire of a Sign.* The subtitle should not frighten anyone concerned with the fate of "the old language," as the translation nicely puts it. Rather than a nod to chic French theory, Latin as the "empire of a sign" echoes the old French reactionary (and most definitely unchic) Joseph de Maistre, who defended Latin as the "*signe européen*" in his 1819 book *On the Pope.*

Waquet focuses on the Latin of the sixteenth to the twentieth centuries, when its fate as a "dead language" was sealed. While Latin had been

---

Originally published in *The New Criterion*, December 2001.

the common language of Europe since the Middle Ages, its role changed after the Renaissance and Reformation. On the one hand, its use as a common spoken tongue faded almost into insignificance; on the other, Latin expanded its cultural and intellectual place in both Catholic and Protestant Europe.

Waquet describes for us "a unitary intellectual Europe in which, until a relatively recent date, learning was expressed in Latin." And not only in science or literature, which were "nothing...compared to the enduring predominance of the old language in the schools and the Church: here childhood memories took over, and there came back to me the memory of a time—not so very long ago—when Latin was a part of people's lives." The influence of *Latinitas* extended from the Old World into the New. Most of the founders (but not all—the physician Benjamin Rush strongly opposed Latin education) thought the classical languages were essential to an informed citizenry, and Roman examples and imagery are staples of early American political culture. In institutions such as the Boston Latin School, the ideals of the Latin educational tradition were continued in America.

The watershed occurred, not surprisingly, in the 1960s. By the end of that decade, Latin was simply no longer considered valuable to Western intellectual life. Not because Latin or its study was out-of-date (of course, it had long since been replaced by the vernaculars), rather, "Latin disappeared because it no longer meant anything to the contemporary world." To the revolutionaries in those heady days, Latin represented all that needed to be overthrown: religion, history, tradition, a system of cultural symbols derided for their "ethnocentric" and "hierarchical" foundations. Echoing arguments used by Rush two centuries earlier, they simply saw no use for Latin. Almost without resistance, the language of Europe disappeared.

Waquet examines Latinity from a variety of historical, literary, and academic sources. The first part, "The European Sign," explores the "familiar world" Latin created. Drawing on Eamon Duffy's work on pre-Reformation England as well as historical research derived from Brittany and elsewhere, Waquet concludes that though formally unknown to the majority of the populace, Latin nevertheless was part of their quotidian lives. The book sheds light on an aspect of the history of the language that is almost incomprehensible in our ironic, postmodern world: simple loyalty to old forms and a deep respect for the power of words. When Latin was overthrown, a new world, and one not necessarily better, appeared: "[t]he disappearance of Latin meant more than the interruption of banal habits, the replacement of simple mechanisms; it disarranged a mental universe in which that unintelligible language had become fully domesticated." This is not a paean to ignorant peasants thumbing unintelligible breviaries: the data suggest, rather, that most of the uneducated in fact knew bits of Latin, from long use if not from formal education. And even for those who did not, Latin provided a background tradition, a "bass line" as Waquet calls it, that made the larger world comprehensible.

The second part, "Standards and Ability," looks with a sometimes sardonic eye on the actual quality of the Latin written, read, and spoken by pupils, scholars, and politicians over the last four centuries. The conclusions Waquet draws are not entirely favorable to those seeking a widespread reinstatement of Latin. According to available records, for example, in the eighteenth century most students achieved only a basic proficiency. Even those who were supposed to be conversant in the old language, such as those submitting doctoral dissertations in Latin, in fact often lacked competence in the classical tongue. In this harsh verdict, Waquet reveals a bias toward "classical" Latin, in which the use of non-Ciceronian vocabulary or word order is considered a flaw. One implication of Waquet's research, however, is that a strict adherence to such a truncated classical model led to Latin's decline.

The final section, "What Latin Meant," expands the field to consider the cultural implications of adhering to a Latin-centered curriculum, even when it had increasingly less practical utility. Why learn Latin if no one needs it anymore? By the late seventeenth century, the now familiar canon of arguments defending Latin had arisen: as background for the modern languages, as general cultivation of the mind, as the language of religion, as a mark of social class, or (as in my high school) as a way into Western culture. Taken together, the arguments contend that Latin releases us from what Eliot called the provinciality of time; the old language is both familiar and strange, and the combination is a fruitful source of intellectual reflection and cultural sophistication.

In its wide scope, *Latin* demonstrates that far from being a "dead" language Latin was rightfully considered a critical component of cultural life for the majority of the peoples whose cultures were heir to that of Rome, from Russia (in which there is now an academy teaching spoken and written Latin) to the United States. In light of the exhaustive detail Waquet provides on the vitality, importance, and sheer cultural weight of Latin in the modern period, comparison with the other "universal language," English, is instructive. English may be the language of international commerce and communication, but it is used almost exclusively as an instrument. It has never developed a broad system of cultural symbols like the one that made Latin the common and unifying language of the West. Waquet's somewhat harsh assessment of English's weaknesses may bear a residual trace of Gallic pride (one wonders at her reaction had French retained its status as the standard international and diplomatic language), but is nonetheless persuasive.

Waquet concludes with a call for a modest Latin revival in order to save it both from the pedants as well as from those who treat Latin as a subject for nostalgia or decoration. Waquet advocates creating a cadre of "professionals of humanist literary culture" who will concentrate on Latin as a subject in itself, in order to "have access to those wellsprings of our own culture, the Fathers of the Church and the *Corpus juris*" and the mass of medieval and early modern documents that have yet to be translated. While one hopes this may not be its ultimate end—one lesson of *Latin* is that the language should not remain the preserve of the academic class—with scholars of Waquet's generosity and ability, the old language might yet have a future.

# *Love and Error*

❧

**Ovid** is not exactly the proper example for Roman greatness. He is the author, after all, of famously lascivious love manuals and erotic poetry, teaching in his *Ars Amatoria* (*The Art of Love*) how to pick up girls outside the Forum and generally mocking the pretensions of early imperial Rome, which caused Augustus to exile him in late middle-age. For generations of schoolboys (myself included), Ovid was excluded from the usual high-school *cursus authorum Romanorum* of Caesar, Cicero, and Virgil. Along with the equally off-color Catullus, Ovid had to wait for the supposed maturity of college.

And yet there is no question that Ovid belongs in the first rank of Roman poets. In the closing lines of the *Metamorphoses*, he predicted that his fame would live on whatever his end, and so it proved to be. His influence was already evident shortly after his death; in the twelfth and thirteenth centuries he surpassed Virgil and Horace as the Roman poet of choice. By the seventeenth century, as Gian Biagio Conte writes in his magisterial history of Latin literature, Ovid had become "thoroughly absorbed within European culture." This interest continues; Mary Zimmerman's experimental retelling of the *Metamorphoses* was recently a hit on Broadway, and in 1994 Michael Hoffman and James Lasdun published *After Ovid*, a collection of retellings of Ovid's tales.

The standard account divides Ovid's work into three broad stages. There is the early Ovid, the love poet who composed the *Amores* (*Experiences of*

---

Originally published in *The New Criterion*, January 2003.

*Love*), the *Ars Amatoria*, and *Remedia Amoris* (*Love Therapy*), and the stylized letters of mythological women to their lovers, *Epistulae Heroidum.* Ovid then moved on to more serious works with his *Metamorphoses* and *Fasti* (*Festival Calendar*). His final years are reflected in the *Tristia* (*Elegies of Lament*) and the *Epistulae ex Ponto* (*Letters from the Black Sea*), which describe his journey from Rome and accommodation to his new surroundings.

Of his life we know little, other than what he himself tells us. That source may not be completely trustworthy, as Ovid was adept in creating and recreating his poetic persona as needed. Publius Ovidius Naso was born of minor nobility in the town of Sulmo, about ninety miles from Rome, lived roughly from 43 B.C. to A.D. 16 or 17, and died in exile. As a young man, Ovid received the rhetorical training traditional for those of his background. Rather than embarking upon the usual political career of a wealthy Roman, Ovid devoted himself to poetry. Ovid attached himself to the literary circle of the Roman aristocrat Valerius Massella but was apparently wealthy enough so as not to need the support of a patron.

When Ovid was about fifty years old, the Emperor Augustus exiled him to the town of Tomis on the Black Sea coast, at the very edge of the Empire, in what is now Romania. The reasons for the exile remain mysterious. Augustus seems to have been displeased with Ovid's love poetry, specifically the *Ars Amatoria*, and ordered them removed from the public libraries in Rome. Ovid himself only obliquely refers to his *error* as some unidentified *culpa* (fault) he learned of by accident. It did not help that, as the evidence suggests, the *culpa* somehow involved Augustus' granddaughter Julia, who was busily, and notoriously, violating her grandfather's renewed emphasis on moral virtue. Despite Ovid's entreaties, neither Augustus nor his successor Tiberius granted him pardon.

Along with his near-contemporaries Propertius and Tibullus, Ovid was heir to the poetic tradition of Callimachus, whose allusive, witty, and complex style suited the jaded sophisticates of the early days of the Empire. The complexity also served as convenient political covering. Augustus achieved full control of Rome only in 31 B.C., after defeating Marc Antony and Cleopatra at the battle of Actium. Augustus then began transforming himself from the *princeps* (first in rank) of the Republic to Emperor. His position was far from secure, however, and the years of Ovid's adulthood were wracked with political and domestic threats. Poets especially needed to be careful, as the Emperor freely used literature to establish his Rome as a "Golden Era." Ovid's exile was only another installment in the imperial drama that continued until after Augustus' death in A.D. 14.

Niklas Holzberg, a distinguished scholar and Professor of Classics at the University of Munich, in *Ovid: The Poet and His Work*, a readable and comprehensive contribution to the Ovidian revival, examines each of the major works individually and as part of what he sees as Ovid's larger poetic project. His Ovid "intended systematically to develop possibilities for literary expression that Ovid's predecessors among the poets of antiquity exploited only rarely, if at all." First, Holzberg maintains, the rules and inner logic of elegy remained with Ovid in all his works, concealing at times political themes, and second, that the concept of "metamorphosis" is used deliberately as a literary device from the very beginning. While erudite, the book is accessible to non-specialists and does not require knowledge of Latin.

Elegiac poetry depicted the erotic enslavement (*servitium amoris*) of a Roman male citizen to a female slave or prostitute, and represented a reversal of both traditional Roman mores and the Augustan morals program. The roles in such poetry were sharply defined: "the unwavering devotion of an upright, poetically talented, young upper-class Roman stands over against the infidelity of a *hetaera* [courtesan];" because of her inconstancy, the male *amator* suffers for his love. Moreover, he is cast out of society for his subjugation to a faithless *dura puella* (tough chick) of an unacceptable social rank. The elegists employed political and military imagery to illustrate the *amator's* attempts to win the loyalty of the puella, as further examples of the reversal of social roles.

Holzberg portrays the early Roman elegists as reactionaries against what they saw happening to their upper-class Roman society under Augustus's elimination of the Republic. They retreated into the world of love poetry, where the usual rules were turned upside down. There was some of this in Ovid as well, but what makes him worth reading now is how he adapted the forms of elegiac poetry for his own purposes. As Holzberg explains by the example of *Amores* 3.7, Ovid "intertwines the speaker's chronologically unfolding lament with the chronology of his recollections of each particular act." The love poetry transcends the formalism of elegy into a real narrative of characters whose psychological and emotional development we can follow. In a section entitled "Amor, Roma and the Moral of the Novel," Holzberg makes a case of Ovid not only as an accomplished parodist of his predecessors, but also as an innovative poet who was exploring what Holzberg calls the novelistic possibilities of Latin verse.

Holzberg convincingly argues that the rules of elegy became a constituent part of Ovid's work, even when his subject matter turned to myth or exile. The best example of this is perhaps the appeals to Augustus throughout the *Epistulae ex Ponto*, in which the Emperor is placed in the position of the *dura puella*, coldly refusing to favor her distressed lover. Using the language common to the *amator*, Ovid unrealistically imagines the Emperor heeding his laments:

> *aut ego me fallo nimiaque cupidine ludor,*
> *aut spes exili commodioris adest.*
> *nam minus et minus est facies in imagine tristis,*
> *visaque sunt dictis adnuere ora meis.*
> Either I am mistaken and am being fooled by an all too violent longing,
> Or there is hope for a more agreeable place of banishment.
> For the face in the image is less and less stern,
> And it seems that the countenance is nodding consent to my words.
> *Epistulae ex Ponto*, II.8, 71–74

His inventiveness with the rules of elegy also informs Holzberg's second theme. In Ovid's poetry, everything is changing: gods and mortals take different forms, men and women assume new roles, and mortals are made divine. The *Epistulae Heroidum*, for example, set up the women as *amatores* and the long-lost men as the *puellae* who have abandoned them for war or adventure. Not even Rome, he implies, is safe; it too will pass away. In the *Amores*, Ovid describes his own transformation into a poet of elegy:

> *Arma gravi numero violentaque bella parabam*
> *edere, materia conveniente modis.*
> *par erat inferior versus; risisse Cupido*
> *dicitur atque unum surripuisse pedem.*
> Weapons in weighty rhythms and violent wars was I making ready
> To sing, and the matter suited the measure.
> The first line was as long as the second. Then Cupid laughed,
> They say, and stealthily stole a foot.
> *Amores* 1.14

The "foot" (*pedem*) stolen by the god of love is the length of meter that transformed the intended poem from epic hexameter to elegiac couplet. Ovid was now to write about love, not war. This is the first of many indications for Holzberg of Ovidian metamorphosis, both poetical and personal. The proem to the *Metamorphoses* transforms Ovid yet again. He asks the gods to look on his project with favor, which they themselves have also "metamorphosed" from something not described into a *perpetuum carmen*, a term for epic.

The experiences Ovid endured as an exile complete his transformation. Holzberg summarizes Ovid's exilic works as those of "a seafaring, patient Odysseus learning the ways of a remote land [who] becomes, after undergoing a living death, a new member of a barbaric people," which "is something unique in ancient literature." With this study, Holzberg provides ample reason for revisiting, and enjoying, Ovid's immediacy, literary skill, and psychological insight.

# *Georgics on My Mind*

TRANSLATING VIRGIL these days is either eccentric or...well, there really is no "or." It is eccentric. Virgil is the archetype for what were called in the heyday of the culture wars "Dead White European Males." After all, Publius Virgilius Maro was the author of the *Aeneid*, an explicitly pro-imperial epic that praised Roman arms and Rome's success in bringing law and civilization to the barbarians. Not the sort of thing, in other words, to garner support at an MLA meeting. Perhaps a new translation that emphasized Virgil's "ambiguous attitude" toward empire would be more acceptable to sophisticated audiences, or one that placed Dido, the wronged queen of Tyre, at the center of the action. But here, Janet Lembke has eschewed the martial for the agricultural and has produced a graceful and supple translation of the *Georgics*, Virgil's great paean to rural life, whose four books are concerned, respectively, with crops, vines, livestock, and finally bees. What is more, *Georgics* is an explicitly Roman poem, extolling the virtues and products of the Italian farmer and praising the military victories of Augustus.

The poem is a perfect fit for Lembke, who has translated a number of other classical works and is also a distinguished naturalist, but it presents a number of challenges for a translator. First, like all of Virgil's extant poetry, it is written in the epic meter of dactylic hexameter, a verse form not readily translatable into English. Not surprisingly, Lembke has not kept to the original meter, but the English lines are generally congruous to their Latin originals, and Lembke is able to maintain a solid rhythm of five

---

Originally published in *The New Criterion*, June 2005.

beats per line, which moves the poem at a proper pace. Second, the poem is full of obscure or arcane farming and husbandry terms, with which even dedicated students of the classics may be unfamiliar. Indeed, with some of these items (such as a common Roman plow), we do not even know what they look like.

Lembke adopts the sensible approach of using contemporary American usages when applicable, and dropping antique phrases or Britishisms adopted from an earlier generation of translations. Lakes Larus and Benacus, for example, are given their current names of Como and Garda, and various nymph names are transliterated into colorful renderings such as Woods Girl and Fancy Leaf; my favorite, perhaps, is calling the wine-god Bacchus the "Body-Relaxer" after one of his Greek names, Lyaeus, which derives from the verb meaning "to loosen." Purists may object, but Lembke obviously has deep knowledge and love for the Latin language, and the names Lembke provides serve the same purpose for us as the originals did for the Romans: as a visual cue to the powers of the deities or topographical features—and, for the most part, they succeed.

The *Georgics* continues an ancient tradition of agricultural poetry that focuses on, among other things, the unremitting nature of farm labor: "[m]oving in great circles," Virgil writes, "work revisits the farmer as the year wheels around in its own tracks" (redit agricolis labor actus in orbem/ atque in se sua per vestigia volvitur annus). Yet despite this labor, the farmer cannot control everything, and must still try to appease the gods to avoid disaster. The poems balance a coldly realistic view with a wistful look back at a utopian "Age of Saturn," during which labor was not needed to stave off starvation. Hesiod's Greek poem *Works and Days* was the standard for this sort of poetry, and was a model for Virgil as he composed the *Georgics*; Virgil's other surviving poems also demonstrate his deep knowledge of Greek models. The *Eclogues*, an earlier collection of ten short pastoral poems, has Theocritus as a model, and of course the *Aeneid* takes up where Homer ended. Closer to home were the Roman treatises on agriculture and the vivid similes of the natural world in Lucretius' great poem of Epicureanism, *De Rerum Natura* (*On the Nature of Things*). As a devotee of Epicureanism, Virgil was no doubt deeply familiar with Lucretius. In the *Georgics*, however, there is little direct appeal to the gods to protect the farmer against nature: labor remains more important. Book III closes with a horrific scene of disease and plague striking down animal and human alike, despite prayers or even work. Interestingly, Virgil's view of politics is seemingly different: by the time he gets to Aeneas, piety, the Roman virtue encompassing proper respect for ancestors and the gods (throughout the epic, Aeneas is repeatedly described as "pius"), becomes the more important virtue.

Virgil lived from 70 to 19 B.C., one of the most tumultuous periods of Roman history. By the time he moved to Naples as a young man from his native Mantua (in what is now Lombardy), Rome had already suffered through decades of civil war. Reformers of the previous generation, such as the Gracchi and Marius, had largely failed to restructure the Roman social system, which turned in part on the protection of the food supply and the difference between citizen and non-citizen. Indeed, the basic privilege of citizenship to those living outside the city of Rome was granted only grudgingly. (Virgil himself, for example, did not become a citizen until the age of forty.) The republic was slowly dissolving under pressure from the new powers in the city, such as Sulla and the young upstart named Julius Caesar. There would be more years of fighting until 31 B.C., when Octavian, Caesar's nephew, collected all power to himself after defeating Mark Anthony in the battle of Actium, which Virgil celebrated in his last poem, the *Aeneid*. The *Georgics* is believed to have been completed earlier, in around 30 B.C., when the fighting had finally ceased, perhaps for good.

What does all this have to do with farms and beekeeping? Actually, a lot. While primarily concerned with agriculture and husbandry, the poem is not without its political referents. It is a lament for the destruction the civil unrest was causing to the traditional ways of Roman agriculture. The years of civil war had disrupted farming, destroyed crops, and dispossessed the farming classes of the Italian peninsula, including (it is thought) Virgil's family. The proem in Book I combines his two concerns:

*Quid faciat laetas segretes, quo sidere terram*
*vertere, Maecenas, ulmisque adiungere vites*
*conveniat, quae cura boum, qui cultus habendo*
*sit pecori, apibus quanta experientia parcis,*
*hinc canere incipiam.*
What makes the crops rejoice, Maecenas, under what stars
To plow and marry the vines to their arbor of elms,
What care the cattle need, what tending the flocks must have,
How much practical knowledge to keep frugal bees—
Here I start my song.

But a few lines further down, Virgil suggests his second theme. He calls upon Caesar (Octavian, now styled Augustus), for approval to begin his work, and he asks that the emperor "with me feel compassion for country people unaware of their way" (ignarosque viae mecum miseratis agrestis). This is a clear reference to the veterans of Caesar's armies who were given land formerly belonging to farmers, and in whose amateur hands the land had suffered. And he closes the poem with a tribute to "great Caesar's lightning struck in war by the deep Euphrates and he, as victor, gave laws to eager people and gained the path to Olympus." There is that pro-empire sentiment again, combined with an argument for rural landholders and traditional Roman folkways: the Roman red states, perhaps. Better call the MLA.

# *Primal Obligations*

The West inherited Greek literature, philosophy, art, and elements of ancient political culture, yet Greece remains, in some respects, a foreign world. Those simple, white classical statues were adorned and painted in vivid colors. The hive-society of Sparta or an Athens drenched in what seems like obscene imagery were not what the Victorians had in mind in terms of classical values. Once one discovers that statues called herms sprouted enormous phalluses (which were allegedly desecrated by Socrates's pupil Alcibiades) and were dotted across Athens, for example, one never again quite sees classical Greece in the same way. Thus, too, in their theater: an all-male cast, wearing masks, performing plays set to music (lost to us) at quasi-religious festivals that trace their connections, some believe, to songs of goatherds presents an arresting picture at odds with how we think the Greeks behaved.

This more nuanced picture of the ancient world has not seeped much into popular culture. Of course, there are mass-culture events such as the recent cinematic take on the battle of Thermopylae, *300* (which, in a window on the culture, is based not on Herodotus or other ancient writers, but on a graphic novel), the *Odyssey*-inspired George Clooney vehicle, *O Brother, Where Are Thou?*, or the truly awful *Alexander*, with Angelina Jolie as the wife of Philip of Macedon, sporting snakes as fashion accessories. There are, however, other encounters with the classics, such as *The Theban Plays of Sophocles*, now in a new edition. The distinguished poet and

Originally published in *The New Criterion*, December 2007.

translator David Slavitt renders into elegant English Sophocles's *Oedipus Tyrannos*, *Oedipus at Colonus*, and *Antigone*, which deal with darker questions of power, unforgivable offense, and desecration that most popular films tend to avoid, but which fascinated the Greeks themselves.

The Greek past continues to shed light on our own time. As Victor Davis Hanson pointed out in an early book, the Greek model of agrarian citizenship still has something to say to us. And although one hears more about imperial Rome, the Greeks too dealt with questions of empire, both as imperialists themselves, through the domination of Athens over the Greek world, as well as with their confrontations with Persia. Even *300* was viewed not merely as a comic book adaptation, but as another installment of the West's competition with, and considerations of, the (non-Greek) "East." Similarly with the plays. *Antigone*, for example, has long been an instrument for expressing politically correct fashions, such as feminism or, more significantly, as an anti-fascist play in Jean Anouilh's 1944 recasting.

One cannot easily see a contemporary parallel to a figure like Sophocles (495–406 B.C.); our culture does not honor its playwrights in the same way (for writing the play believed to be *Antigone*, Sophocles was named a general!), nor are most of them worth the honor. Sophocles was born a few years before the defeat of the Persians at the Battle of Marathon in 490, and lived long enough to be appointed to the body assigned to respond to the disaster of Athens's invasion of Sicily during the Peloponnesian war. Politically influential, he was able to weather the rule of both Cimon and his successor Pericles, and was one of the commanders of the expedition Athens mounted against the island of Samos. Only seven of a body of work estimated at more than one hundred plays have come down to us—another gap in our full knowledge of who these Greeks were. Chronologically, he is the middle figure of the great three Greek playwrights, living between Aeschylus and Euripides. In 468, he defeated Aeschylus, then at the height of his career, in a contest.

Despite the traditional themes of the plays that have come down to us, Sophocles was something of an innovator. For example, some of the action takes place indoors, whereas until then the scenes had been set in front of the various buildings that frame the scenes. Further, Sophocles is believed to have been the first to add painted scenery. Most significantly, he apparently added a third speaking character; previously there had only been two, in addition to the chorus. Further, unlike, for example, the *Oresteia* of Aeschylus, these plays were not performed or written together; indeed, it seems that *Oedipus at Colonus* was not even performed until after Sophocles' death. Written at different periods of Sophocles' life, the plays focus on the story of the exceedingly ill-starred family of Oedipus, whose basic outline is familiar, even if only vaguely remembered from school. Jocasta and Laius, rulers of Thebes, are fated to have a son who will destroy his father and sleep with his mother. So when their son is born, he is abandoned and thought dead. Of course, he is not dead, and Oedipus grows up to fulfill the prophecy, returning to Thebes after accidentally killing his father. After marrying Jocasta and becoming ruler himself, he fathers the sisters Antigone and Ismene, and their brothers Polyneices and Eteocles.

*Oedipus Tyrannos* describes what happens when Oedipus, to his shame, learns the truth. He blinds himself and leaves Thebes. In *Oedipus at Colonus*, we find him after he has wandered around Greece, looking for solace. He dies at Colonus, near Athens, where Sophocles himself was born. In the presence of Theseus, ruler of Athens, Oedipus is taken by the gods after promising to watch over the city. The daughters return to Thebes where Oedipus' sons have taken over as co-rulers of the city, but they have a falling out. They fight and kill each other after Eteocles refuses to share power. In the third play (presented first here), Creon, Jocasta's brother, takes over and refuses to allow Antigone to bury Polyneices, who as a traitor to the city and a rebel can be denied these rights. Antigone does so anyway, and is killed. Creon does not escape either: his son Haemon and wife Eurydice kill themselves, he because of his love for Antigone, and she for love for her son.

The difficulty with translating ancient tragedy is that the language is often too arcane and too direct at the same time. Some of the lines, rendered literally, sound banal. Others, often those of the chorus, refer back to myths that needed little explanation to its original audience, but which can lose their force to contemporary audiences. Slavitt takes a couple of approaches to this problem. He divides up the chorus's lines among speakers denominated "First Chorister" or "Second Chorister." This loses something of the original, where the chorus speaks with one voice, but it enhances Sophocles' emphasis on the individual characters; there is more of a sense of conversation. The lines between characters come across as spare, even aphoristic, accurately reflecting the original. Witness this exchange between Creon and Tiresias, the blind prophet who tries to convince the king not to consign Antigone to death.

> TIRESIAS: Wisdom is a greater treasure than treasure.
> CREON: And foolishness is worse than any disease.
> TIRESIAS: That's what you have, and a very serious case.
> CREON: I dislike speaking rudely to a prophet.
> TIRESIAS: You want to tell me politely that I am wrong?
> CREON: There are some prophets in it for the money.
> TIRESIAS: And many rulers who turn out to be corrupt.

Tiresias is proven right, of course. Despite Creon's last-minute attempt to save Antigone, it is too late. Slavitt also preserves the formality of the text, which is a necessary component of the drama, without rigidity. For example, he renders as "Your words are hardly music to my ears" a line the standard Loeb gives as "canst thou not see/ That e'en this question irks me?" The Loeb is more literal, but Slavitt better conveys Creon's attitude.

The plays confront insurmountable confrontations of primal obligations, but they are usually misunderstood, especially by elite audiences who are unable to reinhabit the Greek worldview. *Antigone* is not, or is not primarily, about conscience, rights, or even resistance against oppression. The problem for Antigone is that her conscience is predetermined: she must bury her brother. Against Creon, she argues that "it was not Zeus who made that [Creon's] law, nor Justice who dwells with the gods below and rules in the world of men and women. Your edict was clear and strong, but not enough to suspend the written, unfailing laws of the gods who live forever." Of anyone, Ismene speaks what perhaps some of us are thinking: "You're a fool. But a good sister." Likewise with Oedipus, who, through no fault of his own, nevertheless remains condemned by the gods. Only at the end of his saga do we get a glimpse of what we may call redemption, when Oedipus is taken by the gods. But even that is ambiguous. The play ends with the chorus saying to Antigone and Ismene, who have been denied their father's burial place, "Accept that this is how things must be."

# PART EIGHT

## *America the Beautiful*

# *The Declaration Now—and Then*

**In 1996,** Barry Alan Shain published his *Myth of American Individualism: The Protestant Origins of American Political Thought.* It was a book that should have shaken professional conservatism to its foundations. At the time Patrick J. Buchanan was a standard-bearer for an America bound by a common cultural and religious tradition and was being resisted by a conservative "movement" that preferred a big-government conservatism based on abstractions and embodied in a centralized bureaucracy. Shain, a professor of history at Colgate University and a child of secular Los Angeles, argued that the generations leading up to and including the founding were not lovers of an abstract liberty or an untrammeled individualism. The sentiments and mores of the colonists were based not in Locke or some post-Renaissance "republicanism," but in small-town Calvinist Protestantism and a strong sense of the heritage of English liberty. This tradition undergirded the founding generations and continued long after the War of Independence.

The language of our founding documents, Shain argues, "does not describe an individualistic disposition. Rather, it reflects a Protestant communal world of ideas in which only a narrow range of behavior could be described as liberty rather than license." To be sure, Americans were influenced by different schools of thought, including classical republicanism and the conviction that the "science of politics...has received great improvement" (*Federalist* 9), owing to the work of theorists like Hobbes and Locke and, above all others, Montesquieu. This latter influence tended

Originally published in *Chronicles*, September 13, 2018.

to stress individual rights. However, the most important formative influence on the early republic remained "the reformed-Protestant character of their political thought, with particular emphasis placed on the strong sense of personal and political limits derived from the Christian dogma of original sin." One cannot, in other words, understand what the colonists were talking about when they discussed liberty or political order without understanding that they assumed the sinfulness of man, the human temptation to license and evil, and the corresponding need for God's grace. In this context, "rights" are more circumscribed and focused on preserving and furthering a truly common good, and liberty must be preserved so man may discover what is right and act upon it, not simply so that he may do whatever he wishes.

The idea that the colonies embodied a deeply Christian culture saturated in Reformed theology does not sit well with our contemporary understanding of the revolutionary generation. We tend to think of those eighteenth-century colonial leaders as protoliberals pursuing happiness apart from faith or custom. But Shain's work went unremarked by most of the conservative movement, even though it complemented the work of conservative thinkers such as Russell Kirk. Shain's work struck at certain conservative tropes, such as the conviction that the American political order expressed in the Declaration and the Constitution was some sort of content-free zone "of natural rights." Some modern conservatives, much as some liberals do, disdained colonial history as the story of small, Reformed Protestant communities. Morals and a common cultural understanding are all well and good, but not connected in any substantive way with the language of our founding documents. Willmoore Kendall, for example, famously criticized Kirk for arguing that our constitutional tradition was not really new. These conservatives rather found the entire American experiment a philosophic enterprise centered in the Declaration, which they considered (in the words of Harry Jaffa) "the best of all guides to educating the guardians of republican freedom."

The Declaration is of course important, but perhaps not so important as some of its partisans believe. It was the result of years-long jostling among the colonies to agree on their desired relationship with imperial Britain. In his new book *The Declaration of Independence in Historical Context*, Shain continues his assault on reigning pieties regarding both the Declaration and American political culture generally. The book is a sober, scholarly collection of just about all of the important writings on the subject. Shain selected his material from the three Continental Congresses that met in the period 1764–66, and again in 1774–77. Exhaustively edited and attractively presented, this book places the Declaration in a wider American and British imperial context and ranges from statements by the king through various resolutions of the colonies (and later, the states) to generous selections of letters and other memoranda. For this reason alone, the book will stand as a lasting scholarly resource.

Important interpretive questions remain, however, and Shain restates here his communalist Protestant position. The arguments of writers seeking to establish a primary role for Lockean and republican influences on the founding generations and the Declaration itself suffer from several flaws. The first is that these theories are "idealist in suggesting that well-developed high-level abstract political theories...served as the principal guides in directing North American colonists to resist British parliamentary imperial governance. . ." Further, they focus on the "we hold these truths" paragraph of the Declaration as "a stand-alone piece of political philosophy that uniquely gives full expression of the American mind circa 1776 while additionally providing that nation's founding and perpetual creed." Pulling back from a minute analysis of the text of the Declaration itself or of the mind of Jefferson, its primary drafter, permits us to look at hundreds of resolutions, statements, and other documents in the years leading up to 1776, many of which involved the very same men who would later vote to approve the edited draft of the Declaration. They display very little support for the contemporary view of the Declaration as the formative influence on the tradition of ordered liberty among the colonists.

This crucial period offers abundant evidence that leading colonists were obsessed with a particular point of British imperial policy: whether Parliament had the right to tax them directly, or whether the colonies stood in a direct relationship to the king as overseas possessions rather than as part of the British realm proper. Kirk, quoting the historian Daniel Boorstin, claimed that "the major issue of the American Revolution was the true constitution of the British Empire, which is a pretty technical legal problem." The Declaration is not only about legality, of course—though in form much of it is a legal brief, and Jefferson's prolix first draft was severely cut back—but to ignore that it is at least in part about legality is to do the Declaration, and by extension the circumstances leading to its promulgation, a disservice.

Shain has divided his book into "Acts," moving from the Stamp Act crisis of 1764–66 through the Coercive Acts in 1774 and the early fighting that produced the Declaration to the creation of the "New Nation" in 1776 and 1777. He has prefaced each section with a rich critical essay, outlining the issues at stake and the shifting positions of both the colonists and the British government on the road to independence. Shain portrays the story dramatically, especially in the period from October 1775 (when George III declared that the colonies were seeking to establish an "independent empire") through the early months of 1776, when the failure of the Canadian campaign became increasingly obvious and the last of those colonists still committed to king and empire began to feel independence was the only remaining option. As Shain shows, the stirring language of the Declaration in its assertion of individual rights is a departure from previous actions by the Continental Congresses. For the Declaration provides "a rich philosophical description of republican political theory, one at variance with the constitutional-monarchical principles and political institutions that three earlier Congresses had defended…" Thus, he concludes that the "We hold these truths" paragraph "turned to a heretofore more or less peripheral republicanism and natural rights theorizing in making its case for the colonies" to be recognized as independent states. And it is perhaps noteworthy that the changes made to Jefferson's draft largely let that paragraph stand and focused instead on the legal grievances against the king—supporting the view that its implications were not generally appreciated. Shain notes the irony of a congressional rejection of claims made in 1776–77 by residents of what was then part of New York to govern themselves rather than to be governed by the state of New York, even as they were relying on the language of the Declaration. And he includes in his book the congressional response of June 1777 to a protest by Vermonters that they could take "no countenance or justification" from the Declaration for their own acts. Self-government, it seems, only went so far.

Barry Shain does not go too far in speculating how Jefferson's stirring phrases came to be included in the final text, though he suggests that their inclusion reflects a long-standing political debate among the colonies, rather than any definitive understanding either of independence or of the basis for the constitutional order—a matter which was not to be considered until more than a decade had passed.

*The Declaration of Independence in Historical Context* fosters an understanding of the Declaration as the result of an awkward, complex competition of interests and ideas, undermining the Whiggish idea of a republican, individualist constitution. It helps us ponder anew just what kind of government the Constitution was meant to establish.

# The Founding Dialogue

**The success** of Lin-Manuel Miranda's *Hamilton* confirms that a large audience still welcomes stories about the founders' lives. But how well have their eighteenth-century *ideas* held up? In *An Argument Open to All: Reading "The Federalist" in the 21st Century*, Sanford Levinson asks this question of each of the eighty-five essays that constitute *The Federalist*, seeking to establish which of Publius' premises and principles should still guide us.

Levinson, a professor of government and law at the University of Texas at Austin, has long been one of the Constitution's most provocative liberal interpreters. He harbors "strong reservations" about our ability to determine the original meaning of constitutional phrases, and clearly believes that parts of the document, however interpreted, make little sense in contemporary America. Still, Levinson argues that "every one of the essays that make up *The Federalist* contains something that should spark our interest today."

Though concerned with the "science of politics," *The Federalist* is not a theoretical treatise, but an attempt to persuade a skeptical audience to adopt the new Constitution. Levinson draws a lesson from Publius' purpose: the Constitution's meaning is to be determined by the various branches of the federal government *and* the American people. Levinson seems to agree with opponents of judicial supremacy: Publius, he writes, "had only a limited faith in what we may term a 'legalized' Constitution, that is one consisting of commands, whose meanings, when ambiguous, should be resolved by judges whose authority gives them primacy over all

Originally published in *Claremont Review of Books*, September 6, 2016.

other interpreters." Judges are important, but "it would be a huge error to ignore the extent to which Publius relied far more on politics, in the highest sense of that term, including a widely shared commitment to 'prudence.'" The contours of that widely shared commitment are not to be invented by judges, in other words; they must reflect the actual political arrangements and understandings of the people themselves.

*Federalist* 78 contains the famous defense of judicial review. The judiciary can neither execute the laws nor spend the public money—it holds "neither sword nor purse," in Publius' phrase—making it the federal government's "least dangerous" branch. But it *can* override legislative enactments that contravene the Constitution. This power, says Publius, "only supposes that the power of the people is superior to both [branches]; and that where the will of the legislature, declared in its statutes, stands in opposition to that of the people, declared in the Constitution, the judges ought to be governed by the latter rather than the former." Thus, the nods toward "emerging international norms" that the Supreme Court occasionally indulges would have no place in a Publian political theory, since it entails the justices substituting their will and purposes for those of the people.

Publius, convinced only a few citizens would possess both the morals and the knowledge needed for judging well, anticipated that lifetime tenure would be sufficient to check judges' ambition for favor and advancement. Levinson is more skeptical: in our age of strong partisanship, lifetime tenure might entrench judges who promote their own ideological or partisan interests over the constitutional will of the people. Since the rise of an activist liberal judiciary in the 1960s, the idea that judges should push the nation toward certain partisan (usually progressive) conclusions has become standard. Watch any confirmation hearing and Publius' confidence in those few "who unite the requisite integrity with the requisite knowledge" will seem misplaced. The judiciary serves as a bulwark against the other branches when they overstep their bounds. When judges themselves exceed their bounds, however, politics intrudes into the world of law.

Publius defends the Constitution's institutional supports—the separation of powers chief among them—that restrict and counteract ambition.

He also presumes certain characteristics of the American people and their elected officials. Americans must respect institutional barriers to power, and govern according to "reflection and choice." But fruitful reflection requires a common set of assumptions about natural rights and the nature of government. Levinson highlights *Federalist* 2's intriguing language, where Publius stresses America's political stability rests on its people being "descended from the same ancestors, speaking the same language, professing the same religion, [and] attached to the same system of government." This was never strictly true, even in 1787. Many in the colonies and the new nation did not share those characteristics, and some were deliberately excluded from the political community. Nonetheless, Levinson invites us to consider whether cultural, linguistic, political, or historical homogeneity strengthens the republic. But such bonds cannot be the only support for constitutionalism. He nicely ties this theme to the need for a "veneration" of constitutional forms, discussed in *Federalist* 49, veneration that must be combined (if tensely) with devotion to public reason accessible to all citizens. The Founders envisioned a critical citizenry that all could join, but one whose criticism must be bounded by a respect for the constitutional structure that gives their criticism coherence.

Levinson is concerned, for example, about how large-scale immigration from countries without democratic traditions will affect our democratic decision-making. This is especially worrisome now that America's culture has lost confidence in its founding documents, and the system those documents established. When Harvard Law School strangles free speech, when the federal government threatens religious freedom, and when every discussion of the founding is preoccupied with denouncing evils of the founding generation, it is unsurprising that the institutional supports Publius relied on have been weakened. These considerations become all the more important in moments of crisis, such as 9/11. *Federalist* 40 and 41 seem to permit the government to set aside the "law" to preserve the nation. However, without a settled understanding from our own history and tradition, how can "we the people" know whether such "illegal" activities should be countenanced or condemned?

*The Federalist*, in Levinson's hands, becomes less a guidebook and more of a dialogue, one reminding and persuading us that a constitutional republic remains possible.

# *The Quintessential Founder: John Witherspoon*

WHO NOW REMEMBERS JOHN WITHERSPOON? Despite his many achievements—a celebrated pastor, president of Princeton, tutor to James Madison and other founders, and the sole cleric to sign the Declaration of Independence—Witherspoon has all but fallen through the memory hole of American history. And yet during his lifetime he was a giant figure in at least three areas in colonial and newly independent America: politics, religion, and education. His career has much to teach us about what we think we know about the founding generation. In this new book, *John Witherspoon and the Founding of the American Republic*, Jeffry Morrison, a professor of government at Regent University, has tried to solve the riddle of Witherspoon's disappearance.

Witherspoon (1723–1794) was a child of the Scottish Enlightenment, having been born in Scotland the same year as Adam Smith and educated at the University of Edinburgh. He was also a child of the Reformation, and was descended, according to family history, from John Knox. Witherspoon was a rising Presbyterian minister in Great Britain, and a well-known defender of the evangelical Popular party that opposed the more theologically liberal Moderate party in his church. He was invited to America by Benjamin Rush, by the trustees of the College of New Jersey at Princeton, as it was then known, and by the evangelist George Whitfield, whose preaching had touched off the first Great Awakening. This

Originally published in *Modern Age*, Spring 2006.

triple invitation presaged Witherspoon's later life in the colonies. Rush, of course, is numbered among the founders; Princeton is where Witherspoon would make his lifelong home; and Witherspoon would throw himself into the development of religious life in America through his participation in the councils of the Presbyterian Church.

Although he was one of the most influential Americans of the eighteenth century, Witherspoon has been overlooked by subsequent generations of historians. Morrison suggests a variety of practical and ideological reasons for this. As a general matter, Witherspoon did not leave many private papers or letters, unlike his more famous contemporaries, and his failure to sign the Constitution, despite his prominence, places him in the second rank.

While not an original intellect, Witherspoon made significant contributions to American letters that have been unjustly ignored by later scholars. For example, his *Lectures on Moral Philosophy* offered the first systematic treatment of moral philosophy published by an American, and he was also the author of the first American treatise on rhetoric. More generally, Morrison surmises that contemporary scholarship is uncomfortable with this minister-founder who "insisted on wearing his clerical garb to the Continental Congress" and who complicates many current notions on what the founding fathers intended.

In a chapter entitled, "Plain Common Sense," Morrison describes Witherspoon's interpretation of the Scottish Enlightenment. As the founding generation understood and used it, the phrase "common sense" expressed "experience and a common moral faculty" that people could use to make moral judgments about society and human nature. This approach, as developed by Scottish philosophers like Thomas Reid (1710–1796), was directed against those thinkers, such as David Hume, who questioned the ability of the mind to know the external world.

Witherspoon had largely adopted the views of the common sense school by the 1760s, and such a position happened to fit nicely with the emerging American character with its emphasis on "self-evident" truths that could be discerned through a faculty possessed by all people. (And let us not forget that Thomas Paine chose the phrase as the title of his influential pamphlet.) By the late 1770s, Witherspoon concluded, through the application of common sense, that it had become necessary (in the words of the Declaration) to "dissolve the political bands" that had connected the Americans to the United Kingdom. This thinking has obvious connections to Witherspoon's Reformation heritage, which likewise places its emphasis on each individual's personal quest for God.

The picture Morrison draws of Witherspoon's intellectual and religious life adds additional nuance to our understanding of the founding era. As he notes, the hegemonic vision of the founders as Lockean deists that held sway for decades has now been all but completely overthrown. A more complicated account has emerged, in which figures such as Witherspoon take on a more prominent place and other intellectual currents are unearthed and given their due weight.

Witherspoon himself combined the Scottish Enlightenment and the new political science of Locke with the heritage of John Calvin. While influenced by Locke, Witherspoon did not take him whole; as Morrison writes, "Witherspoon also pursued a more explicitly Christian formulation of the state of nature than Locke," due in part to the "deep impress of the Reformation" upon him, which shaped his outlook on republican government. In particular, Morrison notes, Witherspoon accepted Locke's thesis on the importance of sense experience as the means by which humans come to know the world, but he rejected Locke's strict empiricism. Instead, he argued that there were some innate ideas, "truths" that sense experience could discover, but which existed independently of the human mind. Thus, for example, the book of nature could be gleaned for evidence of a Providential design.

The influence of political theory on the founding can easily be exaggerated. Americans were a practical people, not much engaged in idle speculation, and theory was most often used merely as a springboard to consider what worked. Morrison retrieves, for example, interesting excerpts from founders as diverse as Adams and Jefferson casting scorn on the dreamy Plato in favor of the more practical Aristotle. In short, the founding generation comfortably inhabited a colonial political world in which Calvinist theology, natural-rights theory, and British republicanism jostled one against the other to form the backdrop for thinking about revolution.

And think about revolution Witherspoon did, with relish. He is said to have been one of the first in the colonies publicly to call for independence. In 1768, the year Witherspoon arrived in American, John Hancock had forced a showdown with the British over inspections in Boston and John Dickinson's *Letters from a Farmer in Pennsylvania* were published. The next year Witherspoon honored Hancock with an honorary degree, thus signaling his sympathies with the colonies, and wrote approvingly of Dickinson's *Letters*. He served on New Jersey's committee of correspondence during the War for Independence, signed the Declaration and the Articles of Confederation, and helped ratify the Constitution in 1787 as a member of the New Jersey legislature. Indeed, Witherspoon played a crucial role in the July 1776 debates leading up to the Declaration.

The more conservative Dickinson had argued that independence was too precipitous a step for the colonies to take, and he counseled caution. Witherspoon responded that the colonies were ready for and needed independence, and were "in danger of becoming rotten for the want of it." Witherspoon's arguments helped carry the day, and for the next six years, until he left the Congress in 1782, he was a central figure, serving on many committees and being asked, in 1781, to draw up instructions for the peace commission in France. So well known was Witherspoon that the Scottish philosopher Adam Ferguson in a 1778 letter places "Johnny Witherspoon," his former classmate, at the head of the rebels.

The only reason Witherspoon was not present as an influential voice in the Constitutional Convention itself in 1787 was sheer happenstance, but the circumstances demonstrate Witherspoon's character. He was himself in Philadelphia that summer, but had been committed a year before to be a delegate to the Presbyterian Synod of New York and Philadelphia, which was meeting in the city at the same time as the Constitutional Convention. Witherspoon spent that summer debating and drafting a constitution (called the "Form of the Government")—but a constitution for the Presbyterian Church, not for the new nation being born at the same time.

As a result of Witherspoon's efforts, the Presbyterian Church was in effect nationalized, with a common catechism and other documents. Both his civil and his ecclesiastical reforms were aimed toward the same end: to inculcate "the ideas and habits of independence." Political constitutions were necessary, but not sufficient, to hold the new nation together; as probably the most powerful intermediary institution in the country, the Presbyterian Synod was an instrument for Witherspoon to stabilize the political victory of 1787.

Although the New Jersey's delegation to the Constitutional Convention arrived without him, Witherspoon was nonetheless there in spirit. Five of his Princeton students, including James Madison, were present. A sixth founder, Alexander Hamilton, was not a Princeton student, but he came to rely on Witherspoon nonetheless in the area of political economy. Morrison explains that Hamilton asked Witherspoon's input prior to writing his "Report Relative to a Provision for the Support of Public Credit" in 1790. Witherspoon responded, and his ideas made their way into Hamilton's report. Unfortunately, Morrison does not provide much detail about what Hamilton borrowed, though he does discuss Witherspoon's defense of hard currency against paper money. Morrison discusses more fully the debt of the authors of the *Federalist* to Witherspoon, noting general influences as well as specific phrasings from papers by Madison and Hamilton that echo Witherspoon.

As "the prototype of the political parson," Witherspoon's understanding of the connections between civil society and religious faith reflected the way in which he synthesized his Enlightenment and Reformed backgrounds within the new American context. He did not advocate what we now term "establishment," but nor did he adopt the anachronistic "separation" between church and state. He was rather solidly in the mainstream of American founding thought in believing that a religious people fostered civic virtue. He was quite convinced, as the author of government-sponsored Thanksgiving prayers perhaps should be, that America owed its existence to the Creator who bestowed self-evident truths upon humanity. Nevertheless, because of his fluency with the many intellectual traditions coursing through the founding era, Witherspoon was quite capable of speaking with sensitivity to audiences beyond his own Protestant fold. In his respect for the civil opinions of others, without compromising on the larger truths of the American experiment, Witherspoon was a prototypical American.

With this book, Morrison has engaged in an act of recovery. Getting to know Witherspoon helps us know aright the other founders and gives us a deeper understanding of the world that created a new nation.

# *Forgotten Founder, Drunken Prophet*

❧

History, it is often said, is written by the winners. The people who say that, however, have never met Bill Kauffman. Since his groundbreaking 1995 study of the America First movement Kauffman has been at the forefront of a new generation of writers for whom the American past is rich with opposition to the corporatist, centralized political and cultural life our democratic capitalism has bought us. Living in his hometown of Batavia, New York, he has reimagined American history to encompass traditions from the Anti-Federalists to Dorothy Day, the opponents of the Interstate Highway System to Gore Vidal, and that has a place for localists of all stripes. Kauffman's most recent contribution is his brief biography of Luther Martin (1748–1826), entitled *Forgotten Founder, Drunken Prophet*, as part of ISI's "Forgotten Founders" series. Martin and his generation get the full Kauffman treatment, as this brave but flawed Marylander is placed at the heart of a debate over what kind of nation would the thirteen colonies become. Martin ended his life as a cantankerous, impoverished drunken mess, but had a long career as a statesman and a lawyer, serving, among other things, as Attorney General of Maryland for almost thirty years and as one of Aaron Burr's defense lawyers in his trial for killing Hamilton.

Kauffman starts with the starkest reality of the American founding: the founders were not supposed to rip up the Articles of Confederation and start to create a government from scratch. Martin, among a few others, smelt a trap, and pounced. He opposed the secrecy of the proceedings,

Originally published in *The Chesterton Review*, XXXV, 3–4, 2008.

for example, and the efforts to effectively nullify the power of the state governments. He spoke, for example, for hours against the Virginia Plan, which favored the large states. In the end, he refused to sign the document emanating from Philadelphia, in part from its lack of respect for federalism and his fear that without a bill of rights, the national government would crush local liberty. Martin raged against almost every aspect of then proposed national compact. Against the six-year terms of Senators, he said, "If [a Senator] has a family, he will take his family with him to the place where the government shall be fixed, that will become his home, and...his future views and prospects will center in the favours and emoluments... of the general government." Paging Senator...well, almost any of them. In the end, Martin's eloquence won few victories, the most important being securing the rights of the smaller states in the Senate.

Martin's speeches during the Convention still read full of ire, amplified by Kauffman's sprightly and impassioned prose. In his notes to the Convention, Madison described one of Martin's tirades as "delivered with much diffuseness and considerable vehemence." After the Convention, Martin became an "Anti-Federalist," the unfortunately named (as they were, after their fashion, actually supporters of a decentralized federation) losers in the constitutional battle when the Constitution was taken on the road for ratification. The winners in the debate, James Madison, for example, or Alexander Hamilton, come off here—from their own words—as defenders of big government, monarchism, and opponents of the true "Spirit of '76"—not quite the history that's taught today, and more is the pity. Martin's fight was with those who wished to scrap the Articles of Confederation in favor of a document that minimized local rights and threatened individual liberties. In the end he could not put his name to the document, and walked out of the Convention because of his concern for the states and individual liberties. The quotes Kauffman unearths by Madison and others about their interest in abolishing the states and making them provinces of a central government makes you glad Martin was there to hold them off (at least for a while, some might say). But these positions did not endear him to his victorious contemporaries or to later historians, especially progressives for whom the argument of men like Martin was beyond the pale.

Martin was a difficult man, at best, even during the height of his brilliant career. In a vignette that speaks volumes about eighteenth-century life, the Maryland bar levied a tax on its members to support Martin in his destitute old age, in recognition of his services. Yet, although a "loser," after a fashion, he represents a tradition that deserves not to be forgotten.

# *The Truth About America's Civil Religion*

❧

THE RECENT RETIREMENT of Derek Jeter's Yankees jersey number had all the marks of a civic ceremony. Old legends and dignitaries were paraded on the field, a plaque presented, and highlight reels played. It was a ritual in every way perhaps but name. Indeed, baseball is one of the nation's most lasting and popularly observed elements of our civil religion. The national anthem, "God Bless America" in the seventh inning, the salute to veterans: each of them is an element in the contemporary American understanding of itself. It is no wonder, then, that baseball has been a frequent subject of conservative commentators as an expression of the national mind. Even Jeter's personal selection of the day for the ceremony—Mother's Day—is an illustration of how public events are commemorated or valued. Religious and even civic holidays fade into the background; others rise to take their place.

To baseball, we can add other elements of the American civil religion: heroes and villains, national memories and documents, military victories and defeats. Debates over subjects from the presence of Confederate monuments on public spaces to immigration are just different expressions of an ongoing conversation about who we are. What gets complicated, and contentious, is when the civil religion changes. Philip Gorski, in his striking new book, *American Covenant: A History of Civil Religion from the Puritans to the Present*, on American civil religion, does not mention baseball or other popular expressions of our civil religions, of which more later. Rather, Gorski explores the key thinkers who shaped the different strands

---

Originally published in *The American Conservative*, August 28, 2017.

of our civil religion. Even better, especially coming from the progressive academy, the book opens with a strong defense of tradition.

Tradition is the intellectual world we live in; although we can examine our tradition critically, we cannot look from "outside" our tradition. And it is certainly not opposed to "reason;" indeed, tradition is in some ways a prerequisite to rational discussion. Moreover, tradition is not fixed, but can be changed by thoughtful emendation, or it can be corrupted and abandoned by thoughtless disregard. He helpfully identifies four characteristics of tradition: canon, archive, pantheon, and narrative. He does this for two reasons: first, to show liberals that tradition is something to value, not disdain, and second, to combat the conservative complaint of a culture in decline. If we can identify the sources of our tradition, we can revive those that are most important.

Gorski, a professor of sociology at Yale, begins with the basic dichotomy of American civil religion, drawing on Robert Bellah's distinction between "covenantal religion" and what he calls "civic republicanism." The former is the largely dissenting Protestant groups who settled America; as Barry Shain and other historians have noted, the American colonists were basically scattered groups of evangelical Protestants. Civic republicanism, on the other hand is a different tradition derived from the example of the ancient republics of Greece and Rome. But Gorski adds an additional pair of approaches, what he calls radical secularism and religious nationalism. Radial secularism is the younger of the two, arising really only with the progressive era of early twentieth century. Religious nationalism is older, and has gone through several iterations, in which America is seen as a godly nation with a divine mission.

However, between the radicals of either side "leaves the rest of us: those of us who don't confuse democracy with empire, who don't think we have a monopoly on truth or morality, who don't believe that religion is always a source of oppression, and who don't think science has all the answers. Or, in positive terms, those of us who are committed enough to the dream of the righteous republic to talk and maybe even walk across the deep trenches that were dug during the culture wars." The righteous republic is

Gorski's term for what he also calls the "vital center," a term made famous by Arthur Schlesinger, Jr. This tradition is stronger than its counterparts, for various reasons. The radical secular view has emphasized autonomy—a legitimate strain of the American civil religion, just not the only one—and will not accept a compromise on protection of endless self-liberation. The religious fundamentalist view has the opposite problem: its correlation between theological orthodoxy and American power prevents it from reaching out to the many well-intentioned Americans without religious commitments. But a righteous republic combines both: a government that is composed of free citizens of all faiths and of none, but one that requires non-governmental limits and civic virtue, including the virtues that can be inculcated by religion.

One key event that changed the nation's civic culture was the Second World War. The war and the subsequent fight against communism undermined two crucial components of the "old" civic republican tradition: fear of a standing army and the association of freedom with commercial prosperity. These two offshoots of the older civil republican tradition still bedevil conservatives. Many seem to think the military and the industries that support it are bulwarks of "the American way" rather than solvents of family and community bonds. The connection between economic growth and the nation is likewise mistaken. Love of money is the root of all evil, as one founding book of our civil religion tells us; and economic man is not necessarily the same as a free republican citizen.

The example of Martin Luther King, Jr. is also an important one in Gorski's telling. I'm old enough to remember when the Martin Luther King, Jr. Day was first established in the 1980s, much to the chagrin and opposition of conservatives. King was a womanizer and a leftist, the arguments went, and why should the country give up a day in honor of Washington or Lincoln to honor a controversial figure? These conservatives were wrong to oppose this inclusion of the holiday, and missed an opportunity to widen the conservative appeal to racial minorities. King, whatever his faults, was a great American, and one deeply placed in the American tradition. Gorski makes a compelling case that he was able to expand the promise of civil religion, to fully include African Americans in the national experiment, precisely because he was working within a tradition whose language and principles could be understood by other Americans. In this context, Gorski brings out the thought of Frederick Douglas, as someone who changed the nation's view of "political time." Rather than moving back to a golden age, Douglas was one who pushed forward what the founding documents meant, in particular he and others "broke once and for all the inegalitarian legacy of classical republicanism."

Gorski has written an intellectual history centered on ideas and thinkers rather than institutions, power relationships, or popular culture. And he is right to focus on the very real ideologies of radical secularism and religious nationalism and threats to a center that is very much worth reviving. But the challenge is that the center can be too static. Changes to the civil religion often come from the margins, as each side tries to pull the civil religion in their direction. Thus compare King with the current controversies around "cultural appropriation." This is not a real outgrowth of the civil religion but an imposition of an ideology. There is no real grammar or discourse around what can be culturally appropriated, and it runs counter to a long American tradition of a relatively free mixing of culture, cuisine, and styles.

This points to one minor amendment to Gorski's learned and thoughtful analysis (aside from a quibble that Gorski takes, I think, at face value too much of Obama's civic rhetoric). It is true that religious nationalism "is often accompanied by ritual violence against cultural and racial 'others'" who threaten the godly order. Religious nationalists often simply object to their opponents with the language of sin or the mistaken view that Christianity and American patriotism are the same thing. But the common mode of radical secularists is also theological, in a way that Gorski perhaps underplays. That is, both play with apocalyptic tropes and the current progressive left, with its own rituals and purges, seems just as theological as the religious nationalists Gorski has in mind. Gorski calls out the "Enlightenment fundamentalists" who "insist that science has all the answers and will not deign to enter into dialogue with the great unwashed." True, but as the description reveals, the "science" of at least some of these fundamentalists is simply a god in a lab coat.

Which leads us back to that ceremony at Yankee Stadium. As historians like Christopher Dawson like to remind us, people naturally seek the transcendent. It is the tragedy of recent American history that we have lost that common language, ether of a shared theology or devotion to republican principles. More people have seen Jeter play than ever will read Cotton Mather or James Madison, much less Arendt or Douglas. Video games, sports, and concerts are the main sources of engagement in our time, and they largely reflect the liberal secularism described here. Gorski has set the intellectual baseline to understand the differing strands of our civil religion. Those who wish to preserve the vital center need to translate those strands into a new fabric for the vital center.

# *Lessons on Citizenship, Place, and a Humane Economy*

Land and Liberty: The Best of Free America, a handsome, lavishly produced book, rescues from obscurity a critical piece of American intellectual and literary history. Among the many disruptions the Second World War caused was the realignment of American ideological camps. The long American tradition of populism and decentralization was reaching new heights in the 1930s in the face of rapid social and economic dislocation, but it was derailed by the postwar fight against communism. As a result, a strong national government was defended by "conservatives" mobilizing in response to the threat of the Soviet Union, which also helped big business position itself as a defender of freedom. With this collection, we see a different America, where those championing the values of community also opposed rampant capitalism in a way that became foreign to conservatives for decades. In an age suffering from recurrent polio outbreaks, the Great Depression, the emergence of fascism abroad, and centralization (governmental and commercial) at home, *Free America* asked questions about sufficiency, citizenship, economics, and governance in defining and defending the kind of citizens the country needed.

*Free America* reflected that critical moment of realignment, as the older, more quixotic America was eclipsed by more ideologically driven camps. It was a quixotic, composite project, intentionally so, of two main groups. On the one hand were the Southern Agrarians, especially the

Originally published in *The American Conservative*, June 28, 2020.

Twelve Southerners who published *I'll Take My Stand* in 1930. This group, loosely affiliated with Vanderbilt University, included Allen Tate, Donald Davidson, Andrew Nelson Lytle, and John Crowe Ransom. The Statement of Principles to that book states that the "communities and private persons sharing the agrarian tastes are to be found widely within the Union. Proper living is a matter of the intelligence and the will, does not depend on the local climate or geography, and is capable of a definition which is general and not Southern at all."

Tate thought that the book's title was needlessly adversarial and would invite dismissal from critics; his proposed title, *Tracts Against Communism*, perhaps better conveyed the focus of at least some of its contributors. Tate proved prescient. As it happened, the Agrarian critique of urbanism, industrialism, and centralization was overshadowed by a perception that it was simply a defense of the South, including its racial hierarchies—a criticism that is not without some support. Six years later, some of the Twelve Southerners would join with future *Free America* contributors and others to publish *Who Owns America?* The title indicated a more direct attack on the concentrations of wealth and power.

On the other hand were the distributists, a more loosely-organized group of economists, writers, publicists, and dreamers located mostly in the North, who traced their lineage to other sources. Most of these sources were English, such as G.K. Chesterton and Hilaire Belloc, but they also included native influence such as the tax theories of Henry George and the Catholic rural life movement. But they too were overwhelmed by the war, and much of the infrastructure and momentum of the distributist and agrarian revival of the 1930s was gone by, say, 1948.

*Free America* lasted until 1946, and original copies are exceedingly difficult to find. The journal was the brainchild of three people: Herbert Agar, Ralph Borsodi, and Chauncey Stillman. Agar is perhaps the best known of the three. Although born in New Rochelle, New York, Agar spent time in London where he worked for *G.K.'s Weekly*, among other journals, and absorbed distributist arguments about the dangers of concentrated power and property whether denominated "socialist" or "capitalist." In 1933, he won the Pulitzer Prize for his history of the presidency, which draws on distributist arguments to make the case that the country was founded by "small farmers, artisans, and merchants, with productive property owned by the vast majority of families."

Borsodi was a more straightforward anarchist, and advocated intendent, fully productive homesteads. Stillman perhaps balanced the two. He was no stranger to concentrations of wealth—he came from a wealthy Texas family whose ancestor was a founder of what became Citigroup—but he turned his attention rather to the country life than finance. He agreed to finance *Free America* but made additional substantive editorial contributions of his own, especially in the area of sustainable and innovative farming, which were methods he practiced at his estate in the small New York town of Amenia. His essay, "Challenge to Famine," argues for biodynamic farming as a solution to soil exhausted by factory farming methods.

In his excellent introduction to *Land and Liberty*, Allan Carlson puts these disparate movements into context. Despite policy and practical disagreements, the editors "would test every existing or proposed economic, political and social matter by a common measure: how the things at issue would affect the small and the human." In the inaugural issue, Agar makes the point that the contributors were united in their opposition to collectivism and plutocracy, and the journal would serve as "the meeting ground for those who are equally opposed to finance-capitalism, communism, and fascism," which were incompatible with democracy, since democracy could only survive when anchored by the widespread possession of property. The journal gathered contributors across from what we now would consider the ideological spectrum. Belloc contributed an essay, on "The Enemy," as did the editor of *Commonweal*, Michael Williams, on "The Great Tradition."

The journal combined theoretical analyses, like Borsodi's two-part essay on decentralization, with more practical concerns. (Carlson includes samples in sections titled "Recovering Homecraft," "The Productive Home," and "Practical Homesteading.") The underlying theme of both kinds of articles was, as Wilson says in his afterword, "the belief that cultural form, the way of life of a people, is partly dependent on the material 'base' or economic structure." This is no Marxist notion, but reflects a simple truth. If a society valorizes (and materially rewards) the high-flying management consultant who leaves her home to live in temporary dwellings across the country (or world) through much of her early adult life, then that creates a certain type of culture. A society that counsels instead that the children of management consultants should go out into the country to start a farm and reject the global capitalist machine would create another, even if not every institution in the country were run on distributist bases. Similarly with property: a society that believes intangible financial "assets" create and sustain wealth in the same way as actual goods and skills will reflect that belief in its societal arrangements.

Now, one should not idolize farming. It can be hard, grueling work. The distributist idea fails if it is to force everyone to be a small-scale farmer. Rather, the idea is to recognize that the material conditions that create massive agricultural concerns may not be as economical as advertised, and also that the culture such concentrations create is incompatible with a free society. In this connection it may be worth noting the antipathy most *Free America* writers had towards war, and for the same reason: it favors bigness, which in turn transforms free citizens into "consumers" and derails improvements in technology or machinery that could have been for the benefit of all.

The mistake critics of distributism or agrarianism often make is in thinking that writers like those in *Free America* required a country to be all distributist, or agricultural, or not at all. Instead, it is the mass culture that requires uniformity and projects onto distributism a totalizing attitude distributism largely lacks. I see no necessary problem in a distributist society with large cities or large-scale industry, and indeed debate over how to combine distributist principles with America as it then existed peppers the pages of *Free America*. The options are varied, as H.A. Highstone noted in a 1943 essay. The challenge is in forming institutions such that they serve the citizens, rather than vice versa.

In one sense, the world conveyed in this book is now almost impossible to imagine. It is an America where many people were still familiar with the rhythms of rural life and the scrim of machinery and technology had not obscured the natural realities of community. The yeoman farmer as the national role model yielding to the soldier, the factory worker, the ad man, the "knowledge worker," and the town or small city to the "metropolis." In 2020, for example, it is difficult to see how we might turn away from mass agriculture, but it is not difficult to imagine an economic system that favors families and communities over financial institutions and global corporations.

And even mass agriculture need not be accepted as is. In "Fallacy of Mass Production," Borsodi sounds at first unrealistic in railing against the evils of factory flour production in 1937, but his point makes more sense now, perhaps. It is not simply the means of production (mass versus artisanal). Rather, one should look at "the part which favoritism in freight rates, taxation and other forms of government assistance to manufacturers played in enabling the 'giant' mills to undersell their smaller competitors," allowing these favored enterprises to engage in predatory pricing and misleading advertising with the public.

In considering the future of distributism, Peter van Dresser expressed a "degree of discouragement" given the explosive growth of the state and corporate power but hoped that distributive principles could be "an 'enclave' within our present managerial civilization" and "broaden its associations and alliances." Still good advice, seventy years on.

# *The Uses of American Government*

❧

THAT THE REPUBLIC has degenerated from a Protestant-inflected localized republic to a centralized bureaucratic imperial state is something most conservatives take for granted. The reason for such a transformation, however, sometimes becomes more assumed than proved. This compounds the difficulty of convincing liberals, and even some "conservatives," that such a transformation has occurred. The secular Whiggism of the major media outlets and academia is so overwhelming that actual American history is obscured or willfully ignored. Since the 1960's, the aggrandizement of the central government and the judiciary by both parties has effectively effaced real federalist checks on national power. Local differences in political habits or mores are treated with suspicion or as obstacles to "rights" rather than as a support for liberty.

Even among conservatives this history is largely unknown despite three decades of "conservative dominance" of the Republican Party. The establishment conservatism of the Beltway and Wall Street similarly see centralization as inevitable, though for them it is usually hidden behind the economic language of "efficiency" or culture-war language that mirrors the ideological obsessions of the left. Invocations of federalism, as in the gay-marriage debates, are not serious because judicial interference or executive orders are invoked on subsequent issues, if such would further a political agenda. There are some exceptions, of course. The Southern Agrarians were strong proponents of federalism. Russell Kirk wrote important pieces on federalism and Orestes Brownson's view of "territorial

Originally published in *Chronicles*, April 2014.

democracy." More recently, Bill Kauffman has excavated a regionalist antiwar tradition of which more conservatives should be aware, and others, such as Gore Vidal, have focused on the depredations of Washington.

The general neglect of what is perhaps the most distinctive American contribution to political thought is curious because, as Jeff Taylor notes in *Politics on a Human Scale: The American Tradition of Decentralism*, "Americans have traditionally been suspicious of highly centralized government because it tends to be directed by remote elitists and administered by remote bureaucrats." Both the Tea Party and the Occupy movement represent aspects of what has long been mainstream American opinion on government, money, and the role of each in a republic:

> Both are frustrated with a corporate-dominated status quo where Washington seems to be a rigged game while the middle class—or the 99 percent—are given empty promises by politicians who are discreetly leased by a financial elite.

The objects of their opposition may differ, but they both reflect a long-standing American distaste for the centralization of power. Unfortunately, the two movements share another characteristic all too common in American opposition movements: Both are in the process of being completely taken over by the organs of the political establishment and the financial interests that support the establishment.

For Taylor, decentralism comprises four elements: democracy, liberty, community, and morality. Thomas Jefferson is initially the central figure here, as his work includes aspects of all four of the decentralist elements; Taylor explains why this makes Jefferson of continuing importance to the American political conversation. In a sense, Taylor bases his history on the classic Jeffersonian-Hamiltonian dichotomy. There remain two ways of seeing America, and where many pundits and politicians use Jeffersonian rhetoric, Taylor exposes the Hamiltonian language underneath.

*Federalism* is a useful term, but the perspective Taylor delineates is broader than a simple adherence to the division of power between the national government on the one hand and state governments on the other. Rather, it means "minimalistic government at every level." It is a liberty-biased perspective that provides the overarching principle of particular decisions and arrangements of government power. The people who hold a decentralist position range from ethnic enclaves who want to preserve their cultures to secular liberals; as Taylor notes, the arguments for decentralization have appeal across the spectrum, in part because these arguments transcend that spectrum.

Taylor is charitable to all sides, and he acknowledges the disasters of the American experiment in regionalism, including Jim Crow. He resists demonizing those who sought greater centralization or to destroy communities; such results need not have been a reflection of evil motives. Nor is there an easy urban-rural divide to draw. Although in some circumstances rural life tends to reinforce those virtues and habits supportive of Taylor's four elements, that need not always, or exclusively, be the case. Indeed, given the desolation of America's rural communities in the present day—thanks to the centralization the great Midwestern tradition embodied by William Jennings Bryan and Robert La Follette tried to stem—towns and other urban areas may be more fertile sources of decentralist resistance right now. Taylor's analysis is generous enough to include this possibility, as well as to give respectful attention to progressive or other movements whose aims are inspired by decentralist ideas.

Decentralization is no sure cure for political ills, but that is the point. Government power—contrary to fantasists of both parties—cannot solve all human problems, nor cure the effects of original sin. The argument for widely dispersed power is prudential as much as principled. "The existence of a multitude of small-scale sovereignties provides for avenues of individual escape if community reform cannot be achieved." Having many points of government power reduces the malevolent reach of any one of them. It is a simple truth that has been sent down the memory hole, replaced by the assumption that individual wants must trump, with government power if necessary, the considered views of the community; and that these wants, moreover, must be uniformly enforced across the nation.

This book is engagingly written, and the notes and source materials would provide the raw materials for a true conservative renaissance. The text itself, after an introductory chapter setting the stage, is divided into eight chapters tracing the decline and fall of the decentralist ideal in each of the major political parties, as well as three appendices dealing with William H. Murray and George C. Wallace as "other populists with national ambitions," Woodrow Wilson, and the tale of Thomas Bayard and Grover Cleveland.

Perhaps the high points in the political influence of the American decentralist tradition occurred during the late nineteenth and early twentieth centuries, and again just after World War II. In a chapter titled "The Path Not Taken by the Progressive Era and New Deal," Taylor discusses the Jeffersonian tradition as it was embodied and sustained by the once immensely popular but now almost forgotten Bryan and La Follette. These men were progressives, but not progressives as we understand them; no proponents of the modern welfare state (as they are often claimed to be), they were rather "Midwestern agrarians [who], being populists, disliked unnatural largeness in the economic and political spheres." Taylor carefully documents how important progressive goals were subverted by the centralizing impulse. Thus, history books credit—when they mention them at all—progressives like Bryan with the crusade against the trusts. That may be true, but the federal agencies and laws established to fight the trusts worked against the progressives' goals, which were to disperse the power of enforcement in order to prevent the trusts from doing what they eventually did—control agencies like the Federal Trade Commission and, at a financial level, the Federal Reserve. "[O]ne wonders," Taylor wryly notes, "if occurrences of bait and switch can really be tallied as wins for the agrarian movement."

The Southern Democrats, perhaps the most Jeffersonian wing of their party, maintained this tradition the longest, by Taylor's estimate through the 1970's. But they too have largely succumbed, in part because of their own centralizing compromises but also because even

> when they were at their most conservative they often expended their political capital to conserve the worst of their traditions. By invoking states' rights in defense of segregation, they used an honorable means for a dishonorable end.

Indeed, the unimaginative recalcitrance of Southern conservatives on civil rights has perhaps been the most severe blow to the decentralist cause, and any evocation of states' rights or federalism remains tainted, even when it is used by those with no connection with, or interest in, the South.

Taylor is no less sparing in his assessment of the Republicans: "Decentralization of power—at home and abroad—is not a priority for most Republican administrations and legislators because they like power...as long as it is wielded by themselves and their allies." They too battled intramurally over what kind of America they stood for. On the one hand was the Eastern financial and political establishment, represented by such figures as Wendell Willkie. This wing has triumphed, perhaps permanently, over the more conservative segments of the party. In retrospect, the Reagan years have made no difference at all and indeed may have made conservatism's position worse, Reagan having cloaked even solid conservative impulses in universalist rhetoric lifted from Thomas Paine.

As an historian, Taylor can be said to argue simply not to put your trust in princes. Elites, especially Eastern elites, will always choose centralized power over geographical and political diversity. But the other crucial contribution Taylor makes is to draw the connections between and among the men and women who have decided America's fate. Elite Americans sometimes like to believe that abstract principles govern human affairs: "equality," perhaps, for the left, and "capitalism," typically, for the right. Taylor acknowledges the force of ideas, but it makes a difference when these ideas are discussed, and by whom. That George W. Bush's Cabinet was composed of men of his father's era, who shared old connections with the Eastern Republican establishment, is significant. That Rockefeller interests were so closely intertwined with one of the nation's largest banks over generations is important. Taylor, without unduly attributing people's views solely to their backgrounds, nevertheless puts in fuller context the facts of how political change is affected in this country. This is humane history, in other words, which paints the individual at the center of historical change.

*Politics on a Human Scale* is both solid history and inspiring polemic. Although as an historian Taylor takes a pessimistic view, he retains a Christian hope that the current moment provides an opportunity to revive a humane political tradition. Let us hope that he is right.

# PART NINE

## *Understanding the Culture*

# *Liberalism: The Great Anti-Tradition*

❧

Writing in 1955, Russell Kirk cited the German thinker Carl J. Friedrich to the effect that "[T]o all intents and purposes, the United States is today a highly traditional society, in the sense that arguments from tradition carry a great deal of conviction." Few would agree now, or at least not in the way Kirk intended. What defines much of American popular discourse today, among elites especially, is a conviction that appeals from authority not only have little resonance but also that tradition itself is suspect. Or to be more specific, reliance on tradition for any authoritative position that would restrict or limit individual freedom is almost completely out of bounds. In other words, tradition can be discussed only where it has no authority. Thus, we see attacks on institutions and practices—the Boy Scouts, Catholic schools, gender-specific sports—that are seen to embody "traditions" that are not inclusive.

Tradition is one way, we are told, that conservatives differ from liberals. Conservatives wish to conserve something; liberals, supposedly, do not. Indeed, liberalism is the great anti-tradition. But too often conservatives are left to mount only an attenuated defense of tradition; they seek to show liberals that some practice or tradition is in accord with "reason" and therefore sensible to retain, or that submitting to a tradition is more useful or advantageous than not. But this ultimately is no defense of tradition at all. It values tradition only insofar as it meets the standard of some other metric, such as utility, or it assumes the liberal separation of tradition from "reason" as valid, when it is not.

Originally published in *The American Conservative*, April 22, 2019.

In that same essay, Kirk distinguished between tradition and ideology. "Individualism" or "democracy" in the abstract, he thought, could not form a tradition. Although Kirk's rejection of ideology is controversial in some conservative circles, in general he meant an overarching system that purported to give answers to all earthly problems, typically imposed by a self-selected political elite. Traditions, in contrast, "are not abstractions; they are particular beliefs and customs closely related to private life and faith. The American Republic has its traditions, and so has the Cambodian Kingdom; but traditions are not created by political authority, and ought not to be debased into party slogans."

Because traditions are not ideological, there could be several kinds within a political community. In America, the bulk of traditions come from the Christian religion and our British heritage, though there are pockets of French and Spanish traditions as well. "These traditions are very numerous, and some are in conflict with others," Kirk said, "yet, provisionally, we may take for examples of American traditions such received opinions as the following: belief in a spiritual order which in some fashion governs our mundane order; belief in political self-government; belief in the importance to human persons of certain natural private rights; belief in the value of marriage and the family."

Now that may all be well and good, but how do we know when a tradition should change, and how do we determine how people should think about and defend traditions? The recent debate over Confederate statues and monuments is one example. Some conservatives argued for them to be kept as a recognition of history, but others argued they did not represent the best of our traditions—better to have monuments to the Underground Railroad and its heroes, for example. This major study from Mark T. Mitchell is titled *The Limits of Liberalism: Tradition, Individualism, and the Crisis of Freedom*, but one of its main themes is how we can think about tradition, because one of the things that has become clear from the body of conservative thought is that we are tradition-making animals.

We are, in George Scialabba's words, "situated beings" living in a particular place and time with family and economic circumstances that shape us. Even when we are thrust into an unfamiliar situation, we take our traditions with us and seek to recover them, or to adapt them, in order that we may retain them. An example based on historical precedent is the TV series *Deadwood*. Deadwood was an actual town in South Dakota which for a brief period was "without law," since the law of no state nor of the U.S. Constitution applied to it. Yet it mimicked—at some points less well than others—the traditions its inhabitants brought from elsewhere.

Mitchell recognizes that "an errant account of tradition may entail an errant account of knowing, which in turn may give birth to social and political maladies." One kind of errant account of tradition is evident in liberalism. The liberal person is an autonomous self whose ultimate goal is liberation from every idea and restraint except for the idea that restraint is unacceptable. Mitchell writes that the first stage of liberalism still relied on the Christian, traditional society in which it lived. But the second stage of liberalism, which he defines as beginning in the late eighteenth century, threw off even these restraints:

> First wave liberalism, because it relied (despite its explicit claims) on resources rooted in tradition, entailed a general agreement about substantive goods, including some notion of the good life, both individually and corporately. Second wave liberalism is characterized by an increasingly explicit and energetic reaction of any claim to a universal, substantive good. What matters in second wave liberalism is merely a procedural framework that creates the maximal space for individuals to determine their own good.

And because there are no just limits to liberal autonomy, second-wave liberalism furthers what Mitchell calls cosmopolitanism, "the ideal of the autonomous chooser combined with a cosmopolitan impulse that seeks to eradicate differences, even as it celebrates the unconstrained choices of individuals." Note that this description encompasses certain forms of free-market absolutism as well as liberalism. In their underlying assumptions about tradition, the Democratic Socialists of America and Silicon

Valley global capitalists are not so different. Liberalism in this second stage, though theoretically cohesive, is as a practical matter unstable. Because it disregards the validity of common traditions that should shape our conduct, it has no limiting principle.

The bulk of the book examines three of the most astute interpreters of tradition: Michael Oakeshott, Alasdair MacIntyre, and Michael Polanyi. Oakeshott developed a sophisticated defense of tradition, one made notable because it dispensed with any appeal to religious faith or natural law as a grounding of any particular tradition—or as Oakeshott later called it, "practice." The lack of any sure baseline for when we can distinguish a good tradition from a bad one therefore opens Oakeshott up to criticism that he is simply a partisan of the status quo. But this would be unfair. According to Mitchell, Oakeshott was attempting to explain the conditions of how we think. Liberal critics think of the mind as a neutral instrument that is applied to a problem; for Oakeshott, "when an innovation is needed one simply cannot find a solution outside of what is available. And what is available constitutes one's tradition."

But at its best, tradition reflects not just epistemology but anthropology. Customary social practices reflect what we think a human being *is*, and whether there are practices that hinder or further personal flourishing (within, in some contexts, a common good). For this, Mitchell turns to MacIntyre. In his writings, MacIntyre considers how we can judge among traditions—something that was not explicitly part of Oakeshott's account. MacIntyre thinks that, although we are all bound by our specific traditions, those traditions may nevertheless partially reflect and give access to truths beyond any one tradition. It is that commonality in objective truth that makes development within, and communication between, cultures possible. MacIntyre thus tries to answer the main challenges to his account of tradition: from the Enlightenment partisans who believe there is some universally applicable truth that can crush all customs and traditions to the postmoderns who deride MacIntyre's search for any universal reality. But the MacIntyrean process of judgment is not easy, because it involves having to learn another tradition from the ground up.

Polanyi contributes for Mitchell a theory of knowing, or "tacit knowledge," since not all valuable knowledge is articulable in logical precepts. Like MacIntyre and Oakeshott, Polanyi does not really think a "tradition-less" position is possible, but what is possible is knowledge of an objective reality. He develops a theory of knowing that relies on what Mitchell calls a fiduciary relationship: to know something, we must submit to the authority of someone who already knows that thing. In other words, there is an element of conscious participation in the knowledge we are obtaining because otherwise—if the truth were just presented to us without our assent to understanding—we would not be able to understand it, a process Polanyi describes as objectivism leading to nihilism.

So far, so good. Mitchell has written a deep and compelling account of the school of thought that defends tradition. It will long be a resource for conservatives and others who want to understand how tradition can represent an alternative to modern rationality that both recognizes objective truth and our personal rootedness, which paradoxically is what gives us the means to understand that truth. It furthers the project that Kirk and others initiated. We are tradition-minded beings, despite the Enlightenment delusion, and our rationality is tied up with our historical and cultural situations.

If that was where Mitchell ended, the book would be useful but little more. What makes it of real value is that Mitchell knows this analysis is not enough, for conservatives have heard this all before. The question is not how we can explain tradition in a world without tradition. As Mitchell explains, there was always within liberalism—in its first or second phases—an illiberalism, which is itself a tradition. This illiberal liberalism has developed even as it was throwing off older traditions in the name of liberation. The question is what to do with the liberal tradition that has already developed. This is made more complicated by the very fact that we are swimming in that liberal tradition—that is what we know, in an Oakeshottian sense. As Mitchell acknowledges, the theme of liberation—from the Puritans to the abolitionists—is deeply woven into the American character.

Mitchell discusses this in his chapter entitled "The Incoherence of Liberalism and the Response of Tradition." Liberalism, in Rousseau's phrase, will force us to be free. We can choose whatever we want except that which questions liberalism. And that means, as we have seen, that contemporary liberalism is very comfortable with punitive measures against those actors (Christian bakers, for example) who choose goods contrary to it. Liberalism has its liturgical calendar and its eschatology, its saints and demons, and it has developed customs and traditions from this that are recognizable lineaments of a kind of tradition. Liberalism may have rejected traditional authorities of church and state, but it has put other authorities in their place. The conservative lament that liberalism is only "procedural" in its rejection of tradition is incorrect, largely for the reasons Mitchell adumbrates.

Several strategies therefore present themselves. One is MacIntyrean. Conservatives must learn the liberal tradition as it exists now, not simply as many think of it—as a poor offshoot of Western Christendom. Those seeking to defend tradition must then infiltrate its institutions and shift them in a non-liberal direction when warranted and able. Law professor Adrian Vermeule has proposed something similar in light of liberalism's dominance. With Polanyi, we must also participate in our traditions and seek ways to express the universals in ways that both liberalism and tradition can understand. Only then can we start to recover a way back to tradition.

And that brings us back to Kirk. The frustrating thing about most conservative discussions of tradition is that for a topic that is so place- and context-specific, there are too few analytical discussions of what those traditions might be. Simply to tell liberals that their cosmopolitanism does not take into account the irreducibly local and personal nature of human relationships, or that one should submit to those knowing more about a practice than you, will persuade few people. In part, this is because Mitchell is right: liberals have their own traditions, so this line of critique is not that effective. Similarly, there is surely a hierarchy of traditions that deserve more conservative reflection on their interrelationship and reliance on one another. Our tradition of public recognition of the divine, for example, is more important than my grandmother's tradition of cooking fish on Christmas Eve. The World Series is an important cultural moment in our national tradition, but not more important than, say, our tradition of an impartial jury of one's peers, and so on.

For Kirk, as the quote above demonstrates, traditions in the private sphere were just as important if not more so than political ones. He saw an organic and real connection between tending your own garden and the development of virtue, between public holidays and self-government. How we spend our time locally dictates what we care about nationally. More important, his own life was a paean to rootedness, which makes his work all the more attractive. Mitchell recognizes this need too and develops somewhat in this direction, but this is not such an instruction manual. Therefore, this book needs to be read alongside the work he and others have done with the website Front Porch Republic, where more concrete examples of lived tradition are discussed.

Perhaps what is needed instead is a reverse MacIntyrean strategy. Conservatives need to "translate" liberalism so that they can better explain its failings—something Mitchell does well. But conservatives also need to persuade liberals to translate conservatism. To do that, conservatives need to find potentially sympathetic interlocutors (such as Scialabba) and live lives that spark interest from those inclined to disdain tradition.

# *Unholy Holidays*

**My commuter railway** sent out the warning on a Friday afternoon in late December: No alcoholic beverages would be allowed on the trains this weekend. It was not a new temperance message or Bloombergian attempt to control our vices, just a safety announcement on the eve of SantaCon, an event in New York and many other cities, during which Kris Kringle-disguised revelers drink themselves silly through a weekend before Christmas.

Holiday alternatives are multiplying. One can proceed from a SantaCon party to Festivus ("for the rest of us," as the *Seinfeld* episode says, a holiday, as Peter Augustine Lawler recently noted, which neatly inverts Christmas themes) through the obscene circus that Valentine's Day—or, sorry, "V" Day—has become, and then, with only a slight bump for Good Friday, enter an Easter of chocolate eggs and bunnies before the real holiday in this new calendar, Earth Day. And in the fall comes the re-paganized Halloween, not to mention lesser celebrations like Movember and the truly hideous, retail-industry invented day of Thanksgetting.

The secularization of the culture proceeds apace, and it is never clearer than in what and how we observe holidays. A generation ago, American society observed the major Christian feasts, even if sometimes in the breach, and had that supplemented with a series of days of national importance. One could observe, or not, but the calendar maintained what the larger society considered worthy of public recognition.

Now no more. New and competing sets of holidays displace traditional

Originally published in *First Things*, January 14, 2015.

feasts. Concerns over which holidays to observe have become so fraught that some school districts have dispensed with holidays altogether, for fear of offending some group, say, Muslims, who observe different religious holidays, or atheists, who observe none. The University of Missouri has identified pagan or Wiccan holidays as among those for which students can be excused from taking an exam.

And a new ideology has transformed many of them from the inside. This change in our civil religion is as important, perhaps more so, as the more public legal and political battles in the public square. Historian Christopher Dawson liked to say the word *culture* derives from "cult," the process of organized worship. It makes a difference whether people publicly acknowledge the God of Abraham and Isaac rather than Wotan or the invented religions of science fiction television shows. People going to Burning Man rather than Midnight Mass will necessarily have different attitudes and produce a different culture. And Earth Day is very different from the localist, humane Arbor Day that is has replaced.

Three distinct movements have caused this explosion of different celebrations. The first is the increasing de-Christianization of the country. Where citizens either are embarrassed by, or do not acknowledge, the Christian roots of our calendar, it is no surprise that SantaCons reign, Christmas becomes the "sparkly season," schools break for a generic "winter holiday," and every connection with a holiday's religious roots is banished. The remaining public displays of traditional religious holidays face legal challenges, resulting in the tortuous religious liberty jurisprudence over how many reindeer can de-sacralize a crèche in a city square. Many of these assaults on holidays have come from those opposed to the Christian tradition in the first place. Thus the recent controversy in Detroit, when the Satanic Temple was allowed to place its own display on the lawn in front of the State Capitol.

The second movement is the growing diversity of our society. In some school districts, Ramadan is more important than Easter, and so other holidays are filling school and work calendars. Many workplaces already recognize their employees will not necessarily want Good Friday, Christmas, or Yom Kippur as holidays. This is a salutary recognition of the nation's enduring theism, and of humanity's natural urge toward transcendence. However, it is often joined to an aggressive multiculturalism that uses the pluralism of our society to impose a secularist ideology. This movement has a counter-current as well; groups of "traditionalist" Christians fighting to return neglected aspects of the Christian calendar back into public view.

The final piece of this puzzle is the nonstop commercialization of everything. Thanksgetting, which I first heard on commercials this year, is an example. Black Friday was bad enough; now the entire weekend is being treated as an exercise in consumerism. As Alexis McCrossen remarks in her 2001 book *Holy Day, Holiday*, which is a history of "the American Sunday," debates over the meaning of setting aside days for worship or "rest" are part of the national character, and in a nation as large as ours, many traditions can and should be accommodated. Recent transformations of the notion of holiday contain new elements of irreverence, however, such as the antipathy toward any public recognition of religious faith. They aren't out to diversify our days of worship. They aim to eliminate the holiness of holidays altogether.

# *Sparking Renewal:* The Benedict Option

❧

WITH HIS 2006 BOOK *Crunchy Cons*, and a writer's knack for identifying emerging currents in the zeitgeist, Rod Dreher drew attention to the emergence of a new cultural movement outside the post–Cold War divide between liberal and conservative. *Crunchy Cons* identified people who shared beliefs about autonomy, community, and a humane scale of living but who did not map onto then-current political or ideological categories. A growing number of more traditional conservatives had become disillusioned with the Republican Party in politics (especially its insistence on prosecuting wars in the Middle East and elsewhere after the Cold War), yet were also uncomfortable with the cultural leftism of the Democrats. At the same time, these conservatives became alienated from their own culture, as its largely Christian presuppositions were questioned, then rejected.

Dreher's argument is that the left-right divide is outdated, an argument that is more common among conservative intellectuals and others now than it was in 2006. Both left and right share an anthropology that is essentially modern in character and constructed largely without reference to theological understanding of humanity. On the left, the liberationist rhetoric of the 1960s has led to an obsessive focus on the individual and its endless narcissism. Everything is rights all the way down, no matter the social cost. On the right, the obsession with global capitalism has made the morality of the market the standard measure of worth, and the individual a mere cog in an economic machine. This corrodes traditional bonds of community and family, and, combined with the conversion of

---

Originally published in *The Intercollegiate Review*, March 2017.

the traditional Republican emphasis on a strong national defense into a mandate for endless war, in fact complements progressivism's hostility toward those same things. Whether the government or the market provides the solvent for tradition, reverence, or preservation of local communities makes little difference in the end.

Along the way, Dreher has carved out his own space against that toxic culture and has called that space and that which he saw others creating "the Benedict Option." The name is an homage both to Pope Benedict Emeritus XVI and the famous closing sentence of Alasdair MacIntyre's influential book *After Virtue*: "This time...the barbarians are not waiting beyond the frontiers; they have already been governing us for quite some time. And it is our lack of consciousness of this that constitutes part of our predicament. We are waiting not for a Godot, but for another—doubtless very different—St. Benedict."

This is our cultural moment, despite who occupies the White House or Congress, and with his unerring cultural radar, Dreher has written the book for this new moment: a central point in *The Benedict Option: A Strategy for Christians in a Post-Christian World* is "put not your trust in princes." Culture is more important than politics, and the currents of modernity did not change on Election Day. And one thing conservatives, and especially Christian conservatives, should understand is that they have lost the culture war, and, indeed, it was their obsession with politics—and their assumption that the culture and major institutions such as big business would always support them—that partially caused that loss.

Dreher summarizes our current cultural barbarism with the phrase "moralistic therapeutic deism" (MTD). This he describes in the opening chapter of *The Benedict Option* as the operating morality of Americans, even those who describe themselves as Christians. This perspective is, in essence, all about the believer and not about God. Its main features include that "the central goal of life is to be happy and to feel good about oneself" and has little about sin, obligation, or transcendent morality to which we as humans owe obedience. Dreher notes that "the problem with MTD, in both its progressive and its conservative versions, is that it's mostly about improving one's self-esteem and subjective happiness and getting along well with others. It has little to do with the Christianity of Scripture and tradition, which teaches repentance, self-sacrificial love, and purity of heart, and commends suffering—the way of the Cross—as the pathway to God."

But why is this a problem? MTD doesn't sound so bad—why shouldn't people feel good about themselves and slough off the inherited worries that burdened our superstitious ancestors? Dreher has two responses to that. The first is a larger cultural point that conservatives have long made: MTD does not work. Our culture can be extremely corrosive and destructive of authentic human flourishing. MTD has no standard against which to judge—let alone "resist," to borrow a cant phrase from today's progressives—that culture's imperatives. On issues ranging from stagnating wages to the attack on the family, Dreher argues that MTD makes us slaves rather than free persons, slaves to economic and political systems we cannot control and barely understand.

Second, in Dreher's telling, there is a war against Christians to drive them out of public life and to stigmatize their beliefs. Christians should stop pretending that they live in a culture or a political system still sustained by Christian norms, even the attenuated Protestantism of the last century. MTD, it turns out, is not as tolerant as it proponents would like us to believe. It is in fact a totalizing ideology that has its own value system. That system cannot tolerate Christianity, which has claims beyond self-esteem and beyond any specific political system. What has surprised some on the right (though not Dreher) is that often big business—supposedly liberalism's adversary—sides with cultural elites against local communities. For Catholics, the Obama administration's campaign against the nuns who refused to sign on to the contraceptive mandate imposed by the Department of Health and Human Services was the clearest example that the cultural winds have shifted, perhaps permanently. (Not that Dreher, who left the Catholic Church because of the sex abuse scandals and is now a member of an Eastern Orthodox community, is blind to the many sins of religious institutions.)

But Christians are enjoined to be both in and of the world. The "Option" must include engagement as well as isolation. As an example, Dreher cites Václav Havel and other dissidents within communist countries who had to create "an antipolitical politics" in the face of an oppressive regime. This kind of "parallel polis is not about building a gated community for Christians but rather about establishing (or reestablishing) common practices and common institutions that can reverse the isolation and fragmentation of contemporary society." This is a Christian moment, but one different from the height of the influence of, say, evangelicals, in the 1980s. This moment is about retrenchment and relearning, so as *better to engage the world*—a point lost on many of the book's harsher critics. "In other words, dissident Christians should see their Benedict Option projects as building a better future not only for themselves but for everyone around them."

Although the book contains a large amount of historical and cultural analysis, and reflects Dreher's wide reading and deep thinking, it is not a work of intellectual history. Those who have read Dreher know that passion is not long concealed beneath analysis. Therefore, throughout the book Dreher offers admonitions, instructions, and suggestions about how to live out the Option. The book is really trying to be a new Benedictine Rule of how we should live in our age of liquid modernity, combined with a jeremiad about our dissolving culture. James K.A. Smith has called the Benedict Option a symptom of the "new alarmism"; in a sense, when has the Church *not* been at odds with the world? What may be passing is simply an age when the relationship was a little less contentious. As a matter of tone, perhaps the criticism is valid: the world described in *The Benedict Option* still has much hope in it, a hope that was more clearly expressed (and thus more open to those who did not share his thesis) in *Crunchy Cons*. But as Dreher explains, the Option, though it can be lived variously, is meant both to protect Christians and also to allow them to live in the world, but to do that, one must sound alarms when needed. The drop-off of church attendance and the simple lack of comprehension or acceptance of traditional Christian language and practice in contemporary culture are things about which one is right to be alarmed.

*The Benedict Option* is depressing and exhilarating by turns, sometimes on the same page. Depressing because Dreher shows how far we have fallen and how much work there is to be done, made more so because the cultural issues he describes are at times very personal, which affect every family in America. As a father in a post-Christian world, the stress and real presence of spiritual danger can be almost overwhelming. But the book also proves exhilarating because Dreher reminds us of the great history of Christianity in sparking renewal, and shows us how it is being done, today, now, in our own communities if we have but eyes to see. Hope, in the end, remains our most important cultural inheritance. In the catacombs of ancient Rome, in the Soviet-era Eastern Bloc, and in places like China today, the Church has modeled a society that is a witness to a different kind of polity. It is that moment again.

# *Seedbed of Renewal*

❧

MANY PEOPLE who consider themselves conservative are woefully ignorant of the culture they claim to defend. The list of causes is long: Television has largely destroyed storytelling, public school denigrates the idea of a common culture, and the internet has killed off lingering remnants of community. The music industry has replaced popular songwriting and songmaking with prepackaged "pop stars." In response, too many conservatives cling to talk radio and conservative "best of" lists, cursing the darkness.

Gregory Wolfe is not among them, a youthful sojourn among the right-wing chattering classes notwithstanding. He has been the editor and driving force for two decades behind *Image*, a journal devoted to contemporary art and literature that draws upon the Western religious tradition. This is a quixotic project, to say the least, in a political culture dominated by economic ideologues of left and right. But, unlike many projects on the establishment right, it is devoted to creating the seedbed of cultural renewal rather than political victories.

In the arts the progressives have too often seized the high ground, claiming the purpose of art was *épater la bourgeoisie*, yet ignoring "the deeper wellsprings of human and divine order" that give rise to lasting art. Instead, contemporary art succumbs to fad and ideological fancy, and so loses even the weakest connections to the source of its value. In response, Wolfe turns to the tradition of Christian humanism and its defense of beauty in all its guises against the ugliness of modernity. Wolfe invokes the language of prophecy and imagination, art and faith, which must interact.

Originally published in *Chronicles*, November 2011.

> Faith asks art to be about something more than formal virtuosity and to consider that meaning itself is already inherently metaphysical, even religious. Art asks faith to become incarnate in the human condition without compromise—or evasion—and remain compelling.

This collection features essays on subjects ranging from Thomas More to Malcolm Muggeridge, Andrew Lytle to Gerhart Niemeyer, as well as more thematic pieces on the role of the artist in a fractured, postmodern world and the place of the Catholic novelist in a secular society. Drawing on such writers as Walker Percy, Wolfe argues that the collapse of the secular imagination is a welcome event for the religious artist, dissolving the false modern dichotomy between faith and reason and allowing a third element, the imagination, once again to work between them.

Wolfe's artistic tradition begins with the Gospels and moves through to the modernism of Eliot and Flannery O'Connor, which seeks to express traditional norms in new forms. But his modernism does not stop with Eliot, or even D.H. Lawrence, whom he appreciates for the questions the novelist raises in his work, even as he disagrees with the answers. Wolfe embraces contemporary writers like Larry Woiwode and Ron Hansen, as well as lesser-known ones such as Harold Fickett. But, unlike many conservative critics who disdain most of the cultural products of our age, Wolfe is engaged with images as well as words. As its name implies, *Image* has long nurtured and considered painting, film, and other visual arts. Included here are essays on the painters Fred Folsom, Mary McCleary, and Makoto Fujimura, artists who combine skill with moments of transcendence. Fujimura, for example, drew upon Eliot and Dante in his collection of paintings called *Water Flames*.

Wolfe believes traditionalism is dead, desiccated by leftist ideology and rightist philistinism. What is needed, as Russell Kirk knew, is a revivified imagination for what he called the Age of Sentiments, when images on a screen will be more important than words on a page. Indeed, "beauty will save the world" echoes Kirk's own statement that "imagination will save the world." Wolfe finds much to admire in the Michigan man of letters, whom he includes in a separate essay entitled "Politics and the Imagination," along with essays on similar authors, such as Marion Montgomery, Lytle, and Wendell Berry, in whose work Wolfe has found inspiration. Wolfe notes Kirk's sacramental vision, in which it is "impossible to separate Kirk's sense of transcendence from his love of particular people, places, and things." This vision, defined by Kirk as the moral imagination, reflects what Wolfe calls "one of the truest and most inclusive visions of our cultural inheritance." It is this vision that conservatives must recover, lest they become (or remain?) irrelevant as a cultural force.

Wolfe is not a political philosopher, and neither he nor we would likely wish some of the principles espoused by his favored artists established in law. His argument is aesthetic, and catholic in its holistic appreciation of various expressions of the deepest truths of human existence. But one should not (and Wolfe assuredly does not) mistake art for politics. Beauty will save the world, not govern it.

# *The Age of Addiction*

**The age of industry** was—is—also an age of addiction. We like the luscious apple or the beautiful sunset or the rush of sugar or alcohol, not to mention stronger substances; the problem is we can't get enough of them. Throughout most of recorded history, pleasure (except perhaps that of sex, and that usually of males at the expense of females) was sufficiently unavailable such that no one, not even the rich, got too much of it. This was especially true of intoxicants, which were generally preserved for ritual or ceremonial occasions; when they were not, different societies have gone through spasms of addiction, from opium dens to gin-soaked England.

That balance has changed radically over the last two centuries. Pleasures once obtainable only rarely and typically only by the upper classes now have a much broader reach. Massive factories churning out ice cream (one of the "packaged pleasures" of the title) are not necessary if only an elite can purchase their wares. This broad reach is possible because of a series of improvements in the way humans can preserve and package sights, sounds, and tastes. The ability to preserve pleasure indefinitely and release it on command has become an often-overlooked feature of modernity, in the shadow of equally impressive achievements in areas such as medicine or farming.

Now we—all of us—can have pleasure almost anytime, anywhere, in multiple forms. But our bodies have not changed: our desires for pleasurable sensations have not lessened and the risk of addiction, and indeed harm, is thus ever present. The evidence of such addiction has been

Originally published in *The University Bookman*, November 3, 2019.

voluminous even if we sometimes have not seen it, from obesity and substance abuse to endless porn. Whether our obsession with technologically assisted pleasures has reduced our ability to enjoy and take part in unenhanced experiences is a question left to the end of this scholarly yet engaging book, *Packaged Pleasures. How Technology and Marketing Revolutionized Desire.*

Gary Cross and Robert Proctor characterize our age as one of "packaged pleasures" because it is defined to an almost unimaginable degree by the ability to carry around and use a variety of manufactured and preserved products and experiences. A beautiful song was once something never heard again, and known only to the people who had heard it directly; it was an immediate, non-replicable engagement. Now that song can be relayed millions of times and shared easily, becoming no longer unique in the process. At the same time, this deep penetration of pleasure into ordinary life allows an unprecedented individualism to occur; where feasting, listening, and watching were communal events, now they need not be and often are not. This democratization of pleasure can be dangerous, the authors imply; our bodies may not be meant for the constant availability of sensory overload.

Technology has always been used to extend what the authors call "the power of the human sensorium." But in the modern age such technologies have been combined with industrialization, that set of techniques, innovations, and inventions that enabled mass production and distribution of those power-enhancers. After a brief survey of how early humans tried to extend pleasurable experience through techniques such as the fermentation of alcoholic beverages and curing meat, Cross and Proctor, both academic historians, focus on specific improvements in how certain pleasures have been targeted to individuals (called now consumers) over the last two hundred years. In that time period, "[m]odern people learned how to capture and intensify sensuality, to preserve it, and to make it portable, durable, and accessible across great reaches of social class and physical space." The cellophane wrapper and the pressurized tin can, the record player and the pop-top allowed previously unimaginable access to tobacco, the flavor of soda, the blast of sugar, and the repetition of sound.

One way to tell the story of pleasure is through the growth of industrial corporations that took advantage of the human desire for sensory pleasures and grew fat from it, without regard for consequences. And there is some of that in *Packaged Pleasures*. But another way to tell this story of the packaged-pleasure revolution is one of liberation from tradition, hierarchy, and the cycles of planting and harvest, to say nothing of space or time. Although religion- or class-based laws restricting pleasures to certain groups or times have existed throughout history, massive technological changes rendered them unenforceable beginning in Europe and the New World beginning in the early modern era. Because the desire for sensory pleasure is a human constant, people choose, and have chosen, these pleasures as freely as they could. Mass-produced sugary drinks and high-calorie, high-fat foods satisfy, for a time, and are economically affordable. Listening to music on your phone is cheaper than going to a concert or trekking out to a nature preserve to hear "natural" sounds. Yet as Cross and Proctor note, the very success of the "package revolution" has been an increase in health problems and social dislocation; it disrupted "the traditional relationship between scarcity and desire," of which more later.

But the packaged revolution did not simply preserve pleasure. The new technologies also created new pleasures. The candy bar is not just a sugar-delivery device, though it is that. Thanks to repeated innovation and increased sophistication, candy bars hit several pleasure centers of the brain at once, in a combination of smells, colors, and tastes. Such combinations do not exist "in nature," and unlike a song or even a natural substance like alcohol, there is literally nothing else like it. In an analogy repeated several times here, the carrot, with its monocolor and subtle taste, is no match for the candy bar.

The concept of "tubularization" acts throughout the volume as a connecting thread. The mass production of cheap tubes was a revolutionary innovation. As syringes, they could deliver medicine (but also refined forms of opiates such as heroin); as cigarettes, they delivered tobacco; and tubes of a thicker and fatter shape—cans—tubes preserved foods indefinitely.

Although many such packaging types have been known for a long time, their consistent and popular use is remarkably recent. Paper, for example, was made from cotton or flax until the middle of the nineteenth century when manufacturers found ways to make paper from wood pulp instead. The paper bag was introduced only in 1844. "Paper packaging solved a host of problems for manufacturers, reducing handling costs and waste (from vermin) while also saving retailers time.... Paper packs and cartons also allowed goods to be distributed more easily more cheaply, and over greater distances to people who usually had no idea who had made them to where they came from." These advantages only increased in the twentieth century with the advent of plastic; cellophane dates from 1914.

Although *Packaged Pleasures* is not a work of political theory, the book does much to undermine two prominent understandings of the individual, the libertarian and the liberal. For the libertarian, the individual is sovereign; the market exists to satisfy individual desires and will self-regulate to maximize that set of desires. The liberal self, too, is sovereign, a "mind" that chooses freely and that should be free of all coercion or impediment to that free choice. Philosopher Charles Taylor has called this the unencumbered self. It is a product of the modern age, even as the technologies that have emerged also seem to serve that conception of the individual.

But both of these selves are an illusion. To an extent ignored by libertarian and liberal alike—but not by corporate public relations departments or scientists—the self is an enfleshed mind. Our choices cannot be separated from our physical bodies. This, as Proctor and Cross note, is the unstated gap in the championing of consumer choice. Yes, a person chooses to smoke. But that initial choice is made in the context of advertising, government approval (or disapproval), and marketing. Later "choices" are constrained by the design of the product itself, which is created with extreme care to heighten sensation, and in some cases to encourage physical dependence.

It is the fiction of unconstrained choice that clouds what is in certain cases really occurring. The libertarian would trust to the market to regulate our (insatiable) natural urges, perhaps, by providing "low calorie" or healthful alternatives. But that only ignores the brute facts of our physical existence.

The liberal self fails for similar reasons to grapple with the implications of packaged pleasure. Although it is more skeptical of the market, the liberal view shares with its libertarian counterpart the idea that there is an "I" that can see through marketing and resist harmful temptation; early forms of liberal thought also believed there could be no wrong choices for this "I," only uneducated ones. It too ignores the physical dependence such substances or experiences can cause, at least in some circumstances.

And liberalism's reliance on governmental supervision also posits a disinterested state that is more ideal than reality. Regulation, at least in the American tradition, is understood to be broadly reflective of the desires of the electorate. If the voters want sugar-rich drinks of any size, government will, eventually, allow them. Moreover, government involvement is not always beneficial. The American addiction to fructose, for example, has much do with the political power of the corn lobby. And government sales of alcohol to native Americans (for example) in the course of our colonial history does not speak well of placing the power over pleasure in the hands of the state. As the authors note here, government power was used to overcome initial consumer resistance to packaged goods. Americans preferred and trusted the local merchant rather than the far-off manufacturer, so companies went to work, lobbying for laws meant to place them at an advantage, such as inspection regimes that could be best met only by larger firms.

The risk of a combination of market and state power to control pleasure comes through in their chapter on the amusement park, "Packaging Fantasy: The Amusement Park as Mechanized Circus, Electric Theater, and Commercialized Spectacle." That last clause is the critical one. The modern amusement park has three main sources. First there are the medieval festivals and fairs, in which traditional roles were reversed and people celebrated a brief period of abundance amidst ever-present scarcity. Second are the eighteenth-century pleasure gardens, largely restricted to the wealthier parts of society. And the third source Proctor and Cross identify is the most recent, the international exhibition or world's fair. The modern amusement park ride—to say nothing of the organizational and efficiency innovations of behemoths like Disney—overlays all of these sources and makes the modern park possible. Like the other technologies *Packaged Pleasures* details, the park heightened and intensified experience. The experience of the park, however, more so than other pleasures, also infantilizes us.

The modern amusement park is geared toward adults as much as children, to let us relive the intense experiences of childhood. They combine "the saturnalian intensity of the traditional festival, the sensual relief of the pleasure garden, and the dense clustering of display and spectacle of the world's fairs—all in a technologically dazzling and commercial form." That is to say, the modern park is a commercially defined space sanctioned by the state, indeed assisted by the state. As the history of the late medieval fairs illustrates, the modern state does not like spaces that permit or celebrate unrestrained subversion of authority. The state destroyed those spaces and helped create limited commercialized space. Political and hierarchical subversion was broken, and the space for amusement and distraction was removed from the traditional cycle of seasons and of scarcity and plenty. Rather like Vauxhall in London or Coney Island in the 1890s, self-expression and sheer intense experience, untethered by context or culture, was to become the defining paradigm.

The packaging of pleasure is easy to understand when it comes to eating and drinking (or smoking or injecting), but less so with seeing or hearing, for example in the cases of pornography or video games. There is not insubstantial research (alluded to here in passing) that such images can hit the same pleasure centers in the brain as other kinds of stimulants. Their chapter on visual imagery, "Packaging Sight: Projections, Snapshots, and Motion Pictures" begins by acknowledging the importance of the visual to us as human animals. In some ways, it is the most pervasive of the packaged pleasures. To get to consumers, advertisers have to catch their eyes; thus the explosion of advertising and marketing in the nineteenth century. The legendary Madison Avenue ad man was only a stage in a long process.

> It is hard to understand modernity without understanding a kind of obsessive exploitation of visuality. Technologies for extending the visual for elites were developed in the seventeenth century—think telescope and microscope; later these technologies gave the less-than-wealthy similar visual enlargements.... A new age of intensified and extended imagery liberated people form the visual constraints of the past and brought much of the world—or at least its appearance—into immediate experience in ways never before even imagined.

As Susan Sontag noted, photographs "package the world" even as they are themselves packaged into albums, books, or films. Proctor and Cross take us through the succession of visual stimuli from the camera obscura and magic lanterns through the photograph and movie. These innovations moved the visual image in two opposite directions. The initial appeal of early photography was its *uniqueness*; the daguerreotype, for example, was more like a portrait. Its cumbersome development process made its products one of a kind. But the technology could not be stopped, and the rise of easier and less expensive methods of photography led to what we now think of as its defining trait: the limitless reproducibility of images, a trait only accelerated and magnified in the era of Instagram and YouTube.

People no longer understood photographs as making them closer to a unique event. Instead, and unexpectedly, photography now emphasized the distance between the thing itself and the thing photographed. As Jacques Rancière has noted in his treatise, *The Future of the Image*, photography, like other arts, does not simply re-present is original. Rather the arts produce an "alteration of resemblance." For Proctor and Cross, the important thing about photographic technologies is that they enable people to experience the visual in new and more exciting ways. Moviemaking techniques allow us to see things that previously could not be seen, but they worry that this visual "wow" has "dulled our sensibility toward the greens, browns, and grays of nature and the pace of a gathering storm or a sunset..."

Of the two ways to tell the story of packaging pleasures for mass consumption, Proctor and Cross, as the above quotations indicate, lean towards the liberal view of the person, but only mildly so. They place different experiences into different categories based mostly on what we now think of as their health effects Tobacco should likely be banned, for example, and they seem favorably disposed toward proposals such as the "Twinkie tax," imposed on high-sugar and caloric foods. This is a paternalistic liberalism, trying to protect those who perhaps cannot protect themselves. But unlike the most dominant form of liberalism, which assumes adult rational decision makers, Proctor and Cross recognize that a lot of the packaged pleasures are directed at children, not just through sugary foods but also diversions like video games. Unlike perhaps in traditional societies, which had specific activities reserved for children, the cultivated tastes for these pleasures are to continue through adulthood.

And they are concerned about waste; as the ease of amassing pleasures has increased, "this amassing raises the obvious questions about how much any person, class, or nation should possess, especially when the packaged pleasure emerged in a context of growing inequality, resource depletion, and seemingly unstoppable carbon pollution." Because they do not want to seem censorious, their suggestions are mild and more to inspire discussion than agreement. The story they tell is complicated, which they acknowledge, and includes a range of good and bad results. If more people gained access to the same pleasures, more local or unique experiences were lost. "Items came to be desired as much for their labels and associations as for their flavors and nutritive value. Old taboos disappeared, but so did seasonal, ritual, and festive foods and drinks.... The packaged pleasure may even have made us more hedonistic, with consequences we have not really though about, even today." We can now live in self-enclosed bubbles of pleasure, but these bubbles have costs, both social, and personal, that we are just beginning to acknowledge and which, for their own reasons, neither the liberal nor libertarian perspectives can fully address.

Perhaps the rise of the "artisanal" or organic food movements, although not discussed here, represent a hopeful opportunity to address some of the issues Proctor and Cross identify. Those pleasure are by definition more ephemeral than mass-produced alternatives. The locally sourced grains can travel only so far, or the preserved foods that are produced only in small batches by definition limit their reach. Those are elitist pleasures, not yet packaged and distributed to the masses. And like the sacred ceremonies or sumptuary laws of the past, which connected access to intoxicants or rich food to a priestly caste or the wealthy, these movements implicitly connect such pleasures with virtue. Yet perhaps these movements, with their rejection of homogenous uniform packaged pleasures, can be joined with the technological innovations described here to generate a new interest in what lies outside the package.

# *Thriving with Thrift*

❧

**Waste not, want not.** A penny saved is a penny earned. A bird in the hand beats two in the bush. Phrases like these were once part of America's common economic wisdom. Especially in the twentieth century, Americans learned, through the Great Depression and two world wars, that it was better to hold on to your resources and use them wisely than to spend them recklessly or to gamble with them in the hope of making a greater gain. Indeed, the 1920s saw the rise of the National Thrift Movement, which took its inspiration from our nation's thriftiest Founder, Benjamin Franklin. Many Americans who grew up in that era never forgot its privations, which imposed at least a partial check on their characteristic economic optimism.

These venerable phrases haven't been heard much over the last twenty years, however. First came the Internet era, which seemed to suggest that there was no limit to the Dow Jones Index or to our personal fortunes; then the subprime-housing bubble, in which overly easy credit was joined to an unrealistic view of the free market and a failure of nerve in Washington. Traits like frugality and thrift were regarded as arcane ideas from another time, as if those practicing them wore the top hats and frock coats of somber Victorian burghers.

In his new book, *Thrift: Rebirth of a Forgotten Virtue*, the impressively named Theodore Roosevelt Malloch seeks to return thrift to its place among commercial society's respectable virtues. After all, the word "thrift"

Originally published in *City Journal*, a publication of the Manhattan Institute for Public Policy, Inc., on February 12, 2010.

is cognate to the verb "thrive," and it is Malloch's view that thrift, properly understood, should be joined with a constellation of other characteristics that make society more just and ultimately more prosperous. Thrift does not mean poor, and its opposite is not wealth but waste. Tracing its roots to the Scottish Enlightenment, Malloch describes thrift as "a matter of the wise use of assets—accumulating where this was possible, investing where this promised a return, and avoiding waste." Thrift is, in a sense, a principle of good stewardship and could apply to caring for the environment as well as to tending one's bank account. It requires judgment, reflection, and the forging of sound habits that will lead to happiness. One can be generous and thrifty; the term need not, as Malloch makes clear, be equated with stinginess.

*Thrift* ranges widely across intellectual history, from Aristotle to the Enlightenment, from George Weigel's reflections on European malaise to the policies that the developed world should adopt toward less developed nations, from economic theory to debates over the religious causes of prosperity. The result is a sometimes-chaotic ride through several complex subjects. Malloch is concerned, among other things, with the transition into a new kind of capitalist economy:

> Instead of an economy based on saving and thrift, which launched Europe on its path of growth and prosperity,...we have an economy based on consumption, debt, and credit, in which saving is discouraged not only by the culture of affluence but also by the fiscal policies of governments.

Economic policy, he argues, should be directed toward reinforcing good habits of saving and proper consumption.

That doesn't mean greater government involvement or expenditure. The rise of the welfare state over the last century, for example, has contributed to the corrosion of thrift. A government that promises everything eventually convinces the populace that it need not save or prepare for anything. This position becomes ultimately untenable, Malloch argues, sapping people's ability to develop the habits necessary to maintaining a free society. Reliance on the government also masks the reality that government resources ultimately derive from a prosperous populace; if government action reduces those resources, its own effectiveness becomes limited. It's curious, though, that Malloch offers not a word of complaint against the private institutions that helped further our economic troubles. While it's true that Washington failed to restrain debt spending or to inculcate thrift, the boom and inevitable bust in housing wouldn't have been possible without thousands of private, profit-seeking individuals and firms seeking to cash in on the frenzy.

No doubt Malloch would say that an emphasis on virtue and community-building would help lessen such destructive private actions. He notes that in a society focused on consumption, "the insatiable urge to acquire things, whether or not they are needed, has reached epidemic proportions" and "has caused severe social and cultural dislocations and warped the basic values of American society." His shorthand solution for restoring the balance is "spiritual capital." Michael Novak and others have long argued that a disciplined capitalism requires a complex structure of social sanction, education, and often, if not always, religious belief. While Malloch concedes that calculating spiritual capital is difficult, he brings to bear an impressive array of data that shows a correlation between prosperity and traditional religion.

Shifting at times from diagnostician to sectarian, Malloch may lose some readers, but his analysis addresses the fault lines of our current predicament. A nonjudgmental secularism combined with an amoral economic system is a recipe for economic loss and cultural degradation. Perhaps it is time to bring Franklin back into the picture.

# *Our Once and Future Catholic Culture*

**Some years ago** the poet Dana Gioia published a piece on "The Catholic Writer Today." His argument was that Catholic fiction has declined since the golden days of Flannery O'Connor, Walker Percy, and other major figures, and that despite being the nation's largest religious group, the presence of Catholics in the fine arts was almost nonexistent. Others, such as Paul Elie, sounded the same note, calling the contemporary place of the novel of faith "something between a dead language and a hangover." Not all were convinced. Gregory Wolfe, for example, has argued that religious fiction is alive and well if you put aside rose-tinted nostalgia and know where to look.

But that debate addressed only one side of the literary world. The other, arguably as important, was that of non-fiction: history, criticism, philosophy, commentary, and the sciences, all of which were subjects of a specifically Catholic culture during the same time Gioia identified as a golden age of Catholic fiction. If Catholic fiction remains a still, small voice, Catholic nonfiction is a whisper, and that should equally be of concern.

For Catholics, reality is comprehensible through reason, and any subject can be studied to reveal eternal truths about the human condition. Moreover, these truths can be discussed in an open public square with anyone of good faith. Kevin Starr describes how that works in a useful broadside published by the redoubtable Wiseblood Books: *The Lost World: American Catholic Non-Fiction at Midcentury.*

---

Originally published in *The Catholic Thing*, April 13, 2016.

There was a time where Catholics were influential figures across a range of genres in a secular world. Moreover, at midcentury, Starr, former Librarian for California, argues that "the plenitude of this nonfiction helped create the golden age of belletristic writing."

The decline of non-fiction has many causes. Most people do not read much, if anything, anymore. Then, contemporary liberalism disdains any strong notion of the truth or the common good. Even its former bulwark, the language of rights, now has become largely a weapon to force a preferred agenda, as the recent debates over religious freedom attest.

Your race, orientation, or gender now define your principles: your motives become more important than your arguments. In this world, Catholics are reduced to simply another interest group and they cannot, for example, be enunciating ethical principles available to all of good faith—or a historical perspective that is informed by faith but open to all. Few have escaped this trap of liberal ideology.

Starr outlines the cultural moment at midcentury, at which point American Catholics had gained a strong enough of a foothold in the nation to become a potent cultural presence, but before the Second Vatican Council. He begins the account of this cultural moment in late nineteenth century England with John Henry Newman, G. K. Chesterton, and Hilaire Belloc, who were equally influential in the United States. British authors such as Fr. Vincent McNabb and Monsignor Ronald Knox continued to have significant American sales into the post-war period. Native-born Catholics, such as the inimitable Orestes Brownson, also contributed to the tradition.

And throughout the early decades of the twentieth century Catholic publishing houses and magazines were founded. But more importantly, these writers convinced secular publishing houses that Catholic books could sell. Thus, Doubleday launched its Image paperback series of Catholic classics in 1954, something that is inconceivable today. Consider its list: Chesterton, Christopher Dawson, and St. Francis de Sales' *Introduction to the Devout Life* (!). And as Starr notes, secular college campuses permitted Catholicism to a greater degree than previously to enter academic intellectual life. For example, the great Catholic historian Carleton J. Hayes was president of the American Historical Association in 1945 and a year later was awarded Notre Dame's Laetare Medal. (You only need look to this year's recipients of that award to see how Catholic culture has suffered in the interim.)

It's easy to overemphasize the vigor of this culture, and by portraying its variety I do not think Starr is arguing for some kind of return to that era, which is in any event not possible. He reminds us that this period was in some respects "a time of theological indecision and even confusion, [but] was not devoid of multiple levels of commentary, ranging from the popular to the profound, that created a force field for Catholic novelists and poets to absorb from their very environment the color, context, profundities, and dissonances of the American Catholic experience."

Starr's role rather is primarily that of an historian, and for that he should be commended for reminding us of this aspect of Catholic culture. Arguably, Catholics of the 1940s, 1950s, and 1960s were more exposed to non-fiction writings of all kinds, including spiritual writings, as a natural part of being "Catholic" than the authors, great as they are, being lauded by Gioia and Elie.

But there is a contemporary lesson in Starr's work. Catholics must support those engaging culture from a perspective of faith but in language open to all. Writers like *New York Times* columnist Ross Douthat and scholars like Princeton's Robert George come to mind. Moreover, Catholics must look to enrich other cultural forms—movies, television, the Internet—since that is now the world most of us inhabit more fully than the books and magazines Starr profiles. A new cultural moment is upon us. Looking backward will perhaps help us move forward.

Made in the USA
Middletown, DE
20 October 2024

62450451R00274